Visions from the Past

Visions from the Past

THE ARCHAEOLOGY OF
AUSTRALIAN ABORIGINAL ART

M. J. Morwood
Illustrations by D. R. Hobbs

Smithsonian Institution Press
Washington, D.C.

Published in 2002 in the United States of America
by the Smithsonian Institution Press
in association with Allen & Unwin
83 Alexander Street
Crows Nest NSW 2065
Australia

ISBN: 1-58834-091-0

Library of Congress Control Number: 2002100935

National Library of Australia Cataloguing-in-Publication Data available

Text design and typesetting by Bookhouse, Sydney, Australia
Printed in Singapore, not at government expense

08 07 06 05 04 03 02   5 4 3 2 1

Contents

Acknowledgements

I would like to thank John Iremonger and Colette Vella of Allen & Unwin and Liz Feizkhah for their consistent advice, encouragement and patience. I would also like to thank the following.

For financial assistance: Australian Research Council, University of New England, Australian Nuclear and Scientific Technology Organisation, Julie Everett and UNE Faculty of Arts.

For practical assistance: Terry Bailey, Paul Cooper, Charlie Dortch, Bryndon Harvey of the National Museum of Australia, Nicky Horsfall, Penny Jordan, Pat and Peter Lacy, Bob Layton, Scott L'Oste-Brown, Angie McGowan, Ken Mulvaney, Maree Parsons, Sarah Pizzey from Kakadu National Park, Peter Randolph of the WA Department of Indigenous Affairs,, Leonn Sattertwait of the Queensland University Anthropology Museum, Madge Schwede of the WA Department of Indigenous Affairs, Claire Smith, Moya Smith of the Western Australian Museum, Athlea Sullivan of the Kimberley Land Council, Will Stubbs of the Buku-Larrnggay Mulka Centre, Project Officer Jack Williams with Mumbultjari Community, Walter Zukowski of the Central Australian Land Council, the School of Human and Environmental Studies (UNE), and students of my rock art units from 1982 to 2000.

For permissions and assistance during fieldwork: Many traditional owners and organisations including the Bidjara Elders Corporation (Rockhampton) and the late Fred Lawton (central Queensland highlands); King-kiara Aboriginal Corporation (north Queensland highlands); Ang-gnarra Aboriginal Corporation, Tommy George, Laura George and George Musgrave (Cape York Peninsula); William Bunjuk, Alphonse

Fredericks, the late Vincent Frederickson, Louis Karadada, Jack Karadada, Rose Karadada, Billy King, Father Anscar McFee, Sylvester Mangolamara, Clement Maraltdj, the late David Mowaljarlai, Mary Pandilo, the late Manuella Puran, the late Hector Tungaal, the late Austin Unghango, the late Dicky Udmarra Unghango, the late Laurie Utemara, the late Daisy Utemara, Ester Waina, Laurie Waina, Neil Waina, the Kalumburu Community Council and the Wunambal-Gambirr Corporation (Kimberley).

For permissions to use figures: Jacqueline Angot-Westin, Fachroel Aziz, Robert Bednarik, Noelene Cole, George Chaloupka, Jean-Jacque Cleyet-Merle of the Musée National de Préhistoire des Eyzies, Bruno David, Iain Davidson, Robert Edwards, Bill Harney of the Wardaman Aboriginal Corporation, Historical Society of Cairns, Peter Keegan, Anne and John Koeyers, Darrell Lewis, Josephine McDonald, the family of Mataman Marika, Scotty Martin, Sven Ouzman, Gordon Pontroy of the Mumbultjari Community, Andrée Rosenfeld, June Ross, Mike Smith, Kate Sutcliffe, Nebo Tjukadai of the Haasts Bluff Community (Ikuntji), Percy Trezise, Patricia Vinnicombe, Grahame Walsh, Kurt Wehrberger of the Ulmer Museum, Richard Wright, Ang-gnarra Aboriginal Corporation, Ballanggarra Aboriginal Corporation, Bidjara Elders Corporation (Rockhampton), Hungarian National Museum, John Oxley Library, National Museum of Australia, the Dodnun Community, Musée National de Préhistoire des Eyzies, the Mumbultjari Community, Ngarinyin Aboriginal Corporation, Tasmanian Aboriginal Land Council Aboriginal Corporation, Ulmer Museum, University of Queensland Anthropology Museum, Western Australian Department of Indigenous Affairs and Western Australian Museum.

For additional line drawings: Kathy Morwood and Michael Roach.

For comments on drafts: Robert Bednarik, Peter Brown, Paul Clark, Dorothea Cogill, Iain Davidson, Josephine Flood, Luke Godwin, Penny Jordon, Darrel Lewis, Ian McNiven, Josephine McDonald, Kathy Morwood, John Mulvaney, Bert Roberts, Andrée Rosenfeld, June Ross, Claire Smith, Annie Thomas and Dave Whitley. Kathy Morwood also prepared the glossary and the index.

Finally, Chapter 3 on the history of rock art research incorporates a paper previously published with Claire Smith in *Australian Archaeology*.

Mike Morwood
October 2001

Introduction

The urge to decorate is one of the defining characteristics of modern human beings (*Homo sapiens sapiens*). There are odd pieces of 'art' known from earlier contexts, including the polished section of mammoth tooth stained with red ochre from Tata in Hungary and estimated to be between 78 000 and 116 000 years old, but art does not appear as part of a coherent, visual system until around 40 000 years ago. Its arrival is associated with human evolutionary and technological changes in Europe, Africa and Asia, and the initial colonization of America and Australia. Since this time, human beings have consistently decorated themselves, their implements and, where available, rock surfaces.

The implications of this artistic watershed for advances in the ability, or need, for new types of social communication are still being argued about, but the fact that art, or symbolic expression, was practised in all human societies over such a long period means that artistic material forms a reasonable proportion of the archaeological record: Upper Palaeolithic cave art, Mayan murals and New York subway graffiti are very different in character, but can all provide information on value systems, social institutions and ideologies, if the right questions are asked.

There are many books, theses and articles dealing with art generally and with specific art assemblages. These range from well-illustrated coffee-table books with mediocre text to excellent regional syntheses such as Patricia Vinnicombe's *People of the Eland*, Wellman's *A Survey of North American Indian Rock Art,* and André Leroi-Gourhan's *Treasures of Prehistoric Art.* However, none of these provide an overview of the potential, problems and methods of approach used in the study of past art. Students seeking a good starting point are thus forced to read a large number of works to get a feel for the topic. This is a pity, since there is clearly wide interest in prehistoric art, reflected not only in the number of colleges and universities that offer courses in the subject, but also in the relatively recent formation of organizations such as the American Rock Art Research Association, the Australian Rock Art Research Association and various government-funded Rock Art Research units.

An overview of developments in the archaeology of art and the relationship between art and other types of archaeological evidence would also be useful to professional, 'non-art' archaeologists. Over the past ten years or so, they have become increasingly aware of the light that art can throw on changes in human behaviour, technology, economy and ideology which might not be reflected in other types of archaeological evidence. There are various reasons for this shift, including greater interest in social explanations for aspects of the archaeological record, and the efforts of such researchers as Meg Conkey and Clive Gamble, who have made good use of data on art styles to interpret aspects of European prehistory.

This book is concerned with the archaeology of Australian Aboriginal rock art, partly because of my personal interests and experience, and partly to restrict the scope of the topic to manageable (and readable) proportions. Nonetheless, it has to be seen in the context of historical, methodological and theoretical developments in other disciplines and other parts of the world, which have both influenced and been influenced by it. By archaeology I mean the study of the human past using surviving physical evidence. Art is more difficult to define but has the following characteristics:

- It is produced by deliberate, modification of objects or surfaces by changing their form, removing sections and/or applying other materials, such as pigments. More specifically, rock art involves modification of natural rock outcrops. Marks produced incidentally during other activities, such as sharpening of implements on sandstone, do not constitute art.

- It is a visual symbolic system in which the modifications can stand for other things or concepts. For this communication to occur there have to be conventions about meanings, which are shared by the artist and intended audience. Symbols used in writing and sign-language also have these attributes but their conventional meanings are more specific and fixed.

Those who think that the archaeology of Australian Aboriginal art is only of interest to specialists should consider that symbolic systems such as art, dance, music, style in material culture, dress and language are universally defining cultural characteristics. In fact most people would automatically think of Australian Aboriginal culture in terms of boomerangs, the distinctive sound of clapsticks and the didgeridoo, the dynamic portrayal of Dreamtime events in dance, the X-ray bark paintings of Arnhem Land, and Central Australian geometric art in 'dot' style.

Ethnographic information (Chapter 4) makes it clear that artistic symbolic systems serve as important group-defining characteristics within Aboriginal culture as well. They are central to the corporate identity of land-owning and social groups, and to the way this identity is maintained and reinforced. In other words, symbolic systems are not just peripheral decoration for the core elements of the culture; they are integral to cultural definition and operation.

Since archaeology is the study of past human behavioural systems and how cultures have changed over time, it cannot afford to ignore such evidence for symbolic systems. In Australia, rock art is the most common surviving evidence for past symbol use. If we ask the right questions of it, then it should be possible to reconstruct the ways in which the fundamental basis of Aboriginal society has changed since humans first came to this continent.

In the past, archaeologists have generally relied on 'hard' evidence, such as stone artefacts, the remains of meals, and human skeletal remains in their reconstructions of the past. However, these do not tell us much—if anything—about many important developments in Aboriginal ideology, territoriality, resource use and social organization. Symbolic evidence, such as rock art, on the other hand, can provide crucial insights into these core aspects of Aboriginal culture, particularly when it is assessed in the context of other types of archaeological and palaeo-environmental evidence.

Australian Aboriginal culture is unique to this country and one of our few defining national icons. Certainly, many international tourists here purchase items of Aboriginal manufacture (or connotation) as mementoes of their visit to these shores—bark paintings, T-shirts with Aboriginal motifs, didgeridoos, boomerangs. In fact, a survey by the Australia Council in 1990 showed that half of these visitors are interested in seeing and learning about Aboriginal culture, and 30 per cent purchased Aboriginal art or items related to Aboriginal culture. Furthermore, it has been estimated that the Aboriginal arts and crafts market is worth about $200 million per year, with about half of this associated with tourism. The commercial value of such intellectual property and the means for compensation are important issues currently being debated (Chapter 11).

Aboriginal art and culture are important and integral parts of Australia's identity. The archaeological investigation of this art and the way it has developed in response to past environments, population levels, relations within and between groups and outside contacts, need not be just an esoteric, specialist interest. Aboriginal art has undergone major changes in the past, just as it is changing today for a whole variety of political, technical and commercial reasons. Understanding 'how and why' adds to our general appreciation of Australian Aboriginal culture, and of what it is to be Australian.

In this book, I will dwell on several crucial points; that the archaeological study of art is important; that an understanding of past art systems is predicated on our understanding of present-day art and how it functions; and that art evidence cannot be looked at in isolation. These points will be reinforced by examining case studies from the central Queensland highlands, the north Queensland highlands and southeast Cape York Peninsula.

CHAPTER 1

Aboriginal archaeology in context

Who exactly were the first Australians? Where did they come from? When, and how, did they get here? Once they arrived in Australia, how did they adapt to—and modify—their new environment? While most of these questions still provoke lively debate among archaeologists, in at least some areas a broad picture is becoming steadily more clear.

The first humans

Humans did not evolve in Australia but arrived relatively recently, between 40 000 and 60 000 years ago. They must also have made a number of substantial sea crossings from mainland Southeast Asia. We know this because before humans arrived, the only Asian animals that managed to get here were those capable of making sea crossings—by swimming, rafting on flotsam or flying—in sufficient numbers to establish biologically viable populations (such as seals, rodents and bats). Similarly, the few marsupials found on east Indonesian islands (such as cuscus and wallabies in the Moluccas) were almost certainly transported there by humans. The sea barriers that separated Asia and Australia enabled the distinctive Australian fauna dominated by marsupials to develop over millions of years.

Southeast Asia may have been the immediate source area for the first Australians, but to find the earliest part of humanity's family tree we must turn to Africa, where we can trace back a distinctive hominid (human) lineage for 6 million years, beginning with the Australopithecines. Major steps in hominid evolution then included the emergence of our genus *Homo* about 2.5 million years ago; our ancestral species *Homo erectus* 1.7 million years ago; archaic members of our species, such as the Neanderthals *(Homo sapiens neanderthalis)* 200 000 years ago; and finally fully modern humans, *Homo sapiens sapiens*, around 130 000 years ago (Figure 1.1).

On present evidence, *H. erectus* was the first of the human line to disperse out of Africa. This hominid then radiated out into the Middle East, Europe, South Asia and East Asia (China, Thailand,

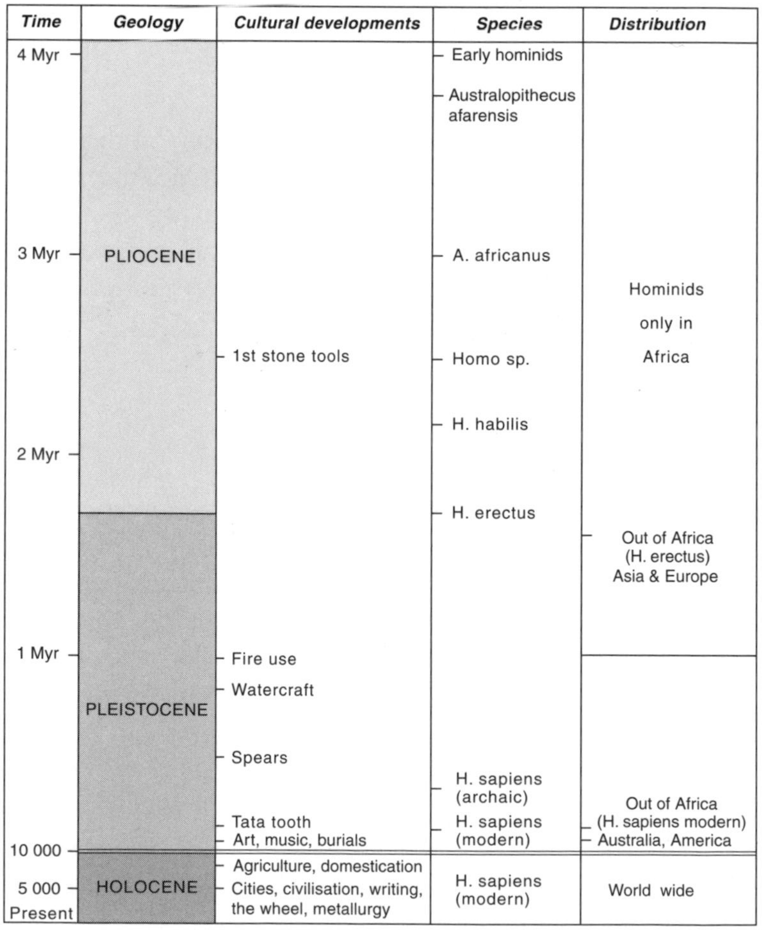

FIGURE 1.1

Timeline of the last 4 million years of hominid evolution and cultural development. Art and decoration appear very late in the sequence and are only associated with fully modern humans.

Time	Geology	Cultural developments	Species	Distribution
4 Myr			Early hominids	
			Australopithecus afarensis	
3 Myr	PLIOCENE		A. africanus	Hominids only in Africa
		1st stone tools	Homo sp.	
			H. habilis	
2 Myr			H. erectus	
				Out of Africa (H. erectus) Asia & Europe
1 Myr	PLEISTOCENE	Fire use		
		Watercraft		
		Spears	H. sapiens (archaic)	Out of Africa (H. sapiens modern) Australia, America
		Tata tooth	H. sapiens (modern)	
10 000		Art, music, burials		
	HOLOCENE	Agriculture, domestication	H. sapiens (modern)	World wide
5 000 Present		Cities, civilisation, writing, the wheel, metallurgy		

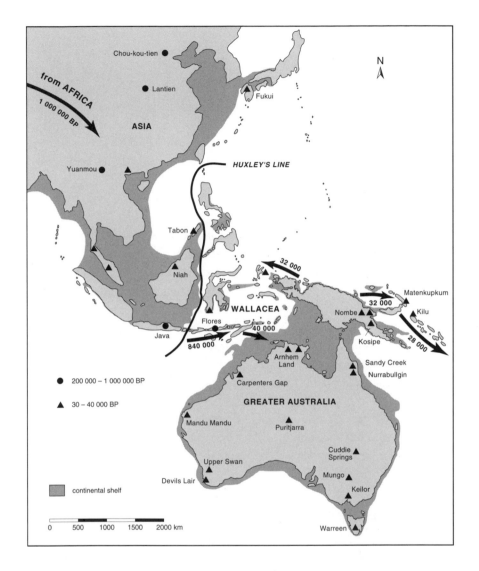

FIGURE 1.2

Hominid colonization of Southeast Asia and Australia. The earliest phase involved the dispersal of Homo erectus *from Africa to the Middle East, Europe, South Asia and East Asia. Fully modern humans,* Homo sapiens sapiens, *appeared in Africa around 130 000 years ago and later spread to all parts of the Old World, Australia and the Americas. On the basis of the Australian evidence, modern humans had reached Southeast Asia by 60 000 BP.*

Indonesia). It is important to note that it was possible at that time to reach all these areas simply by walking—even Java, the most distant point of all, and the one closest to Australia, was periodically connected to the Southeast Asian mainland by land bridges during times of low sea level. Consonant with this, Java formerly had a full range of Southeast Asian mainland animals (Figure 1.2)—*Homo erectus* was not the only large mammal to walk across these land bridges.

Once ancestral humans arrived in the islands to our northwest about 1 million years ago, what happened next? Investigation into this question spans about a century, but there are still crucial and tantalizing gaps in our knowledge. Research on early hominids in the area began in Java, with the work of Eugene Dubois, a Dutch anatomist who came to Indonesia in 1887 with the express aim of looking for the missing ape–human link in Darwin's theory of human evolution. From 1890 to 1896 Dubois carried out a major excavation at Trinil, a site on the bank of the Solo River in central Java. He discovered a hominid skullcap and thighbone, and named the species *Pithecanthropus erectus* (or upright ape-man). It was later renamed *H. erectus*; Dubois' discovery is actually the type specimen for this species.

Subsequently, hominid fossils have been discovered at many other localities in Java (such as at Ngandong, Mojokerto, Sambungmacan and Sangiran). The earliest such fossils are a little over a million years old (Figure 1.3); at the other extreme, Ngandong is not well dated, but fossil animals from the site indicate that it is more recent than most other *H. erectus* sites in Indonesia—an age of around 300 000 years is probably a reasonable estimate. It is therefore significant that the Ngandong fossil crania show evolutionary changes in the 'modern' human direction. They are less robust than hominid crania from Trinil and Sangiran, and have larger brains. A more recent find from near Sambungmacan, designated SM-3, still has not been dated, but anatomically it is even more 'modern' in appearance; physically, it appears to be transitional between *H. erectus* and our own species, *H. sapiens*.

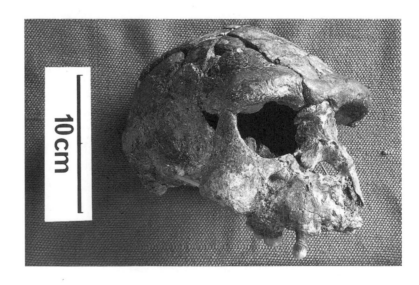

FIGURE 1.3

Sangiran 17, the most complete Homo erectus *skull found in Java. This fossil is about 750 000 years old. Later Indonesian specimens show physical changes in the modern direction with larger brains, finer features and the development of a forehead.*
(Photo F. Aziz)

This brings us to one of the most fundamental issues in Australian archaeology. Was there in fact genetic continuity between early *H. erectus* populations in this part of the world and the Asian ancestors of Australian Aborigines, or did the latter originate from a later dispersal of fully modern *H. sapiens* 'out of Africa'? Unfortunately, there is a gap in the Indonesian archaeological record between about 300 000 BP, the most recent likely date for *H. erectus*, and 40 000 BP, when sites containing the remains of fully modern *H. sapiens* appear. At this point, we simply do not have any direct archaeological evidence as to what was going on among the hominid populations in Indonesia during these critical millennia. We must try to infer the answer from data gleaned on either side of that time gap.

On one hand, as an anatomically 'transitional' *H. erectus/H. sapiens*, SM-3 would suggest that there was regional continuity at least up to the stage of archaic *H. sapiens*—that perhaps the very earliest Australians did indeed stem from these ancient populations. However, on the other side of the time gap, looking at modern populations, we find that studies of mitochondrial DNA from modern human populations worldwide indicate that the female ancestor of all modern humans lived in Africa a mere 100 000 to 200 000 years ago. If this is correct, then the far older Indonesian *H. erectus* population must have been an evolutionary dead end, a species independently evolving such 'modern' features as bigger brains, but eventually dying out or being supplanted by more modern populations in a more recent dispersal event out of Africa. If so, it would be descendants of these later populations that then moved on into Australia. My feeling is that the jury is still out on the matter; we simply need more evidence.

SM-3 also had bilateral asymmetry of the brain and enlarged frontal lobes, suggestive both of heightened intelligence and a capacity for proto-modern human language. A quite different line of evidence for the abilities of Indonesian *H. erectus* comes from the island of Flores in east Indonesia. Remember that at times of low sea level, Java was connected to the Asian mainland and animals, including hominids, could have walked there. Consequently, Java and Bali had a full suite of Asian animals, including elephants, pigs, deer, cattle, rhino, monkeys and tigers. But it was never possible to walk further east to the islands of Lombok, Sumbawa, Flores, Timor, Sumba or Sulawesi. We know that there have never been land bridges connecting the islands of east Indonesia to either the

FIGURE 1.4

A flaked stone tool excavated from Mata Menge on the east Indonesian island of Flores. Such stone artefacts first appear in local sites about 840 000 years ago associated with the remains of Stegodon (an early type of elephant) and Komodo dragon. They provide conclusive proof that hominids had reached Flores by this time, which must have involved sea crossings. However, there is no evidence that people had the ability to make the much longer sea crossing to Australia at this time.

(Photo Australian Museum)

Asian or Australian continental areas because, prior to recent human intervention, these islands had very few land animals—the only land mammals to colonize islands east of Bali were elephants, such as *Stegodon*, and rodents. (Elephants are large, buoyant, strong-swimming herd animals and are therefore surprisingly good island colonizers, whereas rodents can cross water barriers on natural rafts of flotsam, following flooding.) With these exceptions, then, the islands east of Bali are devoid of mainland species—in fact, the sudden drop-off in animal species on islands east of Bali corresponds to a major biogeographical boundary known as Wallace's Line.

Yet despite the sea crossings, which proved insurmountable to most Asian land animals, there is indisputable evidence that *H. erectus* had reached Flores by 840 000 years ago. Stone artefacts have been found associated with the bones of *Stegodon*, a primitive type of elephant, sealed in by layers of volcanic tuff of this age (Figure 1.4). These findings challenge the commonly held view that *H. erectus* did not have the brains or technology to make sea journeys. The recent discovery of well-designed, well-crafted and possibly composite spears at the 400 000-year-old Schoningen kill site in Germany supports this view; no simple 'upright ape' would have been capable of crafting such spears. The technological capacity of early hominid populations may have been seriously underestimated.

Furthermore, there is a general consensus that the foresight, planning and organization needed to build water craft capable of transporting a biologically and socially viable group is impossible without language. Previously the organizational and linguistic capacity required for sea voyaging was thought to be the prerogative of modern humans, and to have appeared much later: indeed, the human occupation of Australia between 40 000 and 60 000 years ago was the earliest generally accepted evidence for such distinctively 'human' abilities. The clear implication of the recent Indonesian finds, though, is that *H. erectus* must have had language of some sort fully 840 000 years ago.

Language is a communication system in which sounds or signs are used as symbols. That is, sounds or signs stand for something other than themselves; each is assigned a conventional and arbitrary meaning, which has to be learnt. *H. erectus* clearly was neurologically capable of symbol use.

Art is also a symbolic system, in which visual signs—marks in pigment, scratches, carved bone or stone—stand for something other than themselves, but at this stage there is no evidence that *H. erectus* or archaic *H. sapiens* populations had art. Isolated examples of non-functional, aesthetic 'art objects' of this age are known. For instance, fragments of red pigment with ground facets have been recovered from Twin Rivers in Zambia (200–400 000 BP), Mogaroop in western Kenya (290 000 BP) and Klasies River Cave in South Africa (120 000 BP), while a ground and possibly ochred section of mammoth tooth was found at Tata, Hungary, in deposits between 78 000 and 116 000 years old (Figure 1.5). However, art does not appear as part of a coherent visual system until after 45 000 years ago, associated with fully modern humans.

Presumably the need for art and personal decoration as a means for asserting and reinforcing personal and social identity was not present until this time. Some of the earliest evidence we have worldwide for art comes from Australia and this is broadly contemporaneous with similar evidence from Africa and Europe. The fact that this artistic watershed occurred at the same time as the emergence of long-distance exchange systems and the first evidence for deliberate burial of the dead, as well as the colonization of the New World and Australia, is clearly not a coincidence.

Colonization of Australia

Human occupation of Australia began during the Pleistocene, a time when there were constant fluctuations between warm and intensely cold global climates—termed interglacials and glacials respectively (see timeline in Figure 1.1). The last glacial maximum occurred between 25 000 and 15 000 years ago, when temperatures were about 6–10 degrees lower than today, a large proportion of the earth's water was tied up in polar ice sheets, and sea levels were as much as 130 metres lower than today's (Figure 1.6). When sea levels were this low, the Australian continental shelf was exposed, so adding 2.5 million square kilometres to the land area, with broad land bridges connecting New Guinea, Australia and Tasmania (that is, Greater Australia). Sea crossings between Indonesian islands and Australia, though always required, were much reduced in length. Conditions during the last glacial maximum 18 000 years ago were not only colder but also drier, with about half of today's rainfall and a much-expanded arid zone.

FIGURE 1.5

This sectioned and possibly ochred mammoth tooth from Tata in Hungary is between 78 000 and 116 000 years old. It is older than the appearance of modern humans in Eastern Europe and shows that people of the time had the intelligence and dexterity to produce art, but generally did not. Art seems to have arisen as a way of showing the affiliation, status and trustworthiness of people at a time when information exchange became far more extensive. (Photo I. Davidson)

FIGURE 1.6

Changes in sea level over the last 140 000 years. At times of maximum glaciation the sea level was around 130 metres lower than today's and the continental shelves were exposed. At such times New Guinea, the Australian mainland and Tasmania were all joined, but there was never a land connection to Southeast Asia. (HP = based on data from the Huon Peninsula uplifted terraces in New Guinea; NJS = the temperature-corrected isotropic sea-level curve) (After Chappell 1993, Figure 2)

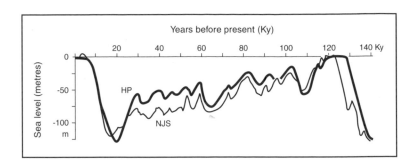

FIGURE 1.7

Possible routes taken by the first people to reach Australia. Recent archaeological findings suggest that the southern route along the Lesser Sunda Island chain, from Java to Timor, was the most likely one used. (After Birdsell 1977)

At the end of the last glacial period, conditions warmed, sea levels rose to flood the continental shelf, and rainfall increased. Over the past 6000 years, there have been only minor fluctuations in sea level, of up to 1 metre.

What of the route taken by the early Australians? There are a number of possibilities, but the most likely was a series of island hops along the Lesser Sunda Island chain, with the final water crossing from Timor to northwest Australia being about 100 kilometres at times of low sea level (Figure 1.7). We will never

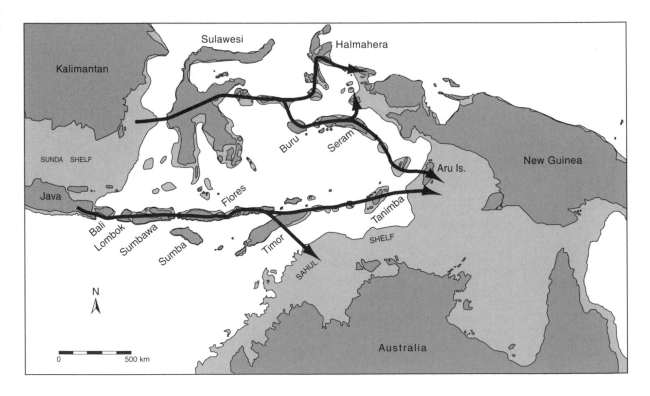

FIGURE 1.8

The experimental bamboo raft Nale Tasih 2 *successfully crossed from Kupang in West Timor to Melville Island near Darwin. It was an efficient ocean-going vessel, coped with very heavy seas and reached the Australian continental shelf in six days. This is its predecessor,* Nale Tasih 1, *which failed because the bamboo was not properly cured and became water-logged.* (Photo R. G. Bednarik)

know exactly what type of watercraft was used, but bamboo rafts are certainly a likely candidate. Recently, Bob Hobman and fellow researchers made an 18-metre bamboo raft, named *Nale Tasih 2*, using only the tool technology and organic materials available to the first colonists (Figure 1.8). They took six days to sail from Kupang in West Timor to the edge of the Australian continental shelf, which would have been the coastline at times of low sea level, and thirteen days to reach Melville Island off the Northern Territory.

Whatever craft was used to make the first crossings to Australia, the fact of that crossing does suggest something about the culture and means of subsistence of the earliest colonizers. They almost certainly were a people comfortable with and expert at water transport. It seems likely, then, that coastal peoples in Southeast Asia at that time had a maritime technology, in which watercraft were used to exploit littoral resources.

It is also likely that the crossing was deliberate, for it was not a one-off event. Greater Australia later served as a jumping-off point for the colonization of adjacent islands. By 32 000 years ago people had reached New Britain and New Ireland to the northeast of Papua New Guinea; by 28 000 BP they had reached the Solomons; and by 20 000 BP they were moving obsidian from New Britain to New Ireland for stone tool manufacture, and had reached Manus Island, which involved a minimum journey of 200 kilometres across open sea. Speakers of East Papuan languages still occupy parts of these islands, while cuscus and wallaby, both marsupial species, were introduced from New Guinea around 20 000 years ago to supplement the game available for hunting. There is also evidence that the

Moluccas Islands of northeast Indonesia were settled some 32 000 years ago by a back-movement of people from the west Irian Jaya region of Greater Australia, rather than directly from Southeast Asia. Speakers of languages belonging to the West Papuan language family still occupy the area, and the cuscus and wallaby were also introduced to these particular islands about 10 000 years ago.

Exactly when people first reached Australia is still uncertain, but there are two main schools of thought, neither of which has the upper hand at this stage. The first school accepts the oldest radiocarbon dates for Australian archaeological sites at face value—suggesting initial colonization around 40 000 years ago. The problem is that this age is also at the limit of standard radiocarbon dating—the technique simply cannot reliably record a date much older than this. However, two prominent adherents of the '40 000-year school', Jim Allen and Simon Holdaway, have pointed out that radiocarbon dates obtained with accelerator mass spectrometry (AMS) for non-cultural deposits, such as peat bogs, go back to 60 000 BP, in marked contrast to those obtained at archaeological sites.

The second school dismisses the 40 000 year limit as an artefact of radiocarbon dating methods, and accepts dates provided by thermoluminescence (TL) and optically stimulated luminescence (OSL). These two latter techniques measure how long sand grains have been buried away from sunlight, and can date samples up to 300 000 years old. Using TL, Bert Roberts, Rhys Jones and fellow researchers obtained dates of between 50 000 and 60 000 years BP for the first occupation of Nauwalabila and Malakunanja II, two rockshelters in western Arnhem Land. Similarly, on the Huon Peninsula in northeast Papua New Guinea, uranium series dates for uplifted coral reef terraces indicate that massive stone artefacts comprising waisted blades and core tools are between 50 000 and 60 000 years old.

If radiocarbon dating has its limitations, though, so do TL and OSL. The problem with their use is that, particularly in rockshelters, sand samples can be contaminated with quartz grains derived from the weathering of other older sources, such as bedrock or rockfall. Since these grains have been effectively 'buried' for millions of years, spurious results can be obtained. This is exactly what happened when TL dates of 116 000 years BP, and possibly 170 000, were claimed for human occupation of Jinmium Rockshelter in the Keep River area of the Northern Territory. The claim made headlines and created media interest around the world. New dating evidence now shows that Jinmium was first occupied around 5000 years ago.

To overcome this confounding factor, Bert Roberts and his colleagues have now pioneered the dating of individual sand grains rather than bulk samples. When enough grains are dated to be statistically valid, older contaminant grains can be easily identified and removed from the age calculation. This was done when checking the original TL results for Malakunanja II, and this more sophisticated grain-by-grain OSL dating method has confirmed the dates previously obtained by TL.

Claims for much older occupation have also been made, primarily on the basis of a quite different line of evidence; an increase in the number of fires and associated changes in vegetation. For instance, pollen specialists Gurdip Singh and E. A. Geissler found that the pollen sequence in deposits from Lake George near Canberra showed a shift from casuarina woodland to eucalypt forest associated with an increase in charcoal particles. They initially argued that the change occurred around 125 000 years ago, and that it reflected human modification of the environment, a claim that would put the human colonization of Australia back another 60 000 to 70 000 years. Apart from the fact that the evidence is open to other interpretations (it could reflect human impacts, or it could reflect quite independent climatic change), the 125 000 date was later revised to around 60 000, which better fits the existing archaeological evidence—and the TL results. Currently, then, most researchers would accept 50 000 to 60 000 years BP as the most probable date range for initial human occupation of Australia.

With all this movement, it seems most unlikely that, after the initial colonization event, all contact between Australia and its northern neighbours ceased. Whether there were continuing *substantial* migrations from Southeast Asia is not certain, but the possibility is there, and has been used to explain variation in both ancient and modern Aboriginal populations. For example, Joseph Birdsell explained geographic variation in recent Aboriginal populations in terms of three distinct waves of migration; in order of appearance, Negritos, Murrayians and Carpentarians. Alternatively, though, long-term processes of genetic change combined with later gene flow from Southeast Asia and Papua could easily explain the differences seen in modern populations.

Other models for the genesis of Australian Aborigines have been put forward using human skeletal evidence. For instance, Alan Thorne argued that two distinct human populations occupied Australia and that the characteristics of modern Aboriginal people were derived from later mixing. At sites like Kow Swamp and Cohuna in Victoria, 'robust' individuals with thick-walled skulls, sloping foreheads and other archaic traits were said to be directly descended from *H. erectus* in Java and to represent the first wave of Australian colonists. In contrast, 'gracile' individuals, such as Mungo 1 and 3, were assumed to be representatives of a population, which migrated more recently into Southeast Asia and Australia from southern China.

One problem with Thorne's model is that the oldest human skeletal material recovered here is in fact 'gracile'. Mungo 3 is between 28 000 and 32 000 years old, while the oldest, 'robust' Kow Swamp burials date to between 13 000 and 9500 BP. In addition, other researchers, such as Colin Pardoe, Colin Groves and Peter Brown, have argued that obvious differences in these early peoples result from sexual dimorphism, not race; men were bigger and more robust than women.

Modes of dispersal

Having arrived in Greater Australia, how did people then go about dispersing across the continent? They could have achieved this in a number of ways (Figure 1.9). Birdsell reasoned that the migrants must have already been well adapted to a maritime life based on collecting of foods from the tidal zone and seas of island Southeast Asia. However, population increase would next have forced rapid

FIGURE 1.9

Different models for dispersal of the first Australian colonists. From left to right: Birdsell's radiational model, Bowdler's coastal colonization model and Horton's 'well watered regions first' model.
(After Flood 1995, Figure 5.1)

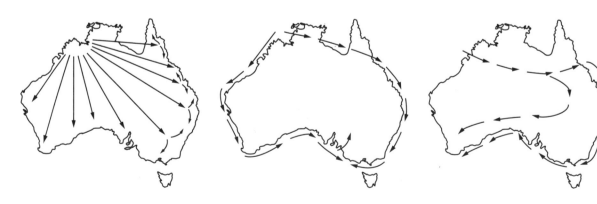

⋮ *12*

adjustments in culture and technology, and this in turn would have enabled the exploitation of land resources. Birdsell used historical data on rates of human population increase to show that, once land-oriented economies developed, it was possible for the whole of Greater Australia to have been filled to saturation point within 5000 years. In this scenario, human occupation would have radiated out from the initial beachhead as a 'bow wave' in a virtually instantaneous process, with no perceivable difference between the earliest colonization dates for any parts of Australia.

In contrast, Sandra Bowdler argued that people most probably stuck to what they knew, and diffused first along the coastline and up the major river systems, where their coastal economies could be translated to freshwater conditions. In her 'coastal colonization' model, areas away from the coast and major river systems were not settled until much later; less than 12 000 years ago, when the occupation of desert and montane regions began in earnest. Discoveries made since Bowdler proposed her model, especially the 32 000-year-old Puritjarra site in Central Australia, now show that her suggested late timing for the development of land economies is not correct.

As the archaeological evidence for the occupation of all major resource zones by 25 000 BP has accumulated, so models for the nature of subsequent population growth and the effects of long-term climatic change have become less mechanistic. They have been constructed with more awareness of the differences in human carrying capacity of different resource zones, and the likely impacts of climatic change upon regional occupation sequences. Peter Veth, for instance, distinguished three broad biogeographical zones in Australia: 'refuges', where fresh water was always available and people could have remained even during the last glacial maximum; 'corridors', which would have been occupied or abandoned depending on climatic conditions; and 'barriers', like desert dunefields, which were particularly difficult environments and were only occupied much later (after people developed survival aids such as kangaroo-skin water bags and the ability to dig deep wells for tapping groundwater). Veth's model fits the available evidence very well. Occupation sites in identifiable 'corridor' areas were abandoned at the last glacial maximum, as his model would predict, and the oldest sites in the harshest, sandy deserts are less than 3000 years old (Figure 1.10), suggesting that they were indeed 'barriers'.

FIGURE **1.10**

Peter Veth's biogeographical model for Australian colonization. He argues that 'refuges' with permanent water were occupied first and then continuously; 'corridors' were occupied intermittently when climatic conditions allowed; and 'dunefield barriers' were only occupied within the past 5000 years after people had developed kangaroo skin waterbags, the ability to dig deep wells to tap ground water and extensive social networks. (After Veth 1989)

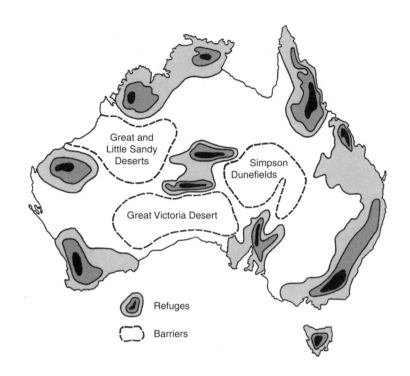

Great and Little Sandy Deserts

Simpson Dunefields

Great Victoria Desert

Refuges

Barriers

Early Australians

The history of Aboriginal occupation of Australia can be divided into two broad phases. The first, from the initial arrival of people up to the mid-Holocene (that is, about 5000 BP), was marked by relatively low populations, comparatively little technological variation, and by (rock) art traditions that were long-lived, widespread, and uniform over large areas—at least, compared with what followed. The second phase, from the mid-Holocene to the time of European impact, is distinguished by rapid increase in population densities, and an efflorescence of technological and artistic variation.

This is not to say that in the first phase, nothing happened. True, in most regions there are few early archaeological sites of this age and they tend to be ephemeral in nature, implying that population density was relatively low (Figure 1.11). But by 25 000 years ago people had spread to occupy all major resource zones—coastal, montane, desert and rainforest. A wide range of resources was used right from the initial phase of human settlement, including marine and freshwater fish and shellfish, and land animals.

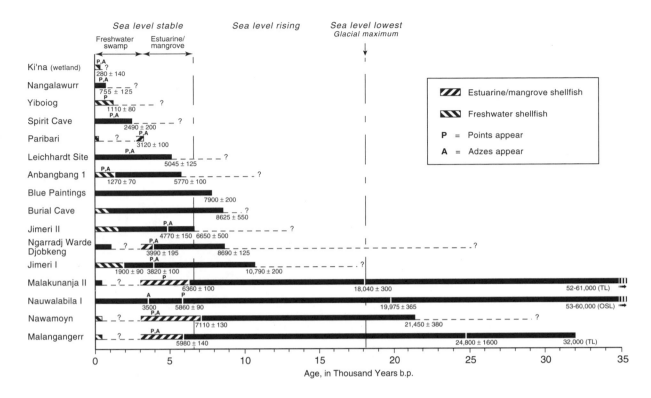

FIGURE 1.11

The history of occupation for excavated sites in western Arnhem Land. The earliest sites are between 50 000 and 60 000 years old, but a rapid increase in number of sites (and probably people) began when sea level stabilised around 6 000 years ago. This was also the time when the regionally distinctive X-ray rock painting style began.
The formation of rich and productive freshwater swamps over the past 1500 years led to further population increases, associated with more elaborate rock painting styles. (From Morwood and Hobbs 1995; Figure 3)

People also set about modifying the natural environment to better suit their needs. For example, evidence from New Guinea shows that from this time people were modifying the landscape with fire, while the transporting of the cuscus (an agreeably slow-moving prey item and a substantial meal) to the Bismarck Islands in West Melanesia indicates that people were actively manipulating the animal resources to their advantage. By 9000 BP, the management of 'wild' resources in parts of the New Guinea Highlands had intensified to include the planting of crops and the construction of drainage canals.

Across the rest of the Australian continent, human firing and hunting may also have been a major contributing factor in vegetation changes and in the extinction of many animals, particularly large-bodied (megafauna) species, such as *Diprotodon, Procoptodon* and *Genyornis* (Figure 1.12). In his book *The Future Eaters,* Tim Flannery put forward a *Blitzkrieg* model of human colonisation, in which an advancing wave of colonists had an unsustainable impact upon

FIGURE 1.12

The giant short-faced kangaroo (Procoptodon) *grew to 3 metres in height and browsed on scrubs. This and many other megafaunal species appear to have become extinct by 40 000 years BP.*

(Drawing by Kathy Morwood)

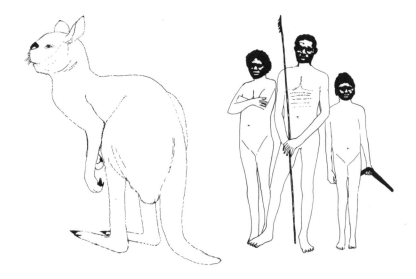

animals that had no previous exposure to humans. Recent OSL dating of megafauna sites by Tim Flannery and Bert Roberts suggest that he might be right—a major extinction event around 46 000 BP seems to have been contemporaneous with the arrival of humans, not with climate deterioration.

With regard to technology, we have two major categories of evidence. The first of these are recovered artefacts, and foremost among these are stone artefacts, simply because they are the most common technological items preserved in Australian archaeological sites.

In the first phase of occupation, stone tools were predominantly the simple unhafted flakes and cores of the Australian Core Tool and Scraper Tradition (Figure 1.13). Small grindstones were also used for the preparation of ochre and plant foods. The stone toolkit of this time appears to have been fairly basic and rather uniform across the continent, but regional variation is also apparent. Some of this variation we can put down to differences in the range of suitable rock types available, but there are also some quite peculiar, and to date inexplicable patterns of distribution. For instance, edge-ground axes, which in recent times were used in most areas of mainland Australia (for woodworking, removing honey and possums from trees, and as weapons), occur in the earliest occupation sites in the Kimberley, Arnhem Land and southeast Cape York Peninsula, but do not appear elsewhere in Australia until 5000 years ago at most

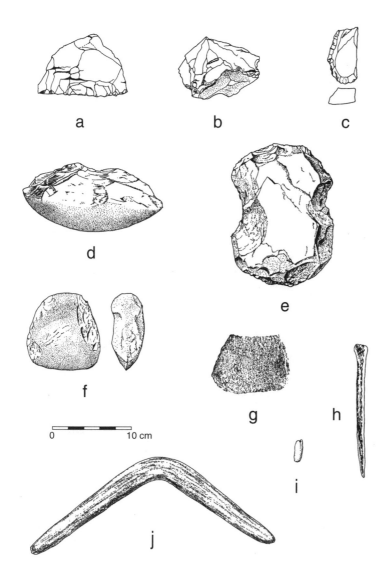

FIGURE 1.13

Early Australian artefacts: (a), (b) core tools; (c) retouched flake scraper; (d) pebble tool; (e) waisted blade; (f) edge-ground axe head; (g) small grindstone; (h) bone point; (i) bone bead from Devil's Lair; (j) wooden returning boomerang from Wyrie Swamp in South Australia. (Drawing by Kathy Morwood)

0   10 cm

(Figure 1.14). Why such a useful technology did not spread rapidly is a mystery.

Occasionally, under favourable conditions, organic artefacts and items are preserved. For instance, 25 wooden implements dated to between 10 200 and 8990 BP were excavated by Roger Luebbers at Wyrie Swamp in South Australia. The find included 'a simple short spear, at least two types of digging stick, and a barbed javelin fragment carved from a single piece of wood' (Luebbers 1975).

FIGURE 1.14

Dates for edge-ground axes in Australia. These occur in the earliest occupation levels of sites in the Kimberley, Arnhem Land and parts of Cape York Peninsula, between 60 000 and 40 000 years ago. However, they did not spread down the east coast until 5000 BP at the most. In Central Australia edge-ground axes do not appear until 1000 years ago, while further to the southwest, they were adopted even more recently—if at all. (Morwood and Trezise 1989, Figure 1)

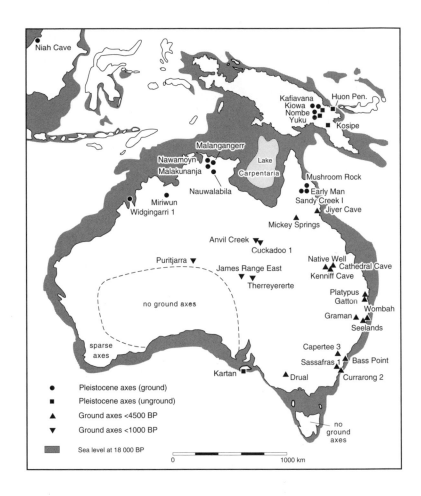

Bone points were also used; they have been recovered from Devils Lair in Western Australia, Cloggs Cave in the Victorian Alps, and Cave Bay Cave on Hunter Island in Bass Strait. In addition, we can at least *infer* that the first colonists had watercraft and that they used nets: they had to have watercraft to reach Australia, while the size range of fish caught at Lake Mungo indicates they were netted, not speared or hooked.

Artefacts can give us more than bare examples of technologies of the past. For example, we know that early peoples in Australia were also decorating themselves just as modern humans do; this is evident in the 22 pierced shell beads recovered from the lowest levels of Mandu Mandu rockshelter on North West Cape, Western Australia, dated to around 32 000 years ago. Most likely these were part of a necklace or headband (Figure 1.15). Long-distance exchange of goods (which included aesthetic, prestige items) is also evident at a number of early sites. For instance, fragments of baler shell and pearlshell recovered from Koolan 2 on Koolan Island in the southern Kimberley are dated to 28 000 and 19 000 BP respectively. The pearlshell was transported to the site at a time when the coastline was 200 kilometres away, indicating that people occupied the now-drowned coastal shelf, and were moving or trading items and materials over considerable distances. Similarly, in Central Australia, red ochre from 30 000-year-old levels at Puritjarra Rockshelter came from the Karrku ochre source, about 150 kilometres away and across a dune field. This ochre find brings us to the second major window into the remote past in Australia—art.

Red ochre and other pigments have been found all the way to the base of the earliest sites of human settlement in Australia. It seems that they were used for a range of ceremonial and decorative purposes, including rock painting. At Lake Mungo, for example, a burial was sprinkled with red ochre 30 000 years ago, while at Carpenter's Gap shelter in the southern Kimberley the local people had painted a section of the shelter wall by 39 700 years ago; this is the earliest evidence for rock art anywhere in the world. Evidence of rock painting dating to 28 000 BP has also been found embedded in mineral accretions covering the original rock art surface at Walk-Under Arch and Sandy Creek 2 in northeast Queensland.

In most parts of Australia, the rock surfaces are dynamic—that is, they either erode away quite quickly, or are fairly rapidly obscured by mineral deposits. This means that finds such as those at Carpenter's Gap are rare, the consequence of some lucky chance of preservation, or unusual local condition. In contrast, the unusual hardness and slow weathering rates of rock outcrops in western Arnhem Land and parts of the Kimberley mean that some of the earliest rock paintings created in these regional sequences are likely to be still visible on the rock surfaces.

In both the Kimberley and western Arnhem Land, the earliest paintings known are large red ochre paintings of animals, fish and yams, plus a few 'humans' and weapons. It is intriguing to note that the paintings include depictions of some large animals, such as *Palorchestes*, the marsupial tapir, which probably became extinct in the initial phase of colonization, suggesting that these still-undated paintings do indeed survive from the very earliest period of

FIGURE 1.15

Necklace of Conus *shell beads excavated from 32 000-year-old levels at Mandu Mandu rockshelter on North West Cape, Western Australia. This is the same age as the earliest necklaces found elsewhere in the world. Personal decoration and art seem to have been features of Aboriginal culture from initial occupation.* (After Noble and Davidson 1996, Figure 37)

occupation. Also associated with the earliest paintings in these two regions are stencils of hands, boomerangs and other items. Such stencils provide unique and fascinating evidence for organic items in the toolkits of very early populations—the actual outline of someone's hand or personal belongings, tens of thousands of years ago, recorded on the rock surface.

Hand stencils older than 12 000 BP have also been found in the limestone caves of southwest Tasmania, indicating that this art form was widely distributed throughout the continent at the time. Elsewhere in Australia, during the first phase of settlement, there was a widespread and relatively homogeneous rock engraving tradition, the Panaramitee, dominated by circles and tracks (Figure 1.16).

On the other hand, in contrast to all this homogeneity, stylistic similarities between the earliest rock art styles in the Kimberley and western Arnhem Land set them apart as a distinctive rock art province. Darrell Lewis, for instance, regards Bradshaw and Dynamic figures as regional variants of the same rock art tradition. The distinctiveness of the northwest is also seen in the distribution of early edge-ground axes and the distribution of non-Pama-Nyungan Aboriginal languages. In later chapters we will see more evidence of the 'oddity' of this corner of the continent—for now, we can note that from the very earliest times, people and cultures in the northwest corner of Australia stand out as different.

This apart though, and compared with what followed, the first phase of settlement was a time of *relative* uniformity of culture and technology, both across time and space. In this context, it is striking that what we do know of the richness and complexity of Greater Australian culture and ideology comes from rock art, language dispersal, and other types of symbolic evidence. If we relied solely on the most commonly surviving evidence in the archaeological record, stone artefacts, our picture of Australia's earliest populations would be impoverished indeed.

A world in transition

The Holocene period—from 10 000 BP to the present—was a time of massive environmental, social and economic change. We see the beginnings of it as early as 15 000 BP, in the dying days of the last

FIGURE 1.16

Pecked engravings at Panaramitee Station, South Australia. Kangaroo and bird tracks are the predominant motifs, followed by a range of geometric designs, such as circles and groups of dots. Similar panels of deeply weathered pecked engravings occur over most of Australia and have been termed the Panaramitee Tradition. (From Mountford and Edwards 1963)

glacial period, as the globe warmed and rainfall rose. By 10 000 BP, climatic conditions in Australia were much as they are today, and the pace of Aboriginal technological and cultural change in the region began to pick up. This rate of change, though, escalated abruptly from 5000 BP; from this point onwards, we see a mass of continuing changes in the archaeological record.

In the northern highland fringes of Greater Australia, the early Holocene, from about 9000 BP saw the development of horticulture, probably involving the cultivation of yams and taro. Evidence for cultivation comes from the site of Kuk in the Wahgi

Valley of the New Guinea Highlands by 9000 years ago, well before the land bridge between Australia and New Guinea was flooded. Over subsequent millennia, the 'invention' of horticulture began to have its own impacts on human populations. The expansion of the Trans-New Guinea section of the Papuan language family across New Guinea and to the east Indonesian islands of Alor, Pantar and Timor prior to 4000 BP probably reflects population movement and growth resulting from this development. Greater Australia at this time was not just a passive recipient of cultural and economic innovations and population movements from areas to the west, but was itself a source of innovation and movement.

There were clearly exchanges of cultural traits, resources and probably people between Greater Australia and adjacent regions. Some 5000 years ago, Austronesian-speaking horticulturists began to spread from Taiwan across island Southeast Asia and then the Pacific. They arrived in east Indonesia around 4000 years ago, bringing a range of cultivated plants and domestic animals, including the dog and pig. Around the same time, the dog (or dingo) was introduced into Australia, presumably from Timor, where dingo-like skeletal remains of this age have been excavated.

The introduction of the dingo coincides with widespread technological, economic, demographic, linguistic and symbolic changes in Aboriginal culture (Figure 1.17) (The single and singular exception to this was in Tasmania, which was cut off from the mainland by rising seas 11 000 years ago.) One of the major debates in Australian archaeology is the reason for this swathe of changes, which included:

- A general reduction in Aboriginal size and robusticity. This was a worldwide trend also seen in many animal species, presumably as a response to global warming: in general, Ice Age animals, including humans, tended to be larger than their Holocene counterparts.
- The spread of the Pama-Nyungan language family across 80 per cent of the Australian continent, implying large-scale population movement at this time.
- A dramatic increase in the number of archaeological sites, and an apparent increase in the intensity of use of some archaeological sites. This increase seems to reflect a major increase in population.
- Exploitation of new food resources, specifically the appearance of labour-intensive food procurement strategies, such as the

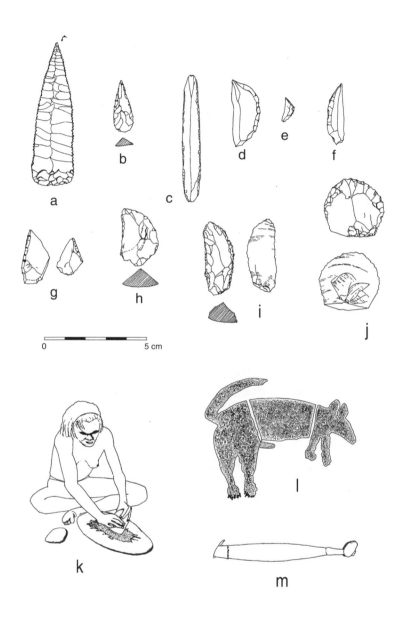

FIGURE 1.17

Additions to Aboriginal culture over the last 5000 years: (a),(b) bifacial and unifacial points; (c) blade; (d),(h) backed blades; (i) elouera; (i) burren adze slug; (j) thumbnail scraper; (k) grinding of acacia and grass seeds; (l) dingo; (m) North Queensland spearthrower.
(Drawing by Kathy Morwood)

0   5 cm

grinding of grass seeds and the elaborate processing of cycads to remove toxins. This again seems to speak of increased population: it also appears to coincide with the first evidence for large-scale ceremonial gatherings of the type observed in historic times.

- The addition of new stone artefact technologies: first, a general reduction in artefact size, with more controlled flaking; and second, the appearance of new implement types, such as backed blades and adzes. More efficient use (that is, rationing) of stone for flaking was very likely a general response to increased demands on this resource because of population increase. The new implement types included some with a long developmental history in Australia (such as edge-ground axes and burren adzes) and others, more novel, which may have been introduced from Southeast Asia. In either case, the spread of new technologies suggests a basic change in alliance and information exchange systems, towards an increasing flow.

• The appearance of a greater diversity of regional rock art systems. This seems to reflect the closure of social networks as groups became more concerned with emphasizing their ownership of particular tracts of land and resources (see Chapter 7).

There has been much debate about whether the primary cause for many of these changes was external contact, population increase and dispersal, or intensified social demands on production systems. Although the arrival of the dingo, at least, is indisputable evidence for some external contact at this time, we will see that most aspects of culture change over the past 5000 years can be satisfactorily explained in terms of indigenous Australian developments. These included new mechanisms for the wider diffusion of previously localized technologies, such as edge-ground axes and burren adzes.

In some regions, for example, population growth from this time seems clearly to be related to the generally more people-friendly climate, which usually brought an increase in the resource base. For instance, in western Arnhem Land high, stable sea levels over the past 6000 years and the more recent formation of freshwater swamps led to a huge increase in food resources for local people. Similarly, in southeast Cape York Peninsula, most freshwater swamps, which were important sources of plant foods and drinkable water, formed during the Holocene, particularly over the past 2500 years.

But in other areas, there was either little environmental change or actually deterioration in local resources during the Holocene. For instance, higher rainfall between 9000 and 6000 years ago should have allowed for population growth in arid areas—but in fact we do not see population growth in the Victorian Mallee and Central Australia until much later. In the case of Central Australia, it seems that technological change was the key; exponential population growth did not begin until around 1500 years ago, and is associated with the first evidence for large-scale processing of grass and acacia seeds, a labour-intensive activity which in historic times was a dietary mainstay for both domestic and social consumption. In fact, the large ceremonial gatherings that characterized recent Central Australian culture would not have been possible without this 'seed economy'.

So the mid-Holocene 'efflorescence' was not completely simultaneous, nor completely Australia-wide; it was only the starting point for a series of changes that continued right up to recent times. In southeast Cape York Peninsula, for example, technological developments in stone artefact manufacture can be detected as early as 15 000 years ago, but were not apparent at some sites in the region until the last millennium (see Chapter 10). In the central Queensland highlands, a whole suite of new traits appeared at 5000 BP (see Chapter 7, while in Central Australia, a major restructuring of Aboriginal land use began 1500 years ago in the central ranges, but did not reach more outlying areas, such as the Simpson Desert, until a mere 600 BP.

These differences in the timing and specific nature of these changes in Aboriginal culture in different parts of Australia suggest that both general and local factors were responsible for the multitude of changes that we find from this time on. The point is best made by looking in more detail at a case study, in southeast Queensland (Figure 1.18).

Close-up: southeast Queensland

In recent times, southeast Queensland was a rich area for hunter–gatherers and supported high population levels, but this has not always been so; major components of this resource abundance were a result of climatic change, which triggered a cascade of changes.

At the height of the last Ice Age, 18 000 years ago, when sea levels were 130 metres lower than today, the coast here was some 40 kilometres to the east of its current position, at the edge of the continental shelf. This meant that beach gradients were steep, and the littoral zone relatively unproductive. The area could not, and did not, support a large human population.

All this changed, though, when at the ending of the last glacial period the sea rose and flooded the lower Brisbane River Valley to

FIGURE 1.18

Southeast Queensland showing tribal areas and movement of people to the bunya feasts. Gatherings of up to 2000 people were reported in historic times, with people coming from as far away as Port Macquarie on the central coast of New South Wales— a distance of 550 kilometres. Coordination of such population movements required collecting, exchanging and assessing information, which in turn relied on ways of assessing the status and trustworthiness of information sources. Symbolic markers, such as body paintings, cicatrices (body scarring) and shield designs played an essential role here. (After Morwood 1987)

form an area of shallow seas and enclosed waters—Moreton Bay. This change has been followed by 6000 years of stable sea levels, a stability unique during the timespan of human occupation of Australia. Mangrove mudflat areas of great biological productivity developed in the shallow and stable littoral conditions, and there is good evidence that dugong, turtle, fish, shellfish and crustaceans all had well-established populations in Moreton Bay by 4000 years ago.

Not only was there an increase in the abundance of resources, but regional resource structure also changed. The long-standing summer bonanza of bunya nuts in the Blackall Range and Bunya Mountains was now matched by huge winter runs of fish, such as mullet, in Moreton Bay (Figure 1.19). While the richer littoral and marine resources over the past 6000 years would have provided scope for population growth, it was the development of cultural mechanisms for the more efficient use of these geographically and seasonally patchy gluts of resources that further raised the regional carrying capacity for local Aboriginal people.

Prior to 6000 BP

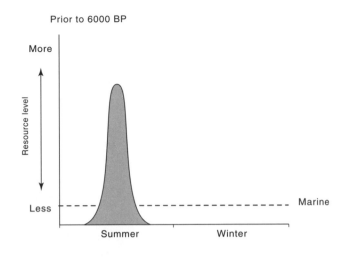

FIGURE 1.19

Changes in resource structure in southeast Queensland. Prior to 6000 BP sea level was lower and constantly changing. Over the last 6000 years it has been relatively stable, estuarine mudflat areas have developed and marine resources became far more abundant with a distinct peak in winter corresponding to huge runs of fish, such as mullet. From this time, an inland/summer glut of bunya nuts and a coastal/winter glut of fish promoted seasonal movement of people and the development of economic exchange.
(After Morwood 1987)

After 6000 BP

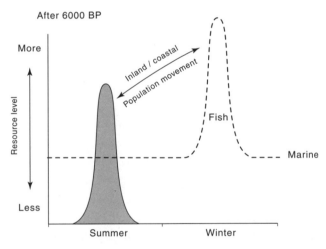

WHAT ETHNOGRAPHY TELLS US

There are two main strategies for the efficient use of resource gluts: one can use storage techniques, such as the drying of fish, to extend the seasonal availability of foods over the lean times between; or one can establish a system which allows people to cluster or disperse depending on food availability. With a few exceptions, Australian Aborigines chose the latter strategy—demographic flexibility—and this was certainly the case in southeast Queensland.

In historic times, the movement of people within and between group territories and regions in southeast Queensland, for initiations,

FIGURE 1.20

Decorated shields, removal of teeth, decorative body scarring and body paintings symbolized an individual's affiliation and status, and therefore their trustworthiness in information exchange and decision making. The ribbed designs painted on Gaiarbaul/ Willie Mackenzie's body refer specifically to ferns, which characterized his country in the sub-coastal ranges of southeast Queensland.

(Photo Winterbotham Collection; courtesy Anthropology Museum, Queensland University)

ceremonies, corroborees, fights and feasts, is well attested. For instance, the bunya festivals in the Bunya Mountains attracted gatherings of up to 2000 people from as far away as the central Queensland highlands and the Kamilaroi area of northern New South Wales. Although local people did store bunya nuts and fish for short periods, it was clearly the movement of people that made efficient use of food surpluses far beyond the needs of a local group.

The flexibility in population dispersal may have been underwritten by resource gluts, but it also would not have been possible without a distinct social infrastructure involving an established network of contacts, rights and obligations based on marriage, trade and ceremonies. Further, it required sophisticated monitoring of resource availability, a means for disseminating the information needed for constant adjustments to population distribution, and ways of controlling the level of violence between disparate groups at large gatherings.

Means for collecting, exchanging, verifying and acting on information about resource levels characterized Aboriginal culture in southeast Queensland. For instance, local people could predict when possums would be at their fattest, or the size of the coming mullet run, by observing the flowering of certain trees, the behaviour of birds, and so on. The information was then passed on in a number of formal and informal ways. Messengers with distinctive shield and body paintings and carrying message sticks as symbols of their authority would be sent to invite other groups to attend gatherings (Figure 1.20). At large-scale gatherings senior men would formally relate what had been occurring in their areas, corroborees would sometimes depict actual events, and gossip would be exchanged.

Tensions between groups were reduced through competitive games, and when violence did break out it was usually minimized. For instance, knife duels between individuals were supervised: cuts could only be inflicted on the back and legs, and the 'umpires' evened up the score at the end of the fight. Similarly, fights between groups generally had equal numbers of participants on each side, and hostilities stopped when someone was killed or wounded.

There were also established means for displaying and assessing the degree of authority, allegiance and trustworthiness of individuals involved in information exchange and decision making. These included shield and body paintings, body scarring, the removal of

FIGURE 1.21

The Gatton rock engraving site in southeast Queensland. This was the first rock art site in Queensland to be scientifically investigated—in 1884 by Henry Tryon of the Queensland Museum, who commented that some of the pecked designs resembled the distinctive cicatrices (body scars) of local people. Archaeological excavations have shown that this rock engraving site was first used around 4000 years ago—a time of rapid population build-up.
(Photo M. J. Morwood)

the left little finger of 'coastal' women and possession of esoteric knowledge about creation events and the associated meaning of rock paintings, carved trees, and so on (Figure 1.21). The same symbolic markers encoded information about group and status similarities and differences. In fact, the use of multi-media, symbolic paraphernalia, which could be distinctive or shared, was an integral part of Aboriginal social complexity in southeast Queensland.

WHAT ARCHAEOLOGY TELLS US

On the basis of what we know about Holocene changes in resource levels and structures, as well as the ethnographic evidence, we can suggest that the Aboriginal population in southeast Queensland grew substantially from about 6000 years ago because of the increase in resource levels, but that the honing of cultural means for making more efficient use of resources subsequently led to yet further population increases. Archaeological evidence for population increase could include:

- more sites
- more intensive use of sites
- more intensive economic strategies, particularly those that target small-bodied plant or animal foods
- movement into more marginal areas.

Evidence for increases in socioeconomic complexity could include:

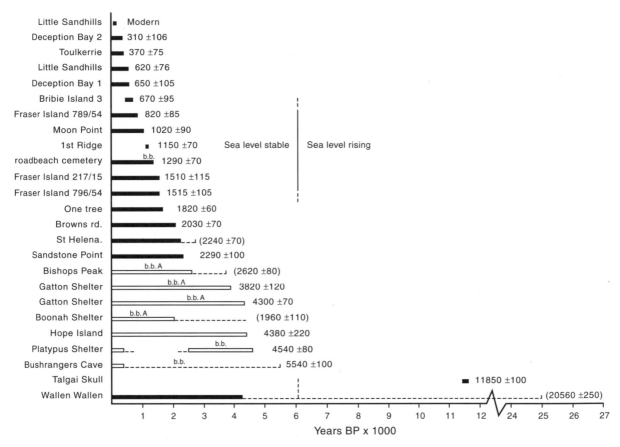

FIGURE 1.22

Dated Aboriginal sites in southeast Queensland. The figure shows that initial occupation of the region had occurred by 30 000 BP, but a rapid increase in population occurred in the last 6000 years after stabilization of sea level and more estuarine resources. There is also evidence for increasingly complex social networks and population movements from this time—facilitated by new means for exchange and assessment of information on the availability of resources. All dated rock art sites in southeast Queensland are less than 5000 years old, indicating that they played an important role in these developments.
(After Morwood 1987)

• more sites concerned with symbolic activities, such as bora rings and rock art sites
• the appearance of exotic items and technologies
• social gatherings of increasing size.

All of these suggested lines of evidence do indeed occur in the archaeological record of the region (Figure 1.22). There is an exponential increase in site numbers over the past 6000 years, with all of the dated rock art sites in the region being less than 5000 years old. There is an expansion of the diet, with greater emphasis on smaller animals such as shellfish and fish on the coast, and possums and koalas at inland sites. Around 5000 BP many new stone artefact types and technologies appeared in the region, including backed blades, adzes and edge-ground axes, signalling major developments in regional (and Australia-wide) communication systems. Furthermore, the loss of backed blades from the inventory around 1000 years ago seems to coincide with a change in hunting techniques, from individual hunting strategies in which single kangaroos and wallabies were speared, to cooperative hunting involving drives and nets. Strategies like this allowed large gatherings to be fed on large numbers of animals caught in nets, as we know from early European records.

There is certainly evidence that the scale of gatherings continued to increase markedly very late in the cultural sequence. Thus, when Europeans arrived in the area, ceremonial gatherings of up to 2000 Aboriginal people were observed at Sandstone Point near Bribie Island north of Brisbane, and bora rings used for initiations, a stone fishtrap and extensive middens testify to the richness and importance of the area. However, use of Sandstone Point—even transient use— seems to have commenced only about 2300 years ago. Use of fish at the site began 1500 BP, and the first evidence for intensive, large-scale use dates to the last 1000 years. The large social gatherings recorded by early Europeans in the area thus appear to have been a very recent development indeed, suggesting that population expansion and the cultural innovation this brought was still accelerating.

In summary, changes in the resource levels in southeast Queensland over the past 6000 years allowed populations to increase, while the new resource configuration seems to have promoted the development of demographic flexibility, the required reciprocity network and further population increases. Extrapolating from this case study, it seems most likely that the changes we observe in the Australian archaeological record from 5000 BP resulted from a complex of interacting factors.

As we move from consideration of a single regional culture to larger areas, we can also add to the agents of change the possibility of diffusion of the new social models themselves. The adaptive advantage given by new social mechanisms, which facilitated the more efficient use of resources and higher population densities, means that they would then have spread to all parts of mainland Australia from 'catalyst' areas like southeast Queensland and Arnhem Land. Here, close examination of historic examples of cultural contact between Aboriginal Australia and external groups can help us understand cultural change in the archaeological record. Thus, recent case studies such as those involving cultural contact with island Southeast Asia and New Guinea show that the results of outside contact were not always simple, predictable or one-way. The archaeology of symbolic evidence, such as rock art, will play a prominent part in our future investigations of the way in which Aboriginal culture developed over time.

Recent Australian cultural contact and change

Australian Aboriginal culture did not develop in isolation. For much of the relevant timespan Australia and New Guinea were joined, and there has probably always been contact between Australia and Asia: it begins, after all, with the first colonization itself. The complexity of outside contacts has probably been much underestimated, as shown by documented cultural interactions in recent times.

For instance, at the time of European contact a trade network existed between New Guinea and Cape York across Torres Strait (Figure 1.23). This trade involved canoes, spears, spearthrowers, pigments and human heads. Some aspects of northeast Australian Aboriginal culture were definitely Papuan borrowings (for instance, the use of outrigger canoes, snakeskin drums, pineapple-headed clubs, ritual, mythology). The boundary between Australian hunter–gatherers and the food-producing Papuan peoples was also fuzzy: people on the eastern and northwestern islands of Torres Strait had permanent coastal villages with a predominantly horticultural economy; those on the central islands had a hunting and gathering economy supplemented by small-scale horticulture; and people on the western islands were hunter–gatherers. The complexity of past contact and population movements is reflected in the distribution of language types in the strait. Miriam, spoken on the eastern islands, is related to Papuan languages, while western islanders speak Mabuiag, which is related to Australian Aboriginal languages with a strong Papuan overlay.

It is significant that Australia was not a passive recipient in this cultural contact. Outrigger canoes, fishhooks and other items may have been introduced to northeast Australia across Torres Strait, but Aboriginal spears and spearthrowers were much sought after in Papua, while the distribution of harpoons in northern Australia, Torres Strait and Papua indicates that in this region they were probably an Australian invention.

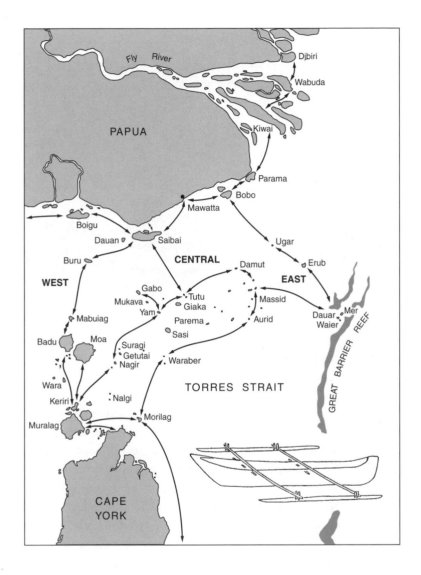

FIGURE 1.23

Trade routes across Torres Strait. Trade items included canoe hulls, weapons, ochre and human heads. As a result of such trade, Aboriginal groups in parts of Cape York Peninsula adopted the outrigger dugout canoe, fishhooks, pineapple-headed clubs and hero cults—but they did not take up the bow and arrow or gardening. The reasons for cultural change occurring (or not occurring) as a result of outside contact are complex. (After Moore 1978)

Turning to northwest Australia, the most intensive Asian–Australian contact in recent times involved Indonesian seafarers. We know that Macassans, Bugis, Butonese and Bajau people, from islands such as Sulawesi, Madura, Flores, Timor and Roti, visited parts of the north Australian coast to collect marine resources such as trepang (sea slugs or sea cucumbers), pearlshell, turtleshell, clam meat and shark fins.

There is a range of historical evidence for these visits to Australia, which on the basis of Dutch East India Company records began

An Indonesian trepang processing site on the Arnhem Land coast drawn by Harden S. Melville, artist on HMS Fly, *about 1843–45. The view is somewhat idealized. Remains of such Asian industrial sites are still found along the coasts of the Kimberley, Arnhem Land and the Gulf of Carpentaria. They include lines of stone hearths, wells, graves, layers of ash and scatters of broken pottery.* (The Queen, 8 February 1862)

around 1725 CE. Nineteenth-century European navigators, such as Matthew Flinders, encountered Macassan trepang fleets in the north (Figure 1.24). They reported that Indonesian trepangers came to Australia in summer on the monsoonal winds and returned on the trade winds, and that up to 2000 men were involved in the Arnhem Land industry. Systematic Indonesian trepang collection and onshore processing occurred along two sections of the northern Australia coastline—the Kimberley, known to Indonesian seafarers as *Kaju Djawa*, and Arnhem Land, known as *Marege*. It was processed onshore, taken back to Macassar, the chief port on the east Indonesian island of Sulawesi, then shipped to China, where it was used as a flavouring in soups and as an aphrodisiac (Figure 1.25). It is sobering to think that Australia's first commodity to be valued in international trade was not wool or gold, but sea slugs.

Although large-scale visits by Indonesians to the Kimberley and Arnhem Land ceased in 1900 and 1907 CE, respectively, these regular visits also left a range of archaeological evidence along the Kimberley and Arnhem Land coastlines, in the form of shipwrecks, processing sites, graves and tamarind trees. They also had social, linguistic, technological, economic, artistic and genetic impacts on local Aboriginal people. For instance, Indonesians probably introduced both smallpox and the cat to northern Australia. Malay also became the *lingua franca* along the coast; while Macassan and

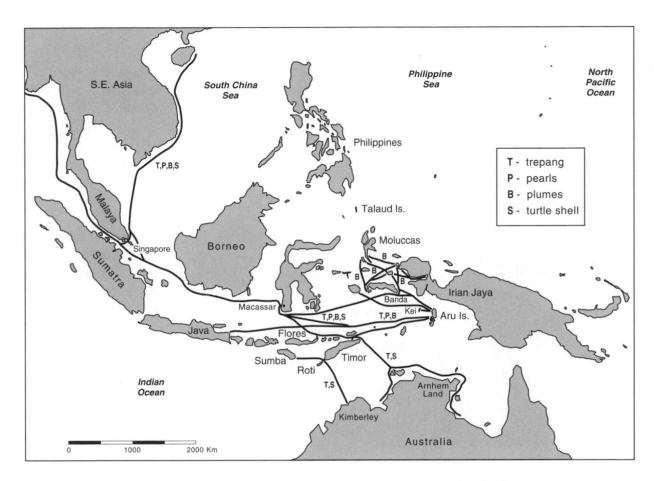

FIGURE 1.25

Part of the east Indonesian trade network in historic times. This included regular, large-scale visits to the North Australian coast to collect trepang, pearl shell and turtle shell. Processed trepang was shipped from regional collection points, such as Macassar in Sulawesi, to China, where it was used as a flavouring in soups and as an aphrodisiac.
(After Healey 1980 and Macknight 1976)

Sama (Bajau) words were incorporated into local languages for some places and personal names, and for introduced items. The latter included the dugout canoe (*lepa-lepa* in Macassan and *lippa-lippa* in Arnhem Land languages); the long wooden smoking pipe; and iron, which was used for making harpoon heads and shovel-nosed spears.

However, the most complex effects of Indonesian contact were in the symbolic sphere—in legend and ceremony and, of course, in art. Macassans are portrayed in rock and bark paintings (Figure 1.26); while on Groote Eylandt carved burial poles imitate the posts on Macassan graves. Macassan boats are also depicted in stone arrangements and in ceremonies, while some items of material culture became Aboriginal ceremonial totems—the square-faced gin bottle and *prau* sails being just two examples.

FIGURE 1.26

A bark painting from northeast Arnhem Land showing Macassans boiling down trepang in cauldrons, praus and a mangrove tree. Painted by Mataman Marika at Yirrkala in 1964. (Courtesy family of the artist and the National Museum of Australia)

The culture of Aboriginal hunter–gatherers was thus enriched, particularly in the sphere of art, ceremony, myth and language. However, it is significant that, despite such long-term contacts with groups who practised horticulture, had a range of domestic animals, and used pottery and metal, the fundamental basis of hunter–gatherer Australian Aboriginal society did not change. The main reason is that in recent times neither the Indonesians nor the Papuans were interested in permanent occupation of the contact areas of Australia which were not suitable for cultivation. No foreigners were, until the establishment of a British penal colony at Port Jackson in 1788.

European settlement of Australia is clearly documented in the 'post-contact' subjects in rock art panels. It is also recorded indirectly, in changes in the character and distribution of rock art sites. In the Victoria River District, for instance, there appears to have been a brief post-contact efflorescence in rock painting because of local population displacement by European pastoral incursions; in many other parts of Australia, the last phase of rock painting is characterized by the use of white, and the paintings were roughly executed. With a few exceptions, the painting or engraving of rock surfaces is no longer a part of Aboriginal culture. Its very absence is a form of record, testimony to the destruction of traditional Aboriginal life.

CHAPTER 2

Australian Aboriginal rock art

Australia is the rock art capital of the world. It has many thousands of sites, with huge variation between regions and over time in motif range, technique, style and context. All areas of Australia with suitable rock surfaces have rock art, although in some (such as Victoria and southeastern Queensland), the number of known sites is small, while others (such as western Arnhem Land, the Kimberley, the Pilbara, southeastern Cape York, the central Queensland highlands and the Sydney Basin) have enormous numbers of rock art sites of national significance.

In a few remote areas rock art is still occasionally done by Aboriginal people, but in most areas its production ceased soon after European contact. This means we have little or no direct evidence on its meaning, either because the early European settlers failed to record relevant ethnographic information (as in Sydney), or because the rock art tradition is of considerable antiquity (as in the Bradshaw art of the Kimberley).

Art was a feature of Aboriginal life right from the time people first colonized this continent. Used pigment fragments excavated from Malakunanja II in western Arnhem Land show that Aboriginal painting has a minimum antiquity of between 52 000 and 61 000 years. More specifically, as we have seen, excavated evidence from Carpenter's Gap site in the southern Kimberley shows that rock painting was being done in Australia at least 39 700 years ago. At present this is the oldest evidence for rock painting in the world.

Early rock paintings are also evident at Sandy Creek 2 in southeast Cape York Peninsula, where a layer of pigment embedded in mineral crusts on the rockshelter wall dates to 27 000 years ago. The earliest figurative paintings from western Arnhem Land and the Kimberley also date back to the Pleistocene. For instance, a mudwasp nest overlying a Bradshaw painting is dated to at least 17 000 years old, and other archaeological evidence indicates that such paintings are at least 21 000 years old.

Other Pleistocene rock art sites include Koonalda Cave on the arid Nullarbor Plain, where finger markings and incised lines on the soft walls of the cave are probably contemporaneous with flint mining deep underground between 22 000 and 15 000 years ago; and the Early Man site, in southeastern Cape York Peninsula, where 14 000-year-old deposits cover a panel of pecked circles, dots, connecting lines, and bird tracks. The number of dated rock engravings increases as we move to more recent times.

There are hundreds of published and unpublished reports that refer to Aboriginal rock art in various parts of Australia, with the earliest dating virtually from the time of first European contact. For

FIGURE 2.1

Major rock art regions in Australia. There are many other regions with rock art concentrations which have not yet been investigated. (After Layton 1992a)

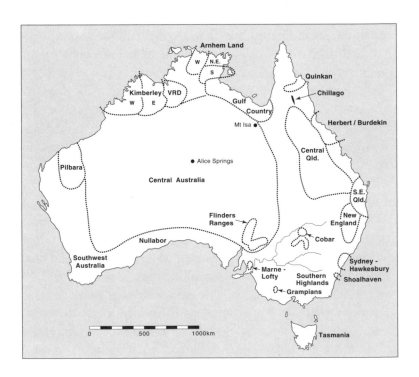

instance, in 1789 John Stockdale commented: 'in all these excursions of Governor Philip, in the neighbourhood of Botany Bay and Port Jackson, the figures of animals, of shields, and weapons, and even of men, have been carved upon the rocks, roughly indeed, but sufficiently well to ascertain very fully what was the object intended'.

Most published reports, however, are poor in quality, restricted to the most obvious aspects of a site, repetitive and virtually non-analytical. Even so, they do illustrate the large number of sites, their uneven distribution across the continent, the regional diversity of Aboriginal art, some of the changes that have occurred over time, and the range of techniques employed by Aboriginal rock artists.

They have also encouraged more systematic investigation of the art in some areas—though in many other areas no site recording work has yet been undertaken. The rock art bodies in some of the better-known areas are described below (Figure 2.1).

Central Australia

The art of Central Australia has a distinctive style characterized by the use of geometric motifs (circles, spirals, arcs, lines, dots) and tracks. This style can be seen in modern canvas paintings, sand drawings, body paintings, designs on weapons and sacred items, rock paintings and rock engravings. Many rock painting and engraving sites have been recorded in this vast region. Claire Smith has demonstrated the homogeneous nature of recent Aboriginal art in the resource-poor Western Desert region.

Although we have good ethnographic information on rock painting sites, there are very few references to the making of rock engravings. However, in 1937, Charles Mountford observed Aborigines in the Western Desert engraving geometric, track, figurative designs and alphabetical symbols by pounding through the dark-red patina on the surface of rocks to expose the lighter-coloured rock underneath (Figure 2.2). This engraving method is quite different from that used in many deeply pecked and patinated rock engraving assemblages in the region, which local Aborigines usually denied were made by humans. Bob Edwards noted that 'old' Central Australian engraving sites share a number of constant features, including close proximity to water, association with occupation debris, an advanced state of weathering and surface patination, and the consistent relative

FIGURE 2.2

Recent lightly pounded engravings in Central Australia. These include depictions of European subjects. (After Mountford 1955, Figures 3 and 4; 1976, Figure 9)

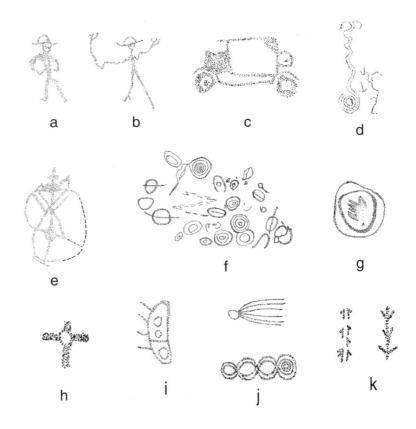

frequencies of motifs, with an emphasis on circles and tracks (Figure 2.3).

Edwards compared the relative frequencies of tracks, circles and 'other designs' at a number of sites—Tukulnga Rockhole, Florina, Panaramitee, Tiverton, Winnininnie, Cleland Hills—and found that they were remarkably similar in their percentage of the various motifs, even in sites 1300 kilometres apart (Figure 2.4). Edwards concluded that a simple rock engraving style might have been used over a wide area of the Australian continent and that 'these motifs predate the time when tribal boundaries became rigid and separate cultural entities developed'.

There is a range of evidence indicating that these old pecked engravings are part of an art tradition extending back into the Pleistocene. Although more recent engravings in the region have been made by shallow pecking and battering, the emphasis on geometric designs and tracks has continued. Surviving Central Australian rock

FIGURE 2.3

Top: *General view of Ewaninga, a typical Panaramitee style engraving site in Central Australia. The rock outcrop is located next to a claypan, which provides an ephemeral water source. The wooden platform was built to enable visitors to see the main engraved panel clearly without venturing onto the rock surface.* (Photo J. Ross)

Bottom: *The main panel of pecked engravings at Ewaninga. This ancient engraving site shows an emphasis on circles and tracks.* (Photo J. Ross)

paintings are probably no more than a few thousand years old at most, but have a similar emphasis on geometric designs and tracks, as do recent dot paintings produced on canvas at Hermannsburg.

The range of motifs used in Central Australian rock art does depend upon the context of production, however: sacred and secret art is almost exclusively made up of geometric designs and tracks, while art in secular, domestic situations places more emphasis on figurative motifs (Figure 2.5).

FIGURE 2.4

Ancient Panaramitee engraving sites in Central Australia emphasize circles and tracks, but also have a small percentage of figurative motifs. Among the best known of these are the engraved faces at Cleland Hills, west of Alice Springs.

This photograph shows a general view of an engraved pavement at Cleland Hills with circles, line mazes and an anthropomorph. (Photo M. A. Smith)

FIGURE 2.5

Public rock paintings at Walinga Cave (Owalinja) in the Musgrave Range south of Uluru (Ayers Rock). These occur in the living area of the site and can be viewed by women and uninitiated men. They have a much higher figurative content than panels of 'restricted' art in the same site. The site was originally on the lands of a Yankunjatjara clan of the Honey-ant totem. Its mythology focuses on the travels of the Kungkarungkara (seven virgin sisters), their protecting pack of dingos and an ancestral hero named Yula (meaning penis).

(After Mountford 1976, Plate 12)

Tasmania

Tasmania appears to have been first settled soon after people reached Australia: the oldest Aboriginal site, Warreen, is 35 000 years old. During the Pleistocene, when sea levels were low, Tasmania was connected to the Australian mainland by a wide land bridge across present-day Bass Strait, but this was cut by rising waters about 11 000 years ago. Since then it has remained an island and local

Aboriginal culture developed in isolation. Tasmanian rock art provides a useful comparison with art from other parts of Australia.

The best-known rock art sites in Tasmania comprise twelve open engraving sites, mostly along the northwest coast. George Augustus Robinson reported the first such site in 1833. Circles are the predominant engraved motif, and these range in diameter from over 1 metre at Mt Cameron West to 3 centimetres at Mersey Bluff. There are also concentric circles, spirals, and rows of dots. Non-circular linear designs are the next most common; figurative motifs—which include depictions of animal tracks, a shell, and an emu—occur at only four sites (Figure 2.6).

In addition, a number of rockshelters and caves contain red hand stencils. The first such site to be reported was near Ellenbrae in 1959. More recently, 23 red hand stencils and a number of pigment smears were discovered at Ballawinnie Cave in the Maxwell River Valley, and a further 23 were located at Wargata Mina Cave (Judd's Cavern) in the Cracroft Valley. The consistent presence of red ochre in the deposits of many caves in the region shows that art was definitely a feature of Tasmanian life during the Pleistocene. Further finds are expected.

Prior to 10 000 BP, when conditions were colder and drier, southwest Tasmania was a more open environment and more attractive to hunter–gatherers. The numerous caves and rockshelters here were occupied between 35 000 and 12 000 years ago. As conditions then

FIGURE 2.6

Below left: *Engraved circles at Preminghana (formerly Mt Cameron West) in northwest Tasmania. The emphasis on circles and tracks is similar to that found in Central Australian engraving sites.*
(Photo R. Edwards)

Below right: *Engravings at Sundown Point Reserve.* (After Flood 1997)

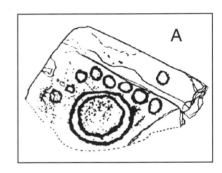

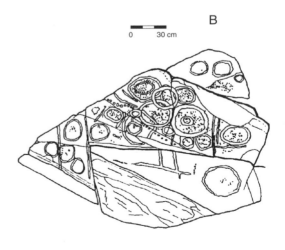

warmed, thick rainforest scrub took over much of the region and most sites appear to have been abandoned.

Sydney

There is a huge concentration of rock art in and around Sydney. The emphasis (80 per cent) is on figurative motifs, which are simplified silhouettes and strongly standardized. Generally, humans are depicted frontally, animals in profile, snakes and lizards from above. Fine details of the anatomy and body contours are not shown, nor is surface texture, nor any bodily features except eyes (Figure 2.7).

The best-known rock art motifs in the region are the large engraved figures—outlined by pecking or by the manufacture of pits by rotation, then finished by abrasion—on the horizontal sandstone platforms of the region. Subjects include macropods, fish, whales, humans and reptiles, some of which are of gigantic size (up to 18 metres long).

Within the region, there are also local variations in the art. Some seem culturally determined: south of the Georges River, for example, there are no profile human-like figures (anthropomorphs), culture heroes, emus and contact motifs, while to the north there are no anthropomorphs with a 'bird beak' projection on the side of the head. Other differences in rock engravings relate to local context: sites near

FIGURE 2.7

Typical anthropomorph (human-like) engraving at an open-air site near Sydney. The outline of the figure was first pecked then the groove was abraded.

(Photo M. J. Morwood)

the coast have a higher proportion of marine fish and mammals, those inland have more emphasis on inland animals such as emus and kangaroos.

The sandstones of the Sydney region are relatively soft, and it has been estimated that the engravings would generally only last 2000 years at most. In addition, the fact that a few engravings depict European contact subjects—including sailing ships—tells us that the practice of rock engraving clearly continued into historic times. In spite of this, there is virtually no ethnographic information on the significance of the engravings to local Aboriginal people. Only one account survives, that of 'Queen Gooseberry', widow of a local Aboriginal chief, who on questioning some time before 1847 said her father had told her 'black fellow made them long ago' and that people kept away from the engraved sites except during dances and ceremonies because 'too much debble walk about'.

Rock art assemblages in shelters include paintings, drawings, stencils and engravings. Although these are generally contemporaneous with the open engraving sites, there are significant differences in motif emphasis between shelter and open rock art sites assemblages. In a few very sheltered locations, deeply pecked and patinated circles and tracks also occur (Figure 2.8). These are more similar to the pecked engravings found in Central Australia and seem to represent a much older rock art tradition.

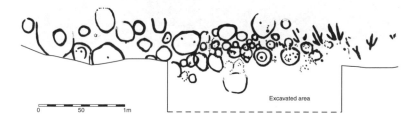

0   50   1m
Excavated area

FIGURE 2.8

Engraved circles and tracks at Yengo 1 in the Sydney Basin. These are thought to be a regional variant of the Panaramitee engraving tradition and probably predate 4 000 years BP. (After McDonald 1994, Figure A1.4)

Southeast Cape York Peninsula

This is one of several areas in Australia where rock art recording and research were largely initiated by the enthusiasm and labour of one man, Percy Trezise, a pilot, bushman, author, artist and unrivalled teller of yarns. There are earlier reports. For instance, Logan Jack

FIGURE 2.9

Painting of a horse in a rockshelter near Cooktown, southeast Cape York Peninsula. This painting must date to the early European contact period around AD 1874. Other contact paintings and local knowledge indicate that the practice of rock painting continued in the region until the 1920s.

(Photo M. J. Morwood)

FIGURE 2.10

Deeply patinated and pecked engravings at Yam Camp, southeast Cape York Peninsula. Motifs include pits and rectilinear mazes, incorporating bird tracks and enclosures. They are a regional variant of the Panaramitee engraving tradition. Archaeological excavation at the site yielded a piece of the engraved panel, which had fallen before intensive occupation of the shelter began 1250 years ago. However, the engravings are probably much older. Two white paintings of women, which appear fresh and overlie the pecked engravings have been dated to 700 years BP.

(Photo M. J. Morwood)

described 'cave drawings' on the upper Mossman and Palmer Rivers in 1895, and seven years later Walter Roth noted rock paintings 'at Cooktown, the Bloomfield and on the Palmer'. Wider European knowledge of rock art in the region, however, did not begin until the 1960s, when workers on the Peninsula Highway rediscovered rock paintings at Split Rock near Laura. The resulting publicity led to Trezise's systematic exploration and recording program, which has now yielded over 1000 rock art sites.

Rock art in southeast Cape York Peninsula is characterized by large colourful, figurative paintings of anthropomorphs, humans, macropods, flying foxes, dingos, echidnas, fish, birds, reptiles and occasionally plants and tracks. This art has been termed the Quinkan rock painting style, after some of the prominent and very distinctive depictions of Quinkan spirits. Depicted subjects and a range of excavated evidence indicate that this rock art style dates to the last 4000 to 5000 years, contemporaneous with a significant increase in use of sites and the appearance of technological innovations.

Despite the spectacular nature of many Quinkan paintings, they can be categorized as crudely naturalistic, with many similarities to Sydney–Hawkesbury figurative art: humans are depicted frontally, animals from the side and reptiles from above. In addition, figures tend to be 'stiff', static and stereotyped and lack any fluidity of movement. Motifs are sometimes placed to represent compositions, but infrequently. Many paintings have internal patterns of vertical and/or horizontal lines marking regular body divisions, while a few paintings also have internal organs illustrated in X-ray fashion.

There is no clear sequence evident in the paintings, the most recent of which include post-contact subjects such as Europeans with guns, horses and pigs (Figure 2.9). However, in some sites, paintings overlie very weathered and patinated engravings of deeply pecked geometric shapes, circles, pits, meandering lines and tracks. Excavations by Andrée Rosenfeld at Early Man shelter has shown that this 'geometric and track' engraving style is at least 14 000 years old (Figure 2.10).

Victoria River District

Colloquially referred to as the 'Land of the Lightning Brothers', two creation beings who feature in local stories and rock art, the Victoria River District lies to the southwest of Katherine in the Northern Territory. Best known through the work of Howard McNickle and Josephine Flood, large numbers of rock paintings, drawings, stencils and engravings are found in the numerous sandstone rockshelters of the region (Figure 2.11). Motifs include anthropomorphs, faces, macropods, dingos, birds and other animals painted or engraved mainly in a simple naturalistic style. However, some motifs, such as paintings of the Lightning Brothers, are more complex in format. Engravings are also common, particularly abraded grooves. In historic

FIGURE 2.11

Rock paintings at Yingalarri, a Wardaman site in the Victoria River District. These are 'complex figurative' in format. Archaeological excavations indicate that this distinctive rock painting style dates to the last 1000 years and that some of the sites may reflect social changes resulting from European disruption of traditional land tenure.
(Photo B. David)

times the cutting of such grooves was a way of making the rock 'bleed' and so ensuring rain.

Local Wardaman people distinguish two categories of rock art: *bulawula*, secular rock paintings or engravings, which are acknowledged to have been made by humans; and *buwarraja*, or Dreaming pictures, which are said to have been made by creation beings in the Dreamtime.

Secular rock art was done for a variety of reasons—as play art, decoration, love magic, to record a visit to a site, or to illustrate a story. Subjects depicted include European contact items and activities, such as sailing ships, horses and droving scenes.

In contrast, the primary purpose of *buwarraja* art is to symbolize the events of the Dreaming. Most are large anthropomorphs with elaborate internal decoration, which are placed at the centre of the sites. These are very regionally distinctive in style and are usually painted (or engraved) at places where the creation ancestral beings came to rest or 'painted themselves on the rock'. The best known are the Lightning Brothers, the Rainbow Serpent, the Moon and the Devil Dingo. Some of the anthropomorphs are very similar to those in the Wandjina paintings of the Kimberley.

Because of the softness of the sandstone in the region, most of the rock paintings date to the last 1000 years at most. During this period archaeological excavations by Josephine Flood and her co-researchers show a significant increase in painting activity at the sites.

In fact, many of the best-known paintings in the region probably postdate European contact. Pecked and abraded engravings, on the other hand, can survive much longer—as shown by the recovery of engraved rocks from Yingalarri, which are between 5000 and 7000 years old.

Arnhem Land

The Arnhem Land plateau and escarpment is one of the richest rock art areas in the world. Estimates of the number of sites vary, but in the southern escarpment country, which forms part of Kakadu National Park, there are probably 5000 to 6000. Like the art of the Kimberley and Pilbara regions of northwest Australia, the figurative art of western Arnhem Land includes paintings which are more complex and less stereotyped than figurative art found elsewhere in the continent.

The rock art of western Arnhem Land is best known through the work of Eric Brandl, George Chaloupka, Darrell Lewis and Paul Taçon, although earlier work by Baldwin Spencer, Charles Mountford and A. P. Elkin helped define its scope.

Brandl distinguished two main phases of rock painting in the area. 'X-ray' art features large, multicoloured images of humans, macropods, birds, fish and reptiles with decorative or descriptive infill depicting internal organs (Figure 2.12). These are associated with

FIGURE 2.12

Complex figurative X-ray paintings of fish in western Arnhem Land. There was an increased emphasis on depiction of fish late in the regional sequence and artists included enough visual cues to enable species to be readily identified. (Photo R. Edwards)

FIGURE 2.13

Dynamic (Mimi) figure rock paintings in western Arnhem Land. A male figure with a headdress is spearing an emu with a hand-thrown multi-barbed spear. The emu has ribs shown in incipient X-ray style and has dashes from the mouth, perhaps representing a cry. (Photo G. Chaloupka)

stencils, prints and beeswax figures. The Mimi art style comprises small red naturalistic figures, in which movement is skilfully portrayed (Figure 2.13). On the basis of superimpositions, content, stylistic development and present-day cultural significance, Brandl showed conclusively that Mimi art was the older style. In fact its depictions of the extinct thylacine (Tasmanian tiger) suggest that Mimi paintings may be of considerable antiquity. Brandl also noted some evidence for an earlier art style characterized by large paintings of animals and humans.

The painting sequence also reveals changes in material culture over time. For instance, Brandl separated 'early' Mimi from 'late' Mimi art on the basis of the disappearance of the boomerang as a hunting weapon and the appearance of the spearthrower.

Since 1958, Chaloupka has recorded about 2000 rock art sites in Arnhem Land, as well as associated mythological and historical information gathered from Aboriginal informants. Some 40 years of work have been distilled into his *Journey in Time*, an authoritative book of great beauty. Chaloupka defined the Arnhem Land rock art sequence in far more detail than was attempted by Brandl. By combining the evidence of superimpositions, differential weathering, defined styles and changes in the range of depicted animal species and their environmental contexts, he inferred four broad artistic periods. These incorporate many art phases, which are defined on the basis of degree of stylization, naturalism and subjects.

The *Pre-estuarine Period* includes the earliest rock paintings. The name refers specifically to the period before the rise of sea level, which resulted from global warming over the past 10 000 years. At this time the Arnhem Land escarpment was up to 300 kilometres from the coast.

Pre-estuarine paintings are characterized by depictions of inland animal species, such as thylacines, Tasmanian devils, kangaroos, emus, snakes, freshwater crocodiles and possibly megafauna. These are associated with handprints, stencils, and depictions of human beings in various styles and with spears, baskets, head-dresses and other items of material culture. In Chaloupka's scheme the earliest art comprises handprints and imprints of grass and other thrown objects, followed by large naturalistic figures of humans and animals, including extinct species. Mimi figures, which Chaloupka refers to as Dynamic figures, also belong to the Pre-estuarine Period.

The *Estuarine Period* began when the sea rose to its present level about 6000 years ago. In some areas this led to estuarine conditions and associated marine animals in the major river systems right to the base of the escarpment. Estuarine Period paintings are characterized by depictions of saltwater fish and crocodiles, and people with items such as stone-tipped spears.

The *Freshwater Period* began around 2000 years ago when freshwater swamps began to form in the floodplains between the escarpment and the coast. Paintings from this period include new animals, such as magpie geese, and new items of material culture, such as goosewing fans and the didgeridoo.

The *Contact Period* is characterized by the appearance of Indonesian and European contact subjects (such as Macassan boats and horses) in the rock art. On present evidence large-scale Indonesian contact with Aboriginal groups along the Arnhem Land coast began around 1725 CE.

Lewis recorded many rock art sites in Arnhem Land and has targeted depicted items of material culture as a means of identifying a rock art sequence featuring, in order of appearance, the Boomerang, Hooked Stick, Broad Spearthrower and Long Spearthrower Periods. This sequence rests on the assumption that artefacts, such as spears and spearthrowers, can be 'temporally ordered'.

Because of the hardness of the rock, engravings are not common in Arnhem Land. Simple abraded lines are the most common motifs, but the oldest are made by a combination of pecking and abrasion.

These emphasize pecked cupules, which are usually grouped on vertical walls and sometimes on ledges and boulders. The most extensive panel of these occurs at Yuwunggayai Shelter. Engraved depictions of animal and human tracks, fish and birds also occur.

Kimberley

The Kimberley plateau also has a large concentration of rock art. As in Arnhem Land, some of the basal rocks are extremely hard and thus aid the long-term preservation of rock paintings as well as engravings.

The rock art of this area is best known through the work of Ian Crawford, Grahame Walsh and David Welch. Although there are differences between the various chronological schemes for Kimberley rock art, they more or less coincide. Since 1978, Walsh has recorded about 1000 sites and on the basis of superimpositions and differential weathering has constructed a detailed rock painting sequence with three main 'epochs', Archaic, Erudite and Aborigine (Figure 2.14). This terminology is not generally accepted because it implies that only the most recent epoch is associated with Aboriginal people, but the actual sequence of styles, and the presence of two marked gaps in the rock art sequence, can be identified.

1 The earliest phase of Kimberley rock art comprises handprints and imprints of grass and other thrown objects, followed by large naturalistic figures of humans and animals, including extinct species. Pecked cupules are also found.
2 The second phase comprises a developmental sequence of Bradshaw figures, which are exquisite depictions of humans with associated ceremonial garb and material culture.
3 The most recent phase comprises the stylistic sequence, which culminated in the development of the regionally distinctive anthropomorphs or creation beings known as Wandjina. (See Chapters 4 and 6).

Of particular interest is the fact that the earliest art of the Kimberley sequence is very similar to that encountered in Arnhem Land. Bradshaw figures, for instance, seem to be regional variants of the Dynamic/Mimi figures found in the rock art of Arnhem Land.

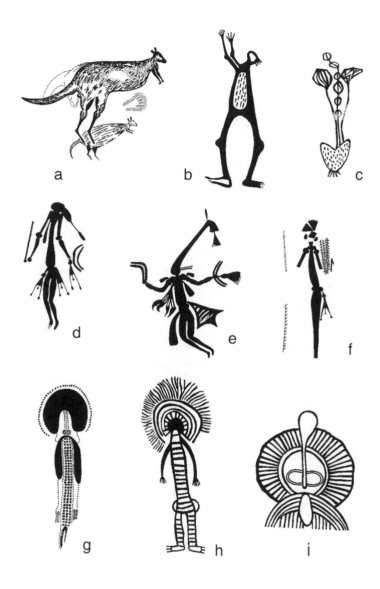

FIGURE 2.14

Rock art styles in the Kimberley in order of appearance. Irregular Infill Animal Period: (a) Macropod, (b) Anthropomorph, (c) Yams. Bradshaw Period: (d) Tassel Bradshaw, (e) Sash Bradshaw, (f) Clothes Peg Figure. Clawed Hand Period: (g) Horseshoe head figure, (h) Ceremonial figure. Wandjina Period: (i) Classic Wandjina. (After Morwood et al. 1994)

Pilbara

The Pilbara has been described as 'without doubt the richest and most exciting region of rock art engravings in Australia' (G. Walsh 1988). In this semi-desert area, rock engravings occur on and around low, conical hills of weathered granite boulders dotted about an almost treeless spinifex plain (Figure 2.15). The engravings have been made by pecking away the brown patina of pavements and

FIGURE 2.15

Rock engravings at Gallery Hill in the Pilbara region of Western Australia. (Photo Western Australian Department of Indigenous Affairs)

boulders to expose the yellow undersurface. They are best known through the recording programs of Robert Bednarik and Bruce Wright.

The artists appear to have been very selective in their choice of locales—some large areas of suitable rock are devoid of engravings. The engravings are associated with pools or rock holes containing permanent or semi-permanent water, and many also occur very close to seed-grinding grooves.

The majority of Pilbara engravings are simple figurative depictions of human-like figures, macropods, birds and other animals. However, some—formerly known as Gurangara figures but now referred to as Woodstock figures after the locale where they were first discovered—are more complex: they are long, sinuous, have split hands and are often shown engaged in sexual activities.

The age of the engravings is unknown. The degree of patination of some engravings indicates that they are of considerable antiquity, while others are fresh and unpatinated in appearance. Patination and superimpositions also show an early style of broad abraded outlines of life-size and larger subjects, including thylacines, and much later unpatinated styles dominated by life-size subjects executed in pecked infill. But there is little local Aboriginal knowledge about the original significance of even the most recent engravings.

The big picture

A point worth emphasizing is that the distribution of Australian rock art is highly correlated with regional geology. It is hardly surprising that regions that have few rock outcrops (such as western Cape York Peninsula) or that have unsuitable or rapidly weathering rock surfaces (such as Southeast Queensland) have relatively few or no rock art sites. In contrast, major concentrations of rock art occur where there are extensive exposures of suitable rock. Geology also determines the distribution of regional rock art styles and the nature of their boundaries. For instance, the abrupt western boundary of the Central Queensland rock art style occurs where the sandstone uplands give way to the blacksoil plains of western Queensland.

A number of researchers have attempted to summarize the regional and chronological variability evident in Australian rock art with a continent-wide sequence. The earliest of these, Daniel Sutherland Davidson, was influenced by a theoretical approach used by

North American anthropologists of the time: Geographical Trait Distribution Theory held that cultural traits spread out ripple-like from their centre of origin, to replace earlier analogous traits, and that mapping their geographical distribution would provide evidence for the chronology of trait development.

In 1937 Davidson applied this 'age-area' principle to many aspects of Australian Aboriginal culture, and mapped the continent-wide distribution of different types of spear, spearthrower, club, basket, netting, watercraft, social organization and art. For his study of decorative art, he plotted the distribution of design types, such as concentric circles and zigzags, to identify five design areas (Figure 2.16). By interpreting the non-contiguous distributions of design elements in terms of the development and spread of new designs 'at the expense of other patterns', Davidson suggested that there had been many changes in the distribution of designs in the past. He also interpreted the central design area, with its emphasis upon concentric circles, as being more recent than peripheral design areas because of its central, relatively restricted distribution, which in historic times appeared to be spreading outwards.

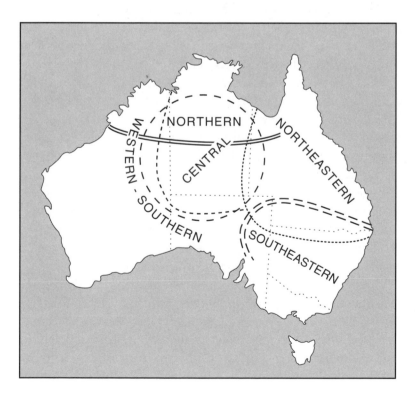

FIGURE 2.16

D. S. Davidson's map of his five Australian Aboriginal design areas. According to the age-area model, which Davidson adhered to, the Central Australian decorative complex was most recent because it was more geographically restricted in distribution. (From Davidson 1937)

Davidson's study plotted only a small number of design elements, and he failed to take relative frequencies of occurrence into account. However, in her later assessment of Australian rock art studies, Lesley Maynard concluded that this approach had good potential for future research if the distributions of a wider range of design elements were investigated using modern techniques of multi-attribute analysis.

The next rock art researcher of note to attempt an overall synthesis of Australian rock art distribution and chronology was Fred McCarthy, whose 1958 book, *Australian Aboriginal Rock Art*, was very influential. It describes the characteristics of rock art throughout the continent, attempts to classify it and proposes a pan-Australian sequence. For instance, McCarthy distinguished four phases of engravings. From earliest to most recent these comprise:

1 Abraded grooves arranged either singly or in simple patterns.
2 Pecked and/or abraded outlines of humans, animals and items of material culture.
3 Pecked linear designs.
4 Pecked solid or silhouette figures and a number of variant styles.

However, the sequence is based on a small number of engraving superimpositions that McCarthy recorded at one locale, Port Hedland, while the categories used are not hierarchically consistent in the way they are derived or applied.

The work of Andreas Lommel, beginning in 1959, is not as well known, and is now mainly of historic interest. He proposed that Australian art could be divided into two basic styles: naturalistic and linear/geometric. Like Davidson, he then plotted the distribution of these two styles across Australia and found that the linear/geometric style occurred in an area roughly corresponding to Central Australia. He concluded that naturalistic art must be more recent because it is restricted to the northern and eastern peripheries, and probably 'traced its origin to external influences' on northwest Australia. Lommel's argument was based solely on the evidence of geographical distribution and his own value judgements about artistic merit.

In 1959, Mountford used the same argument. He plotted the distribution of art styles and techniques, then decided that: 'Working on the assumption that the simple motifs of the southern peripheries... are more ancient than the motifs of the high development areas of the northern coasts... it is possible to construct a tentative chronological sequence of cave paintings.' He suggested that the rock painting sequence began with stencils, then progressed to linear paintings, monochromes, bichromes, polychromes, and so on.

Lesley Maynard was the first to integrate a range of dating evidence with information on geographical distribution to derive a general Australian rock art sequence. As originally outlined in her 1976 Master of Arts thesis, the three-part sequence comprises:

1 the Panaramitee Style
2 Simple Figurative Styles (e.g. Sydney, southeast Cape York)
3 Complex Figurative Styles of northwest Australia (e.g. the Kimberley, western Arnhem Land, the Pilbara).

THE PANARAMITEE STYLE

Following on from the work of Bob Edwards, Maynard recognized that remnants of the old 'geometric and tracks' engraving style found in Central Australia were also present in regions around the coastal fringe, where more recent rock art traditions emphasized figurative motifs. She called this old engraving style 'Panaramitee' after the type-site on Panaramitee Station, northeast South Australia.

Classic Panaramitee-style engravings occur at widely distributed sites in Central Australia, from the Manunda–Yunta drainage area of South Australia to western Queensland and western New South Wales. They are characterized by an emphasis on tracks (62 per cent) and geometric motifs (34 per cent); figurative motifs form a minor component. The engravings are composed of bands and solid forms. Overall, the motif range at sites in the core arid zone is remarkably homogeneous over huge distances.

Similar sites occur outside the arid zone, with deeply pecked, patinated engravings emphasizing geometric and track motifs, but in different proportions to those of classic arid zone sites. They are found in the central Queensland highlands, the Queensland Gulf country, southeast Cape York Peninsula, around Sydney and in Tasmania (Figure 2.17). Maynard assimilated these sites into the Panaramitee style and proposed that this style may have been continent-wide in distribution.

The Panaramitee engraving style is clearly very old. The panel of engravings at the Early Man site in Cape York is partially covered by deposits 14 000 years old, while at the Ingalaadi site in the Victoria River District, John Mulvaney excavated fragments of rockfall with pecked tracks and abraded grooves from levels dated

FIGURE 2.17

Open engraving sites in central western Queensland with deeply patinated and weathered pecked engravings. These have a range of motifs, composition and site context not characteristic of more recent, regionally distinctive rock engravings. Sites such as the Bull Hole, Twelve Mile Crossing and the Plateau are considered to be regional variants of the Panaramitee engraving tradition.

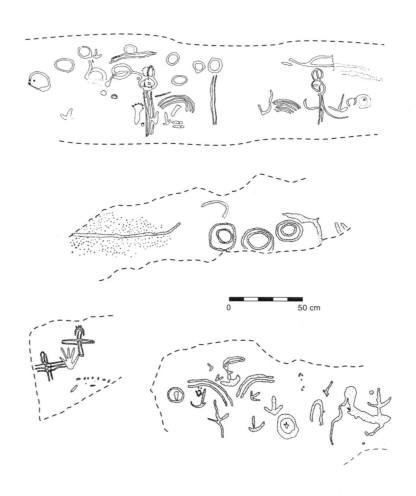

to between 5000 and 7000 BP. If the Tasmanian engravings are from the same rock art tradition, then the Panaramitee predates the formation of Bass Strait 11 000 years ago.

Maynard concluded that in terms of the range of motifs used, modern-day Central Australian art was directly descended from the Panaramitee and that this was largely because of the innate cultural conservatism of the region. Elsewhere, around the margins of the continent, the emphasis on geometric and track motifs was superseded by art traditions with greater emphasis on figurative portrayals.

SIMPLE FIGURATIVE STYLES

These regional rock art styles are characterized by crudely naturalistic depictions. There is considerable regional variation in techniques used and motif size, but all the styles are strongly standardized in format:

humans are almost invariably shown from the front, mammals, fish and birds from the side and reptiles from above. The figures lack fine anatomical details and contours, and decoration is relatively simple. Examples include the Sydney engravings (80 per cent figurative) and the Quinkan paintings of southeast Cape York Peninsula (84 per cent figurative).

Simple figurative styles occur around the margins of the continent, and each is relatively localized. In a number of regions, superimpositions, differential weathering and absolute dating evidence indicate that the Panaramitee preceded Simple Figurative style engravings.

Maynard also established a relative chronology for rock engravings in the Broken Hill area of western New South Wales. Here three engraving sites occur in close proximity: Sturt's Meadow, Mootwingee and Eurowrie. Maynard used differences in degree of motif patination and weathering at the sites to infer relative ages: those at Sturt's Meadow (very patinated and weathered) were oldest, those at Eurowrie ('fresh' in appearance) were most recent, and those at Mootwingee (intermediate in condition) fell in between. She argued that differences in the proportions of motifs at the three sites show sequential changes in motif use, from an early emphasis on tracks and geometric motifs to a late emphasis on figurative and geometric motifs (Figure 2.18). In other words, in this area there was evidence of change from an early Panaramitee rock engraving tradition to one placing more emphasis on simple figurative motifs.

FIGURE 2.18

Top: *Panel of pecked engravings at Mootwingee. These are lightly patinated and therefore of intermediate age between the very patinated engravings at Sturt's Meadow and the fresh lightly pecked figures at Euriowie.* (Photo M.J. Morwood)

Bottom: *Panel of lightly pecked engravings at Euriowie. These are fresh in appearance and overwhelmingly figurative in motif emphasis.* (Photo M. J. Morwood)

Below left: *The change in motif use at three rock art sites of different ages in western New South Wales. On the basis of weathering, Sturt's Meadow is the oldest site, Mootwingee is of intermediate age and Euriowie is the most recent. There is an early emphasis on track motifs which changes to a greater emphasis on figurative motifs in recent times.* (From Maynard 1979, Figure 4.2)

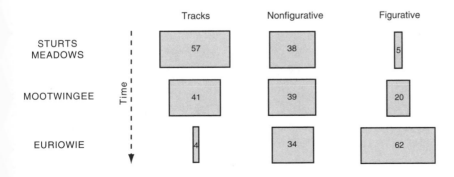

Tracks   Nonfigurative   Figurative

STURTS MEADOWS: 57 | 38 | 5

MOOTWINGEE: 41 | 39 | 20

EURIOWIE: 4 | 34 | 62

Time

Examples of Bradshaw (top) and Dynamic (bottom) paintings from Arnhem Land and the Kimberley, respectively. Because of the stylistic similarities between these early rock art styles, some researchers, such as Darrell Lewis, have argued that a single rock art style may have existed across both regions and that there was later divergence in style.
(After Walsh and Morwood 1999)

COMPLEX FIGURATIVE STYLES

These occur only in the northwest of Australia—in the Pilbara, the Kimberley, Arnhem Land and the Victoria River District. They are very diverse but, as well as featuring Simple Figurative depictions, Complex Figurative styles include varying proportions of motifs which are 'more sophisticated than crudely naturalistic'. For instance, the related Bradshaw and Dynamic Figure paintings of the Kimberley and Arnhem Land, respectively, are often highly decorated, show exquisite anatomical detail, depict a range of associated material culture, and skilfully portray movement (Figure 2.19).

More recent Complex Figurative rock painting styles include large colourful figures with regionally distinctive characteristics: Wandjina paintings of the Kimberley, for instance, usually have a white background, a halo, eyes and nose, but never a mouth. The pounded engravings of Gurangara figures in the Pilbara are also highly stereotyped, with their beaked faces, elongated bodies, large genitals, long flowing limbs and emphasis on sexual themes (Figure 2.20).

ASSESSING MAYNARD'S MODEL

In contrast to other models for the Australian rock art sequence, Maynard's three-part sequence does seem to explain much of the pronounced spatial and chronological variation. Evidence from Tasmania and the Laura area indicates that the relatively homogeneous Panaramitee engraving style was widespread prior to 5000 years ago but that its use later contracted to Tasmania and the conservative core area of Central Australia. Elsewhere this art style was replaced by styles which placed greater emphasis on figurative motifs, and which showed greater regional variability. The Complex Figurative style is more restricted in distribution to the coastal areas of northwest Australia, and may reflect external contacts with Asia.

Maynard's approach to chronology and research provided the basis for later work on the archaeology of Australian art—a point most researchers now acknowledge. And her three-part sequence is still a useful baseline for overviewing geographical and chronological change in Australian rock art. This is not to say that her scheme does not have 'problems'. For instance, some eastern regions, such as the central Queensland highlands and southeast Queensland, do not fit comfortably into her scheme, while none of the Complex

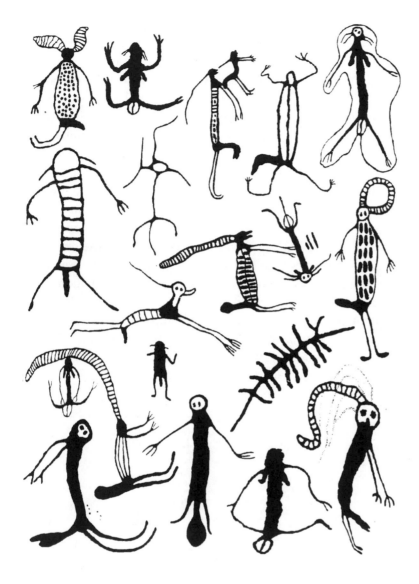

FIGURE 2.20
Engraved Woodstock (or Gurangara) figures at Gallery Hill in the Pilbara region of Western Australia often have exaggerated sexual features. (After Mountford 1965b, Figure 5)

Figurative art regions of northwest Australia appear to have earlier Panaramitee-type or Simple Figurative art.

In addition, Maynard offers no real explanation as to why the changes occurred except to note that there are some parallels between the rock art and stone artefact sequences—both show a change from 'early', relatively homogeneous and widespread traditions (Panaramitee, Core Tool and Scraper) to later, more localized and regional traditions. She makes little attempt to examine artistic trends in the context of the general patterns of economic, technological and demographic changes indicated by mainstream archaeology, or to consider the correlation between art and other aspects of Aboriginal culture. For instance, the relative homogeneity of Australian rock art and stone artefact technologies prior to 5000 BP is consistent with the 'open' social networks required by low-density populations to maintain social and biological viability in harsh environments, while an emphasis upon non-figurative motifs, which are ambiguous, esoteric and multivalent, provides evidence for the circumstances in which social knowledge was shared or restricted (see Chapter 4).

The fact that some regions during this time had quite distinctive styles (such as Mimi art) represents a 'problem' if the aim of the exercise is simply to categorize. But if our goal is to relate art to its context, it offers an opportunity for comparative assessment. In ethnographic times both artistic and linguistic differences between groups served a social bounding function, and it is significant that the areas of greatest linguistic diversity in Australia are those with longstanding, regionally distinctive, Complex Figurative rock art bodies such as Arnhem Land and the Kimberley (Figure 2.21).

Similarly, evidence from southeast Cape York and Central Queensland suggests that the development of many regional rock

FIGURE 2.21

There is a close correspondence between the geographical distribution of non-Pama-Nyungan languages and Complex figurative rock art styles in Australia. Archaeological excavations show that major differences between the northwest corner and the remainder of Australia are long-standing. For instance, edge-ground axes older than 30 000 years are found in the Kimberley, Arnhem Land and southeast Cape York Peninsula, whereas they only appear in other parts of Australia within the last 5000 years. (After Dixon 1980)

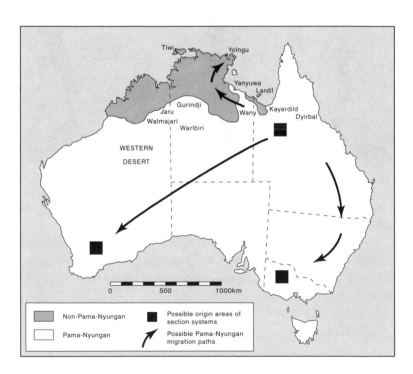

art styles and ideologies may have coincided with significant increases in population, more intensive resource exploitation and an increase in the scale of ceremonies. Most (but not all) such regional art traditions placed greater emphasis upon figurative motifs, which are more specific in reference, less ambiguous, are potentially much more diverse and are generally for 'public' rather than 'restricted' contexts. Changes in the distribution, context and content of Australian rock art over the past 5000 years are likely to reflect such factors as the development of more bounded social networks corresponding to increases in population densities, restrictions on territorial access and more formalized interaction between groups.

In his work on the rock art of North Queensland, Bruno David has demonstrated that regionally distinctive rock art styles appeared around 3500 years ago, at the same time as other archaeological indicators of population increase. He also argues that there is a major stylistic divide in recent rock painting styles. Regions north of the Walsh–Mitchell Rivers in Cape York Peninsula have a heavy emphasis on figurative motifs, which are often bichrome. In contrast, rock paintings in the regions to the south are monochrome, predominantly linear and are largely of tracks and geometric symbols. This division appears to reflect major differences in the nature of social networks (Figure 2.22). South of the Walsh–Mitchell divide, extensive trading networks and inter-group contacts acted against the development of distinctive regional rock art styles. To the north, on the other hand, there was intensive but short-distance interaction between groups.

With a few exceptions, the most recent rock art studies have tended to be regional, or site-specific, in approach, and more quantitative. There has also been greater emphasis upon the investigation of art in its material and social context—as manifest in the ethnographic, archaeological and environmental records.

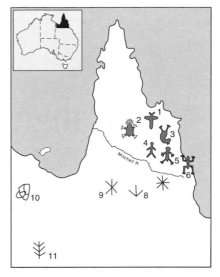

FIGURE 2.22

Over the past 3500 years, rock art in different regions became far more distinctive. This appears to have been a way of symbolically bounding territories when local populations increased and ownership of land became more formalized. For instance, in northern Queensland a major division between regions north and south of the Mitchell River developed. To the north, figurative motifs predominated, even though each region had its own rock art style, while non-figurative motifs were favoured to the south. In recent times, the pattern of trade followed similar lines: there was much long-distance movement of goods between regions south of the Mitchell River, while to the north trade links tended to be shorter.
(From David and Chant 1995, Figure 113)

CHAPTER 3

Australian rock art research

The archaeological study of art began with basic documentation of the number, diversity and chronology of the various art traditions. Despite differences between regions in the timing of discoveries, there are remarkable parallels in the way research has progressed. This is clear when comparing aspects of the history of research in Europe, America, South Africa and India. It will be apparent that rock art research in many parts of the world is still mainly concerned with basic site recording and description.

International beginnings

EUROPE

The earliest publications on prehistoric art in Europe date to the 17th century. However, the scientific study of prehistoric European art really began with the discovery, early in the 19th century, of decorated objects in the limestone caves and rockshelter deposits of the Dordogne area of southwest France and the Cantabrian region of northern Spain. This material, which includes images of mammoth, reindeer and wild horses engraved on bone, was excavated in fairly ruthless fashion from sites like La Madelein, Laugerie Basse and Le Mas d'Azil.

The discovery that these same caves and rockshelters sometimes contained rock art is generally attributed to de Sautuola at the cave

FIGURE 3.1

Above left: *Rock painting of a bison at Altamira, Spain. When rediscovered by de Sautuola in 1879, the scientific establishment refused to accept the art at Altamira as of genuinely Palaeolithic age. However, AMS radiocarbon dating of rock paintings at the recently discovered site of Grotte Chauvet-Pont d'Arc in southern France now shows that people had begun decorating cave walls by 32 000 years ago.* (After Leroi-Gourhan 1965, Figure 26)

Above centre and right: *Art appears abruptly in the European archaeological record in a number of localities around 32 000 years ago, which coincides with the appearance of modern humans in the region. For instance, limestone blocks bearing paint, as well as engraved animals and symbols, were recovered from Aurignacian levels at the French sites of Abri Cellier, Arcy sur Cure, La Ferrassie and Laussel. Some of the symbols are generally interpreted as vulvae (above centre). Similarly, Aurignacian levels at Hohlenstein, Geissenklosterle and Vogelherd in southwest Germany have yielded mammoth ivory statuettes of horses, lions, mammoths, bears and humans, as well as numerous plaques with incised marks (above right). The fact that the items from each region are not isolated finds and that they share stylistic features distinguishes them from earlier, isolated 'art objects' found in the archaeological record.* (Courtesy Les Eyzies Museum and Ulmer Museum)

of Altamira, Spain, in 1879. 'Experts' of the time at first refused to accept that the art might date from Ice Age times, but further discoveries led to a gradual change in attitude (Figure 3.1). The turning point in the debate was the publication in 1902 of Carthaillac's paper 'Mea Culpa d'un Sceptique' (Confessions of a Sceptic), in which this famous archaeologist from Bordeaux publicly accepted that the paintings and engravings were of Pleistocene age.

The earliest attempts to interpret this art focused on mobile art objects recovered in various excavations. In 1864 Lartet and Christy argued that these objects reflect the very rich resources available to Palaeolithic hunter–gatherers. This abundance had led to leisure time, which in turn fostered an interest in art. It was thought that given the 'primitive' nature of Palaeolithic society, the decorative arts would not have symbolic value but would be 'art for art's sake'.

Views about the primitive nature of hunter–gatherer societies changed markedly with the appearance of the first detailed ethnographic information on extant hunter–gatherer groups, particularly in Australia. Seminal works at this time included Tylor's *Primitive Cultures* (1880), James Frazer's *The Golden Bough* (1890) and Spencer and Gillen's *The Native Tribes of Central Australia* (1899). Reinarch was the first researcher to cull this ethnographic literature as an aid in interpreting the significance of European

Palaeolithic art. In 1903 he put forward the idea that the cave art was concerned with sympathetic magic for ensuring success in hunting and the maintenance of faunal resources. He pointed out that most animal species depicted in the cave art were food species or potential food species, and that the art was often located in relatively inaccessible areas deep underground, implying that it was not merely decorative and was not for general viewing.

Of the many researchers concerned with the recording and documentation of European Paleolithic art, the most prolific and influential was Abbé Henri Breuil, who was the first to develop a comprehensive chronology based on superimpositions. In his *Four Hundred Centuries of Cave Art* (1952), he argued for two successive cycles of artistic production, the Aurignacian-Perigordian and the Solutrean-Magdalenian, with each cycle developing from simple to complex forms. Throughout his long career, Breuil expanded upon the 'sympathetic magic' explanation for the rock art. For instance, he argued that on the rare occasions when other predators were depicted, the artist had been trying to eliminate competitors. Breuil's two-cycle chronology was generally accepted until André Leroi-Gourhan proposed an alternative in his *Treasures of Prehistoric Art* (1965).

During the last 45 years a number of new approaches to rock art analysis have been developed. In particular, far more attention has been paid to the relationships between rock art and other material evidence to infer symbolic behaviour—relationships which are thought to reflect the connection between art and its cultural context. André Leroi-Gourhan, the best-known exponent of the structuralist approach, developed an idea first advanced by Annette Laming in her work at the site of Lascaux—namely that the placement of rock art within sites was not random, but deliberately thought out. Breuil, by contrast, had seen no ordering or patterning in the arrangements of artistic motifs within sites. Leroi-Gourhan argued for a 'topographic' approach in which consistent groupings of motifs in specific areas of sites were quantified, then interpreted in terms of a supposed Palaeolithic world view or system of thought that was based on a dualistic division of the world into male and female components.

More recently, researchers have been concerned with analysis of European prehistoric art as a means for inferring a range of social and ecological information. For instance, Clive Gamble, Iain Davidson and Meg Conkey, among others, have used prehistoric art to investigate social aspects of Palaeolithic society. The recent literature on European Palaeolithic art is extensive and very diverse.

In reviewing developments in the study of European Palaeolithic art, Conkey thereby distinguished three broad periods of study and research:

1 *1879–1902:* The initial period of exploration and discovery, when the antiquity of the finds was still much debated.
2 *1902–60:* The period when the antiquity of such art assemblages was accepted and work was concerned with exploration, discovery, ordering and classification.
3 *1960 to the present:* The period when a number of new approaches to rock art have been developed and far more attention has been placed on the natural and cultural context of rock art assemblages.

Although they are of high public profile, there are only about 300 known Palaeolithic rock art sites in Europe. In contrast there are thousands of rock art sites of more recent date. These include major concentrations of Mesolithic, Neolithic, Bronze Age and Iron Age rock art in Scandinavia, the Spanish Levant and the Alps. In recent years, research on these sites has also concentrated on their cultural and natural contexts as a basis for inferring function.

NORTH AMERICA

The earliest reports of North American Indian rock art sites also date to the 17th century, and the first systematic collation of such sites was undertaken in 1886 by Lieutenant-Colonel Garrick Mallery while a member of the Bureau of Ethnology. His *Picture Writing of the American Indians* described art on a range of media, including rock, and is still a generally acknowledged starting point in the history of American rock art research.

Mallery's work was not followed up until the early 1920s, when Julian H. Steward studied Californian engravings, a study which was influenced by the work of the anthropologists Kroeber and Wissler on the geographical distribution of cultural traits. The questions of the relationship between rock art and other aspects of cultural systems were first seriously considered by Heizer and Baumhoff (1962) in dealing with the rock art of the Great Basin. As with earlier studies, they mapped the distribution of Great Basin design types to define five engraving styles and one painted style. However, their

FIGURE 3.2

Above top: *Rio Grande style rock engravings are found in the Pueblo region of New Mexico, USA, from AD 1300. They were produced by shallow pecking, which removed the patina on basalt boulders to reveal the underlying yellow of fresh rock.*
(Photo M. J. Morwood)

Above bottom: *Barrier Canyon Anthropomorphic style rock paintings in the San Rafael Swell, eastern Utah, USA. This distinctive style of rock painting, characterized by dark red, immobile anthropomorphic figures often flanked by smaller figures or tiny birds and animals, is probably associated with hunter–gatherers who occupied the region around AD 700.*
(Photo M. J. Morwood)

study went further to include a contextual approach to investigate art function. It was found that rock art sites tended to be associated with game trails, blinds, etc., indicating a role in hunting. Since Heizer and Baumhoff's classic work, many other rock art studies have similarly examined the natural and cultural context of American rock art (Figure 3.2).

The first general synthesis of North American rock art was undertaken in 1967 by Grant, who structured the information into nine rock art areas. A similar approach was used by Wellmann in his comprehensive and indispensable *Survey of North American Indian Rock Art* (1979). These overviews indicate the great regional and chronological diversity of American rock art.

In 1962, Heizer and Baumhoff commented that 'the study still remains in the initial (that is descriptive and classificatory) stage of development and interpretive or explanatory analysis has been tentative, speculative, or subsidiary'. To a large extent this emphasis on site recording and documentation continues. Partly this situation reflects the fact that much of the data were collected in the course of salvage archaeology, which has stimulated a huge increase in books and articles on North American rock art. This in turn fostered the creation of groups such as the Canadian Rock Art Research Associates (CRARA) and the American Rock Art Research Association (ARARA). The relative lack of problem-oriented research also reflects the fact that rock art studies were until recently regarded as peripheral to the mainstream of American archaeological interests, but this is clearly changing.

SOUTH AMERICA

The first reports of rock art in South America arose in the 17th century, in this case from Spanish and Portuguese missionaries. But here, unlike in Europe and North America, research has been unsystematic and largely descriptive, and the literature is scattered. However, Dubelaar has produced a useful overview of petroglyph characteristics and locations together with preliminary analyses of motif distribution.

Recent work by joint Brazilian–French teams on Brazilian rock art is also rapidly increasing the tempo of research and the quality of information available. These multidisciplinary projects have included excavation of a range of stratified evidence for rock art chronology and context, including a painted panel at Toca do Baixao do Perna 1 dating back to 9540 BP. They have also attempted to

FIGURE 3.3

Panel of Sao Francisco Tradition rock paintings at Lapa do Caboclo, northeast Brazil. French–Brazilian research teams have constructed dated rock art sequences on the basis of rock art superimpositions, as well as excavations at a number of rockshelters in the region. (After Prous 1986, Figure 30)

interpret dated rock art sequences from central and northeast Brazil to provide evidence for past technological and economic change (Figure 3.3). Descriptive summaries of rock art in some Andean regions (such as Bolivia) and Patagonia (in Argentina and Chile) have also been undertaken. The formation of organisations, such as the Bolivian Rock Art Research Society (SIARB), and their associated conferences and publications has lifted the profile of rock art in South America, as has the declaration of Sierra de Capivara National Park in northeast Brazil, the first area in the Americas to be listed on the World Heritage principally to protect rock art.

SOUTH AFRICA

Although the first reports on rock art in southern Africa date back to 1752, research on the area's rock art really began in the 1870s with the salvage ethnographic work of W. H. I. Bleek and C. Lloyd with /Xam informants, and similar work by J. M. Orpen with the Maluti San of the Lesotho region. This largely unpublished work provided a wealth of contextual information on myths and beliefs of the San and the /Xam Bushmen, which have proved crucial in recent interpretations of South African rock art. Overviews of South African prehistory by Burkitt in 1928 and Willcox in 1968 all but

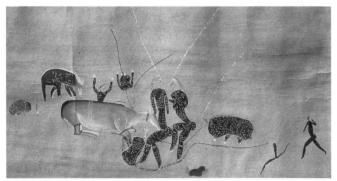

FIGURE 3.4

Top left and right: *The eland is the most commonly depicted animal in the San rock art of the Drakensberg region, South Africa. This tallies with the mythological and symbolic importance of the eland to the San people of the region in the 19th century. Some panels could be taken as a simple record of diet and the animals in the local environment (left). However, other painted compositions seem to depict the visions experienced by shamans during trance. The latter include dying eland, imaginary animals, and humans with lines of power emanating from their heads (right).*
(Photos Patricia Vinnicombe)

Above: *In the Namibian region of southwest Africa, San rock engravings, depicting humans and animals, are more common than paintings.*
(Photo Sven Ouzman)

ignored this rich database. David Lewis-Williams interprets this oversight in terms of the dominant 'empiricist geological paradigm', which emphasised the study of sequence and distribution, rather than the investigation of "meaning"'.

In the 1970s, the work of Vinnicombe in the Drakensberg region and Maggs in the western Cape gave a new direction to Southern African rock art research. From quantitative analyses of rock art data, both were able to demonstrate that the artists were highly selective in their portrayal of animal species and that their choices bore little relation to the animals' frequency in the natural environment or in the diet; in other words 'the paintings are neither a menu nor a check list' (Vinnicombe 1976). The eland is the most commonly depicted subject in the art, while other extensively exploited species such as black wildebeest are almost absent (Figure 3.4). This selectivity was explained through using ethnographic information on Bushman ideology and practices. More recently, Lewis-Williams has used detailed analyses of San ethnographic sources to interpret the function and significance of the rock art. He has shown that the art can only be understood in terms of the beliefs, values and metaphors evident in San mythology and ceremony, and that much of the art portrays the visions seen by medicine men experienced during trance, the central religious experience of San society.

INDIA

The 'exploratory' phase of research on these sites began with the discovery by Carlleyle of rock paintings in the Vindhyas in 1867–68, but the first publication dealing with the topic did not appear until 1883, when J. Cockburn described the discovery of a rock painting site.

FIGURE 3.5
Many rock painting sites occur at Bhimbetka near Bhopal, central India. These seem to range in age from the Mesolithic, 10 000 years ago, up to historic times. Cattle were symbolically important to Indian artists throughout the whole sequence. (Photo M. J. Morwood)

Prehistoric (and historic) rock paintings and engravings have since been found in many parts of the Indian sub-continent, but over 90 per cent of known sites occur in sandstone rockshelters of the Vindhya, Kaimur and Mahadeo hill regions of central India near Bhopal (Figure 3.5). The earliest rock paintings appear to be of Mesolithic Age on the basis of depictions of spears and arrows set with microliths. However, the recovery of a piece of engraved ostrich shell and ostrich shell beads from Upper Palaeolithic levels shows that the regional art sequence goes back possibly to 25 000 BP (Figure 3.6). There is also stratified evidence from excavations that some pecked cupules may be much older.

So far, Indian rock art research has focused on recording, description and identification of subjects to reconstruct aspects of past cultures, and dating the art sequences by superimposition analysis and subject range. There have been no detailed analyses of rock art context or selectivity on the part of the artists.

FIGURE 3.6
Ostrich eggshell beads recovered from Palaeolithic levels in central India indicate that decoration and art may go back at least 25 000 years in the sub-continent. (Photo M. J. Morwood)

The study of Australian Aboriginal rock art

In 1969, John Mulvaney wrote:

> It is difficult for a prehistorian to assess Aboriginal art. Until recently it possessed no time depth...Neither can an Australian prehistorian escape the conditioning influence of ethnographic

data. A prehistorian may infer the methods of application or techniques of engraving from observation, but comment concerning motivation and meaning is beyond the scope of normal archaeological activities.

This statement aptly sums up the attitude towards archaeological research on rock art that prevailed until the 1970s. Despite a long history of rock art recording and the efforts of individuals such as D. S. Davidson, Andreas Lommel, Charles Mountford and Fred McCarthy (see Chapter 2), rock art was still seen as irrelevant to the major issues then being addressed by Australian archaeologists. Times have changed.

Nevertheless, Mulvaney was justified in his opinion. Indeed, a range of ethnographic sources have shown that the specific meanings, or even identification of subjects, in rock art cannot be reconstructed without knowledgeable informants and that, in addition, a specific motif or rock art panel may have many meanings depending upon the particular context of interpretation. Controlling access to esoteric knowledge, including the 'stories' encoded in art, was, and is, funda-mental to the creation, maintenance and perpetuation of status and decision-making hierarchies in Aboriginal society.

The idea that any given rock painting can have a complete, definitive and unchanging meaning is not tenable. However, A. P. Elkin pointed out the solution to the apparent problem of using rock art assemblages as archaeological evidence. He cautioned that the 'meaning' of Aboriginal art was best considered, not in terms of superficial narrative content, but in the light of its functional relationship with ideology, social organization, rights to resources and the general inheritance of culture. It is now generally accepted that 'meaning' in the latter sense—that is, as systems of meanings—is the proper target for both the anthropological and archaeological study of Australian Aboriginal art.

The development of Australian rock art studies over the last 25 years has been strongly influenced by the work and ideas of overseas researchers; the appointment of professionals with a commitment to rock art research at Australian universities and other institutions; a cumulative increase both in the number of known rock art sites, and the evidence of their diversity and antiquity; the passing of federal and state Heritage legislation; the emergence of the Aboriginal land rights movement; the founding of the Australian Rock Art Research

Association and its journal *Rock Art Research*; and technological developments. All these factors set the historical context for developments in rock art research, but the part played by individuals at particular times has been critical.

PEOPLE

The 1970s saw an increasing professionalization of rock art studies in Australia and consequent changes in approach. A similar phenomenon had occurred in Australian archaeology generally in the previous decade. This led to an increase in the pace and calibre of research and to greater emphasis upon quantification by researchers such as Lesley Maynard and John Clegg in their studies of rock art in the 1960s and 1970s. The arrival of Peter Ucko in Australia in 1972 to take up the position of principal of the Australian Institute of Aboriginal Studies (AIAS), was a turning point. Ucko was primarily responsible for the hugely influential 'Schematization in Art' symposium in 1974. He also promoted a change in AIAS funding priorities that gave rock art greater precedence than before and encouraged other European researchers with a commitment to rock art studies, including Bob Layton and Michel Lorblanchet, to come to Australia.

At around the same time, Andrée Rosenfeld was appointed to the Australian National University (ANU) in Canberra. Like Ucko, she had already established an international reputation in rock art research, and after her appointment at ANU she moved quickly to initiate an archaeological project in southeast Cape York Peninsula, which attempted to relate rock art to changes in the material uncovered by excavation.

The appointment of academics with a commitment to rock art research at Australian universities and other institutions was crucial to the development of rock art studies in two principal ways. First, they were a necessary precursor to the establishment of rock art studies as a subdiscipline within the teaching of archaeology. As a result, there has been a significant increase in the number of archaeological and anthropological research theses on Australian Aboriginal art, especially at the ANU under Andrée Rosenfeld—although archaeological courses in rock art are now only taught at four Australian universities: the University of New England, Flinders, Melbourne and Sydney.

Second, the increase in the number of studies on Australian Aboriginal art was associated with the use of new methods and theories—some of local origin; others influenced by work overseas. A healthy aspect of this work was the continuing high level of interaction between anthropological and archaeological approaches, which was particularly apparent at the ANU, where Professor John Mulvaney actively encouraged such interaction.

THEORY

In the 1960s and 1970s archaeologists began reassessing their theories and research methods. The focus of this reassessment was the work of the American researcher Lewis Binford and other proponents of the now inappropriately titled 'new archaeology' (or processualism). They advocated an emphasis on cultural process rather than culture history; the explicit 'testing' of ideas using deductive logic; quantification; and the investigation of contemporary processes as a means of better understanding the archaeological record. The triumph of processualism in Australian archaeology has led to a shift away from an emphasis on cultural diffusion as the explanation for chronological changes in Australian Aboriginal art to investigations that seek to understand the integrating function of art in Aboriginal society; how art and its distribution encode a range of social and economic information; and how rock art may reflect fundamental changes in social organization, group interaction and land use. Such investigations require information on the cultural and natural contexts of rock art production, whereas previous studies had tended to focus on rock art in isolation.

Lesley Maynard and John Clegg took important steps in the development of current perspectives on the study of Australian rock art. Both called for a purely archaeological approach to the analysis of rock art. Maynard contended that meaning is always 'highly specific and usually esoteric' and, as such, is 'probably completely intractable'. She concluded that the analysis of rock art had to be undertaken using standard archaeological techniques for organizing any archaeological evidence into intelligible patterns. These techniques included typological studies, absolute and relative dating, distributional studies, and correlation with other aspects of culture and environment.

Clegg extended this position, arguing that, given the impossibility of reliably ascertaining either the subject or motivation of the artists, it was pointless trying to establish the meaning of the motifs. To indicate that he is allocating names, not labels, to motifs Clegg puts an exclamation mark before his categorisations. Some other researchers have adopted this convention, and Clegg's fundamental point has long been absorbed into the Australian rock art literature. However, the issue of whether we can reconstruct artists' intentions is still under debate overseas.

As well as general changes in theoretical perspective, the work of particular individuals in Europe and South Africa has had considerable influence on Australian rock art research. For instance, publications by André Leroi-Gourhan on European Palaeolithic art, and later by Patricia Vinnicombe on South African rock art, indicate the value of structural approaches to analysis—demonstrating the lack of randomness in much of the rock art's placement within sites, portrayal of animal species, and so on. Such structuring clearly reflected ideological concerns on the part of the artist. Taking up and extending this principle, a number of Australian studies have examined within-site structure, the distribution of motifs between sites within the same artistic system, and selectivity in the cultural context of rock art.

Another turning point in Australian rock art studies was the broad academic shift to viewing style as a means of communicating information. The theoretical foundation for this was semiotics, the study of signs. This reassessment of the potential uses of style in archaeology was partly attributable to the increasing influence from anthropological studies of cultural material, which demonstrated the communicative capacity of style. The first major manifestation of this was the 'Schematization in Art' symposium at the AIAS biennial conference in 1974 (later published as *Form in Indigenous Art*). The thematic and interdisciplinary focus of the symposium provided a unique forum for the exchange of ideas between people working on different aspects of Australian Aboriginal art.

The increased emphasis on social explanations that emerged in archaeology in the 1980s manifested in rock art studies primarily as a concern with information exchange theory. One of the most influential exponents of this theory was Martin Wobst, who suggested that the main functions of style are related to cultural processes such as group integration and differentiation and boundary maintenance. This notion was extended by Clive Gamble, whose ideas were shaped in part by ethnographic information on the role of art in central Australia.

There was a time lag of several years before rock art researchers in Australia started to use the concept of information exchange as an explicit theoretical tool for interpreting rock art, but since then it has been used to interpret a wide range of rock art. I developed a contextual approach to the archaeology of art, which integrates the function of rock art with regional archaeological sequences. Through co-examining the characteristics and chronology of economic, technological and artistic evidence, I have been able to identify a tightening of social networks through time. My general approach is based on the notion that the functional interdependence between art and other cultural components, which is so evident in ethnographic case studies, suggests that art, and changes in art (both spatial and chronological), can tell much about the complexity of past cultural systems. This same interdependence indicates that archaeological studies of art need to take into account all available contextual evidence, including resource use. Fundamental to this approach is the notion of style as information.

Another early foray into this area of research was made by Darrell Lewis, who related changes in the perceived degree of regional homogeneity in northern Australia rock art to changes in environment, population densities and alliance networks. He argued that stylistic similarities in the early rock art of the Kimberley and Arnhem Land point to a relatively open social network in the Pleistocene, and he contrasted this with the greater stylistic heterogeneity of more recent rock art, which he linked to an increase in territorial bounding through time. The important point about the use of information exchange theory in Australian rock art studies is that it moves beyond a simple correlation between stylistic similarity and social interaction to embrace consideration of the causes underlying these interactions. However, the lack of independent dating evidence is still a major problem in many studies.

INCREASE IN THE DATABASE

By itself, growth in the number of recorded Australian rock art sites did not lead to changes in method and theory. But it helped. By the 1970s there was detailed information from many parts of Australia on rock art numbers, diversity and character. There was also some evidence for rock art chronology. Overwhelmingly, these records resulted from the activities of committed individuals rather than institutions—Robert Bednarik, Margaret Nobbs, Andrée Rosenfeld, Bruno David, George Chaloupka, Noelene Cole, Josephine Flood, Ben Gunn, Darrell Lewis, Fred McCarthy, Howard McNickle, Percy Trezise and Grahame Walsh are some of the fieldworkers who have added hugely to our knowledge about Australian rock art sites (Figure 3.7). The same trend continues today.

These records provided the basis for continent-wide overviews of the geographical and chronological variation in Australian Aboriginal rock art. In many cases, extensive site recording programs led to more specialist work on rock art chronology and excavations of associated cultural deposits. For instance, the recording work of Percy Trezise in southeast Cape York Peninsula over the past 30 years has provided a platform for all later researchers in the region.

In a few instances, rock art recording programs have been initiated as part of environmental impact assessments. This occurred in the Pilbara in response to the industrialization of the Burrup Peninsula, and in western Arnhem Land in relation to uranium mining and as part of the assessment of cultural resources in the region by the Australian National Parks and Wildlife Service. In other cases, organizations officially responsible for site management have obtained funding to 'take stock' of previous site records and other documentary sources. These syntheses have stimulated further work and in some cases have shown inadequacies in the database that need to be rectified in future site recording programs. For instance, rock art researchers and site managers now require a higher quality of contextual data and more accurate site locations. There is thus a feedback apparent between the increase in the database on Australian rock art, the amount of research initiated and further developments in method, theory and the database.

TECHNOLOGICAL DEVELOPMENTS

More than anything else, the problem of dating rock art has been the major impediment to its acceptance as useful archaeological data. The advent of radiocarbon dating in Australia in the 1950s allowed researchers to estimate absolute dates for some rock art, but only in a very restricted range of circumstances. For instance, engraved fragments and 'buried' panels or fragments of rock engravings have both been found in archaeological excavations. Rock art can also be stratified when covered by mineral or biogenic coatings, which may be datable using the standard radiocarbon technique.

FIGURE 3.7

A relatively small number of researchers have added substantially to our knowledge of Australian Aboriginal rock art. Andrée Rosenfeld on the top right, formerly of the Australian National University, has encouraged and supervised young researchers for over 25 years and has undertaken rock art research in many regions, including Europe, Cape York Peninsula and Central Australia. She is shown here with Mike Morwood at the Bendemeer rock painting site on the New England Tableland. Grahame Walsh (below) has worked extensively recording rock art sites throughout Australia, especially in the central Queensland highlands and the Kimberley. He has published many books on Australian rock art, including Bradshaw Art of the Kimberley.
(Photos M. J. Morwood)

FIGURE 3.8

Above left: *Alan Watchman taking samples of mineral deposits and pigments from the painted panel at Magnificent Gallery, southeast Cape York Peninsula. His geochemical work enables the composition of pigments to be identified and sometimes sourced. Some of the sampled mineral deposits and pigments can also be dated using accelerator mass spectrometry (AMS).* (Photo M. J. Morwood)

Above centre: *At Texas A & M University high vacuum techniques with low temperature oxygen plasma are used to selectively remove organic carbon in rock paints and so avoid contamination from rock carbonates. The organic carbon is then sent for dating. Marvin Rowe and colleagues have successfully used this refinement of the AMS technique for dating of American and Australian rock paintings in limestone caves.* (Photo M. J. Morwood)

Above right: *Richard Roberts and colleagues have pioneered the use of Optically Stimulated Luminescence (OSL) for dating mudwasp nests over or under rock paintings to obtain minimum or maximum ages for the art, respectively. Here Richard is measuring background radioactivity at a rock painting site in the Kimberley, Western Australia. The technique already indicates that the Bradshaw rock paintings of the region are more than 17.000 years old. Potentially OSL dating of associated mudwasp nests could provide dates for the entire Kimberley and Arnhem Land rock art sequences.* (Photo G. L. Walsh)

The development of the accelerator mass spectrometer (AMS) for radiometric dating has allowed us to calculate the ages of extremely small samples of organic matter (as little as 0.02 milligrams) and thus significantly increase the number of dating options for rock art (Figure 3.8). Although it has been known since the early 1980s that the AMS might be useful in the dating of organic material in rock art pigments, it was not so applied to Australian rock art assemblages until the early 1990s. Since then, however, there has been rapid progress in the development and application of technical refinements for dating rock art and associated materials. The dates for Australian rock painting, for instance, have now been pushed back to a minimum of about 40 000 years. For the first time, there is also the possibility of obtaining well-dated rock art sequences for comparison with other evidence for cultural and environmental changes. The establishment of the country's first high-precision AMS facility at the Australian Nuclear Science and Technology Organization in 1993 should accelerate this process. One of the facility's major aims is dating rock art.

Cation ratio (CR) dating was another technique applied to extremely small samples of rock varnish overlying engravings. CR and AMS dates of up to 40 000 years were obtained for varnishes covering pecked engravings at the Olary site, in northeast South Australia. This was claimed as the oldest direct dating of Australian rock art, but the processes by which rock varnish accumulates are not well understood, and these results have always been questioned. In fact, Ron Dorn, pioneer of the technique, has now conceded that CR is an 'inferior' method because of the complexity of factors affecting cation ratios in rock varnishes. It is no longer accepted as a means for validly dating rock engravings. Research by Rhys Jones and Bert Roberts is also in progress on the use of optically stimulated luminescence (OSL) for dating mudwasp nests overlying or underlying rock paintings in the Kimberley and West Arnhem Land.

New techniques for the analysis of geological samples have also been applied to rock pigments and associated mineral coatings. These techniques include X-ray diffraction spectrometry (XRD), X-ray fluorescence spectroscopy (XRF), proton induced X-ray emission (PIXE) and use of the scanning electron microscope (SEM). Such techniques can be used to study the processes of rock art deterioration, identify the composition of paints and track their sources.

The availability of computers and software for mathematical analysis and data display has revolutionized the way all categories of archaeological evidence, including rock art, are processed. Mainframe computers were first used for rock art analysis and production of graphics in Australia in the late 1970s and early 1980s. Mainframes were relatively difficult to use but, through software such as the Statistical Package for the Social Sciences (SPSS), they enabled researchers to perform frequency calculations, cross-tabulations between variables, cluster analyses, factor analyses and so on. The development of user-friendly personal computers with the power to undertake such analyses over the past ten years means that multi-variate analyses are now standard fare in most academic theses on rock art. Sometimes these approaches have yielded very useful results for the interpretation of rock art variability. In other cases, a black-box approach to computer and software use (in which researchers simply enter data and uncritically accept the results) has resulted in rock art analyses of appalling standards.

Computer-based geographical information systems (GIS) are now increasingly used by state and federal authorities concerned with the management of cultural and natural resources. GIS allows the distribution and context of sites to be viewed at many levels, and therefore would seem an ideal tool for the contextual analyses of rock art sites. This is a likely development in the near future.

Technological developments are also affecting the way in which rock art sites are recorded. Computers are now routinely taken into the field both to archive information and begin analysis of the data, while digital cameras allow electronic downloading, image enhancement and long-term storage. Hand-held and vehicle-mounted global positioning systems (GPS) are also increasingly used to accurately pin-point rock art site locations—thus overcoming a major problem apparent in many previous site recording programs.

AURA

Another turning point in the development of rock art research in Australia was the founding of the Australian Rock Art Research Association (AURA) in 1983, and the publication of the first issue of *Rock Art Research* in May the following year. Robert Bednarik was the motivating force here and acted in response to his perception that interest in rock art research was not being met by the journals of the day. AURA currently has 850 members and has been instrumental in encouraging a higher level of Aboriginal participation in rock art research. Its basic aims are:

> To provide a forum for the dissemination of research findings; to promote Aboriginal custodianship of sites externalising traditional Australian culture; to co-ordinate studies concerning the significance, distribution and conservation of rock art, both nationally and with individuals and organisations abroad; and to generally promote awareness and appreciation of Australia's prehistoric cultural heritage.

The stated commitment to Aboriginal custodianship of sites was considered quite radical at the time that AURA was established and demonstrates that AURA, along with the Australian Institute of Aboriginal and Torres Strait Islander Studies (formerly AIAS), has been in the vanguard in recognizing indigenous rights in cultural heritage; indeed, its influence can be perceived in some of the research now being carried out with indigenous people in other parts of the world.

AURA convenes an international congress every four years. The first in Darwin in 1988 saw the establishment of the International Federation of Rock Art Organizations. The second was in Cairns, and the third in Alice Springs. All were very successful, with the Darwin congress attracting 340 registered participants and the Cairns congress 450, including 59 Aboriginal delegates. These congresses have resulted in a number of important publications. *Rock Art Research* and the AURA Occasional Series are today major international publication outlets for rock art studies.

It is notable that the current pace of rock art research in Australia is not reflected in the two mainstream archaeological journals in Australia—*Australian Archaeology* (*AA*) and *Archaeology in Oceania* (*AO*). Of 401 major articles published in *AA* between 1974 and 1994 only thirteen were on rock art. Similarly, *AO* published thirteen articles during this period. In addition, there has been a noticeable delay between the appearance of breakthroughs in rock art method, theory or results, as reported elsewhere, and its reporting in these journals. In the early days, this time lag probably reflected the relatively marginal place of rock art studies in archaeology, but more lately may be due to publications on rock art published in other forums, such as *Rock Art Research* and *Antiquity*.

LEGISLATION AND CONSERVATION

In the mid-1960s Robert Edwards was instrumental in the establishment of a major site recording program funded by the AIAS. The passing of federal and state legislation during the 1960s aimed at protecting cultural heritage sites led to the establishment of professionally staffed administering bodies and archives for site documentation. One important role of these bodies was the funding of site recording programs.

In the mid-1970s and early 1980s these heritage institutions became increasingly concerned with conservation issues, including those relating to rock art. Under the auspices of the Joint Academies' Committee on the Protection of Prehistoric Places, a symposium on rock art recording, management and conservation was held in Sydney in 1980; a smaller meeting of the people most closely concerned with these matters was held in Canberra in 1981. The Canberra meeting formulated a number of proposals concerning directions and priorities in rock art conservation. One of its recommendations was for a study of the behaviour of tourists visiting rock art sites in Kakadu National Park; this was eventually conducted by Fay Gale and Jane Jacobs, and funded in part by AIAS. Another recommendation was that funds be sought to commission a review of current knowledge on rock art conservation applicable to Australian conditions. This study was undertaken by Andrée Rosenfeld for the Australian Heritage Commission. It was an important first step, which drew together all existing research and experimental data that had a bearing on rock art conservation in Australia. The report was designed for those concerned with, but not necessarily working in, the field of rock art conservation.

Graeme Ward and Sharon Sullivan point out that around this time the federal government was encouraging public discussion of Aboriginal demand for land rights. A public opinion survey commissioned in 1985 found that rock art was one of the very few

Aboriginal associations which were viewed favourably by the public. Ward and Sullivan suggest that this finding contributed to the federal government's decision in 1986 to provide AIAS with supplementary funding to develop a rock art conservation program. The three main aims of this program were the physical preservation and management of endangered sites, including those threatened by the natural elements, interference from humans or other animals; survey and documentation of new and major sites; and research on the significance of sites to contemporary Aborigines. Since then, the program's annual grant of $150 000 has been used to support twelve to fourteen major projects each year.

The rock art protection program also funded the publication in the Institute Report Series of two important studies that complemented the seminal work of Rosenfeld. The first was a regional study of Victoria River rock art and its significance for the local Aboriginal communities. Concluding that 'physical intervention by Europeans has the potential to seriously undermine Aboriginal cultural significance' (Lewis and Rose 1988), the authors then outlined a series of conservation proposals with the view of protecting both the sites themselves and their cultural significance. A second volume in this series recognized the needs of people actively working in the field of rock art conservation and has been especially useful to 'the Aboriginal site officers, rangers and others who are increasingly taking on responsibility for managing their own communities' sites' (Dix 1989). More recent volumes on rock art conservation, management and recording include the two AURA publications *Rock art and posterity* (1991) and *Preservation of rock art* (1995).

In 1989, a one-year full-time graduate diploma course on the conservation of rock art was conducted at the Canberra College of Advanced Education, with financial assistance provided by the Getty Conservation Institute. The course, under the direction of Alan Watchman, attracted fourteen Australian and overseas students. Despite the intensity, depth and breadth of the curriculum and its emphasis on practical experience, few of the Australian graduates are now actively involved in rock art conservation and none have permanent jobs in this field. There are two obvious lessons here. First, state and federal agencies responsible for rock art management should start employing qualified rock art conservators on a permanent basis. Second, the need for long-term planning and funding to meet future rock art conservation requirements is not met by one-off training courses or sources of funding.

In 1995, the Australian Cultural Development Office allocated $500 000 towards a program aimed at the protection of indigenous cultural heritage sites, with particular emphasis on rock art. The project, which was overseen by the Australian Cultural Development Office, the Australian Heritage Commission and the Australian Institute of Aboriginal and Torres Strait Islander Studies, was structured to include a high level of input by indigenous Australians. The principal consultants were Kate Sullivan, Katharine Sale and Nicholas Hall. The main goals of the program were to prepare guidelines for the protection, management and use of indigenous cultural heritage sites; to run a training course on site management; and to conduct an exemplar site management project. Despite unreasonable time constraints and other concerns, the level of funding of this program indicates a strong political commitment to cultural heritage matters and to a high public profile for Australian rock art.

INDIGENOUS INVOLVEMENT

Indigenous involvement in the management and control of rock art sites has increased greatly over the last twenty years (Figure 3.9). However, this has to be seen in a wider sociocultural perspective, especially in terms of the changes in community attitude and legislation, which have affected Aboriginal land rights. Events of particular importance include the beginning of the modern Aboriginal land rights movement in 1966, when the Gurindji walked off Wave Hill Station; the 1967 referendum, which overwhelmingly supported the inclusion of Aboriginal people in Australian census figures; the 1972 election of the Whitlam Labor government with its platform of major changes in Aboriginal social policy; the setting up of the well-publicized Aboriginal Tent Embassy in the grounds of Parliament House in 1972; the passing of land rights legislation by the states, beginning with the Northern Territory in 1976; and the recognition of Native Title by the High Court of Australia in 1992 (the Mabo decision).

Property and political rights are fundamental aspects of land rights, and the increased control of cultural heritage sites is just one manifestation of the recent empowerment of Aboriginal communities. The trend is likely to continue, at least partly because of Aboriginal

FIGURE 3.9

Top left: *Tommy George and George Musgrave, two elders of the Laura community, at Mushroom Rock in southeast Cape York Peninsula. They have both played a prominent part in the Ang-gnarra Aboriginal Corporation, which is involved in management and control of cultural heritage sites in the region.* (Photo M. J. Morwood)

Centre left: *Mike Morwood (left) with the late Hector Tungal, a senior Ngarinjin man at Kalumburu, north Kimberley. Hector had a deep and extensive knowledge about Wandjina rock paintings and their associated ideology. His permission was required in order to undertake research in specific parts of the region. Permission also had to be obtained from the Kalumburu Community Council and the Sites Department of the Western Australian Museum.* (Photo M. J. Morwood)

Bottom left: *Inkarta Peter Bullah, a senior man from Central Australia, with June Ross at a rock painting site. He is singing a song associated with the site and its Dreamtime significance. Such information on the wider cultural context of rock art has seldom been recorded.* (Photo June Ross)

Far right: *Aileen George taking notes during the 1990 archaeological excavations at Sandy Creek 1, a rock art site in southeast Cape York Peninsula. At the time Aileen was a Cultural Heritage Ranger with Ang-gnarra Aboriginal Corporation.* (Photo M. J. Morwood)

people's concerns with the legislative processes that affect their cultural material and the high level of indigenous politicization in Australia. Rock art has been important to the reaffirmation of Aboriginal corporate identity in many regions, and is thus integral to indigenous political processes. In addition, rock art sites have been an important component of Aboriginal land claims in the Northern Territory since the passage of the *Aboriginal Land Rights (Northern Territory) Act 1976,* as often these sites are the material embodiment of aspects of the Dreaming. Aborigines, with the support of archaeologists, and anthropologists, have worked to establish the legal validity of these indigenous relationships to land.

However, there is also potential for conflict between the Aboriginal significance of rock art sites and other heritage values. A recent example, that of the 1987 controversial repainting of Wandjina sites in the Kimberley, illustrates the complexities of such issues and reminds us that rock art research and management are not undertaken in an ethical or political vacuum (see Chapter 11).

PUBLIC INTEREST

Over the past twenty years, there has been increasing public interest in Aboriginal culture and art. Relevant factors include legislative changes, increased leisure time, higher levels of population mobility and greater interest in ecotourism. In addition, Josephine Flood has recently produced a series of books aimed at a general audience, emphasizing Aboriginal rock art and enhancing public interest. Visitor census figures at major heritage sites, such as Uluru and Carnarvon Gorge, clearly show a compounding interest in Aboriginal cultural heritage sites during this period. Longer-term changes in the way people have used Aboriginal art sites and responded to rock art are evident in a study of dated graffiti at rock art sites. These reflect a progressive increase in visitor numbers from the 1950s, with a corresponding increase in vandalism until the passing of state Heritage legislation in the late 1960s, which proscribed inappropriate behaviours. After this time, the proportion of visitors vandalizing sites fell abruptly.

Rock art sites remain a focus of public interest in Aboriginal culture. However, heavy visitation or scientific investigation can constitute a serious threat. Some recent rock art research has been directed towards monitoring the affects of visitor impact and developing methods through which this might be minimized.

Trends and developments

Anthropological and ethnoarchaeological studies of Aboriginal rock art have been very influential on archaeological investigations of art here and elsewhere in the world. Australia is one of the few places where it is still possible to obtain detailed information on the functions of indigenous art and how these may be reflected in the archaeological record. The anthropological emphasis in Australian rock art research will therefore continue, although the political context of research in Aboriginal communities has changed substantially. Katherine Sale has highlighted some of the social and political complexities involved in the practice of re-marking (or renewing) rock paintings, while Claire Smith has analyzed the influence of social and material context on style in an Aboriginal artistic system in the Beswick–Barunga region.

The work of Paul Taçon in West Arnhem Land, Andrée Rosenfeld in Central Australia and Josephine Flood with Bruno David in the Victoria River District has established a more fine-grained understanding of Aboriginal artistic systems. Many of these studies show greater concern with forms of social identity, especially as influenced by processes associated with contact. They also demonstrate an indeterminate boundary between archaeology and anthropology in rock art research. This trend—which runs counter to the general tendency (noted by Peter White) for social/cultural anthropology and archaeology to diverge—is likely to continue.

Regional studies involving contextual analyses and the dating of rock art are becoming increasingly sophisticated. Taçon, for instance, has shown that the recent rock art of Arnhem Land is more stylistically complex than earlier rock art in the region. He interprets this as reflecting a change in the character of group identities, involving an increase in territoriality and an associated need for rock art to encode more levels of meaning. Other recent or current work along these lines includes that of Darrell Lewis on the way local and regional patterns of social interaction are reflected in the rock art style of the Victoria River District; Bruno David's multidisciplinary investigation of Aboriginal land use in northeast Queensland, which emphasizes rock art evidence; Noelene Cole's study of regional and chronological variation in the rock art of southeast Cape York Peninsula; and Josephine McDonald's investigation of the contextual problems posed by a dual media rock art system in the Sydney region and the different degrees of homogeneity exhibited by local rock paintings and rock engravings.

An associated trend is to establish well-dated regional rock art sequences for comparison with other evidence for cultural change and environmental fluctuations. Further developments in technology, minimal-impact sampling and on-site measurements will accelerate this trend. On a broader scale, Bernard Huchet's comprehensive overview of regional styles in body art and rock art is aimed at assessing the relationships between patterning in these art forms and Aboriginal regional identity before and since European contact.

New systems of classification are being developed. Kelvin Officer has developed an approach to motif analysis that crosses the artificial boundary between figurative and non-figurative art, which has been a fundamental problem for Australian rock art studies since Maynard's seminal research in the 1970s. Natalie Franklin has used an analysis of spatial variation in Australian rock art bodies to reassess Maynard's stylistic categories. Josephine McDonald has incorporated gender into her analysis of Sydney Basin rock art and has evidence that men, women and children participated in the stencilling of hands and implements. This is important because records indicate that most recent rock art in Australia was the business of men. McDonald's work provides a timely reminder that the contexts in which Australian Aboriginal rock art was produced over many thousands of years are likely to have been far more diverse than is currently documented.

The nexus between art and ideology means that rock art has been, and will continue to be, important to the ways in which indigenous people see themselves. It is therefore likely that Aboriginal people will take a closer interest in rock art sites than in, say, stone tools. A number of universities now run courses in Aboriginal site management, and this is indicative of future developments. The increasing participation of Aboriginal people in rock art research and conservation, as well as management, will give rise to important changes in method and theory.

Rock art data is now highly relevant to some fundamental problems in Australian archaeology, including human settlement on the continent, the emergence of language, and changes in social organization and land use. The recovery of high-quality pigments from the lowest levels of the earliest occupation sites excavated in Australia shows that people were engaged in some type of artistic activity between 50 000 and 60 000 BP. This has implications for human cultural and evolutionary development worldwide. Similarly, early dates for Australian rock art and later evidence for the regionalization of rock art systems provides important evidence about changes in Aboriginal resource use and the emergence of group ownership of land.

Conclusions

In the last twenty years rock art research has emerged as a distinct and viable sub-discipline of Australian archaeology. As part of this general development, there has been a marked increase in the number of archaeologists who are recording, managing and researching rock art. Rock art studies are an exciting and important part of Australian archaeology. The high standard of rock art research in Australia is recognized internationally. As the 1991 annual report of the Rock Art Association of Canada noted:

> Australian scientists have become the leading authority on nearly every issue of prehistoric rock art studies, including: conservation, site management, research ethics, Native involvement issues, scientific dating and recording, educational articulation, etc. There is not an organisation in the world which could embark upon formulating their particular rock art strategies and policies without due consideration of the Australian experience.

CHAPTER 4

How we study Australian Aboriginal rock art

There is a general principle called 'uniformitarianism', which states that the present is the key to the past. It was first proposed by James Hutton in 1785 and is fundamental to all disciplines concerned with reconstructing the past—such as geology, palaeontology and archaeology. According to this principle, if we try to study Aboriginal cultures through rock art without knowing how modern-day Aboriginal societies produce and use art, we are unlikely to reach sound conclusions. Although Aboriginal art in all regions of Australia has undergone major changes in motif use, technique, context of production and ideological significance over time, contemporary art systems can still provide insights, cautionary tales, ethnographic analogies and, in some cases, direct historical connection with earlier art systems.

Research has shown that the function of Aboriginal art can only be understood within the context of other types of symbolic behaviour, social and ceremonial organization, and resource use. The study of Aboriginal art systems can also aid in the archaeological interpretation of art elsewhere in the world. The principles that underpin rock art research, however, are best understood in the context of archaeological research generally.

Explaining the evidence

Archaeology's main aim is to understand how past cultural systems functioned by examining their material remains—which often do not include any kind of writing. The crucial problem in this exercise is the means by which links are established between the nature of the material evidence and the nature of the original cultural context. Archaeologists study the hard bits, or 'bones', of past systems, to draw conclusions about their cultural anatomy. Whether we are looking at stone artefacts, food remains, sediments, or rock art, the same crucial problem must be faced: how to relate this evidence to the culture that produced it.

By itself archaeological evidence cannot tell us anything unless we can establish some principles for interpreting its significance. Hence the concept of 'middle range' theory, which aims to bridge the gap between data and its implications. In archaeology, middle range theory has largely been concerned with establishing the principles of site formation, as it is generally recognized that the nature and distribution of archaeological evidence are the end results of a range of natural and cultural processes. Much research has been aimed at acquiring an understanding of these processes. For instance, researchers can make and use copies of early tools or observe the way modern peoples behave to obtain information on the workings of specific economic, technological and ideological systems and the way in which that material evidence will be produced and represented in the archaeological record.

Such concerns have not been well articulated in studies concerned with the archaeology of hunter–gatherer art, where a working knowledge of its role in recent hunter–gatherer societies has not been seen as an essential prerequisite for the interpretation of past art assemblages. This was not always the case. At the end of the 19th century, European researchers concerned with the discovery and interpretation of Palaeolithic art were heavily influenced by new ethnographic studies which emphasized the importance of totemism in 'primitive' ideology.

In the 1890s, the work of Baldwin Spencer and Frank Gillen described the totemic context of rock art in Central Australia. The result was that the concept of totemism was lifted directly out of the ethnographic literature and used to explain art of the European Upper Palaeolithic period (40 000 to 10 000 BP) as being concerned with sympathetic magic. Such crude use of analogy later led some researchers to reject the use of ethnographic parallels or 'the comparative method' in interpreting prehistoric art. Instead it was argued that interpretation must be based on the evidence alone. In the words of André Leroi-Gourhan, doyen of French rock art research:

> Without recourse to materials other than Palaeolithic, questions can be addressed to the dead informant: he is of course mechanically limited in his replies by what has actually survived of his creations, but these replies are at least expressed in his own language, and not in the accents of nineteenth-century Tierra del Fuego or the contemporary Sudan.

Some Australian researchers also draw a sharp line between 'ethnographic' and 'archaeological' approaches to the analysis of art. But such distinctions virtually ignore the extensive literature dealing with the relationship between ethnography and archaeology.

In the 1960s, archaeologists began to approach their discipline as a branch of science and to base their work on the experimental method that had proved so valuable in fields such as optics, astronomy, physics and chemistry. This involves: observing the facts; forming a hypothesis which, if true, would account for those facts; deducing from this hypothesis a set of consequences that can be tested by experiments or further observations; and finally, checking the results of those experiments or observations against the hypothesis. If repeated testing supports the hypothesis, it is granted the status of a theory. Contemporary scientists readily concede that there is more to developing and evaluating hypotheses than pure logical reasoning. But this does not alter the fundamental basis of the experimental method, namely that what determines the soundness of a hypothesis is not the way it is arrived at, but the way it holds up when tested.

In 1865, the chemist Friedrich August von Kekulé was trying to figure out how the benzene molecule was structured. One day he had a dream about snakes coiling around to bite their own tails. When he awoke, he realized that the benzene molecule must be ring-shaped. Despite its non-rational origin, this explanation became generally accepted because it was one that accounted for the observed chemical and physical properties of benzene.

The implication of this example for archaeology is that, so long as our hypotheses are robust enough to explain all aspects of the material evidence, it does not matter whether they arise from ethnographic or purely archaeological data. In some cases, detailed ethnographic information on present-day people's beliefs has enabled us to come up with (and test) sophisticated explanations for the content and structure of rock art. In the far more common cases where we have no such information, we may develop explanations—albeit somewhat rougher ones—from a variety of other sources, including the general ethnographic literature. Although rock art studies have a unique database, they are concerned with material evidence for past human behaviour and are therefore part of the wider scientific discipline of archaeology.

From most parts of the world there is minimal useful information on the functional relationship between art, social organization and resource use, and art site formation processes (that is, information of the type useful in the archaeological investigation of art). A number of Australian examples serve to illustrate some important general principles.

Meaning and function of Aboriginal art

It is generally acknowledged that Australia—with its remarkable cultural continuity over tens of thousands of years—has unique potential for the study of hunter–gatherer rock art in its broader social and economic context. Australian researchers have access to some of the most detailed ethnographic information on hunter–gatherer art available anywhere in the world. As in the case of the work of Spencer and Gillen, such information has helped shed light on prehistoric rock art in many countries.

Rock art continued until recently in parts of Central Australia, the Kimberley, Arnhem Land and the Gulf country. Richard Gould encountered two Western Desert men painting a sacred design on a cliff face in the Rawlinson Range as late as 1966, while the most recent known rock paintings in western Arnhem Land were undertaken in 1972. Even though production of rock art no longer appears to be an integral part of Aboriginal culture, many individuals still know a great deal about it, and in some areas traditional art that was once painted on rock is now done on other media.

Despite this, we still have very little detailed information on rock art's cultural function, even where there are substantial bodies of such art that clearly continued into the post-European contact period. Examples include the engraving sites around Sydney with their depictions of sailing ships, and the painted galleries around Laura in southeast Cape York, which include depictions of Europeans with rifles, horses and pigs. But although ethnographic information is often sparse and superficial, it may provide the only clues to the meaning of the art and the motives of its makers.

In a few regions, though, we can still get very detailed information. In western Arnhem Land, for instance, much is known about the life and work of individual rock artists, such as Najombolmi of the Bardmardi clan, who lived between 1895 and 1967 and produced some of the most beautiful decorative X-ray paintings of the region (Figure 4.1). Najombolmi produced at least 604 paintings at 46 sites and in six clan territories along the Arnhem Land escarpment. These include the 'Main Gallery' at Anbangbang and the nearby Blue Paintings. This rich legacy allows us to look at the way individual artists varied their work within a given rock art style to quantify their contribution to the local rock painting tradition over the past 100 years, and to examine the distribution of his paintings in relation to Aboriginal cultural boundaries.

The first ethnographers to set Aboriginal art in its social and economic context were Spencer and Gillen in their work in Central Australia. Among their many important findings were that one symbol can have many meanings depending on its context, and that the choice of motifs (that is, figurative or geometric) reflects the function of the art. Overall their work clearly shows that Aboriginal art can only be understood in terms of its interaction with other elements of the social system.

These implications, however, took some time to be understood. For instance, during the American–Australian expedition to Arnhem Land in 1948, Charles Mountford did little more than pick out the more appealing figures in the rock art, photograph them and ask Aboriginal informants for 'identifications'. He made no attempt to discuss artistic ideology or function. A. P. Elkin's comment on this approach is worth noting:

Meaning is not obtained by asking the artist or bystander what a certain pattern indicates, nor merely by getting the myth it

FIGURE 4.1

These paintings in Anbangbang Shelter at Nourlangie Rock, western Arnhem Land, were done in the 1963–64 wet season by the renowned artist Najombolmi and his friends Djimongurr and Djorlom. Given the number of paintings produced by Najombolmi, it is possible that most of the thousands of rock paintings in the region were done by a relatively small number of individuals. (Photo G. Chaloupka)

represents. Meaning comes after much travail out of the functional relationship of philosophy, belief, ritual, social structure and the general heritage of culture.

The experience of Neville MacIntosh at Beswick Cave illustrates this point particularly well. He originally recorded and identified the rock art at the site without informants, then later returned with the owner, Lamderod, a highly initiated Djauan man. Even at the basic level of identifying subjects, MacIntosh found he had been wrong in fifteen out of 22 cases. He noted that there are at least four levels of meaning in the paintings, ranging from the identification of figures to their esoteric, religious significance, and concluded that the chance of researchers inferring all of this knowledge was 'lamentably small'.

One implication of MacIntosh's work is that archaeologists who are unable to locate knowledgeable informants must confine themselves to examining what the rock art and other remains reveal about the functional relationships between art, ideology, social structure and resource use. In this light, knowing how recent Aboriginal art systems function in their wider cultural context is an essential basis for interpreting (rock) art evidence in the archaeological record. Areas where such information is available include Central Australia, the Kimberley and Arnhem Land.

CENTRAL AUSTRALIA

The graphic art of Australian desert dwellers is very homogeneous in the use of motifs and in function over a wide area. This was recognized in 1937 by Daniel Sutherland Davidson, who coined the term 'Central Australian decorative complex' (Figure 2.16). It denotes a restricted range of geometric designs and trackmarks used in body paintings, sand drawings, decoration and rock art. They can be painted with ochres, pipeclay, charcoal and bird down, or incised on objects with macropod incisor teeth. The most common motifs are circles, concentric circles, spirals, U-figures, straight and curved lines, dots and stylized animal tracks, although simple figurative designs are also used (Figure 4.2). Along the western boundary of the region, among the Pitjantjatjara and Pintubi, other non-rounded, geometric designs such as concentric squares, angular meanders, zigzags, herringbones and interlocking key patterns became common, possibly as a result of outside influence.

In her classic 1973 work on Walbiri iconography, Nancy Munn discussed the structure of Walbiri designs, their characteristics, their use and the functions of different categories of designs. Central Australian art, she concluded, has discontinuous ranges of meaning in which a given pattern or shape may be used to represent many things with similar shapes: a circle, for example, can represent a waterhole, a mountain, a camp, a yam, a piece of fruit or anything else that is 'roundish' (Figure 4.3).

Munn also noted that in Walbiri cosmology, all ancestral beings shared important attributes: they made camps and left tracks. Elaborate designs associated with specific ancestral beings were made

FIGURE 4.2

This rock painting on an outcrop in the Cloncurry River near Malbon, northwest Queensland, features a typical 'Central Australian' composite of geometric and track motifs. It is regularly submerged by the flooding of the river but is still remarkably clear. (Photo M. J. Morwood)

out of simple multi-meaning elements, such as circles, straight lines and arcs. Each composite design was unique, but all shared a common structure based on a core unit of circles and straight lines. The designs both reflect and serve as metaphors for the way in which Walbiri perceive the world.

Arid Australia is of great importance in the archaeological study of art for a number of reasons. First, the region has provided some of the most detailed information on hunter–gatherer art available anywhere in the world. Second, there is evidence that the Central Australian art tradition is of considerable antiquity, almost certainly older than 10 000 years. This evidence includes the degree of patination and weathering of motifs at some engraving sites in the region (Figure 4.4), and the fact that very similar engraved assemblages occur in Tasmania, which was cut off from the Australian mainland about 11 000 years ago, and at the Early Man Site in southeast Cape York, which is at least 14 000 years old.

Continuous meaning ranges

Yirrkalla

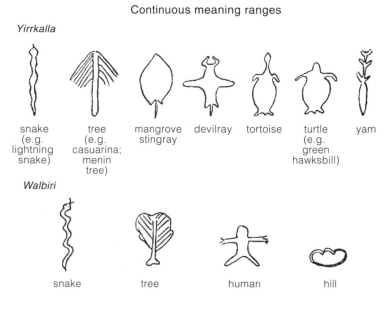

snake
(e.g.
lightning
snake)

tree
(e.g.
casuarina;
menin
tree)

mangrove
stingray

devilray

tortoise

turtle
(e.g.
green
hawksbill)

yam

Walbiri

snake

tree

human

hill

Discontinuous meaning ranges—*Walbiri*

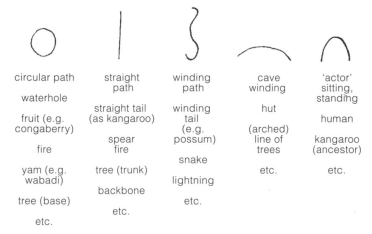

circular path

waterhole

fruit (e.g.
congaberry)

fire

yam (e.g.
wabadi)

tree (base)

etc.

straight
path

straight tail
(as kangaroo)

spear
fire

tree (trunk)

backbone

etc.

winding
path

winding
tail
(e.g.
possum)

snake

lightning

etc.

cave
winding

hut

(arched)
line of
trees

etc.

'actor'
sitting,
standing

human

kangaroo
(ancestor)

etc.

FIGURE 4.3

Motifs with continuous and discontinuous meanings in Yirrkalla (northeast Arnhem Land) and Walbiri art. The former are figurative and therefore have a more restricted range of possible meanings. In contrast, motifs with discontinuous ranges of meaning are used to represent many things with similar shapes. Such motifs are characteristic of Central Australian art.
(From Munn 1966)

Although the motif range in Central Australian art appears to have remained remarkably consistent over time, there have been important changes in its technique and distribution. The earliest surviving rock art assemblages in the Australian arid zone are of deeply pecked engravings of circles, other geometric designs and tracks, located close to water sources. Local Aboriginal informants have stated that such sites were not made by humans, but were the work of ancestral beings. As Robert Edwards notes:

FIGURE 4.4

A very patinated, pecked engraving of Central Australian type in northwest Queensland. In this region, more recent engravings have greater emphasis on figurative motifs. (Photo M. J. Morwood)

They consider these to be a part of the 'dreaming' site and claim they were made when the site was 'created'. Any suggestion of the living people of present and immediate past generations having made the engravings was met with surprise and incredulity. The aboriginals denied any knowledge of the living people having anything at all to do with making the engravings and insisted that they formed an integral part of the ceremonial site and 'have always been there'.

In the historic period, the only rock engravings still being made by the Pitjantjatjara were produced by shallow pounding, a marked contrast to the deep pecking of the older engravings (Figure 4.5). There is also strong evidence that the 'Central Australian decorative complex' was formerly more widespread. Deeply pecked engravings that include circles and other geometric motifs and tracks occur not only in Tasmania and southeast Cape York Peninsula but also in central Queensland, western Queensland and western New South Wales, where they predate more regionally distinctive art styles.

Although these widely distributed engraved assemblages exhibit greater diversity in motif use than those at 'classic' Central Australian engraving sites like Panaramitee, Florina, Tiverton, Pitcairn, Winnininnie, Nackara Springs and Cleland Hills, the similarities have

FIGURE 4.5

A panel of engravings near Mt Isa, northwest Queensland. These are unpatinated and contain red ochre. Figurative motifs have always been part of the 'Central Australian' rock art tradition, but more recent panels have a higher proportion of figurative motifs. (Photo M. J. Morwood)

prompted Lesley Maynard to argue that there was an early widespread art, the 'Panaramitee style' (after the type site in northeast South Australia). Maynard proposed that this style was retained in Tasmania after its separation from the Australian mainland, and that in Central Australia it developed directly into the art tradition that has survived to this day.

Third, Central Australia is important in the archaeological study of art because, even though the region is mostly dry, there is considerable variability in the amount and reliability of rainfall and the nature of the terrain. Montane and piedmont slopes, riverine floodplain, shield desert, stony desert and spinifex sandplains supported different human population densities and resulted in different technological and social strategies. It is worth investigating whether any of these differences are reflected in graphic arts generally and rock art in particular.

The Pitjantjatjara, for example, occupied the Gibson and Great Sandy Deserts—sandy deserts with longitudinal dunes and the occasional low knoll. In this harsh, unpredictable environment, population densities were low (about one person per 100 square kilometres), and mobility was high. Rights to land were flexible— they could be acquired through the father or mother (ambilineal)— and the range of tools and weapons used was very limited.

In contrast, the more forgiving country of the Walbiri and Aranda had higher population densities, a more settled lifestyle and a more elaborate material culture. Land was owned by patrilineal clans, which occupied clearly demarcated tracts of land, or estates. Only during very bad droughts were people forced to leave these clan estates, and the distances moved were very limited.

For Central Australian Aborigines, the landscape is the creation of ancestral beings who travelled widely during the Dreamtime, altering or forming plains, rocks, gullies, springs and caves as they went. Thus all the major features of the landscape are named, and each ancestral being is associated with a particular song cycle about his or her activities at various places. Each site is also associated with one or more sets of designs. Ownership of specific estates is held by common descent groups, either patrilineal or ambilineal depending on area. Each estate traditionally contained a base camp located near a reliable water source and is best thought of as a cluster of sites rather than a bounded territory. In the Western Desert the distance between the centres of Pitjanjatjara estates varied between 35 and 60 kilometres (Layton 1985), while in the area of the MacDonnell Range, near Alice Springs, Aranda estates were about 35 kilometres across.

Except in the most favourable areas, a given group was permitted to hunt and gather not only in their estate but also in the estates

FIGURE 4.6

The paintings at Emily Gap in the MacDonnell Range near Alice Springs are the best known of the many Central Australian rock art sites. They are located adjacent to a waterhole at the entrance to the gorge. The paintings mark a site of great significance for local Aranda people, with the key totemic figure for the site being Intwailuka, *ancestral hero of the caterpillar totem. The painted stripes, which dominate the art, represent the chest decoration designs of participants in the* Intichiuna *ceremonies, formerly held at the site.* (Photo G. L. Walsh)

of adjacent groups. Each estate was crossed by at least two main ancestral tracks. The designs associated with key sites along these tracks could not be copied by men of other estates without permission. Rights to the use of land depended upon knowing the cultural meta-landscape: the associated mythology and the location of sacred sites. Venturing into terrain where one lacked such knowledge was considered 'dangerous'. Estates were spiritually maintained through a range of symbolic activities, including song cycles, dancing and art.

Central Australian graphic arts took the form of decorations on objects, sand drawings and ground paintings, body designs and rock paintings (Figure 4.6). Both secular and ceremonial objects were decorated. The former included weapons and tools, which were customarily covered in red ochre, while shields used in performances sometimes had designs painted on the outer side. Pitjantjatjara spearthrowers could also be incised with geometric designs representing ancestral-being tracks (Figure 4.7). As named waterholes are an integral part of such tracks, song cycles and the designs on secular and sacred objects helped people memorize their location. In arid Australia this obviously had survival value.

A range of decorated objects was also made for ceremonies. These included sacred poles, stringed crosses (*waninga*), and rounded slabs of wood or stone with incised or painted designs known as *churinga* by the Aranda and *kulpidji* by the Pitjantjatjara. *Churinga* were thought to contain ancestral power and were displayed, greased and rubbed with red ochre, by fully initiated elder men during ceremonies. The painted or incised designs were exclusively geometric compositions and stylized tracks, which related to specific places within a clan estate.

At birth, all individuals within an estate became the owner of a 'recycled' or newly manufactured *churinga* associated with their birthplace. However, boys did not see their *churinga* until fully initiated, while women never saw their personal *churinga*, which were normally kept together in a cave or tree storehouse for sacred objects within the clan estate. Women and children would not venture within a certain distance (up to 2 kilometres) of these sacred centres on pain of death. *Churinga* were removed from the sacred storehouse only for major ceremonies but were occasionally loaned to other groups linked by an ancestral track, as a gesture of trust and goodwill.

Each *churinga* design is unique because it is associated with a very

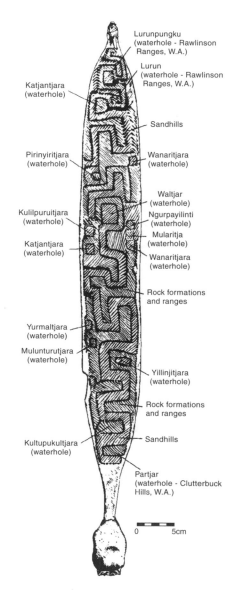

Lurunpungku (waterhole - Rawlinson Ranges, W.A.)
Lurun (waterhole - Rawlinson Ranges, W.A.)
Katjantjara (waterhole)
Sandhills
Pirinyiritjara (waterhole)
Wanaritjara (waterhole)
Waltjar (waterhole)
Ngurpayilinti (waterhole)
Kulilpuruitjara (waterhole)
Mularitja (waterhole)
Katjantjara (waterhole)
Wanaritjara (waterhole)
Rock formations and ranges
Yurmaltjara (waterhole)
Mulunturutjara (waterhole)
Yillinjitjara (waterhole)
Rock formations and ranges
Sandhills
Kultupukultjara (waterhole)
Partjar (waterhole - Clutterbuck Hills, W.A.)
0   5cm

FIGURE 4.7

Pitjantjatjara spearthrower design representing a tract of Gibson Desert over 240 kilometres in length. Waterholes feature prominently in the associated story and so the design also served as a means of memorising the location of water sources.
(After Pfeiffer 1982, p. 171 from an original by Nicholas Amorosi and Richard Gould)

localized topographical/mythological feature, but sets of *churinga* relating to a site or estate tend to share a common core structure. For instance, the *churinga* associated with Uluru (Ayers Rock) all have different designs, but the basis of each design is a linked diamond pattern. The designs on *churinga* from different estates but which relate to places along the same ancestral track may also have similar core structuring.

Churinga are highly valued and carefully looked after: the penalty for their damage or loss is death. It is thus extremely rare for these items to be discarded, but they can make their way into the archaeological record. Caches can be forgotten or lost if the men responsible for their care die. This occurred on the Finke River, when an elderly western Aranda man cleared out the sacred storehouse of his estate because he regarded the younger men as untrustworthy. Despite much searching, its contents have not been recovered.

In another recent instance, Pintubi men who had hidden sacred objects in a rockshelter had to dig up a wide area of the deposits when they forgot exactly where the objects had been buried. The discovery of a *churinga* eroding out of a sandhill in southwest Queensland indicates that similar losses occurred in the past. The collapse of Aboriginal traditional life as a result of European impact has also resulted in many objects being lost.

Sand drawings were used by Walbiri women to keep track of stories as they told them during storytelling, using a continuous, running sand notation, while men used pigments, blood and down to make ancestral designs during ceremonies. Such ground paintings were produced within a limited area of the arid zone encompassing the territory of the western Aranda, Unmatjera, Pintubi, Kukatja, Pitjantjatjara, Iliaura and Warramunga, but not the Eastern or Southern Aranda or the Western Desert people. Like sand drawings, ground paintings consisted almost exclusively of geometric and track motifs, but were more structurally complex. They were deliberately destroyed during the ceremonial performance.

Body paintings comprised simple geometric designs made from pigments or down and were used in public performances or at restricted ceremonies to differentiate people playing different ancestral roles.

Rock paintings in Central Australia included both figurative and geometric components and were used in a variety of contexts, both secular and sacred, but the relative proportions of these two main motif types depended on context: secular art, which could be publicly viewed, tended to emphasize figurative motifs, while sacred paintings associated with specific, totemic ancestors were almost exclusively geometric in form, and were undertaken at specific localities which were prohibited to the uninitiated. Secular paintings were done as 'play-work' or by hunters as they waited for game to arrive (Figure 4.8). The act of painting was intended to hasten the arrival of the quarry. Designs like these and casual designs in caves and other places depicting a hunt or an animal could be publicly viewed.

In contrast, paintings associated with totemic ancestors were owned by local totemic groups and were done at specific localities that were barred to the uninitiated. Charles Mountford provides a good example of this separation at Walinga Hill Cave, where secular and sacred art occupy distinct zones. Paintings in the open, secular area portray ancestors, Europeans and animals, while paintings in the restricted section are geometric, representing sacred objects and body paintings used in the ceremony for the honey ant Ancestor.

Sacred paintings were done in conjunction with a range of other symbolic activities. For instance, Spencer and Gillen observed a fertility ceremony, held at a site called Undiara, which involved the uncovering and rubbing of a sacred stone, chanting and bloodletting, as well as the painting of linear designs on a rock ledge:

FIGURE 4.8

Aranda 'play-work' (secular) paintings, Central Australia. These have a much higher figurative emphasis than art done in restricted contexts. (After Spencer and Gillen 1899, Figure 124)

Red ochre and powdered and calcined gypsum was used, and with these alternate vertical lines are painted on the face of the rock, each about a foot in width, the painting on the left side being done by the Panunga and Bulthara men, and that on the right by the Purula and Kumara. The red stripes are supposed to represent the red fur of the Kangaroo (*Macropus rufus*) while the white ones represent the bones.

Sacred rock paintings are less formally structured than the designs found on *churinga* and are more akin to the body paintings used in the associated ceremonies. In fact, several sources note that one function of rock paintings was to preserve the totemic body designs used at the site on a permanent medium.

WEST KIMBERLEY

The western Kimberley region consists of rugged mountains bounded by the Fitzroy River to the south, the Drysdale River to the east and the Indian Ocean to the west (Figure 4.9). It is an area of great environmental diversity, with interior ranges, stretches of rocky coastline, mangrove-lined inlets, extensive tidal estuaries and offshore islands. It is also monsoonal, with pronounced wet and dry seasons, and is rich in plant and animal resources.

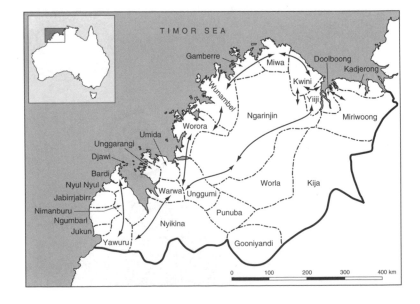

FIGURE 4.9

Aboriginal tribes in the Kimberley. The distinctive Wandjina rock painting style occurs in the areas of the Worora, Ngarinjin, Wunambel and Unggumi. The arrows show the operation of the wunan *exchange system. As well as involving formalized trade, the* wunan *served as a social map for defining the relationship between clans* (After Blundell 1982; Horton 1994; McCarthy 1939)

The western Kimberley is of particular interest because it contains a large number of rock art sites; the art style is regionally distinctive and restricted in distribution; and there is excellent information available on the social role of rock paintings, which remain an integral part of the local people's beliefs.

Western Kimberley rock art is dominated by paintings of large anthropomorphic beings called Wandjina, which are of very standardized form. They comprise heads, or full-length figures, painted in red or yellow on a white background, with horseshoe-shaped headdresses, black eyes, red eyelashes and noses; the mouths and ears are never portrayed. Wandjina are often associated with paintings of plants and animals such as birds, lizards and crocodiles (Figure 4.10). All animal figures are depicted from a distinctively skewed perspective—the head is shown with eyes close together separated by a line running to the nose, ears are perpendicular to the eyes, limbs are stiff and straight and the anus is prominent. The figures are never arranged in narrative sequence.

Other subjects include malicious creatures shown in flat, frontal perspective with no interior details and distorted limbs, as well as representations of the sun, firesticks, ochre, manufactured articles and hand stencils.

Wandjina rock paintings and associated myths appear only in the northern and western sections of the Kimberley. In the southern and eastern areas the emphasis is upon depiction of animal ancestral beings, particularly pythons. There is also evidence that significant changes occurred in the Kimberley rock art sequence (see Chapter 5). Unlike Wandjina paintings, earlier rock painting styles, such as the Bradshaw, were recorded as being of little or no importance to local Aboriginal informants.

Wandjina art occurs in the tribal areas of the Worora, Ngarinjin, Wunambel and Unggumi, which are culturally and linguistically similar. Each language group is divided into clans, which held a defined and named estate. Clan membership is inherited from the father (patrilineal). Local residential groups were fairly flexible in composition according to economic and social circumstances, but usually comprised a core of related male clan members living on their estate, with their wives and children.

Clans were exogamous—meaning that members had to find marriage partners from another clan—and ideally each clan would give women to two other clans and receive them from two different

FIGURE 4.10

A Wandjina-style rock painting of a pair of wedge-tailed eagles painted at a shelter in the Caroline Ranges. They are said to have pursued the central mythological figure at the site, Kadoongoo the female euro, to the site from the northwest. The pair now waits to continue the chase. (Photo M. J. Morwood)

clans. This sequence created a network of alliances that was part of a wider system of ceremonial exchange involving women, ritual objects and implements. This was termed the *wunan* and transcended 'tribal' boundaries.

All people, animals, plants and things, including clans, were assigned to one of two broad exogamous groups (moieties), called Djungun and Wodoi in Worora language, with children belonging to the same moiety as their father. Estates belonging to Djungan clans are called Mamaladba, or Dust Country, and in ceremonies are associated with the colour white (for instance, in body paintings and clan motifs), while Wodai estates are called Monadba, or Bone Country, and are associated with red. Clan estates from the two moieties are located adjacent to each other to form two contiguous, curving areas of country.

Each clan territory contains, and is identified by at least one rock art site in which a named clan Wandjina is depicted. Western Kimberley ideology is centred on these heroic ancestors, who created various natural features, clan estates, and their identifying decorated shelters, and the current social order, including the *wunan*. In fact, the position of clans in the *wunan* is seen primarily in terms of the location of clan estates as marked by Wandjina sites. At the end of their travels the Wandjina are said to have gone into the earth, leaving their 'shadows' on rock surfaces in the form of paintings. Thus such paintings are not thought to be made by humans— though humans were obliged to keep them visible through repainting, and sometimes it was acknowledged that specific individuals were responsible for particular paintings.

Wandjina and other rock paintings are publicly visible symbols of clan identity and cohesion, and their sites are meeting places for clan members on ceremonial occasions. Hand stencils were a means for men to leave a mark of ownership, or of belonging to the place, and could only be done by men with rights in the estate in question. Art sites also served as mortuary areas for deceased, male members of a clan, whose spirits helped protect the paintings.

The responsibilities of male clan members included the repainting of their Wandjina and totemic plants and animals at the end of the dry season. Each art site was said to contain an image of every useful plant and animal species in the clan estate, and regular repainting ensured that these species remained in ample supply. This division of responsibility for maintaining resources served to emphasize clan interdependence, which was integral to the Wandjina belief system. For instance, the end of the dry season was the time when men burnt off the grass on their clan estates during communal hunting drives. Among its many other roles, the repainting ceremony also served as a mechanism for bringing together groups of men for cooperative hunting activities.

In recent times, Kimberley rock art was clearly an important means for validating the social order, but it also contained symbols of the disorder thought to lie outside the *wunan*. These included images of malicious creatures that wandered the country indiscriminately disfiguring Wandjina sites by painting themselves (Figure 4.11). Such paintings were done by sorcerers in rituals drawing on ancestral power to kill or deform enemies.

Most ethnographers who have studied Kimberley rock art have concentrated on the spectacular and publicly visible Wandjina galleries, but these do not display all the motifs in the local people's artistic system. As with other Aboriginal artistic systems, there was also a range of secret geometric designs, such as the stripes and dots of white clay, red and yellow ochre and black charcoal that were painted on wooden objects. These could only be viewed by initiated men, and were hidden away from domestic sites. This component of the Kimberley art system is, therefore, unlikely to be represented in the archaeological record.

FIGURE 4.11
Beeswax depictions of Argulas, or malicious creatures, in two west Kimberley rock art sites. The figure on the left is 38 centimetres high. The beeswax is easily dated using accelerator mass spectrometry (AMS). (Drawn by Kathy Morwood from photos by G. L. Walsh)

THE YOLNGU OF NORTHEAST ARNHEM LAND

Studies of recent rock paintings in western Arnhem Land by George Chaloupka, Paul Taçon and Jennifer Galindo have also provided detailed information on the function of rock art, the behaviour of individual artists and the technology of (rock) art production. Chaloupka, for instance, notes that local people say that the Ancestral Beings taught them to paint, and that they distinguish five categories of rock art:

1 *Mimi bin*: paintings done by Ancestral Beings not people.
2 *Bim gurrmerrinj:* paintings of Ancestral Beings, malevolent spirits and dangerous creatures.
3 *Bim banemeng*: secular paintings of recent times.
4 *Bim bawarde garruy*: rock engravings, which are attributed to the Ancestral Beings, Nagorrgho or Namarrgon.
5 *'Rubbish painting':* crudely executed paintings, usually in white slurry.

These studies have also demonstrated continuity in associated oral traditions since Baldwin Spencer first recorded examples in the early 1900s. Work on other types of Arnhem Land art by anthropologists, including Howard Morphy and Luke Taylor, therefore provide invaluable information for research on rock art, even though production of this type of art has virtually ceased.

In his studies of Yolngu culture, Morphy adopted a perspective in which he saw art (along with song and dance) as integrally related to social organization, rights to land and relationships between landowning groups. As he notes:

> Art objects have a major role in the social, political and ceremonial life. Paintings are produced on a variety of objects in all major ceremonies including a person's body at times when he undergoes a change of status...and on the lid of his coffin after his death. Control over the production of paintings and control of access to information about their form and significance are among the major indices of the power that adult initiated men exercise over the other members of society. Paintings moreover are among the major items owned by a clan as a corporate group and are central both to its definition and the identification of its members with it.

Yolngu society is divided into two exogamous patrilineal moieties: Dhuwa and Yirritja. In fact, everything in the Yolngu universe, including landowning clans and mythological beings is assigned to one of these moieties. Land is owned by patrilineal clans averaging 100–200 members. Authority within the clan depends on how much individuals know about the ancestral beings. This knowledge finds expression in sacred law and objects, song, dance and painting, and is so important to land rights that unauthorized use of clan paintings, for instance, often led to conflict and death.

Morphy found that the Yolngu were constantly seeking to balance:

- Losing control of paintings by spreading knowledge too widely, and losing knowledge by failing to pass it on.
- Maintaining control of a unique inheritance, and releasing paintings as part of the process of perpetuating social and spiritual links. At some ceremonies rights to produce paintings can be passed on to members of other clans whose lands lie along the same ancestral track. This is a way of affirming the reality of the connection.

• Releasing knowledge to younger men to ensure conservation, and maintaining restrictions as a means of exercising control. Rights in paintings are passed on to younger men on the basis of age, primogeniture, subgroup affiliation and trustworthiness. Unruly or indiscreet young men are denied this knowledge and the associated rights and status. A man can also acquire rights in the paintings of his mother's and his mother's brother's clan.

Bark paintings in northeast Arnhem Land encode meaning at many levels. Typically, they have a ground of white or red, a yellow border, delineated feature blocks or segments, geometric representations such as triangles, circles and zigzags, figurative representations which are iconically motivated, and cross-hatched infill which is said to add brightness (Figure 4.12). Geometric representations include clan designs, which are the most specific components of a painting. These are associated with part of a clan territory, with each clan owning several designs. Yirritja clans use variations on the diamond motif, while Dhuwa clans employ variations of squares, curved and straight parallel lines and circles (Figure 4.13). Similarities and differences in form between clan designs reflect mythological and social relations between the groups.

Yolngu art ranges in function from simple decoration to 'restricted' art, which is done in secret by senior initiated men. Public art, including that made for sale to Europeans, tends to be highly

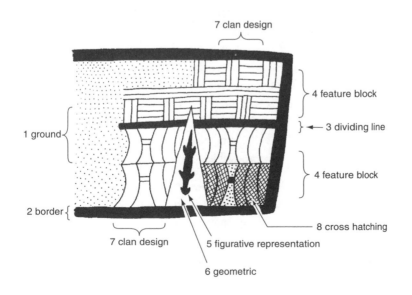

FIGURE 4.12

Components of a northeast Arnhem Land bark painting. The triangular figure represents the molk ceremonial ground, as well as the river at Marribalala. The clan designs, comprising lines at angles to each other, show that this painting belongs to a clan of the Dhuwa moiety, while the specific configuration shows that it is a Marrakulu clan painting. The top clan design represents freshwater, while the lower represents rocky country inland from Marribalala. Bark paintings for public display or for sale emphasize figurative motifs—as in the water goanna shown here. In contrast, paintings produced in restricted contexts usually comprise clan designs and other geometric motifs. (After Morphy 1991, Figure 8.1)

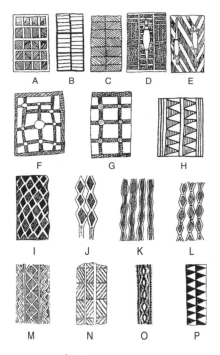

FIGURE 4.13

Clan designs of Yirrkalla, northeast Arnhem Land compared with Indonesian and New Guinea motifs. They all comprise repeated sequences of geometric patterns owned by specific clans or groups of clans within the same moiety. Typically clan designs of the Yirritja moiety consist of sets of linked diamonds, while those of the Dhuwa moiety consist of straight lines at angles to each other. Clan designs: (a) Djapu; (b) Dunalili; (c) Neinmeri; (d) Rirrratjingu; (e) Ngaymil; (f) Unidentified; (g) Djambarrpuyngu; (h),(k),(l) Gumitj; (i) Dhalwangu; (j) Manggilil; (m–o) Cloth designs from Sulawesi, Indonesia; (p) Smoking pipe design, New Guinea. (From Mountford 1956, Figure 61)

figurative, but 'restricted' art consists almost exclusively of clan designs and other geometric representations. Using non-figurative designs serves to make interpretation more difficult but also takes advantage of their multivalent, ambiguous nature to make complex statements about the relationships between things, which cannot be made in other ways.

PRODUCING ROCK ART

There is detailed information available on how, as well as why, rock engravings and paintings were produced. For instance, the outlines of engravings were sometimes first scratched or drawn, while fist-sized cobbles with a pointed end seem to have been the preferred pounding tool. Aboriginal rock painters used a variety of materials as pigments, including haematite and jarosite (red/mulberry); huntite, kaolinite, gypsum and calcite (white); limonite and goethite (yellow); charcoal and magnesium oxide (black); laundry blue and Prussian blue (blue in post-contact sites). When red pigment was not available, it was sometimes produced by heating yellow ochre.

Suitable pigments could be picked up as pebbles from creek beds or widespread geological strata, but in some instances large-scale mining of localized, high-quality ochres took place, as at the Wilga Mia red ochre quarry in the Murchison region of Western Australia (Figure 4.14). In 1939 D. S. Davidson described the site as

a huge hill, which rises high above the general surface of the rough and hilly surrounding country. From the summit of the north side a great open cut varying between fifty and one hundred feet in width and possibly sixty-five feet in depth has been laboriously excavated. On the sides around the bottom are deeper chambers, while underneath them numerous tunnels follow the seams of red and yellow ochre, often for several yards. In some instances admission to these cramped working pockets must be gained by wriggling through such small openings that larger individuals would find entrance impossible.

The size of the Wilga Mia workings indicates that about 19 600 cubic metres of ochre and rock, weighing about 40 000 tonnes, were removed using heavy stone mauls, fire-hardened wooden wedges, shoring and scaffolding. An archaeological excavation by Ian Crawford found that 6 metres of rock debris and haematite dust had accumulated over the past 1100 years. This quarry provided most

FIGURE 4.14
The Wilga Mia red ochre quarry in the Murchison region of Western Australia. The formation of this quarry involved open-cut mining to a depth of 19 metres. Ochre from the quarry was traded widely. (Photo taken in 1910 by W. K. Kretchmer; courtesy Western Australian Museum)

of the red ochre used by Aboriginal artists in the western section of Western Australia—it was known to people 450 kilometres to the northwest, 525 kilometres to the south and 300 kilometres to the northeast.

High-grade red ochre was traded widely throughout Aboriginal Australia, and other famed ochre sources include Bookartoo in the Flinders Ranges, South Australia; Karrku, Lawa and Ulpunyaii in Central Australia; and Tooumbunner in Tasmania. At some pigment quarries (for example, Boohartoo), the mining was done by men; at others (for example, Tooumbunner), it was done by women. The properties and formation of the different pigments were explained in terms of the Dreaming, while the best sources had great religious significance. For instance, the most widely used red ochre in western Arnhem Land comes from Gunnodjbedjahjam, near Jim Jim Falls, and is thought to be the menstrual blood of women accompanying Yanidj, the Ancestral long-horn grasshopper. Similarly, in the Kimberley sources of the highly valued white pigment huntite, which was used for painting Wandjinas, are said to be the excreta or spit of Ungud, the Rainbow Serpent.

People would sometimes go to considerable trouble to obtain pigments from such Dreaming sites for the painting of important mythological and totemic beings. To give an idea of the scale of these enterprises, each year expeditions of some 70 Dieri men would travel up to 500 kilometres along well-established trade routes to obtain Bookartoo ochre. Each man would then return burdened down by prepared cakes of ochre weighing 28 to 35 kilograms each.

For use, hard pigments were ground on flat stone slabs with water, while softer ochres and clays were mixed with water in a container. Storing them in water kept them soft. Wet pigments were painted onto the rock surface with the fingers, the hand or brushes. The latter were made from feathers or by fraying the ends of grass, bark strips, roots or twigs. Paint could also be blown from the mouth to stencil an object; or applied to an object, which was then pressed or hit against the wall to make a print. In addition, pigments were used dry as 'crayons' to draw designs.

Usually, pigments were only mixed with water, but organic fixatives, such as the juice of orchids, were sometimes used to make the painting more durable, as reported by Mountford in northern Australia:

> The orchid bulb is cut in halves, broken slightly by chewing, and in the Oenpelli and Yirrrkala areas, rubbed directly on the surface of the bark or rock surface, or in Groote Eylandt mixed with the colour on the grinding stone.

This addition of organic materials to pigments has important implications for the direct dating of rock paintings (see Chapter 5).

Conclusions

THE MEANING OF ROCK ART

One of the questions most frequently asked about rock art by non-experts is, 'What does this painting/engraving/design mean?'. Australian case studies show that specific meanings are impossible to establish without knowledgeable informants, while the meaning and significance of motifs may change over time. In addition, Elkin made the point that, even where knowledgeable informants are present, the 'meaning' of art is best considered in terms of its functional relationship with ideology, social organization, rights to resources, and so on, while Morphy has shown how such information may be encoded at many levels. A clear implication of such ethnographic work is that the study of past art systems must focus on the same functional relationships as manifested in the archaeological record.

CAUTIONARY TALES

Australian case studies also demonstrate the folly of making simplistic assumptions about how these hunter–gatherer systems operate or about the relationships between art and other aspects of culture. All Australian Aboriginal groups were hunter–gatherers, had totemic beliefs, foraged in flexible bands with changing membership, and were divided into small descent groups that owned land and the songs, myths and designs associated with sites within that land. Yet these groups showed marked regional differences in styles, techniques, motif ranges and the contexts in which they made art within Australia. This should warn against superficially matching specific types of art with specific types of social organization, economy or ideology.

In the case of rock painting, these regional differences were the result of many factors, such as geology and the function of the art, whose influence varied depending upon the nature of resources, population levels and social organization. Understanding how art functions is the key to understanding why it varies in different social contexts, between regions and over time. This is the fundamental basis for the archaeological (and anthropological) study of Australian Aboriginal art.

THE FUNCTION OF ABORIGINAL ART

Australian Aboriginal ceremonial items, ceremonies, songs, dances and designs used in bark paintings, body paintings and rock art all took their meaning from the creation myths associated with particular tracts of country. Since these things served as tangible charters for land ownership, rights to use them were closely guarded. To retain ownership and use of their estates, clans had to maintain the sacred law, perform the required ceremonies and pass on the law to succeeding generations. To do all this they needed knowledge of the stories, songs and art that encoded the sacred law.

The need for people to have localized symbolic knowledge in order to use resources was a way of reducing territorial access. Not knowing the stories for a locale put strangers at a tremendous disadvantage, as John von Sturmer notes: 'Even men of high status are fearful to move until they have been properly introduced to the country, noting the location of "story places" (*awu*) and discovering the direction in which it is safe to go hunting.'

Individuals progressively acquired knowledge about the symbolic landscape and its associated stories and symbols—including rock art—by passing through a series of formal initiation ceremonies. Differences in level of initiation also determined an individual's status and authority in a clan and their entitlement to exchange information with other clans. Within clan groups, knowledge of the symbolic landscape was differentially accessed on the basis of sex, generation, primogeniture and sub-group affiliation. This hierarchy of ritual authority was the fundamental basis of social and economic power in Aboriginal society.

In unpredictable, unproductive environments with low population densities, such as Central Australia, people often had to spread out over a large area in response to environmental conditions and resource availability. Symbolic systems, which served to link widely dispersed groups, were extensive, while changes in symbol use were also gradual. A single rock art style occurs throughout Central Australia.

In more predictable, productive environments with high population densities, such as Arnhem Land, groups tended to occupy a relatively small area, and their symbolic systems were similarly localized (Figure 4.15). Claire Smith has shown that there are major differences in art styles between language groups in northeast, central and western Arnhem Land. Boundaries between art areas also tend to be abrupt.

The same functional perspective is helpful in the study of symbol use within regional Aboriginal populations, which were subdivided on the basis of patrilineal clan, resident group, moiety, section, matri-totemic clan, initiation grade, sex, and so on. Within-group symbolic markers of affiliation and status involved a range of media, some for public display (such as shield motifs and body painting; Figure 4.16), others for use in restricted contexts (such as *churinga)*. Members of these groups could also have rights to produce (rock) art in certain circumstances. For instance, matrilineal totemic clans were probably responsible for mortuary rock art in the central Queensland highlands (see Chapter 8).

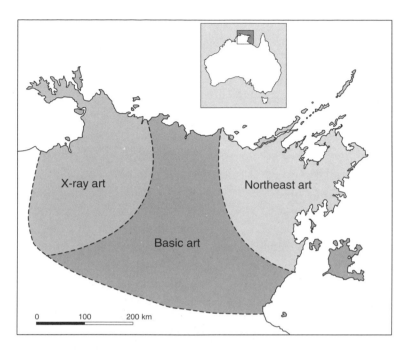

FIGURE 4.15

Distribution of northeast, central and western Arnhem Land art styles. These regional art styles are relatively restricted in distribution, while the boundaries between them are abrupt. Differences in art served as an important means of bounding territory in areas that were productive, low-risk and of high population density. However, some components of the same art system also emphasized ceremonial links between groups.

In contrast, art boundaries in Central Australia usually change gradually between areas. Shared symbolic systems, such as art, helped reinforce and maintain links between widespread groups in high-risk areas of low population density. But some components of the same art system were of limited distribution and served as territorial markers. Art could be exclusive or inclusive depending on circumstances. This seems to be a characteristic of all Australian Aboriginal art. (After Mountford 1956, Figure 2)

FIGURE 4.16

In Australia, public markers of ethnic affiliation and status included body paintings, cicatrices (body scarring), tooth avulsion, linguistic differences and style in material culture, including shield designs and rock art. Rainforest peoples of northeast Queensland had many highly distinctive cultural traits which set them apart from other groups, such as large shields carved from figtree buttresses with totemic designs painted on them, wooden swords and curved spearthrowers. (Photo from the Atkinson Collection, taken c. 1893; courtesy Historical Society of Cairns)

ROCK ART AND SOCIAL CONTEXT

Whether Australian Aboriginal artists used figurative or non-figurative designs depended upon social context and the membership of the participating group. Secular or 'ordinary' rock art placed more emphasis upon figurative motifs and thus its meanings were more specific and easier to 'read'. In contrast, secret rock art emphasised geometric motifs. This made its interpretation highly ambiguous and multivalent; viewers had to be initiated into the 'meaning' of the art and its many levels of interpretation.

In Central Australia, these two basic types of art were done in different places and often on different media. Sacred rock paintings were made at spots closed to women, children and uninitiated men. For example, sacred art in the 'restricted' section of Walinga Hill Cave was geometric, while paintings in the 'domestic' section of the cave were much more figurative. Similarly, only geometric motifs and tracks are found on wooden objects in the Kimberley, *kulpidji* in the Western Desert, and the lids of coffins in northeast Arnhem Land. Although such objects do not usually survive long enough to be found in the archaeological record, analysis of the different types of motifs, techniques and colours on different media and in different locations can tell us much about which are 'secular' and which 'sacred'. Clearly, a researcher concerned with rock art's function cannot afford to study art in isolation.

STRUCTURE AND MEANING

Meaning can be encoded in many ways. A common way in Aboriginal art is the use of formal similarities in design or colour to reflect social groupings (examples are the core structure of *kulpidji* designs in the Western Desert, the shape of clan designs in northeast Arnhem Land and the use of colour to distinguish moieties in the Kimberley). The problem here is that the clan-linked art we find in the archaeological record may reveal more about the complexities of site formation than about the distribution of the clans themselves. In some cases, however, there is a strong relationship between art locations and clan distribution, as in the western Kimberley, where major Wandjina galleries mark the focuses of clan estates. Here, in a landscape with abundant potential rock art surfaces, the positioning of such sites can be used to reconstruct clan distribution, even where there is no specific information available.

In other cases, the situation is more complex. Studying rock art sites in the Western Desert, Richard Gould observed that many of the major Ngatatjara sites held designs associated with other sites along different ancestral tracks. For instance, at *Wi: ntjara*, a site where the totemic Penis (*Yula*) pursued the Seven Sisters, he found designs relating to the carpetsnake, blue-tongue lizard and brush-turkey totems, and concluded that 'paintings are man-made representations of sacred subjects and hence open to a degree of human manipulation'. This also applies, for example, to coffin paintings in northeast Arnhem Land, where designs may reflect the clan affiliation of the deceased, the route chosen for the spirit to the clan well, the place of death and the relational politics of groups participating in the ceremony. Because humans are involved, the designs are not chosen by some rigid formula but are manipulated and negotiated depending upon social context.

URGENT ISSUES

Very few studies have examined the way artistic systems encode social and economic information, and even fewer have been undertaken with an eye to archaeology or to the significance of boundaries between rock art areas. Research on stone artefact manufacture and discard, animal use and discard, and the use of style in items such as adornments, pots, weapons, houses and stone points, has yielded valuable information and insights. Such work is now urgently required on the few hunter–gatherer art systems that still survive.

Just as studies of Australian Aboriginal culture have influenced the way in which researchers have interpreted rock art overseas, so ethnographic research undertaken elsewhere can inform our views on the nature of Aboriginal art. For instance, the work of Martin Wobst on style in Yugoslavian folk costumes, and its role in group integration and differentiation, boundary maintenance and establishing norms, is essential reading for people interested in art anywhere, as is the research of Polly Wiessner on South African San beadwork. There is no merit in being parochial or narrow-minded in the quest for insights into the meaning of art and its significance in the archaeological record.

CHAPTER 5

A question of time: dating Australian rock art

Scientific breakthroughs often happen unexpectedly. In 1994, Bert Roberts and I were eating lunch at Mushroom Rock, a sandstone shelter in southeast Cape York Peninsula. Gazing at the Aboriginal paintings and mudwasp nests on the ceiling, I remarked to Bert that in the Kimberley we were going to try radiocarbon dating of mudwasp nests built over rock paintings, in the hope that this would give us a minimum age for the paintings underneath. Bert immediately got excited. 'Mudwasp nests also contain sand grains, which we should be able to date by optically stimulated luminescence', he said. 'Let's give it a try!' And we did. In the end we found that mudwasp nests contain enough organic material for radiocarbon dating, but optically stimulated luminescence also works well. In fact, the technique may provide the means for dating rock art sequences in the Kimberley, Arnhem Land and other tropical regions throughout the world. Archaeologists should eat sandwiches in rockshelters more often.

We need breakthroughs like this because the biggest problem in rock art research is that the art is difficult to date, and without dates it cannot be considered in the context of evidence from archaeological excavations or the study of past environments. Perhaps this is why few integrated rock art studies have been undertaken. Fortunately, though, that is now changing.

There are two general types of dating technique: relative and absolute. Relative dating allows us to place rock art styles in sequential order. It can tell us that one style is older than another, but not the age of either style. Relative dating methods include differential weathering, superimposition analysis, stylistic analysis and spatial patterning. In contrast, absolute dating methods do allow us to determine ages or age ranges. Such methods include historical evidence, subjects depicted, weathering, the dating of stratified art evidence, association, and direct dating of the art itself.

It is important to understand that relative dating methods are not a poor substitute for absolute ones, although it is true that they are generally cheaper. Their main advantages are that they do not require specialized equipment for collecting the data, and that they can be based on large sample sizes. As well, removing samples for dating, as required for radiocarbon dating, is destructive, and the technologies and procedures involved are often complex and costly. For instance, each radiocarbon date obtained with an accelerator mass spectrometer (AMS) costs around A$1000. So researchers usually work out a relative sequence of rock art styles using the evidence of superimpositions and differential weathering, then date specific points in the sequence on the basis of the subjects depicted, evidence recovered in nearby archaeological excavations and direct dating of the pigments.

Relative dating methods

DIFFERENTIAL WEATHERING

Rock art can weather in many ways. Paints flake off or fade, bits of the rock surface crack and fall away, and mineral deposits (patina) build up on 'fresh' engraved surfaces and eventually return them to the same colour as the unmodified rock.

The use of differential weathering to date rock art is based on the principle that, all other things being equal, a less eroded or patinated motif is younger than a nearby one with greater signs of weathering. But the degree of weathering is not simply a function of elapsed time. It is also affected by the immediate environment, the depth of engravings, the nature of pigments used, and so on. In fact, it is quite common to find different sections of the same rock painting or engraving weathered to different degrees. So this method needs to be used with caution.

Even so, there are many cases where the differences in weathering of rock art do correspond closely to differences in age. For instance, Lesley Maynard has convincingly used differential weathering to show that the mix of motifs at rock engraving sites in western New South Wales changed over time. She noted that engravings at Sturt's Meadows were all very patinated and weathered, those at Mootwingee were patinated but not so weathered, and those at Euriowie appeared unpatinated and 'fresh'. On the basis of differential weathering, she concluded that Sturt's Meadows was the oldest site and Euriowie the youngest. Maynard then looked at the relative frequencies of geometric, track and figurative motifs at the three sites and noticed a shift in emphasis from track motifs to figurative ones (Figure 2.18). She noted that there was similar evidence in other regional rock art sequences. This was one of the lines of evidence she used to construct her general chronology for Australian Aboriginal art (see Chapter 1).

Michel Lorblanchet made systematic use of differential weathering in his study of rock engravings in the Dampier region of Western Australia. To accurately compare their degree of weathering, Lorblanchet took photographic slides of each engraving under the same lighting conditions and using the same film type. He then projected the slides onto a screen and measured the image density of the rock surface within the engraving and immediately outside it using a photoelectric cell. The mean difference between the inside and outside readings gave him a contrast score for the engravings, and this was taken as a measure of relative age.

Lorblanchet used these contrast scores to date rock engravings in a number of ways. First, he examined the range of patination at five sites. Two were dominated by heavily patinated 'old' engravings; one had mainly 'old' engravings with a small proportion of 'fresh' ones, and two had a fairly even mix of contrast scores, implying that they contained engravings of many different ages (Figure 5.1).

Next, Lorblanchet looked at the range of patination for specific motifs, and distinguished four groups (Figure 5.2):

1 *Deeply patinated figures:* punctures, circles, concentric circles, lines, ovals and a few types of human figure.
2 *Patinated figures:* triangles, mazes, bi-lobed motifs, ghost-like figures, human hands, kangaroo-men.

FIGURE 5.1

A lightly pecked anthropomorph near Mt Isa, northwest Queensland. The fact that the engraving is unpatinated and fresh in appearance indicates that it is relatively recent. (Photo M. J. Morwood)

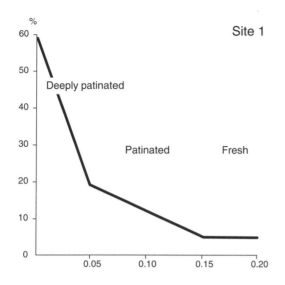

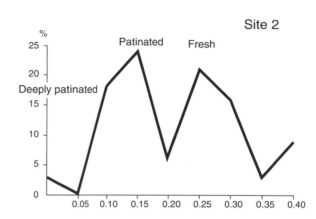

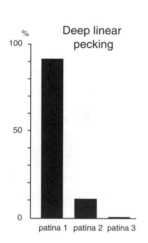 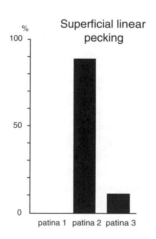

FIGURE 5.2 (above)

Degree of patination of engravings at two sites in the Dampier region of Western Australia. Engravings at Site 1 are predominantly deeply patinated and weathered. In contrast, Site 2 has equal numbers of patinated and fresh, as well as some deeply patinated engravings, indicating that it was in use over a much longer time period. (From Lorblanchet 1992, Figure 10)

FIGURE 5.3 (left)

The distribution of patination states for two rock engraving techniques at sites in the Dampier region: Patina 1 is the darkest and most weathered, while Patina 3 is light and fresh in appearance. The figures indicate that deep linear pecking is the older engraving technique, whereas superficial total pecking was emphasized more recently. (From Lorblanchet 1992, Figure 14)

3 *Fresh figures:* human figures with exaggerated hands and feet, bird-men, snakes, other animals, turtle tracks and boomerangs.
4 *Deeply patinated, patinated and fresh:* human feet, stick figures, turtles, kangaroos, birds, fish, bird tracks, kangaroo tracks, arc, eggs and other geometrics.

Comparing motifs made with different engraving techniques, Lorblanchet found that most deep linear pecked and deep intaglio motifs were very patinated, while the superficial linear pecked, total pecked and abraded motifs were less patinated and therefore relatively younger (Figure 5.3).

FIGURE 5.4

Differences in the distribution of 'deeply patinated' and 'patinated' engravings in Gum Tree Valley, Dampier region, Western Australia, indicate that the main focus for engraving moved over time, with engravers starting in the west and moving east in the upper part of the valley. (From Lorblanchet 1992, Figure 12)

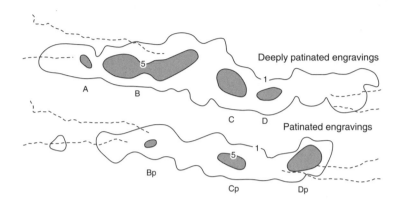

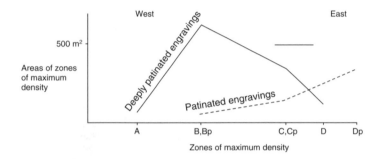

Finally, Lorblanchet plotted the location of groups in the different stages of patination to reconstruct the order in which the engravings had been produced. The results indicated that the main focus for engraving in Gum Tree Valley had moved over time. Engravers had started in the west and moved east in the upper part of the valley (Figure 5.4). Relating this 'map' to the distribution of other types of archaeological evidence helped Lorblanchet estimate the absolute ages of different sites, motifs and techniques (see below).

SUPERIMPOSITION ANALYSIS

The basic 'law of superimposition' for rock art is that a design occurring over or through another, must have been executed later. If there is a consistent pattern to the order of superimposition—for example, if Motif Type A always occurs over Motif Type B, and never vice versa—then this may provide evidence for general changes in the rock art over time.

Superimposition analysis is the most frequently used method for relative dating of rock art. Frederick McCarthy has even said that 'the key to problems of chronology in Australian Aboriginal rock art is the study of superimpositions'.

Simple as that idea sounds on paper though, it presents complications. For instance, recording superimpositions can present technical difficulties, as some colours are more intense than others and tend to come through overlying layers, while others may adhere badly to a pre-existing colour. Darrell Lewis notes cases in western Arnhem Land in which the apparent order of superimposition of two paintings was different at different overlap points. Deciding which of two intersecting engravings was done first presents similar problems. Differences in the depth of each engraving and in their degree of weathering and patination can considerably complicate the issue.

Moreover, artists may deliberately superimpose motifs for aesthetic or ideological reasons. Quantitative studies by a number of researchers overseas have shown that most rock art superimpositions were intentional and obeyed syntactical rules. Because of this, André Leroi-Gourhan rejected superimposition analysis as a dating tool in his classic study of European Palaeolithic rock art.

With such uncontrolled factors influencing the associations and apparent superimpositions of colours, techniques and motifs, superimposition analysis is often best used in combination with other relative dating methods, such as differential weathering and depicted subjects.

Few researchers who have used superimposition analysis to date Australian rock art have explained the assumptions they were acting on. In many studies, regional or even continental rock art sequences have been constructed with insufficient data and no regard for the methodological, statistical or interpretive problems involved in this type of analysis. One of the few quantitative superimposition analyses of Australian rock art was undertaken in the central Queensland highlands (see Chapter 8).

SPATIAL ANALYSIS

This dating technique grew out of the observation that at many Australian rock art sites, specific techniques, colours and motifs tend to cluster together. Almost certainly, this reflects the 'episodic' nature of artistic activities at these sites, as well as the suitability of different surfaces for different artistic techniques. In these cases rock art motifs, colours and techniques that tend to cluster together within sites were probably in use at the same time.

Similarly, at sites with small rock art assemblages, the works are also often very homogeneous in terms of colour use or range of motifs, indicating that they are the products of a single burst of artistic activity. If we assume that in a particular locale the preferred colours, techniques or motifs changed over time, and that sites with small numbers of motifs were probably worked on only a few times during a limited period, then colours, techniques and motifs that often occur together are likely to be contemporaneous.

If that is the case, then the way in which these elements are distributed within sites and between sites should reflect changes over time. Contemporaneous colours and techniques will tend to occur together, while non-contemporaneous ones will tend to be separate.

Spatial patterning of rock art is only useful as a relative dating method if it is based on trends identified from a large database. The degree to which specific motifs, techniques and colours occur together at or between sites can be measured easily, but isolating trends in a large database requires multivariate statistical techniques such as principal components analysis (see Chapter 8).

The real advantages of spatial analysis as a relative dating technique are that it is based on very different assumptions from those underlying superimposition analysis and that it uses information on the distribution of all recorded rock art motifs, not just a sample. But while spatial analysis can show which rock art variables are contemporaneous, it cannot tell us whether one group of contemporaneous motifs, techniques and colours is older than another. This technique thus needs to be used in combination with other relative dating techniques, such as superimposition analysis.

STYLISTIC DATING

It is seldom possible to work out the relative or absolute ages of every single motif in a given rock art tradition. Instead, rock art researchers try to identify chronologically meaningful rock art 'styles' on the basis of distinctive features, colours, subjects, formal attributes and consistent associations. If it can be shown that a rock art style was in vogue at a particular time and place, then relative or absolute dates for a sample of motifs in that style can be extended to all such motifs.

For instance, in the Kimberley region Bradshaw rock paintings have a number of specific features that distinguish them from other regional rock painting styles. Their pattern of superimpositions upon other Kimberley rock art styles is also very consistent: in the regional art sequence constructed by Grahame Walsh, they always overlie 'Irregularly Infilled Animal' paintings and underlie Wandjinas. In addition, differential weathering, superimposition, relative positioning of figures within art panels and developments in associated material culture indicate a consistent pattern of change within the Bradshaw painting tradition. Figures with tasselled adornments are earlier than those with sashes. In turn, Sash Bradshaws predate more static 'Clothes Peg' Bradshaws, which appear to have been painted in two or more colours and often carry spears and spearthrowers.

The general stylistic sequence for Kimberley rock art, which is based on relatively few examples of superimposition and differential weathering, enables us to work out the relative age of most rock paintings in the area. It also provides an overall framework to help us select rock art motifs for absolute dating.

Absolute dating methods

HISTORICAL INFORMATION

Australian Aborigines have often been observed and documented by researchers while doing rock paintings and engravings. Such art is easily dated. For instance, the Aboriginal artist Najombolmi is known to have produced many of the most recent rock paintings in Arnhem Land. Well-known examples of his work include the spectacular frieze at Anbangbang Shelter, Nourlangie, painted during the 1963–64 rainy season.

SUBJECTS

We can often set a maximum or minimum age for rock art by considering the subjects shown. For instance, depictions of extinct animals tell us the minimum age of the art. A good example of this is provided by depictions of thylacines and dingoes in Arnhem Land rock paintings (Figure 5.5). Since thylacines seem to have become extinct on the Australian mainland about 3000 years ago— probably because the dingo was introduced—such paintings are at least that old.

Similarly, depictions of 'new' items or animals can give us maximum ages for the art. Examples of these include stone spear points in the Kimberley and edge-ground axes in southern Australia,

FIGURE 5.5

Depictions of dingoes and Tasmanian tigers (thylacines) provide maximum and minimum dates for rock art respectively. This painting of a dingo at Quinkan Gallery, southeast Cape York Peninsula, must be less than 4000 years old. (Photo M. J. Morwood)

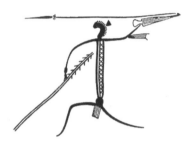

FIGURE 5.6

Depictions of stone spear points and axes in Australian rock art provide good dating evidence because we know from archaeological excavations when these items first appeared. For instance, the stone points depicted in these paintings from Arnhem Land and the Kimberley indicate that they are less than 5000 years old. (After Walsh and Morwood 1999)

FIGURE 5.7

European contact subjects, such as this hunting scene with horse, rider and buffalo painted in western Arnhem Land, provide good rock art dating evidence. (Photo G. Chaloupka)

which both appeared after 5000 BP (Figure 5.6). Depictions of dingoes, horses, pigs, cattle, sailing ships, trucks and planes also provide useful dating evidence (Figure 5.7). Depending on the circumstances, such subjects can allow us to date the art with precision (Figure 5.8). For instance, a painting at Yuwunggayai rockshelter, western Arnhem Land, showing a European with an animal head and holding a gun overhead is likely to represent a member of Ludwig Leichhardt's exploring party in 1845. A few such dates can effectively anchor important turning points in a rock art sequence.

In some cases, changes in the range of animals shown in rock art can be related to already-dated patterns of environmental, economic or social change, enabling us to assign an approximate age band to the artistic sequence. The best-known examples of this in Australia

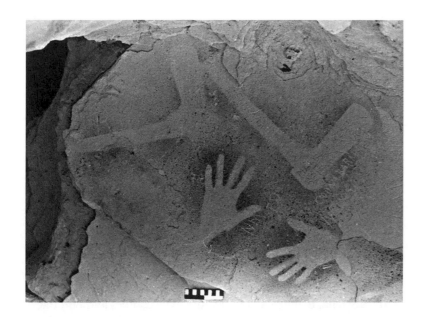

FIGURE 5.8

These stencils of metal axes at Black's Palace in the central Queensland highlands must date between AD 1860, the early European contact period, and 1918, when traditional life in the region collapsed. They are unusual in that the conventional European handle has been retained. In most cases, stencilled axes with metal heads are clearly made from pieces of scavenged metal, such as horseshoes, and are hafted in the traditional Aboriginal manner.
(Photo M. J. Morwood)

are the changes in animals depicted in western Arnhem Land rock art. The earliest paintings show only inland terrestrial or freshwater species, whereas later ones include estuarine species. This correlates to general changes in local environment: at times of low sea level the region was well inland, whereas rises in sea level over the past 15 000 years brought the coast much closer.

The main difficulty of using depicted subjects for dating purposes is establishing the accuracy of the identification (see Chapter 8).

WEATHERING

Chemical and physical weathering start almost as soon as a rock painting or engraving is completed. If weathering goes ahead steadily, then its extent can be used as an indicator of absolute age, but age estimates made on this basis have usually been guesstimates based on scant evidence. More commonly, the degree of weathering is used as a broad indicator of age. In arid areas, where natural weathering rates are low, heavy weathering is assumed to indicate 'great age'.

In addition, Robert Bednarik has pioneered a dating technique based on micro-erosion analysis. This uses the degree of weathering of individual crystals of silica and other minerals to determine the age of surfaces exposed by the action of engraving. It requires specific information on micro-environmental weathering rates for the type of crystal being studied.

STRATIFIED ART

The most common use of absolute dating is in situations where art is 'stratified' in a datable context—in other words, where the art is covered by, or covers, deposits that can be dated at the macroscopic or microscopic level. Depending on the specific circumstance, the results provide maximum or minimum ages.

Stratified art may include art objects; pieces of decorated shelter wall and lumps of pigment that have become incorporated in datable deposits; or rock art panels covered by a build-up of deposits. In a sense, rock art on a surface that was first exposed by a datable rockfall is also stratified.

Until the 1980s stratified art was usually dated by the standard radiocarbon technique, which requires a minimum of 1 gram of carbon. The advent of the AMS, which only requires 50 milligrams of carbon, has vastly increased the scope of radiocarbon dating.

In Australia, fragments of wall with engraved lines and bird tracks were excavated by John Mulvaney in his excavations at Ingaladdi (Victoria River District), while panels of engravings covered by the horizontal layers of occupation deposits were exposed at the Early Man site in southeast Cape York Peninsula (see Figure 10.8), Mickey Springs 34 in the North Queensland Highlands, Cathedral Cave in central Queensland, and in the Skew Valley middens of the Burrup Peninsula (Figure 5.9). Because the engravings could have been in existence for some time before the first datable deposit was laid down, researchers in these cases were able to establish minimum ages for the art. At Early Man, these ages were particularly significant because the date of 14 000 BP for deeply pecked geometric and track motifs provides a minimum age for the Panaramitee engraving tradition, which is found right across central and eastern Australia.

Rock paintings, too, have sometimes been exposed during excavation but they have invariably been so weathered that it is impossible to make out the subjects. At the Early Man rockshelter, though, the upper parts of two flying fox paintings terminated at ground level, and there were still traces of paint on the wall just beneath the top layer of deposits. After comparing these with complete flying fox paintings, researchers concluded that they originally extended some 25 centimetres below the present ground level, implying a minimum age of 1000 BP.

At Devon Downs rockshelter in the Murray Valley, an engraved section of the wall had fallen into the deposits and the exposed rock

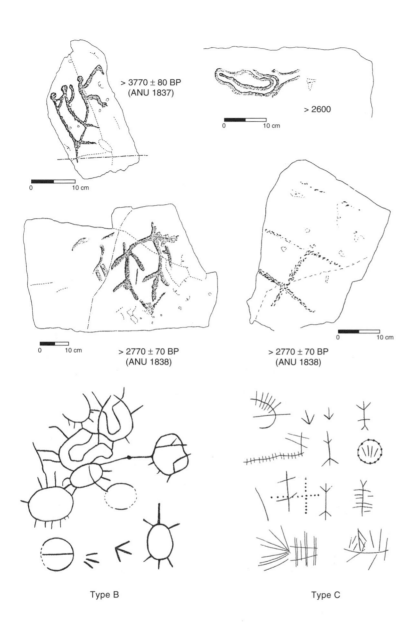

> 3770 ± 80 BP
(ANU 1837)

> 2600

0   10 cm

0   10 cm

> 2770 ± 70 BP
(ANU 1838)

> 2770 ± 70 BP
(ANU 1838)

0   10 cm

Type B

Type C

FIGURE 5.9

Engraved slabs excavated from the Skew Valley shell middens in the Dampier region of Western Australia. The minimum age of each engraving, as based on radiocarbon dating of overlying cultural deposits, is also indicated. The association between the engravings and the middens shows that they are the same age.
(After Lorblanchet 1992, Figure 5)

FIGURE 5.10

'Stratified' engravings at Devon Downs. A three-part rock engraving sequence is evident. Excavated panels show that Type A engravings of grouped sharpening grooves were produced by the earliest occupants of the site. Later, Type B engravings of meandering lines, tortoises, bird tracks and 'sun' designs were done on the shelter roof after a large rock fell from the ceiling. This rock, recovered in the excavation, lay on top of deposits containing an early 'Mudukian' assemblage and so provided a maximum age for the Type B images. Another excavated slab had Type B engravings on its lower side, while Type C engravings of straight-line designs occurred on the new ceiling surface so-exposed. (From Hale and Tindale 1930, Figures 246, 248)

had been used for further engravings, which were stylistically different. By establishing the date of the rockfall, researchers were able to calculate maximum and minimum ages respectively for the two styles (Figure 5.10). A variation on the rockfall theme was evident at Ken's Cave in central Queensland. Here large sandstone slabs had fallen from the roof, covering earlier occupation deposits on the floor. Both the slabs and part of the wall exposed by the fall had been used as surfaces for engraving and stencilling. Dating the rockfall thus provided maximum ages for both groups of rock art at the site.

Australian researchers have not found many portable art objects in excavated deposits, possibly because the decorated objects most likely to survive, such as *churinga*, or sacred stones, tended to be secret and were not kept near areas where people gathered. However, many sites have yielded materials associated with art production, such as pigment fragments and ochre-stained grindstones, which establish the time-frame for artistic activity of some kind.

In most cases, such pigments cannot be directly linked to surviving rock paintings, so it is thought that they may have been used to decorate implements or human bodies. However, at Mount Manning rockshelter, north of Sydney, rock drawings occur in two distinct groups—a stylistically homogeneous group of anthropomorphs, dingoes and echidnas in dark red, and a group of stencils, eels, snakes and kangaroos in light red. Excavation of the nearby occupation deposits found two layers of ochre at different levels. The ochres in the upper layer, dated to about 1400 CE, exactly matched the dark red figures; those in the lower layers, dated to between 1750 and 1830 CE, matched the light red. There is a strong case here for concluding that the two art panels are of the same age as their matched ochres.

At some sites researchers have found that the order in which pigments occur in layers of occupation deposits corresponds to the order in which those colours were laid down in rock art superimpositions. At other sites there is no such correspondence, suggesting that excavated pigments were probably associated with other artistic activities. Still, the concentration of pigment fragments in excavated deposits may indicate changes in the intensity of artistic activities at a site, and this would have implications for the dating of a rock art tradition. For instance, Rosenfeld and her colleagues have argued that an abrupt increase in the use of ochre at Early Man suggests that the distinctive Quinkan rock painting tradition of southeast Cape York Peninsula began 4000–5000 years ago.

Looking at the vertical or horizontal distribution of ochre in occupation deposits can also help us figure out how bursts of artistic production related to other types of activity, such as stone knapping (Figure 5.11). For instance, at some excavated sites in southeast Cape York Peninsula, greater concentrations of pigment paralleled a build-up in stone artefacts. At other sites, when use of pigment

FIGURE 5.11

This ochre-stained grindstone recovered from excavations at Malakunanja 2 in western Arnhem Land, shows that preparation of pigments for painting took place at the site at least 18 000 years ago. Other archaeological excavations have recovered pieces of ochre associated with the earliest evidence for occupation of the region between 50 000 and 60 000 years ago. Although we do not have evidence (yet) that that rock painting was being undertaken at the time, the first people to reach Australia from Southeast Asia included artists.

(Photo M. A. Smith)

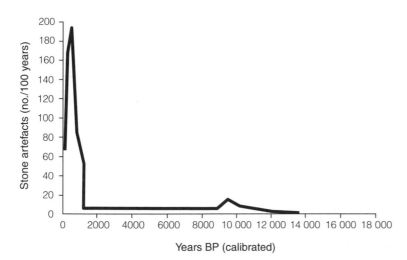

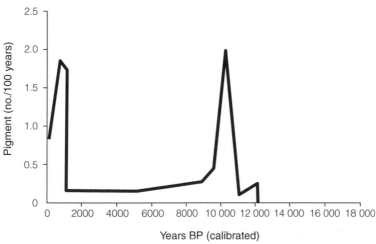

FIGURE 5.12

At Magnificent Gallery, southeast Cape York Peninsula, there is a major peak in pigment use corresponding to high rates of stone artefact manufacture and much more intensive use of the site over the last 1000 years. However, there is also an earlier peak in pigment use around 10 000 years ago, when there is little evidence for other activities at the site. This peak may be associated with an older and stylistically distinctive panel of paintings, which has been sealed in (and preserved by) a silica skin. More recent Quinkan style paintings overlie this skin (From Morwood and Jung 1995, Figures 7.13, 7.15)

was apparently most intensive, no stone working seems to have taken place (Figure 5.12).

Rock art is 'micro-stratified' when it is covered by, or covers, mineral or biological coatings, such as desert varnish, silica skins, oxalate crusts, secondary carbonate deposits, mudwasp nests and lichen. These micro-strata, which may be only 0.05 millimetres thick, can now be dated using the AMS for radiocarbon dating. The results provide maximum or minimum ages for the art, depending on whether the dated deposit underlies or covers the art.

At four rock art sites in Kakadu National Park, Alan Watchman took samples of mineral deposits and used infrared spectroscopy to determine which ones contained the carbon-bearing compound hydrated calcium oxalate; these were selected for radiocarbon dating. The pale brown, multi-layered crusts found at the backs of shelters and on fallen blocks outside were found to have formed at least 8000 years ago, suggesting that some of the rock paintings beneath crusts at Ngarradj Warde Djobkeng have a minimum age of around 8000 years.

Later, at Sandy Creek 2 in Cape York Peninsula, Watchman found that a small flake taken from an apparently unpainted section of the shelter wall contained at least three layers of red ochre sandwiched between microscopic layers of oxalate crust. The layers of red ochre were identical to those evident in rock paintings on the same shelter wall. AMS dates on various layers of the oxalate showed that the paintings had been done in separate episodes about 6655, 15 000 to 16 000 and 24 600 years ago. Similarly, at Walk-Under Arch shelter, near Chillagoe, a mineral crust was found to contain two stratified layers of bright red haematite, plus white clay and yellow goethite. The earliest haematite layer was dated to 28 000 years BP.

Carbonate deposits in limestone areas are equally suitable for dating rock art. At Koongine and Malangine Caves near Mt Gambier, South Australia, laminated secondary carbonate deposits separate several phases of engraving. The earliest engravings were finger lines executed on *montmilch*, a soft limestone deposit. The next ones were engravings of abraded grooves and tracks made on overlying speleothem. In turn these were overlain by travertine, a hard reprecipitated limestone. The most recent engravings, shallow incised lines, occur on and are lightly covered by travertine, which can be directly dated. Robert Bednarik obtained a radiocarbon date of 5500 + 55 BP for carbonates in the dense, laminated travertine between the two most recent phases of rock engraving. However, because the travertine was porous, contamination by younger carbonates was possible and the same layer yielded a uranium-thorium date of 28 000 + 2000 BP. This provides a conservative minimum age for the underlying finger lines as well as the abraded grooves and tracks.

Radiocarbon dating of desert varnish, a distinctive brownish-black patina found on rocks mainly in arid and semi-arid regions, can also give minimum ages for underlying rock engravings. For calcium carbonate deposit which had formed over desert varnish at the Eight Mile Creek site in western New South Wales, Dierdre

Dragovich obtained ages of 7090 years for a bulk sample and 10 250 and 10 410 years for compact, inner carbonate. This suggests that the last major varnishing phase at the site occurred earlier than this. Most engravings at this site, which are Panaramitee-style tracks and non-figurative designs, have a varnish coating suggesting that they are at least 10 000 years old. However, more recent work has shown that the build-up of varnish at the site took place over a long period, and that varnished engravings could have widely different ages. Another complicating factor is that varnish can quickly form again over small 'disturbed' areas when adjacent areas have varnish.

Dating of desert varnish has also been tried using the cation ratio (CR) dating method. CR is based on differences in the mobility of cations or positive ions, in the material. Potassium ($K+$) and calcium ($Ca++$) cations leach out of the desert varnish faster than titanium ones ($Ti+$), so that over time the proportions of potassium and calcium decline relative to titanium. If the rate of cation leaching can be determined accurately, then the varnish can be dated to provide a minimum age for underlying engravings. However, some researchers have argued that the complexity of varnish formation, stripping and replacement, as well as the inevitable exchange of ions between desert varnish and the underlying bedrock, negates the simplistic assumptions of CR dating.

Despite these criticisms, Ron Dorn (who developed the CR method) used it to date desert varnishes over 24 rock engravings at the Karolta site in the Olary region of South Australia. Three AMS dates were obtained from desert varnish samples collected from an adjacent outcrop of the same geological type as the rock art surface. The 'initial cation ratio' found in dust nearby was also determined. Then the rate of cation leaching was calculated, plotted on a graph, and used to date the varnish layers. The resulting age estimates ranged from 1400 to 41 000 BP, and these were later 'confirmed' by AMS dates.

These results would have made some of the Karolta engravings the oldest dated rock art in the world. Since then Dorn has stated that there are 'fatal flaws' in the method mainly because rock coatings are not closed systems but allow contamination by younger or older materials. On this basis, all CR dates for desert varnishes over rock engravings should now be discounted.

Datable mineral deposits always have an organic component. Sometimes this results from the presence on the rock surface of micro-organisms, such as algae and bacteria, which become trapped in mineral encrustations. Larger organisms and their by-products can also provide dating opportunities for rock art. For instance, in some regions rock engravings and paintings are partially covered with lichens, which are slow-growing, long-lived and increase in diameter at a constant rate. This is the basis of lichenometry as a dating technique. A species-specific lichen-growth rate is worked out by measuring lichen diameters on dated rock surfaces; this can then be used to calculate the minimum age of other rock surfaces by measuring the diameters of the same lichen species growing there. Research indicates that lichenometry may be applicable to surfaces up to 3000 years old and that, after an initial growth spurt over the first 100 years to reach a 14 millimetres diameter, growth levels off to around 3.3 millimetres per 100 years. Other aspects of lichen growth, such as the degree of lichen cover and successional stage, may also be useful in relative dating. Lichenometry has not yet been used to date Australian rock art.

Other biological deposits over rock art can also be dated. As we have seen, Bert Roberts and his colleagues have dated mudwasp nests associated with rock paintings in the north Kimberley, using both AMS radiocarbon dating and optically stimulated luminescence (OSL). OSL measures the number of electrons trapped in micro-fissures in mineral grains such as quartz. The electrons are freed by zapping the sample to be dated with laser light (that is, optically stimulating it). The number of trapped electrons is proportional to the background radioactivity of the sample and the length of time that the mineral grains have been removed from sunlight, which 'bleaches' out any trapped electrons. Once background radioactivity is measured, the period for which the mineral grain has been cut off from sunlight can be calculated to give a minimum age for covered-up rock paintings.

OSL can be used to date mudwasp nests; swallows' nests and termite tracks, which contain 'buried' quartz grains. It is possible that a given sample may be contaminated by older quartz grains derived from the bedrock, but examining the distribution of a number of 'single-grain' determinations usually allows such 'outliers' to be identified and set aside.

Mudwasp nests, which are very common in some Kimberley rock shelters, sometimes partly cover, or are covered by, rock paintings. OSL dating does not rely on the nests having an organic component, although the most recent examples have sufficient pollen for comparative AMS dating. Another advantage of OSL is that it need not physically impact upon the art at all. Roberts and his colleagues now have OSL dates for two mud-dauber wasp nests over different styles of Kimberley rock painting. The first mudwasp nest was over a red-pigmented Wandjina painting. The nest was built about 610 years ago, then about 270 years later its stump was used as the basis for a new nest. The Wandjina painting underneath the mud-wasp nest must therefore be at least 610 years old. The second mudwasp nest partially covered a late Bradshaw rock painting and has yielded two OSL dates of 16 400 and 23 800 years. The painting underneath the nest is therefore at least 16 400 years old.

As well as providing dates for associated rock art, some ancient mudwasp nests contain pollen, which can be dated with the AMS radiocarbon technique, and which documents the climatic conditions under which the art was produced. For instance, one mud-dauber nest dating from the coldest and driest part of the last Ice Age, about 17 500 years ago, was found to contain a lot of pollen from gum trees and sedges, indicating that the landscape was fairly open then. Younger nests also contained gum pollen but had much more melaleuca, banksia, wattle, grevillea and grass pollen.

ASSOCIATION

If rock art consistently occurs close to other datable materials, one can often conclude that the two are contemporaneous. This approach can take many forms. For instance, if people use a cave or shelter for a short time, and the entrance is later sealed by a rock fall or a build-up of deposits, then it is highly likely that the rock art and traces of other activities at the site are of a similar age. A number of such sealed rock art sites dating to the last Ice Age have been found in France, but none yet in Australia.

There are other situations where the association between rock art and deposits is less secure, but where we can still infer dates for the art with varying degrees of confidence, depending upon the circumstances. For instance, when specific types of art consistently occur with occupation deposits or implements of a certain age range, or of limited duration, it is often assumed that the painting or engraving and the occupation took place at the same period. If we could date other activities at the site, then we would also be able to date the art. One of the oldest dates for Australian rock art is based on this method: at Koonalda Cave on the Nullarbor Plain in South

Australia, finger markings and abraded grooves on walls deep underground are probably associated with traces of flint quarrying, which took place from 15 000 to 22 000 years ago. After this time, Aboriginal use of the cave seems to have ceased.

Many rockshelter sites in southwestern Tasmania were similarly abandoned around 12 000 years ago, but for different reasons. Today the region is characterized by almost impenetrable, closed-canopy rainforest, but prior to 10 000 BP, when sea level, temperature and rainfall were lower, the region was largely open grassland. Aborigines seem to have begun using local limestone caves as stations for hunting red-necked wallabies about 35 000 years ago, and to have stopped doing so about 13 000 years ago upon the return of warmer conditions and rainforest. This means that the red-ochre hand stencils recently discovered at Ballawinne Cave in the Maxwell Valley and at Wargata Mina Cave in the Cracroft Valley have a minimum age of 13 000 years. Some of the stencils at Wargata Mina Cave are also covered by a layer of calcite, which elsewhere in southwestern Tasmania relates to the more humid conditions around 12 000 years ago.

Michel Lorblanchet used a close study of the spatial distribution of different types of rock art in the Skew Valley near Dampier, Western Australia, as an aid in dating the works. The general distribution of engravings in the valley was found to be highly correlated with that of middens, or rubbish heaps which they mainly face. In addition, some of the middens contain engraved slabs. Lorblanchet argued that the middens and engravings are largely contemporaneous and date from between 2200 and 7000 BP. At one site in Gum Tree Valley, he noted a close fit between the distribution of *Anadara granosa* shells and engravings. This shell species occurs in the top layer of the excavated middens of the area, which are between 2200 and 4500 years old. Lorblanchet concluded that the engravings are of similar age.

At the top of Gum Tree Valley, clusters of deeply patinated engravings occur close to clusters of stone artefacts rather than shell middens, suggesting that they were made before the middens formed. A fragment of *Syrinx aruanus* shell, found among deeply patinated engravings and dated to 18 510 BP, suggests that the shell and adjacent engravings are contemporaneous, but this claim is more tenuous (Figure 5.13).

Another case where spatial association provides evidence for the age of art is at Magnificent Gallery in southeast Cape York Peninsula,

A koala skin bag containing stone artefacts and a piece of yellow pigment found as part of a cache in a rockshelter near Carnarvon Gorge, central Queensland highlands. Such evidence indicates the importance of art and decoration in local Aboriginal culture.

The earliest rock art from the Kimberley and Arnhem Land (pictured) includes large paintings of animals, plants and humans. The age of these is not known at present. Later art styles in both regions are similar (e.g. Bradshaws and Dynamic figures), whereas more recent rock art styles are very different.
(Photo G. Chaloupka)

(a)

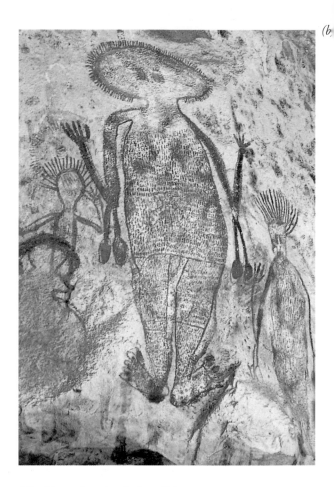

(b)

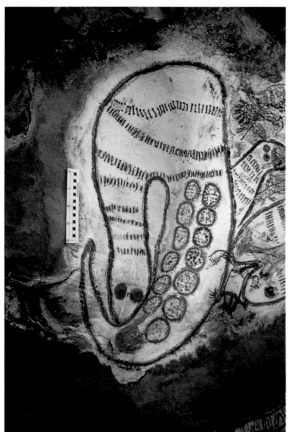

(c)

Wandjina-style rock paintings of the west Kimberley. In each case the paintings are thought to be the 'shadows' of the ancestral creative beings associated with the sites. (a) Waanangga, a 'bee' Wandjina, and his followers, who wear rain robes, at a Sugar-bag Dreaming site, west Kimberley. (b) A Wandjina rock painting in the East Kimberley. This was last repainted about 1996. (c) Snakes are prominent in Kimberley creation stories and their Dreaming trails, which zig-zag across the region, are marked by shelters featuring their painted 'shadows'. The high quality white pigment, used extensively as background in Wandjina-style paintings, was also thought to be the semen, spit or coprolites of the Rainbow Serpent.
(Photos M. J. Morwood and G. L. Walsh)

Stencils of a large, non-returning boomerang and hands at a rockshelter in the central Queensland highlands. No boomerangs of this type were ever collected in this region, but they and many other types of material culture are well documented in stencilled rock art.
(Photo M.J. Morwood)

Pecked engravings of concentric circles at an open site in southwest Queensland. Their degree of weathering and patination indicates they are of great age. However, such geometric designs still predominate in Central Australian art.
(Photo K. A. Sutcliffe)

General view of Mickey Springs 34 showing rock art, occupation deposits and excavations in progress. The site was selected for investigation because the deposits appeared to be deep and panels of pecked engravings continued beneath the sand of the present shelter floor. (Photo M. J. Morwood)

Rock paintings of Native Police at Crocodile 1 Shelter. They probably date to the 1870s, a time of violent conflict between local people and incoming pastoralists and gold miners. The Native Police 'dispersed' Aboriginal groups throughout the region and were the major means for overcoming local resistance. As a means of retaliation, Aboriginal rock artists sometimes depicted police with their horses and rifles in sorcery paintings. (Photo P. Trezise)

A performer at the Laura Dance Festival in 1989. Different styles of costume, decoration, music, dance, song, art and material culture are culturally-defining characteristics for all modern human societies. Archaeological investigations must take evidence for such symbolic behaviours into account.
(Photo M. J. Morwood)

Excavations at Native Well 1 in the central Queensland highlands. These show that the rockshelter was first occupied about 11 000 years ago and that art, as well as stone tool manufacture and use, had been consistently undertaken at the site. However, a major increase in art activities, including the engraving of human vulva motifs, began around 5000 years ago. (Photo M. J. Morwood)

Excavations at Magnificent Gallery showed that the site was first occupied 15 000 years ago, but the most intensive use of the site, including painting, occurred in the past 1000 years. The site was abandoned abruptly in the early European contact period because of its proximity to the main road into the Palmer River goldfields. The use of calico curtains, plastic sheets on the shelter floor and boardwalks minimized the impact of our work at the site.
(Photo M. J. Morwood)

The main engraved panel at Sandy Creek 1 is partially covered by an oxalate crust. AMS dates for the crust have provided a minimum age for the underlying Panaramittee style engravings. Tommy George, an elder of the Laura Community, southeast Cape York Peninsula, is also a Cultural Heritage Ranger and wears the Ang-gnarra logo as part of his uniform.
(Photo M. J. Morwood)

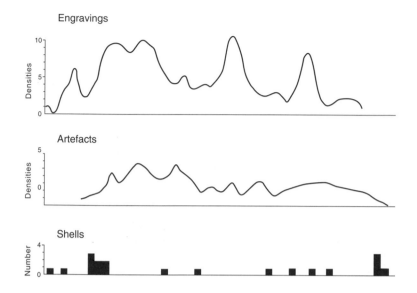

Engravings

Artefacts

Shells

FIGURE 5.13

This figure shows the distribution of rock engravings, stone artefacts and midden shells in Top of Gum Tree Valley, Dampier region, Western Australia. The distribution of engravings is highly correlated with that of stone artefacts, but not shells. Almost certainly, the engravings and stone artefacts are contemporary and predate collection of shellfish. (From Lorblanchet 1992, Figure 9b)

where the artists left a piece of yellow pigment on a grindstone at the foot of the main rock art panel. Visual and geochemical examination showed that the pigment had been used to paint a yellow outline on a nearby anthropomorph. This would have been one of the last paintings done before the site was abandoned in 1875 CE. Similarly, discrete clusters of pigment in excavated deposits have been used to infer the age of rock paintings nearby.

DIRECT DATING

The most direct way to determine the age of rock art is by dating organic materials used in its production. Charcoal, for instance, was often used as black pigment for painting and drawing, while pellets of native beeswax were used to make designs on rock in Arnhem Land and the Kimberley. There are also reliable accounts of Aborigines using urine, blood and plant sap as binders for pigments. Remnants of these in rock paintings could be datable. Other organic materials can be accidentally incorporated in the art: some rock paintings in southeast Cape York Peninsula contain embedded plant fibres from the artists' brushes.

Two methods have been used for direct dating of rock art: amino acid loss and AMS radiocarbon. Amino acids are the building blocks of proteins, which occur in albuminous paint binders such as blood or egg whites. Studies of paints of known age in European cathedrals have shown that the number of amino acids in paints with albuminous binders decreases over time. By calculating the rate of decay, it is thus possible to calculate the age of the paintings. However, because rates of amino acid loss also depend upon micro-organisms and environmental conditions, results from different regions are not directly comparable. In addition, the method cannot be used on paintings older than about 1800 years. It has been used to date rock paintings in South Africa but not in Australia.

Since the advent of AMS radiocarbon dating, which requires mere milligrams of organic material, a number of techniques have been developed for collecting these minute samples with a minimum of contamination. For instance, Alan Watchman has pioneered a method called focused laser extraction of carbon-bearing substances (FLECS-AMS) which enables carbons in very thin layers of mineral deposit to be targeted precisely for extraction. The resulting carbon dioxide is collected for AMS dating. Similarly, because limestones contain inorganic as well as organic carbon, Marvin Rowe and his colleagues use oxygen plasma, rather than heat, to oxidize only the organic component of paint samples on limestone surfaces.

The first AMS dating of Australian rock art was undertaken by Tom Loy and fellow researchers in 1990 at Laurie Creek in the Northern Territory and at Wargata Mina Cave in Tasmania. In both cases small samples of 'pigment' tested positive for the presence of human blood, which in ethnographic times was used as a binder in pigments. Large protein molecules were extracted from the pigment samples and the resulting 40 micrograms samples dated. The two pigment samples from hand stencils at Judds Cavern were dated to about 10 730 and 9240 BP respectively, which corresponds to expectations based on the age ranges of associated deposits. At Laurie Creek a date of 20 320 years was obtained, but repeat analysis of the sample showed that the 'pigment' was a natural deposit of iron oxide, while the identified protein was not from human blood.

Although the potential of AMS for rock art studies is obvious, the uncertainty about the Laurie Creek date illustrates the problems involved in dating very small samples of organic material from geologically and biologically complex substratums. This is well illustrated by the work of Josephine McDonald. In a study of rock art sites in the Sydney Sandstone Basin, she and her colleagues took nine samples from charcoal drawings at three sites: Native Animals, Gnatalia Creek and Waterfall Cave. While collecting the samples, they took great care to avoid contaminating the surfaces with organic substances. The two dates obtained from Waterfall Cave were 635 BP and 'close to modern', which are both consistent and 'reasonable' in the light of other archaeological evidence. However, the AMS dates obtained from a single charcoal drawing at Gnatalia Creek vary enormously: about 6085 and about 29 795 BP. McDonald has suggested possible explanations for the discrepancy:

• One or both samples were contaminated.
• 'Old' charcoal was used in the drawings.
• The dates are correct.

However, until we understand the significance of these dates and explain the discrepancies we cannot accept any of them at face value.

AMS dating of rock art made from beeswax, and the direct dating of charcoal-based black pigments in northern Australia, have been more straightforward. Erle Nelson and other researchers dated a large number of beeswax figures in western Arnhem Land: most date to the last 2000 years, but the oldest—a figure of a short-necked turtle—is about 4000 years old and marks the emergence of the simple X-ray art style. Similarly in the Kimberley, fifteen beeswax figures have been dated to between 200 and 3800 years BP and some have clear stylistic affinities with recent rock painting styles (Figure 5.14).

Direct dating of rock art should never be undertaken lightly, since taking the required samples may damage the art. Moreover, it is not always possible to be certain in the field whether a sample

FIGURE 5.14

Beeswax motifs from rockshelters in western Arnhem Land (left) and the Kimberley (right). AMS dating of such motifs has enabled the age of some recent rock art styles to be estimated. In both regions the oldest examples of wax figures are about 4 000 years old. (Drawn by Kathy Morwood after Chaloupka 1993; Nelson 2000, Figures 166–68; Walsh et al. in preparation)

contains enough organic material for dating purposes. Archaeologists must walk the fine line between keeping sample sizes small enough to protect the art and ensuring they are not too small to give a result. This, and the problem of possible contamination of samples, means the procedure should be undertaken only with expert technical assistance.

It is important to remember that the dating of rock art is not an end in itself, but an aid to viewing the art in the context of the past environments and evidence from archaeological excavations. This can be done at the continental, regional or site-specific level.

The antiquity of Aboriginal art

The earliest evidence for art in Australia is associated with the earliest evidence for human presence, but it is still not certain exactly when these occurred. At Malakunanja 2 and Nauwalabila 1, two rockshelters in western Arnhem Land, pieces of high-quality ochre occur in the initial occupation levels, which have been dated by thermoluminescence and optically stimulated luminescence respectively to between 50 000 and 60 000 years BP. But some researchers have argued that these two dating methods give dates earlier than the actual human settlement of Australia, and that the earliest radiocarbon dates of around 40 000 BP are a better estimate. Even so, it is generally agreed that the first people to live on the continent included artists. This is hardly surprising, as the complex skills and organization needed to build boats capable of transporting settlers from Southeast Asia to Australia imply that those who did so must have had language, and therefore other systems of self-expression and communication, such as art, dance and music.

Red ochre also occurs in the lowest levels of other sites that document the initial arrival of humans. Such sites include Mushroom Rock in southeast Cape York Peninsula and Carpenter's Gap in the southern Kimberley. In fact, most early Aboriginal sites contain pieces of pigment as well as stone artefacts, while an ochre-stained grindstone found at Malakunanja 2 in levels 18 000 years old shows that pigment was prepared at the site (Figure 5.11).

As in recent times, the earliest Australians probably used pigments for a variety of decorative purposes. For instance, the WL3 burial site at Lake Mungo, New South Wales, which has been dated to between 28 000 and 32 000 BP, had red ochre sprinkled throughout the grave. The specific purpose of excavated pigments is not usually obvious, but they were certainly valued enough to be transported considerable distances around the country. For instance, a sourcing study of the red ochre excavated at Puritjarra rockshelter in central Australia and dated to between 12 000 and 30 000 BP, showed that virtually all of it came from Karrku ochre mine, about 150 kilometres away across a dune field.

The earliest specific evidence for rock art in Australia comes from Carpenter's Gap, a limestone shelter in the southern Kimberley. Here a slab of the roof that had been coated with red pigment fell to the floor about 39 700 years ago, although not enough survived for us to be able to tell what was being painted. This is the oldest trace of rock art presently known. In comparison, the celebrated Palaeolithic art tradition of Western Europe began about 32 000 years ago.

Watchman has also found layers of red painting sandwiched between micro-layers of secondary carbonate and oxalate at Walk-Under Arch near Chillagoe and Sandy Creek 2 in southeast Cape York Peninsula respectively. The earliest layer of these pigments dates to about 28 000 years ago. This suggests that the very first Australians were not only painting, but painting on rock shelter walls. However, we do not know what they were painting.

The earliest identifiable rock painting motifs occur in northwestern Australia, where the exquisite Bradshaw rock painting style of the west Kimberley has been estimated at more than 16 400 years old on the basis of OSL dates for an overlying mudwasp nest. But Bradshaws are not the earliest rock paintings found in the Kimberley. Some are superimposed over an earlier style of rock painting, the 'Irregular Infill Animal' style, characterized by paintings of land animals, fish, yams and occasional humans, as well as stencils of hands and implements. These underlying paintings and stencils must be more than 16 400 years old—possibly much older. It is likely that the fragment of red ochre painting recovered from the lowest levels of Carpenter's Gap in the southern Kimberley is from this phase.

Very specific stylistic similarities between Bradshaw rock paintings of the Kimberley and Dynamic Figures of western Arnhem Land suggest that the two traditions were broadly contemporaneous. This means that the distinctive artistic as well as technological traits shared by these two regions date back well before 10 000 BP.

Outside the northwest, the oldest identifiable Australian rock art motifs are engraved. At Koonalda Cave on the Nullarbor, people

FIGURE 5.15

At Koonalda Cave on the Nullarbor Plain macaroni-like scrawls, a grid and concentric circles were incised into the soft walls of the cave with fingers and pointed implements between 22 000 and 15 000 years ago.
(Photo G. L. Walsh)

used fingers and pointed tools to incise spaghetti-like scrawls, a grid and concentric circles into the soft walls of the cave between 22 000 and 15 000 years ago (Figure 5.15). Similar panels of finger marking occur in 25 other limestone caves across southern Australia, from near Perth in Western Australia to Victoria. At some sites finger markings are covered by calcite into which are scored converging lines, dots, groups of grooves, radial figures, circles, mazes and lattices (Figure 5.16). Radiocarbon dating of secondary limestone deposits indicates that these designs, which Robert Bednarik has dubbed the Karake style, are more than 10 000 years old.

Another important early rock art style is the Panaramitee engraving tradition found over much of the Australian mainland and Tasmania. Classic Panaramitee sites emphasize fully pecked geometric designs, such as circles, spirals, arcs, grids, lines, cupules and mazes, as well as tracks (Figure 2.3). They almost invariably occur on open sites near water. Because of their advanced state of patination and weathering, it has long been argued that some Panaramitee engravings date from Pleistocene times, as confirmed by a panel of Panaramitee-like engravings at the Early Man site, which is covered by deposits about 14 000 years old. Panaramitee-style engravings predate a number of more figurative rock engraving and painting styles in eastern Australia.

Deeply pecked cupules at many sites in the Kimberley, Arnhem Land, the Queensland Gulf Country, Cape York Peninsula and elsewhere across northern Australia may be a regional variant of the Panaramitee style although there is no general consensus on this. The fact that some of these motifs are extremely patinated suggests that they could be the oldest surviving examples of rock art in these regions, but differential weathering of motifs on the same surface indicates that they were produced over a very long period. There is also evidence that the practice of pecking cupules in northern Australia may have begun in the Terminal Pleistocene. At Magnificent Gallery in southeast Cape York Peninsula, for instance, pecked cupules must date to less than 15 000 years ago, when people first used the site.

Dates of varying certainty have been established for a number of regional rock art sequences in Australia, including those of southeast Cape York Peninsula, the north and central Queensland highlands, Arnhem Land and the Kimberley. Some major turning points in these art sequences correspond to important changes in the archaeological

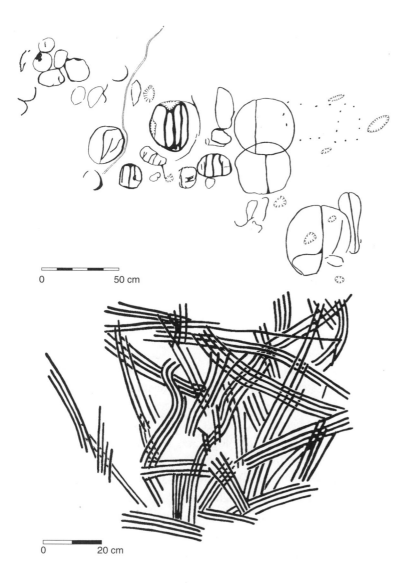

FIGURE 5.16
Deeply abraded engravings on a vertical wall at Paroong Cave, South Australia (top). Robert Bednarik has termed engravings of this type, which occur in limestone caves, 'the Karake style'. At some sites these are cut into calcite deposits, which in turn overlay finger markings, such as those in Koongine Cave (bottom). In these cases, finger markings on formerly soft surfaces seem to pre-date tooled incisions by a considerable time span. (From Bednarik 1986, Figures 4 and 1)

and past environmental records. In fact, rock art has provided a unique perspective on these changes. The Kimberley rock art sequence illustrates this well (Chapter 6).

Dating Kimberley art: a case study

The Kimberley rock art sequence is likely to prove one of the longest and most complex anywhere in the world, rivalled only by the rock art of western Arnhem Land. This partly relates to the hardness and

FIGURE 5.17

Distribution of Kimberley rock art styles and excavated sites. Isolated finds of classic Bradshaw paintings outside their main area of distribution indicate that they were originally more widespread. They now only occur where the rock is particularly hard. In contrast, the succeeding Clothes Peg Figure style is much more widespread and is found in areas where the rock weathers faster. Classic Bradshaw rock paintings may therefore be significantly older that Clothes Peg Figures, even though there is continuity between the two styles. (From Morwood and Hobbs 2000)

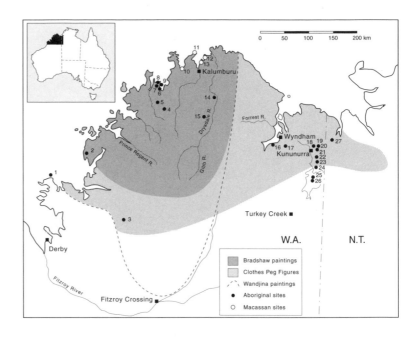

stability of the King Leopold and Wharton sandstones used as the 'canvas' for most of the rock art in the region.

Kimberley rock art has changed greatly over time. It shows chronological changes in subject matter (such as fauna, material culture), local climate, ideology and land use (Figure 5.17). By observing superimpositions, differential weathering and stylistic developments, Grahame Walsh has been able to construct a sequence for this art, which depicts changes in the natural environment, society, ideology, material culture and 'outside' contact. The sequence is being refined and modified on the basis of a continuing site recording program, but it still provides an essential platform for the absolute dating of the region's rock art.

Absolute dates for the Kimberley rock art sequence have been determined in a number of ways, including:

- *Identification of time-specific subjects* in rock paintings—most notably, depictions of thylacine in older painting styles, dingoes in more recent styles and stone spear points in the late Clawed Hand period and Wandjina paintings.
- *AMS dating of materials* used in rock art production: Geochemical analysis of many Kimberley rock pigments shows that these do not contain enough organic material for AMS dating, but

charcoals used in black or grey pigments, and pellets of beeswax, do. AMS has also been applied to oxalate crusts associated with rock paintings and engravings.
- *OSL dating* of mudwasp nests overlying rock paintings.
- Archaeological excavations of cultural deposits to date major changes in the regional sequence, the history of occupation at specific sites, use of pigments and so on.

Using this range of evidence, major turning points in the rock art sequence can now be dated. For instance, as we have seen, excavated evidence at Carpenter's Gap provides a minimum age of 39 700 BP for Kimberley rock art, while OSL dating of mudwasp nests over late Bradshaw paintings establishes that they are at least 16 400 years old. (The fact that AMS dates for overlying oxalate crusts have provided minimum ages for Bradshaw paintings ranging from 1490 to 3880 years does not contradict this.) Furthermore, most Kimberley sites with long occupation sequences were abandoned from about 19 000 to 10 000 BP, when climatic conditions were particularly cold and dry, so Bradshaw rock paintings must predate this exodus (Figure 5.18).

FIGURE 5.18

The Kimberley occupation sequence as based on excavated sites. The core area for Bradshaw distribution in the Kimberley was largely abandoned at the height of the last glacial period from 20 000 to 10 000 years ago. This means that Bradshaw paintings are older than 20 000 or less than 10 000 years. An OSL date for a mudwasp nest overlying a late Bradshaw paintings suggests the former—that Bradshaw paintings predate the period of abandonment. Classic Wandjina paintings only developed in the last 5000 years at most, the same time as a rapid increase in population occurred.
(After Walsh and Morwood 1999, Figure 15)

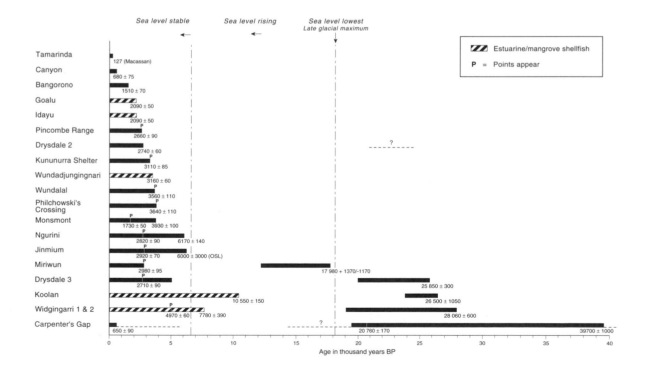

The evidence of differential weathering and superimpositions indicates that there was then a major discontinuity in the rock art sequence between the end of the Bradshaw period and the 'Clawed Hand' rock painting style. Late panels of Clawed Hand paintings include depictions of stone spear points, introduced to the Kimberley between 5000 and 3000 BP, meaning that this style must postdate the period when the Kimberley was largely unoccupied. An age range of 10 000 to 4000 BP for Clawed Hand paintings is therefore a reasonable first estimate. Direct AMS dates for the subsequent Wandjina rock style indicate that it commenced by 4150 BP.

Combining different lines of evidence has been very useful in constructing a chronology and a context for the Kimberley rock art sequence. Even at this early stage, dating the art gives us rare insights into the ideologies, technologies and material culture of peoples long vanished. For instance, the accoutrements and weapons shown in Bradshaw paintings are probably older than 20 000 years. The richness of the Kimberley rock art record contrasts markedly with the threadbare evidence of stone artefacts and food remains recovered from archaeological excavations in the region.

As well as marked discontinuities in the Kimberley rock art sequence, there are also notable continuities—as in the artistic (and probably associated ideological) developments during the Holocene, which ultimately gave rise to the Wandjina painting style. This means that detailed information about Aboriginal people in the Kimberley in recent times can be integrated with that available from rock art, excavations and environmental research.

The potential synergies between different lines of investigation and their usefulness in understanding the past have not been extensively explored in Australia. Rock art studies based on well-dated regional sequences clearly have an important role to play in this process.

Conclusions

The greatest obstacle to the acceptance of rock art as useful archaeological evidence has been the problem of dating it. The advent of radiocarbon dating in Australia in the 1950s allowed us to estimate absolute dates for some rock art, but only in a very restricted range of circumstances. The more recent development of the accelerator mass spectrometer made it possible to calculate the ages of extremely small samples of organic matter, and significantly increased our ability to date a wide range of rock art. Since the AMS technique was first applied to Australian rock art assemblages in the 1990s there has been a surge in its use for dating rock art and associated materials.

More recently, other techniques capable of dating very small samples have been developed and successfully applied—most notably, optically stimulated luminescence. These advances mean that for the first time we can obtain well-dated rock art sequences for comparison with other archaeological and environmental evidence. The establishment of the first high-precision AMS facility in Australia at the Australian Nuclear Science and Technology Organisation in 1993 has accelerated this process. One of the main aims of the facility is dating rock art.

We now have a great range of possible dating techniques for rock art, and no two bodies of such art will necessarily be dated in exactly the same way. But the most convincing dates for art sequences will always be those based on a range of data and the complementary use of relative and absolute dating methods.

CHAPTER **6**

Subject analyses

There are many ways of analysing rock art, but they can be divided into two broad categories, subject analyses and structural analyses, which will be discussed separately in this and the following chapter. The analytical methods in each general category share underlying assumptions and problems, which can be illustrated by case studies.

Subject analyses use the figurative component of art to directly extract information about the artists, their social activities, economy, material culture, ideology and environmental context. Often we cannot infer such information from other types of archaeological evidence. Subject identification is the most common means archaeologists use to reconstruct the cultural and natural contexts of rock artists.

In many places, such as the Drakensberg in South Africa, Bhimbetka in Central India and the Levant of Spain, the degree of composition and attention to detail in figurative rock art provide evidence about past fauna, tools, weapons, ornaments, warfare, economic activities and social activities. For instance, in the Levant, rock paintings depict hats, caps, pendants, feathered head-dresses, bracelets, leg ornaments, belts, loincloths, breeches, skirts, hair and beard styles, pouches, bags, quivers, bows, arrows, digging sticks, the

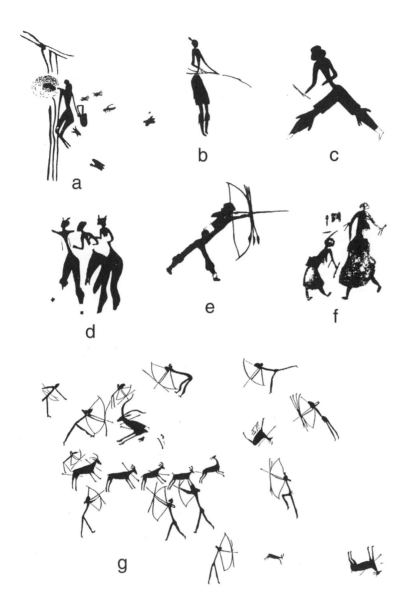

FIGURE 6.1

Items of material culture and activities depicted in the rock paintings of the Spanish Levant. (a) gathering honey; (b–f) styles of dress and hair; (g) hunting scene. These are unlikely to be represented in other types of archaeological evidence.
(After Beltrán 1982)

gathering of plant foods and the collection of honey (Figure 6.1). Many of these items and activities are not likely to be represented in the archaeological record in any other way.

In a few cases such rock art studies have focused on representations of specific items of material culture or animal species, such as bolas, fish traps, humans and horses. A particularly interesting example of this approach is the use of rock art in the Sahara region of

North Africa to plot the former distribution of chariots. These representations are sufficiently detailed to enable us to infer that chariots were used in warfare, in hunting, and as a prestigious vehicle for the elite. The geographical extent of chariot depictions indicates that they were once far more widely used than is documented in historical sources, and were even found in parts of the sub-Saharan region between the Niger and Senegal Rivers, where wheeled vehicles were unknown in later historical times (Figure 6.2).

Subject analyses are particularly useful when the rock art sequence is long and spans major changes in environment, material culture, economy and ideology. For instance, Emmanuel Anati has used the extensive rock engravings found in the Valcamonica area of northern Italy to reconstruct aspects of the artists' daily life, technological level, weapons, tools, animals, economic activities, religious practices and social life, from around 10 000 years ago to the coming of the Romans in 16 BCE (Figure 6.3). Rock art sequences in Central India and North Africa show similarly large changes in the natural and cultural contexts of the artists.

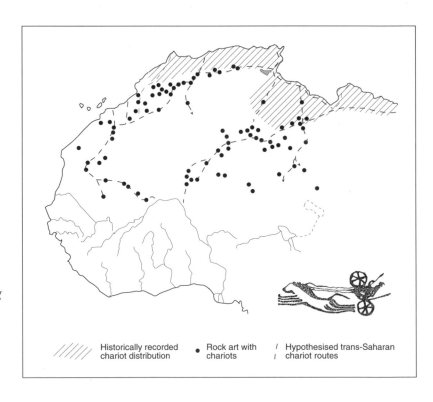

FIGURE 6.2

Distribution of Saharan rock art depicting chariots compared with the historical distribution of wheeled vehicles. It seems that use of the wheel was much more extensive when the engravings were done than in later historical times. (After Camps 1982, Figures 7, 10; Lhote 1982, Figure 1)

///// Historically recorded   • Rock art with   / Hypothesised trans-Saharan
      chariot distribution   chariots   / chariot routes

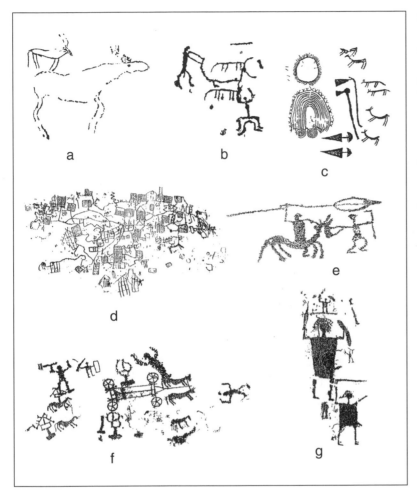

FIGURE 6.3

Aspects of life depicted in rock engravings of the Valcamonica region, northern Italy: (a) Proto-Camunian elk; (b) Neolithic ploughing scene; (c) Chalcolithic weapons, animals and geometrics; (d) Bronze Age map of fields, paths, streams and huts; (e) Iron Age horseman; (f) Iron Age wagon (g) 'Etruscan' warriors. Figurative depictions in rock art are particularly useful when the sequence spans major changes in technology, economy, ideology and social context.

The earliest Valcamonica engravings were produced by stone age hunter–gatherers about 10 000 years ago. Later in the rock engraving sequence the introduction of agriculture, domestic animals, pottery, bronze and iron are shown. The coming of the Romans in 16 BC effectively curtailed this rock engraving tradition, although isolated rock carvings continued to be done into Medieval times (After Anati 1976, Figures 49, 64, 75, 100, 123, 128, 137)

Limitations

The fundamental limitation of subject analysis is that it can only be used when the art is figurative, whereas most of the rock art in the world is non-figurative. It is the specific characteristics of Valcamonica, North African and Central Indian rock art that make them particularly suitable for a direct analytical approach: they are well preserved and are predominantly representational; they feature composed, narrative scenes showing a wide range of activities and material culture; they have clear stylistic differences and superimpositions that allow relative ages to be assessed; and age ranges can be calculated on the basis of dated, 'buried' art and the

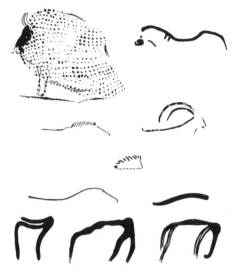

FIGURE 6.4

European Upper Palaeolithic rock art showing stylization for aesthetic purposes, schematization in which only essential traits are shown and abstraction. All art includes aspects of stylization, schematization and abstraction, meaning that the subjects intended by the artist may be impossible to identify. This is one of the major limitations in subject analyses of past art. (After Lorblanchet 1977, Figures 2, 3)

matching of objects illustrated in the art with real, dated objects. Even where rock art assemblages have a figurative component, most are more schematic in format, more selective in subject matter and feature less composition.

A second drawback of subject analysis is the fact that all art uses conventional, stylistic ways of representing subjects, and these conventions in rock art may differ from those familiar to the researcher. Examples include stylization for aesthetic purposes; schematization, in which only essential, diagnostic traits are shown in abbreviated representations; and abstraction, where the art cannot be related directly to reality (Figure 6.4). In some cases the conventions may involve the depiction of imaginary animals or animal–human composites, as seen in European Palaeolithic, South African and Australian rock art; or they may include a degree of deliberate ambiguity. For instance, in recent times the potential ambiguity of non-figurative, geometric motifs, and their ability to encode certain ideas and levels of meaning, has been an important aspect of pre-literate art systems. This is also likely to be true of a large proportion of all non-figurative art. Subject analysis of such art is clearly not possible.

A third drawback in trying to extract information directly from figurative art assemblages is that they are cultural transformations of reality rather than simple windows on the past. Not only do they incorporate schematic and stylistic components that can make subject identification difficult, but they are also selective. They do not portray a random sample of all possible subjects; instead they tend to emphasize some subjects at the expense of others. This means that they cannot be used as a complete or unbiased record of times past. On the other hand, these very biases, both in the choice of subjects and in the way they are portrayed, can tell us much about past values, cognitive systems, beliefs and ideologies (see Chapter 7).

Another complication is the question of the artist's skill in portraying identifiable subjects. For instance, André Leroi-Gourhan interpreted some European Palaeolithic scribblings as 'unfinished' and argued that these were the work of less talented individuals. Similar rough depictions found on portable art objects have been interpreted as the output of students in art 'schools' or 'workshops'. More recently, Jean Clottes has argued that the lack of experience, clumsiness and heaviness of hand evident in some art could easily make it difficult to identify the subjects, given the anatomical errors that are sometimes seen.

Even where figurative motifs were originally well executed and unambiguous, subsequent distortion and fragmentation resulting from weathering or over-painting can still make identifications impossible. This is why Michel Lorblanchet has stressed the need to make accurate recordings and to verify older descriptions of art panels. He has found examples where inaccuracies in recording led to misinterpretation.

Neville Macintosh's experience at Beswick and Tandandjal Caves in the Northern Territory provides a salutary lesson here. He initially recorded the rock paintings and attempted to identify subjects without knowledgeable Aboriginal informants. Later, after he found an informant who could explain and identify the art, he estimated that 90 per cent of his initial identifications were incorrect. His errors had been caused by unfamiliarity with the associated mythology and conventions, deliberate deception on the part of the original artist, and poor rendering of some subjects. Macintosh concluded that to differentiate species in the rock art (for instance, pademelon from rock wallaby), or even tell men from women, a researcher needed particular information about the minutiae of draftsmanship and the conventional norms (Figure 6.5). Even then, he observed, the researcher was totally dependent on knowledgeable Aborigines to gauge the specific purpose and 'thought context' of the art.

In his study, Macintosh became aware of several levels of rock art interpretation: first, simply identifying the subjects depicted; then finding out the art's cultural meaning and purpose; and finally, understanding its inner spiritual meaning. In other words, a depiction of a human, an animal, an object or an event also signified an associated set of ideas, values and beliefs which were not inherent in the depiction, but were prescribed in a culturally specific manner. Using an analogy from linguistics, the rock paintings were signifiers for a range of mental constructs.

In the case of truly prehistoric art, in which no information survives on the associative relationship between things, ideas, values and beliefs, it is impossible to deduce what mental constructs individual depictions signified. This means that studies incorporating superficial use of recent ethnography or personal assessments to 'read' panels of rock art are nonsense. Alexander Marshack's

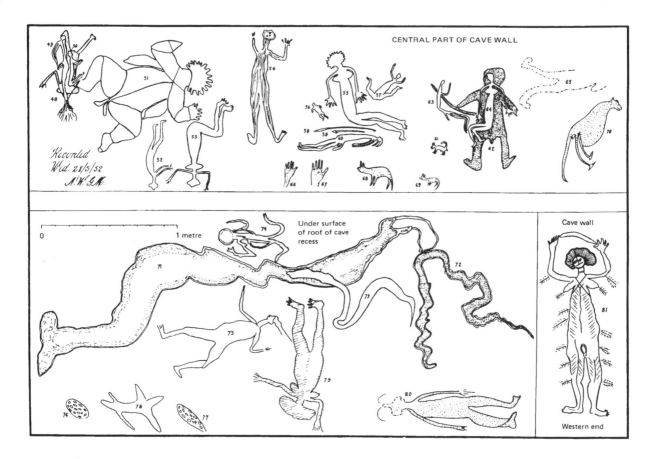

CENTRAL PART OF CAVE WALL

FIGURE 6.5

Panels of rock paintings at Beswick Cave. The site was recorded by Macintosh, a well-known anthropologist, who also identified the subjects depicted in the paintings. When Macintosh later revisited the site with a knowledgeable informant, he found that 90 per cent of his identifications were incorrect. The huge snake (71) belongs to the ceremonial Kunapipi *cycle. The projection from its mouth has multiple significance. It represents the snake's tongue, as well as saliva, lightning and rain being spat out.* (After Macintosh 1977)

unstructured, ethnocentric musings on the meaning of European Palaeolithic rock and mobile art are in this vein. For instance, in analysing a Late Magdalenian composition, he says:

The composition seems to contain an Upper Palaeolithic pantheon, relating a primary animal, perhaps sacrificial, to a sky body and to three subsidiary animals from different realms, a horned and hoofed creature, a fish, and a clawed omnivore, the bear. A number of 'signs' seem to indicate spear, wound, blood, and symbolic water. The relation of the human group to these images does not seem to be aggressive, despite the possible killing of the horse and the bleeding bovine.

A more extreme example is the work of LaVan Martineau, who assumes that North American Indian rock art is the visual representation of gesture language, which has universal elements

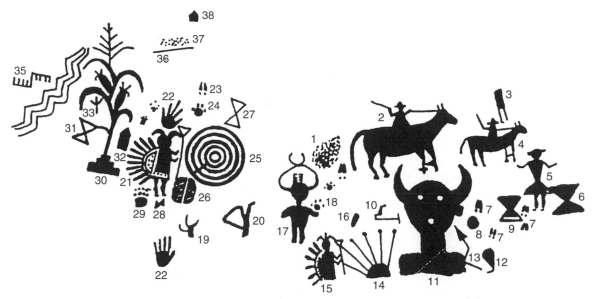

FIGURE 6.6

The North American researcher LaVan Martineau believes that Indian rock art is the visual representation of gesture language and can therefore be deciphered in much the same way as writing. He interprets this engraved panel as the Navajo record of Kit Carson's campaign in 1863–64. For instance, Motif 2 is interpreted as a white soldier; 5 is a Navajo warrior weakened by hunger but attempting to fight, as indicated by the poorly executed war symbol (6); and the deer tracks (7) represent Navajo flight up the canyon, and so on. Interpretive description of this type is merely speculation.
(After Martineau 1973, Figure 49)

and can therefore be deciphered in much the same way as writing. He argues that all art panels basically tell a story, and that one has probably interpreted the story correctly if one's guesses as to the meaning of its parts add up to a coherent whole (Figure 6.6). However scientifically it is put, naive, interpretive description of this type is merely speculation and is not relevant to the mainstream of rock art research.

In contrast, the work of David Lewis-Williams on the rock art of San (Bushman) hunter–gatherers in southern Africa indicates the potential usefulness of specific ethnographic information in the 'reading' of rock art panels with a detailed figurative content. Lewis-Williams has demonstrated that many details in San rock paintings are concerned with communicating the same analogies and metaphors found in modern San myth and ceremony. In fact, many of the rock paintings show aspects of the 'curing' dance, which is the central religious focus of the San today and involves shamans entering a trance and manipulating supernatural power to heal people, control the movements of game and make rain. Some paintings portray seated groups of women clapping, with men dancing, laying hands on people, bleeding from the nose, bending forward with arms bent back and in a state of collapse; all of which are still part of the curing dance as practised by the !Kung San in the Kalahari Desert (Figure 6.7).

FIGURE **6.7**

San rock paintings depict aspects of trance including hunched over position, bleeding from the nose, feelings of elongation, assuming animal characteristics and collapse. Patricia Vinnicombe and David Lewis-Williams both used detailed information on San myth and ceremonies to show that these communicate the same analogies and metaphors evident in the rock paintings. While some San rock art clearly depicts historical events, much is concerned with the sensations and hallucinations seen during trance. The art may have been a way of sharing these experiences with others in the community. (After Lewis-Williams 1986b)

Other San rock paintings portray non-realistic subjects that seem to express the sensations experienced during trances and hallucinations. These include distorted human body size, strange human–antelope composites (called therianthropes and trance-buck), and mythical scenes such as the capture of rain-animals to induce rainfall. The art may have served as a way of 'pooling' trance experiences and thus communicating beliefs and values central to San cultural identity.

San rock paintings encode meaning at many levels. For instance, present-day San make an analogy between entering a state of trance and dying, since trembling, sweating, staggering and bleeding from the nose are common to both. The now-extinct southern San regarded eland antelope as particularly potent symbols of shamanic power, and used dying eland as a powerful metaphor for shamans entering a trance. Thus in the Drakensberg region, eland are the most common animals in San rock paintings because of their symbolic import, not their economic significance.

Once we realize that the meaning of art does not necessarily lie in overt subject content but in the cultural values it communicates, many otherwise inexplicable characteristics of the art may become significant. The work of Lewis-Williams has not only provided new insights into San rock art and ideology, but also prompted other researchers to reassess the way they interpret rock art. However, despite the sophistication of his approach, which is based on a comprehensive understanding of the ideological context of the art, Lewis-Williams still largely relies on the identification of figurative depictions.

This type of analysis is only possible because of specific features of the art: it is naturalistic, and it emphasizes particular subjects, compositions, juxtapositions and superimpositions that can be directly related to the values, beliefs and practices recorded in San ethnography. Most rock art around the world does not share these attributes. Instead, it emphasizes non-figurative components; it is more schematic in format; the relationship between the art and associated value systems is more esoteric (as in the case of most Australian Aboriginal art); and there is no detailed information available on the art. Lewis-Williams' approach, therefore, does not offer a generally applicable way of analyzing rock art but is specific to one regional body of such art.

Where information on the context and underlying principles of rock art is available, researchers can investigate some of the values and metaphors it embodies. But in the vast majority of cases where such information is not available, they are forced to begin by trying to identify the subjects depicted in the art, while acknowledging that artistic conventions, badly drawn subjects, deliberate ambiguity or poor preservation will result in mistakes.

Taking the extreme view, the Australian rock art researcher John Clegg has argued that any claimed identification of subjects in prehistoric pictures can never be verified and therefore 'must be scrupulously rejected'. To emphasize the point he proposes that figurative motifs be labelled as '!people', '!fish', '!whales', rather than 'people', 'fish' or 'whales'. Taken to its logical conclusion, this would mean that figurative art could not be used to infer anything about past things or events, and much of Clegg's work is clearly not undertaken on this basis (see below).

A more practical and consistent view is that the uncertainty inherent in simple subject analyses based on identification of figurative motifs in art has to be balanced against the value of the results in writing about the past. The following Australian examples should demonstrate this value.

The cultural context

Rock art traditions in Australia vary enormously in their degree of visual specificity. Over much of the arid zone, for instance, there is an emphasis on geometric motifs and tracks, and any figurative motifs tend to be simple, with little detail and few explicit cues that might aid in identification. In contrast, some of the Complex Figurative rock art traditions, as identified by Lesley Maynard in the western Arnhem Land and Kimberley regions of northwestern Australia, provide very detailed and precise visual means for identifying animal species, as well as people and their paraphernalia.

The rock art of western Arnhem Land is largely figurative and shares some of the characteristics and potential of Valcamonica engravings. In particular, the paintings have visually specific details allowing accurate subject identification There are also several thousand sites spanning thousands of years and many changes in style and subject, which can be dated by both relative and absolute means. Western Arnhem Land art provides an interesting contrast to that of Valcamonica because, even though it reflects significant changes in environment, material culture, economy, technology, ideology and outside contact, its basic economic context did not change: Aboriginal people in Australia remained hunter–gatherers until recent times.

Western Arnhem Land rock art depicts many cultural elements not usually found in archaeological deposits. These include organic items such as head-dresses, bags and spears; myths featuring anthropomorphic beings and rainbow snakes; and a wide range of social and economic activities (Figure 6.8). In fact, Darrell Lewis argues for a regional rock art chronology based on specific items or animal species which could be found and dated in archaeological excavations. He suggests that such defined periods be named after the identifying marker.

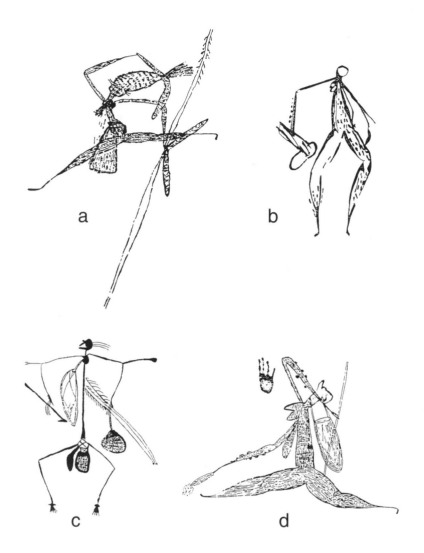

FIGURE 6.8

Items of material culture depicted in western Arnhem Land rock art: (a) Dynamic figure with headdress, pubic apron, multi-barbed spears and boomerangs; (b) Dynamic figure with hafted axe; (c) recent figure with head-dress, multi-barbed spears, spearthrower, bag and goosewing fan; (d) Dynamic figure woman with dilly-bag and digging stick. The paintings offer unique insights into changes in Arnhem Land material culture over many thousands of years. (After Chaloupka 1993 and Lewis 1988)

a

b

c

d

Some of the datable changes represented in the artistic sequence include the replacement of boomerangs, seen as hunting and fighting weapons in the earliest art, by broad spearthrowers and composite spears; the appearance of the hooked stick spearthrower; and its replacement by the broad spearthrower, later replaced by the long spearthrower. Lewis has used these changes to identify major periods in Arnhem Land rock paintings. In order of appearance, these comprise the Boomerang, Hooked Stick, Broad Spearthrower and Long Spearthrower periods (Figure 6.9).

FIGURE 6.9

Darrell Lewis has defined major periods in Western Arnhem Land rock art on the basis of depicted weapons, such as boomerangs and spearthrowers; George Chaloupka used changes in depicted animals for the same purpose. (After Lewis 1988)

Chronology and dating of Arnhem Land rock art

Periods	Identifying characteristics	Years BP (approx.)
Boomerang	Figures in monochrome red with ornate head-dress, carrying boomerangs and/or spears only. Naturalistic perspective usually with allusion to movement. Stencils of hands and material culture items are common. Distribution: pan-plateau.	Maximum: ? (no megafauna) Minimum: 9000
Hooked Stick	Figures with 'hooked sticks' as well as boomerangs and spears, usually with simplified head-dress. Regional variation in perspective and style. Rainbow snake omplex appears throughout the plateau late in period and continues, with changes, until the present time.	Maximum: 9000 Minimum: 6000
Broad Spearthrower	Figures with short, broad spearthrowers, and cylindrical spearthrowers, and a great variety of spear types. Varied perspective, style and colour. In northwest of plateau, long-necked spearthrowers appear to be transitional between broad and long spearthrowers.	Maximum: 6000 Minimum: 1–2000
Long Spearthrower	Figures with long, narrow spearthrower varied perspectives, painting techniques and styles. Includes fully developed X-ray art. Limited variety of spear types.	Maximum: 2000 (probably less than 1000). Minimum: Ethnographic present.

The Arnhem Land art sequence also provides evidence for a degree of continuity. For instance, in historic times rainbow serpent myths were recorded in many parts of Australia. Rainbow serpents are thought to reside in deep, permanent waterholes or in the sea, and are associated with fertility and the creation of rain. In northwest Australia, there are composite beings, with snake-like bodies, macropod or flying-fox heads, tails and various plant and animal appendages. They are the main characters in the major stories and

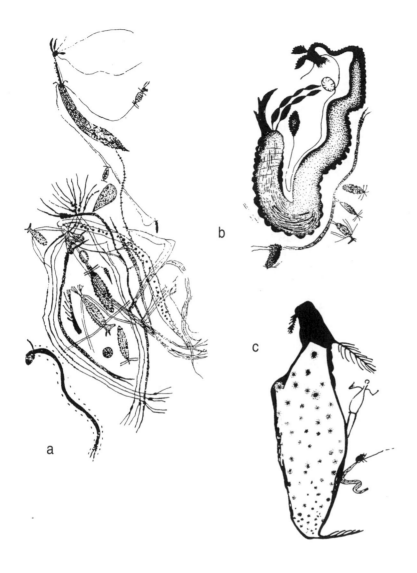

FIGURE 6.10

Rainbow serpents are major characters in the ceremonies, stories and art of western Arnhem Land art. They are generally depicted as composite beings, with snake-like bodies, macropod or flying-fox heads, tails and various plant and animal appendages. Examples (a) and (b) are from rock paintings of the Yam Period, while (c) is part of a bark painting done in 1965.

Rainbow serpents first appeared in the art when sea level stabilized at its present level. There has been artistic continuity in the way they are depicted from then up to the present day—suggesting ideological continuity in Arnhem Land over a 6000-year time span. (After Lewis 1988: figure 120, 121; Brandl 1973, Figure 152)

rituals of Arnhem Land, where they are depicted in rock art and bark paintings (Figure 6.10).

The earliest depictions of rainbow serpents in Arnhem Land rock art occur in the Yam Painting Style by 6000 years ago. This was the time when the most complex compositions involving rainbow serpents and associated subjects were produced. Over time, the depictions of rainbow serpents also changed in other ways: in recent rock art and bark paintings they tend to be larger, and new elements, such as crocodile-like serrated tails, feathered ornaments, prominent teeth, eyes attached to stalks and whiskers, have been added. Even

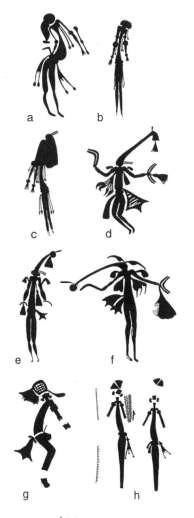

so, there is clear evidence in the art for a continuing, evolving tradition.

Not only does this show the antiquity of a specific ideology but the timing of its appearance and that of other depictions in the rock art indicates some of the factors that may have been responsible. Depictions of rainbow serpents first appeared when sea levels stabilized at their present level around 6000 years ago. This was a time of great environmental change and probable social disruption: the rapid rise in sea level at the end of the Pleistocene must have displaced many coastal groups. This is also the time when the rock art first depicts large-scale battles, although such scenes only became common in the most recent long spearthrower period. Paul Taçon argues that the rainbow serpent story arose as a unifying symbol and that the first depictions in the rock paintings were modelled on sea-horses or pipefish washed up on newly formed shores near the Arnhem Land escarpment.

Rock paintings in the Kimberley region of northwestern Australia have similar, if not greater, potential for showing changes in weapons used, accoutrements and ideology. For instance, early and late Bradshaw paintings can be largely distinguished by ornamental tassels on the former and sashes on the latter (Figure 6.11). In addition, David Welch has argued that many items of Bradshaw regalia can be closely matched with the ceremonial dress worn until quite recently by Aboriginal groups in northern Australia. Other obvious changes in material culture shown in the region's rock art include developments in spear technology, the appearance of the spearthrower and the subsequent disappearance of the boomerang.

Identification of the weapons in Kimberley rock art relies on consistent details in form and contextual association. For instance, spears are linear; relatively long (75–150 per cent of the height of associated humans); may have barbs; are held in 'aggressive' or 'reserve' positions, often with other identified weapons, such as boomerangs and spearthrowers; and may be shown piercing prey or opponents. Spearthrowers are linear; relatively short (13–46 per cent of the height of associated humans); have a distinctive hook or peg shown at one end; and may have a knob or grip at the other. The hook is a crucial identifying feature, and artists sometimes used twisted perspective to show it. In addition, spearthrowers are depicted closely associated with spears, sometimes in the 'launching' position. On this basis, the Kimberley weapons sequence included:

FIGURE 6.11

Bradshaw rock paintings of the Kimberley. On the basis of superimpositions and weathering, Tassel Bradshaws (a–c) are older than Sash Bradshaws (d–f), which predate Clothes Peg Figures (g–h). The figures' highly distinctive regalia allows their relative age of such figures to be quickly assessed, while the amount of visual detail portrayed means that aspects of the artists' material culture and ceremonial life can be reconstructed. Bradshaw paintings, which may be more than 20 000 years old, provide invaluable evidence for the Kimberley cultural sequence. (After Walsh 2000)

- hand-thrown, unbarbed spears and boomerangs in the oldest rock painting style—the Irregularly Infilled Animal period (Figure 6.12a)
- the use of hand-thrown, large-barbed spears in the Bradshaw period (Figure 6.12b–e)
- the appearance of spearthrowers in the late Bradshaw period (Figure 6.12f)
- widespread use of spearthrowers, as well as the appearance of composite spears and curved-tip boomerangs in the Clothes Peg Figure period (Figure 6.12g, h)
- a number of subsequent changes in spearthrower morphology, including a distinctive 'spade handle' spearthrower in the Clawed Hand period (Figure 6.12j)
- the appearance of stone spear points in the late Clawed Hand period (Figure 6.12k)
- the disappearance of the boomerang
- metal spearheads in a few post-European contact Wandjina paintings (Figure 6.12l).

Some major turning points in this sequence have already been dated. For instance, dates for the first use of metal spearheads can be estimated on the basis of historical evidence, while stone spear points first appeared about 5000 years ago, from the evidence of Kimberley archaeological excavations. Since the Clawed Hand rock painting style gradually evolved into the Wandjina style of historic times, this date for stone spear points also provides a maximum age for Wandjina rock paintings and the associated ideology. If confirmed by further work, an OSL date of 16 400 years BP for a mudwasp nest overlying a late Bradshaw painting would provide the earliest date for spears in Australia, as well as the earliest date for boomerangs and spearthrowers anywhere in the world.

The most recent Kimberley rock painting tradition emphasizes deities such as Wandjinas rather than humans. Since Wandjinas used control of cyclones, waterspouts, rain and lightning rather than 'earthly' weapons to administer punishment and death, recent weapons are not well represented in the rock art. Despite such selectivity in subject depiction, however, the art still provides a unique and invaluable archaeological resource.

Very few actual weapons survive in the archaeological record. In fact, at this stage evidence for the antiquity and development of spears

FIGURE 6.12

Changes in Kimberley spear and spearthrower technology as depicted in rock art: (a) simple hand-thrown spears of the Irregular Infilled Animal Period; (b–e) multi-barbed, hand-thrown spears of the Bradshaw Period; (d) first spearthrowers appeared in the late Bradshaw Period; (g,h) spearthrowers became common in the Clothes Peg Figures period, and composite spears appeared, as indicated by two-colour depictions; (i) spade-handled spearthrowers of the Clawed Hand period; (j) stone speartips with denticulated edges shown piercing animals in paintings of the Wandjina Period; (k) spear with a metal point in a late Wandjina painting. Evidence for the antiquity and development of spears and spearthrowers in Australia comes almost exclusively from the rock art sequences of Arnhem Land and the Kimberley.

(After Walsh and Morwood 1999)

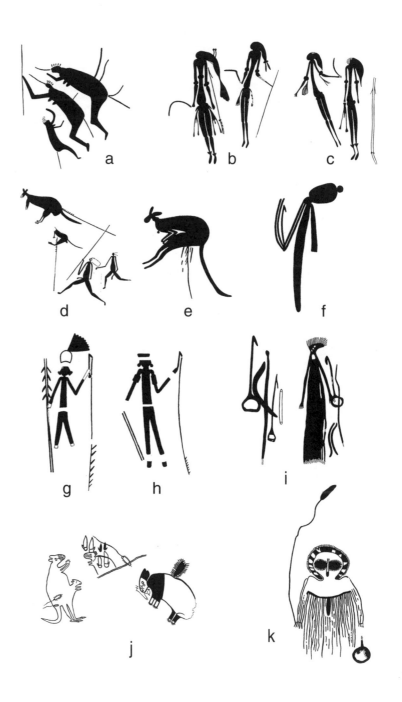

and spearthrowers in Australia comes almost exclusively from the rock art sequences of Arnhem Land and the Kimberley. In both areas rock art shows that the earliest weapons were boomerangs, clubs, hafted stone axes and simple, hand-thrown spears; in both areas spearthrowers and new composite spear types subsequently appeared and developed, while boomerangs were phased out. However, there are also significant regional differences. The 'spade handle' spearthrower depicted in Kimberley rock art of the Clawed Hand period never appears in Arnhem Land art. Conversely, the broad spearthrower cited by Lewis to define a regional art period in Arnhem Land is not depicted in the Kimberley.

Although rock paintings elsewhere in Australia are less easy to interpret than those found in Arnhem Land and the Kimberley, they can still provide useful archaeological data. For instance, stencilling of hands, feet, weapons and utensils was practised in many regions, and stencils have been used in the study of past material culture and communication systems. Stencils of tools and weapons provide information on the range of material culture in a region, especially of organic (wooden and fibre) items, which decay too readily to be preserved in archaeological deposits. As outlines of actual objects, they also have an advantage over paintings, which may be distorted by artistic licence. This is the case in both Arnhem Land and the Kimberley, where early rock paintings depicting boomerangs are contemporaneous with boomerang stencils. The difference is that stencils show the exact size and shape of the weapons (Figure 6.13).

In recent times boomerangs were not made in Arnhem Land, the northern Kimberley or Cape York Peninsula, but in each of these regions they are well represented in the rock art. Local people did, however, know about boomerangs: in Arnhem Land, they were traded in from the Victoria River District, but were only used as clapsticks during ceremonies, not as hunting weapons. On the basis of stencils, George Chaloupka has shown that the full range of boomerangs known from other areas of Australia in historic times was used in Arnhem Land prior to 6000 BP (Figure 6.14). Figurative paintings of the same age indicate that they were used in hunting as well as in ceremonies.

Although relatively recent, stencil art in the central Queensland highlands portrays items never observed in use in the European contact period, while the range of shapes and size of stencilled artefacts is much greater than that seen in museum collections (Figure 6.15). Stencils of exotic or 'contact' items may also tell us about the scope of exchange networks and the chronology of the art. For instance, the occurrence of stencilled Melo shell pendants

FIGURE 6.13

Stencil of a boomerang in western Arnhem Land—an area where boomerangs were not made or used as weapons in recent times. Early rock paintings from the region show that boomerangs were used in hunting and warfare, but that they disappeared when the spearthrower and composite spear were introduced. (From Chaloupka 1993: figure 120)

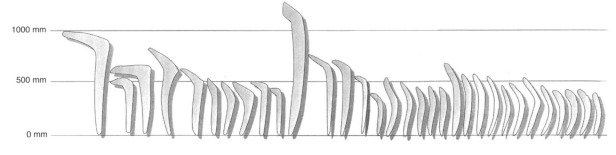

FIGURE 6.14

Rock stencils indicate that a wide range of boomerangs was used in Arnhem Land prior to 6000 years ago. In fact, practically all boomerang types observed in Australia in recent times are evident in this rock art. In more recent times boomerangs were not made in the region, nor used as weapons. Only a few imported examples were used as clapsticks in ceremonies. (After Chaloupka 1993)

FIGURE 6.15

Stencils of axes, spears, clubs, digging sticks, shields and other items are common at rock art sites in the central Queensland highlands. These greatly extend our knowledge of material culture in this region, where historical records are few. (Photo M. J. Morwood)

FIGURE 6.16

Stencil of a Melo shell pendant at Cathedral Cave in Carnarvon Gorge, central Queensland highlands. Melo shell is found on the north Queensland coast. The pendant stencils therefore provide evidence for long-distance movement of goods and ideas through exchange networks. (Photo M. J. Morwood)

in central Queensland highland sites indicates that the local people had indirect contact with far north Queensland. Because individually stencilled items are easy to identify, they also help establish the processes by which rock art assemblages were built up. Precise measurements of 37 stencils of shell pendants in Cathedral Cave demonstrated that these did not represent 37 pendants, but rather 37 stencils of the same item (Figure 6.16). This indicates that large rock art assemblages may have developed in fits and starts, rather than by gradual accumulation.

Stencils of 'mutilated' hands have yielded a range of information about the past. Such stencils occur in rock art assemblages throughout the world and have been interpreted by various researchers as showing the effects of frostbite and disease, the deliberate amputation of fingers for ceremonial reasons and the use of sign language. In Australia, most 'mutilated' hands with missing, partially missing or distorted fingers are clear manipulations of hand position, as used in historic times for sign-talk during hunting or periods of enforced silence (Figures 6.17, 6.18). In central Queensland, their frequent positioning in highly visible but difficult-to-access locations at mortuary sites suggests that hand stencil variants encoded specific cultural information, probably about the totemic affiliation and level of initiation of mourners or the deceased.

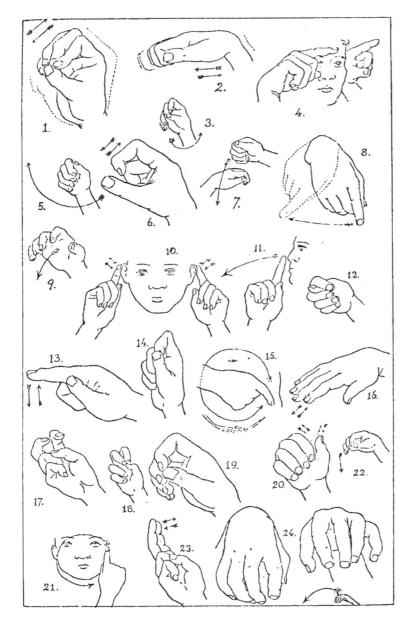

FIGURE 6.17

Aboriginal hand signs observed in northwestern Queensland by Walter Roth. Use of sign language was never recorded in the central Queensland highlands, but some of the same gestures are evident in hand stencils found in local rock art sites. (After Roth 1897)

FIGURE 6.18

These stencils of 'mutilated' hands in central Queensland are just manipulations of normal hand and finger positions— although there are also examples known in which the individual concerned has lost part of a finger. Some of the hand manipulations can be matched with hand signals recorded in northwest Queensland.
(Photos M. J. Morwood)

Hand stencils can be generally categorized on the basis of size as 'adult male', 'female/youth', or 'child'. They therefore provide evidence for the age and sex composition of human groups at rock art sites. In turn this indicates whether the sites were restricted or open. For instance, in a survey of 163 art sites in the Koolburra Plateau region of Cape York Peninsula, Josephine Flood showed that the hand stencils of adult men were concentrated within two large rock shelters which do not contain occupation deposits but which feature zoomorphic 'echidna beings'. Similarly, Bruno and Marie David found that art sites located high in limestone towers in the adjacent Chillagoe region were characterized by hand stencils of adult men and children. Because these sites lacked occupation deposits we can conclude that they were probably used for initiations, as well as disposal of the dead. Hand stencils may also show changes in the characteristics of a group of people over time. For instance, the earliest hand stencils in the Kimberley are huge, much larger than the hand stencils produced during the more recent Wandjina rock painting period, or Aboriginal hands measured throughout Australia by Joseph Birdsell in the 1940s and 1950s.

The natural context

As well as providing information on the operation and content of cultural systems, figurative rock art can document aspects of the natural environment. This is particularly evident in western Arnhem Land, where artists throughout the sequence took great care to provide clues to species identification. Fish are the most frequently portrayed subject in recent rock paintings in the area, and detailed knowledge of local art conventions obtained from Aboriginal informants allows about twelve species to be identified. Both external and internal features are used in identifications (Figure 6.19). Saratoga are depicted with 'prominent barbels forming a V-shape adjacent to the mouth, two large pectoral fins with pointed ends, an elongated almond-shaped body, two broad, curving dorsal/anal fins on either side of a large caudal peduncle and a prominent convex caudal fin' (Taçon 1988). Together with specific internal features of the digestive tract, the nature of the backbone and vertebral processes, and the gill arch, these allow paintings of saratoga to be distinguished from

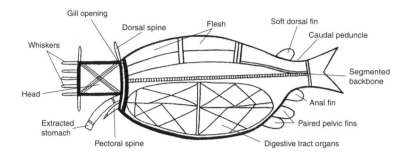

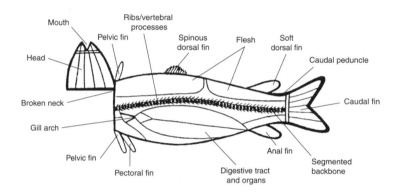

FIGURE 6.19

Generalized paintings of fork-tail catfish and mullet in western Arnhem Land. The artists in the region provide very specific visual cues, including both external and internal features, which enable at least twelve species of fish to be identified. (After Taçon 1988, Figures 3, 4)

those of silver barramundi, eel-tail catfish, mullet, freshwater long-tom, bony bream, black bream, archer fish and other species.

Paul Taçon also found that regional differences in the way fish species are represented within western Arnhem Land rock paintings partly reflect the nature of local environments and species availability, and partly reflect cultural values. This is particularly evident in the distribution of paintings of barramundi, saratoga, forktail catfish and eel-tail catfish, which differs from the natural distributions of these species. The same species also are good eating fish, are carnivorous, and spawn in spring, when people were returning to rock shelters to escape the storms that precede the monsoons. Some of these characteristics may explain their ideological significance in local myth and ceremony as well as rock art.

Rock art assemblages of northwestern Australia contain enough detail to let us accurately identify recently extinct species. For instance, thylacines, which became extinct on the Australian mainland about 3000 years ago, can be confidently identified in the rock art of the Pilbara, the Kimberley and western Arnhem Land

FIGURE 6.20

A number of (locally) extinct animal species are depicted in the rock art of Arnhem Land and the Kimberley. These include the Tasmanian tiger (thylacine), Tasmanian devil and possibly the marsupial tapir (Palochestes). (After Lewis 1988, Figure 64; Chaloupka 1993, Plate 96)

by careful comparison with preserved specimens and photographs taken in Tasmania, where the animals survived until the 1930s (Figures 6.20). In this case and elsewhere, researchers have stressed that accurate identification of mammals, birds and fish in rock art depends upon understanding the local artistic conventions and nuances of style, as well as an assessment of species-specific traits.

The visual specificity in Arnhem Land rock art also provides clear evidence for environmental change over time. Changes in the types of animals portrayed can be related to climatic and sea level fluctuations, as well as to the impacts of people. Chaloupka (Figure 6.21) used these changes in fauna to construct a regional rock art sequence, which includes:

- *the Pre-estuarine period,* with terrestrial animals (thylacine, Tasmanian devil, rock wallaby, emu, python), freshwater crocodile and freshwater fish
- *the Estuarine period,* with estuarine fish (barramundi, mullet, catfish) and salt-water crocodile
- *the Freshwater period,* with magpie geese and waterlilies
- *the Contact period,* with Macassan and European subjects and introduced animals.

Because the general environmental sequence for the region is also known in detail, Chaloupka is able to suggest the approximate age of these major rock art periods (with varying degrees of accuracy).

Where there is little or no information on artistic conventions or the characteristics of particular animals, species identifications in rock

Chronology of the Arnhem Land plateau rock art

Period	Phase	Style/technique	Major or identifying elements
Pre-estuarine	50 000 years ago From this date, haematite and red and yello ochres were used to prepare pigment	*Object imprints*	Handprints; imprints of grass and other thrown objects
	20 000 years ago	Naturalistic	*Large naturalistic figures, complex*	Extinct megafauna; thylacine; Tasmanian devil; terrestrial animals; rock python; freshwater crocodile; human beings; earliest X-ray paintings
		Dynamic figures	Human beings in complex apparel; anthropomorphs; zoomorphs; terrestrial animals; freshwater fish; stencils; hand of 3MF convention, boomerangs; one-piece multibarbed spears; detailed compositions
		Stylization	*Post-dynamic figures*	Human beings in head-dresses, pubic aprons and bustles; macropods; lizards; fighting pick/hooked stick introduced
		Schematization	*Simple figures with boomerangs*	Human beings in head-dresses, pubic aprons and bustles; conflict; fighting pick; single- and multiple-pronged barbed composite spears; possible spearthrower
		Stylization	*Mounted figures*	Human beings (many elongated); spearthrower
		Naturalistic symbolism	*Yam figures*	Anthropomorphized yams; phytomorphized animals; Rainbow Snake; ibis; egret; short-necked turtle; flying fox; long-arm prawn; segmented circle symbol
Estuarine	8000 years ago	Naturalistic	*Early estuarine complex*	Estuarine fish: barramundi, mullet, catfish; saltwater crocodile; variety of spearthrowers
	4000 years ago		*Beeswax designs*	Human beings; anthropomorphs; non-figurative designs
		Intellectual Realism and contemporaneous naturalism	*X-ray complex*	Lightning man; stone-tipped spear; X-ray paintings of animals and humans with detailed and decorative features
Freshwater	15600 years ago			Hook-headed human beings; magpie geese; water lilies; 'goose' spears; goose-wing 'fan'; didgeridoo; complex spearthrower
Contact	300 years ago			Makassan and European subjects; introduced animals; sorcery paintings; decorated hands
	Ethnographic present	*Casual paintings*	

art become extremely dubious. For instance, some researchers have claimed that long-extinct animals such as *Diprotodon*, *Genyornis*, *Thyacaleo* and *Palorchestes* are depicted in the rock art of South Australia, southeast Cape York Peninsula and western Arnhem Land, but these claims have not been generally accepted.

On the other hand, detailed knowledge of animal behaviour and morphology can allow us to distinguish between similar species, as

FIGURE 6.21

George Chaloupka defined major periods in western Arnhem Land rock art on the basis of depicted animals. For instance, his Pre-estuarine Period is characterized by 'inland' animals, such as thylacines, kangaroos, snakes and freshwater crocodiles. Later, with the rise in sea level, estuarine species, such as saltwater crocodile, appear in the rock art. Darrell Lewis used changes in depicted material culture for the same purpose. (After Chaloupka 1993)

has been shown by the work of Josephine McDonald on macropod (kangaroo-like) tracks engraved at Sturt's Meadows in western New South Wales. McDonald began with a study of actual macropod tracks, taking into account species, size and sex differences, gait, speed, nature of terrain and surface type, to establish a species-diagnostic track classification. On this basis she distinguished four groups of engraved macropod tracks ('red kangaroo/euro', 'grey kangaroo', 'megafauna' and 'other'), and concluded that much of the variation evident in the track engravings was attributable to species differentiation.

Tracks are an important species identifier in rock art throughout the world, where animals depicted in profile often have the feet twisted to show them from underneath. The same format is used in many Australian rock art assemblages and reflects the importance of tracks to hunters, as sources of information about the animal's species, age, sex, health, direction and speed of travel, and the time elapsed since it passed.

In other parts of Australia, cues for species identification in rock art are less detailed. For instance, during her research on style and the identification of animal representations in rock paintings of the Laura region of southeast Cape York Peninsula, Andrée Rosenfeld found that naturalism operated at a fairly general level, enabling broad categories such as birds, reptiles, furred animals and humans to be distinguished (Figure 6.22). Some of the clues to more specific

FIGURE 6.22

Generalized kangaroo paintings in southeast Cape York Peninsula. The paintings themselves do not have enough specific features to enable the animals to be identified to species level: contextual information, such as knowing the significance of the site, was probably required for this identification to take place.
(Photo M. J. Morwood)

identification of fauna in Laura art seem to have been encoded in the paintings. Feet were the most useful discriminating features; other clues in the associations between figures, or their location at particular sites, are now beyond decoding.

In this light, depictions of post-European contact subjects are informative. Rosenfeld notes that paintings of horses and pigs incorporate a greater range of explicit clues to species identity, suggesting that contextual information must have been an important identifier in depictions of traditional fauna. There is also a strange combination of standardized and non-standardized traits in many Laura post-contact subjects, including the depiction of long, macropod-like hind legs and shortened front legs in a painting of a horse at Giant Horse Gallery (Figures 6.23, 6.24b). In some cases this may result from the use of second-hand information by the artist, but in others the art provides insights into a different cultural perspective and the psychology of fitting new things into an established worldview. On this basis, the large horse painting at Giant Horse Gallery probably dates to 1872 CE, the time of earliest European contact for the area.

Another fascinating example of contact art occurs at the main Deaf Adder Creek site in western Arnhem Land, in a painting executed in the traditional X-ray style: the painting depicts a European dressed in pants, jacket and boots, but with a spirit's head and holding a rifle in the way a spear is used (Figure 6.24a).

FIGURE 6.23

Painting of a horse at Giant Horse Shelter, southeast Cape York Peninsula. This has more specific cues for species identification than are found in depictions of native Australian animals. The artist could not assume that the intended audience had contextual information to help with identification of this unfamiliar animal.
(Photo M. J. Morwood)

FIGURE 6.24

European contact subjects depicted in Australian rock art: (a) European at Deaf Adder Creek—this possibly depicts the explorer Ludwig Leichhardt; (b) horse at Giant Horse Shelter, Cape York Peninsula; (c) horses and riders in western Arnhem Land; (d) bulls from Bull Cave, Sydney area. Superimpositions show that the black drawings of bulls (left) are more recent than the red drawing. They are also more realistic.

In many areas, the earliest Aboriginal paintings of Europeans, their material culture and their animals have features showing that the artists were not familiar with the subjects. Later paintings of contact subjects tend to be more coherent. (After Chaloupka 1993, Figure 218, p.195; Clegg 1981)

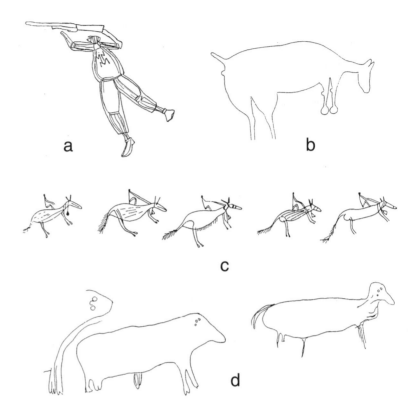

This degree of unfamiliarity and awe suggests that the painting dates to 'first-sight' European contact in the area, and possibly depicts the explorer Ludwig Leichhardt, who passed Deaf Adder Creek in 1845.

Clegg argues that people perceive new, unfamiliar things with reference to known and familiar things, and that their perceptions change as subjects move from unfamiliar to familiar status. He notes that increasing familiarity with new things is likely to be reflected in changes in rock art over time from apparent crudity to a more coherent perspective. Supporting evidence for this comes from Bull Cave in the Sydney area, where two black drawings of bulls overlie (and are, therefore, more recent than) a red drawing of a bull. All the drawings lack horns, and Clegg concludes that these are likely to portray the polled bulls which escaped from the Sydney settlement in 1788, rather than their horned progeny. The drawings are undoubtedly of bulls, but the earlier, red drawing shares some of the characteristics of a bird-like drawing in another, nearby site and looks less bull-like than the black drawings (Figure 6.24d).

Despite the problems of artistic perspective and conventions that beset any attempt to extract biological information from art assemblages, some researchers have used depictions in rock art in combination with information about present-day animal behaviour to reconstruct the behaviour of extinct species.

Conclusions

Australian figurative and stencilled rock art provides a unique and invaluable database for reconstructing past material culture, behaviour and beliefs. Identified subjects (for instance, animals in western Arnhem Land rock art, ceremonial regalia in Bradshaw paintings), also allow some Australian rock art to be sequenced into broad chronological units while some subjects allow us to estimate dates.

The changes in material culture, technology and ideology apparent in the rock art record will be better understood when major turning points in the sequence are better dated, and when more contextual information on changes in past environments, resource use and Aboriginal population size is available. The work of Bert Roberts and his colleagues on Kimberley rock art has shown the potential level of interaction between different lines of investigation and their cumulative contribution towards our understanding of the past. For instance, mudwasp nests in the region not only provide a means for dating underlying paintings but also contain phytoliths (silica secreted by plants) and other evidence of past climates. Evidence for the cultural and environmental context of Kimberley rock art and its age is also being obtained from archaeological excavations.

Although subject studies of rock art are usually non-quantitative in character, subject frequencies, proportions, dimensions, and so on can also be represented graphically or summarized in table form. For instance, in South Africa, Patricia Vinnicombe plotted the frequency of weapons and equipment, method of carrying bows and arrows, and animal species in San rock paintings. Initially she used histograms and tables as an aid to description, but later she realized that her statistics on species representation in the rock paintings could be used to explore the artist's selectivity. Such bias in depiction of subjects is evident in all figurative rock art bodies: European

Palaeolithic art emphasizes animals, especially horse and bison; southern San animal paintings emphasize eland; Australian stencil art assemblages emphasize the weapons of men, and so on.

Vinnicombe's study thus showed that the transition from simple subject analyses of rock art to structural analyses, in which selectivity is demonstrated and explained, is easily made. The next chapter looks at structural analyses, which can be applied to non-figurative, as well as figurative, rock art.

CHAPTER 7

Structural analyses

In her classic study of South African rock art, Patricia Vinnicombe was puzzled why animal species depicted in Bushman rock paintings did not appear in the same relative proportions as they did in the environment or in the diet of the artists. Suddenly it came to her that

> the Bushmen did not paint simply what they saw but selected what was symbolically important to them. Following this came the realisation that the numerical analysis of the paintings could be regarded not merely as a random assemblage of data, but as an ideological structure which reflected a set of values

This is a prime example of a structural analysis. It is always possible to demonstrate selectivity on the part of rock artists—in their use of motifs, techniques and subjects, choice of rock art sites and placement of motifs within sites and in relation to each other. Such selectivity, or structural patterning, tells us much about how a given rock art system operated.

Subject analyses of rock art, discussed in Chapter 6, rely on pictorial content, and thus apply only to figurative art. In contrast, structural analyses apply to both figurative and non-figurative assemblages; in fact, they are widely used on many types of archaeological evidence (such as stone artefacts, food remains). Structural analyses aim to identify spatial, temporal or compositional patterning in the evidence: the patterning can then be explained in terms of economy, ideology, function, discard patterns, site formation processes, and so on. For instance, in the analysis of animal bone at an occupation site, structural patterning could be identified by comparing the relative proportions of animals represented at the site with those found in the surrounding environment. Any quantitative differences between species representation in the cultural and natural assemblages can then be interpreted in terms of human dietary preferences, capture technologies, site formation processes, and so on. If the observed differences are greater than would occur if random, non-selective processes were operating, they are regarded as resulting from human selectivity. In this way the theoretical and methodological perspective used in structural rock art analyses can be seen as part of a general approach used in the analysis of archaeological evidence.

The method can be applied at many levels; it can focus on patterns in space, time, artistic composition, or all of these. However, research is undertaken to solve particular problems, and the analytical level, specific variables and quantitative methods chosen will depend on the problem being addressed.

In the archaeological study of art, we are primarily concerned with identifying structural patterns as a basis for reconstructing the artist's behaviour and other determining factors. These are not inherent in any particular rock art motif or object but are encapsulated in the associative relationships—for instance, between different motifs in rock art panels, in the relative placement of different rock art motifs in sites, and in the location of art sites in their cultural and natural environments. An emphasis on interrelationships and context is, therefore, basic to structural analyses.

The aim of this chapter is to show how structural patterns in rock art assemblages have been demonstrated and explained. As few structural analyses of rock art have yet been undertaken, we will use examples from Africa, America and Europe to demonstrate the potential of the general approach. Australian case studies will then be examined in detail.

Patterns in time

People have been decorating rock surfaces for about 40 000 years. This is just 1.6 per cent of the 2.5-million-year period during which ancestral humans have possessed the cognitive, manipulative and logistic skills to anticipate the need for, and manufacture, stone artefacts. The evidence suggests that rock art, personal adornment, portable art objects and music first appeared at about the same time in Europe, America, India, South Africa and Australia, and contemporaneously with the appearance of modern human populations in these regions. This broadscale chronological pattern—specifically, the relatively recent appearance of art—demands explanation. Two principal explanations have been offered: changes in the cultural sphere and developments in human cognitive capacity.

Proponents of cultural explanations for the appearance of art note that earlier hominids already had the cognitive and manipulative capacity to create, understand and manipulate symbols, as shown by the care taken in the manufacture of hand-axes from 1.5 million years ago in Africa. This is confirmed by the occasional non-functional item found in the archaeological record, such as pieces of red ochre at the French site of Terra Amata, dated to about 230 000 BP, and a polished and pigmented plaque of mammoth tooth from the Hungarian site of Tata, dated to between 116 000 and 78 000 BP. If these are taken at face value, then the sudden appearance of rock art, portable art and personal adornment around 40 000 BP might be best explained in terms of increased social and economic complexity requiring new systems of information exchange, rather than by a sudden increase in human mental capacity.

However, Whitney Davis argues that these early examples of symbol use need not have involved one thing being used to represent another, and that art only developed when it was realized that marks could represent other things. The first indisputable evidence for this 'threshold discovery' is the appearance of image making, or iconicity, in the archaeological record around 40 000 years ago. Similarly, Iain Davidson and Bill Noble take the position that the human capacity to produce the occasional non-utilitarian object much earlier than this does not necessarily imply the capacity to use shared symbolic systems, which require conventions for interpretation and hence a 'reflective, propositional language' (as opposed to vocal communication). They conclude that the cognitive skills required for complex communication systems, such as language and art, only developed relatively recently.

At a more regional level of interest, rock art sequences, as defined by changes over time in motifs, techniques, colours, cultural context and geographical distribution, are often used as descriptive and classificatory devices for the chronological ordering of art panels and sites. However, rock art sequences involve much more than this. They are also a kind of structured database, showing how the artists' selectivity has changed over time. These changes can in turn provide evidence for changes in the artists' natural and cultural context, but few rock art studies have attempted to exploit this potential. For instance, in the central Queensland highlands, three rock art phases have been identified, but only the most general trends in the sequence have been explained in terms of the closure of social networks in response to population increase and more defined territories (see Chapter 8).

PATTERNS IN TIME: AN EXAMPLE FROM THE SYDNEY REGION
In her study of Sydney Basin rock art, Josephine McDonald used 189 instances of superimposed images at 65 rockshelter art sites in the Mangrove Creek catchment. She defined a three-part art sequence comprising:

Art Phase 1: pecked tracks and circles

Art Phase 2: red paintings; white and red hand stencils

Art Phase 3: a proliferation of techniques and colour usage including dry black, dry red and dry white; wet red outline; wet white infill and outline; dry bichromes, polychromes; stencils of various colours; incised; European contact subjects in white stencils and red, and white outlines and infill drawings.

This relative sequence was then used to examine changes in motif preference over time (Figure 7.1): tracks and circles predominate in the Phase 1 engravings, while there is a proliferation of subjects, as well as techniques, in Phase 3, particularly in the range of figurative motifs, such as macropods, snakes, men and women. The number of rockshelters being used as art sites also increased greatly in Phase 3.

There is a range of absolute dating evidence available for this sequence, including the presence of European contact subjects in Phase 3, plus excavated finds from a number of shelters. For Phase 1, pecked circles at Yengo 1 date to around 6000 BP, while the position of engraved emu tracks at Emu Tracks 2 indicate that they were contemporaneous with the earliest use of the shelter, before 4000 BP. For the two most recent rock art phases there is evidence from an excavation at Dingo and Horned Anthropomorph Rockshelter— a date of 581 BP was obtained from just beneath a piece of used

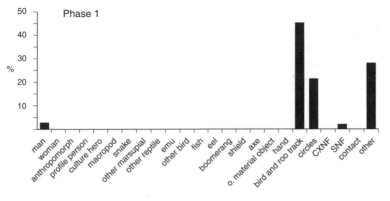

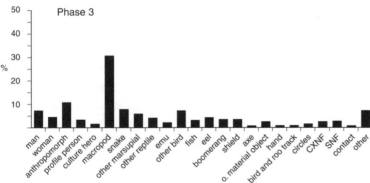

FIGURE 7.1

Changes in motif preference over time at rock art sites along Mangrove Creek, Sydney region. Phase 1 is characterized by an emphasis on tracks and circles and could be considered a regional variant of the widespread Panaramitee engraving tradition. It is older than 4000 years BP. In contrast Phase 3, spanning the last 1600 years, is dominated by a range of figurative motifs, especially macropods and 'humans', and is regionally distinctive. Phase 3 coincided with a major increase in population. (After McDonald 1994, Figure 7.2)

red ochre of the same colour as paintings of the dingo and horned anthropomorphs, which McDonald classifies as late Phase 3. In addition, on the basis of her excavated evidence, McDonald correlates the main phase of Aboriginal occupation at Upside Down Man Shelter with the majority of the rock art at the site (Phase 3). This gives an absolute chronology and cultural context for the Mangrove Creek Art sequence, which she extrapolates to the whole Sydney region:

- *Sydney Art Phase 1:* >4000 years BP, Pre or Early Bondaian
- *Sydney Art Phase 2:* <4000 to >1600 years BP, Early Bondaian
- *Sydney Art Phase 3:* >1600 years BP to European contact, Middle to Late Bondaian.

Despite continued uncertainties about when exactly the art phases began and ended, this dated sequence allows us to assess some changes in the rock art over time in the context of other archaeological evidence. For instance, early low-intensity occupation of the region seems to be associated with a low-intensity art system (that is, Art Phase 1, interpreted as residual Panaramitee engraving tradition), while the main phase of art production (Art Phase 3) coincided with the most intensive period of shelter occupation. In addition, once changes in the art and the intensity and focus of Aboriginal land use are dated, these can be related to environmental changes, such as global warming since 15 000 BP, rises in sea level and the resulting appearance of new food and water resources.

Patterns in space

The spatial distribution of rock art reflects a range of natural and cultural factors which operated at many levels to determine where rock art was produced, whether it survived, and in what form. These determining factors include geological context, the nature of human land use and the function of the art.

ROCK ART AND GEOLOGY

Throughout the world the spatial distribution of rock art is determined by the distribution of rock outcrops suitable for painting or engraving. Many regions of Australia with extensive areas of suitable rock have high concentrations of rock art. Circumstances also have to be right for the preservation of rock art. Thus it is particularly prolific in those regions where decorated rock surfaces are hard and relatively inert chemically, such as Arnhem Land, the Kimberley and parts of Central Australia—all regions where rock art of very different ages has been preserved and is still visible.

SPATIAL DISTRIBUTION OF ROCK ART STYLES

Rock art styles may be localized or widespread, depending on the social and environmental context, and it is of particular significance that many rock art sequences throughout the world seem to have involved a reduction in the extent of style zones over time. The general Australian rock art sequence is marked by the same trend, with a widespread rock art tradition, the Panaramitee style, present over much of the continent prior to 5000 BP, and the subsequent appearance of regional rock art styles of more limited geographical extent.

Some researchers have argued that such changes in the geographical extent of style zones reflect changing demographic and social circumstances. They assert that widespread artistic homogeneity is associated with the open social networks characteristic of low-density populations in high-risk environments, while increased artistic heterogeneity and regionalization are associated with the emergence of higher population densities and more closed social networks (see Chapter 4).

Clive Gamble's seminal study on the distribution of Venus figurines in the European Upper Palaeolithic uses this principle. Venus figurines are a well-described class of art object found in settlement occupation debris from the Atlantic west into European Russia (Figure 7.2), and most share stylistic features in the way the breasts, abdomen and pelvic region are grouped, and the absence of feet and faces. Gamble notes that well-dated examples seem to fall between 29 000 and 23 000 years BP—a period when conditions were becoming colder, with an accompanying decrease in animal resources and increase in the area over which herd animals had to range. He argues that in such a deteriorating environment, low-density and mobile human populations may have required standardized, visual systems of information exchange to help maintain the extensive alliance systems required for social, economic and biological viability. Venus figurines, he says, indicate the development of such systems.

In a similar way, climatic changes and their implications for developments in Australian social and economic systems are invoked by Darrell Lewis to explain aspects of the rock art record in Arnhem Land. He notes that 18 000 years ago, when conditions were coldest and driest in the last glacial period, the vegetation in the region would have been similar to that now present in the semi-arid country 400 to 600 kilometres to the south. On this basis, the sociolinguistic territories of Arnhem Landers at the time are likely to have been comparable in size to those observed in this semi-arid country (15 300 square kilometres in the case of the Tjingili of southern Arnhem Land, compared with 6000 square kilometres for the Kakadu clan territory in Arnhem Land).

This estimated size of larger sociolinguistic territories tallies quite closely with the area of distribution for 'early' style Boomerang

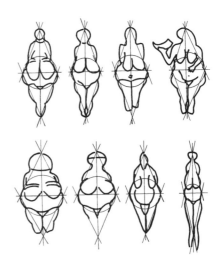

FIGURE 7.2

Venus figurines have been found in France, southern Germany, Italy and European Russia, but not in Spain. They date between 23 000 and 29 000 years BP. The widespread distribution of such stylistically distinctive items at a time when glacial conditions were particularly severe may indicate the development of more open social networks. These examples are from (top) Lespugue, Kostienki V, Dolni Vestonige and Laussel; (bottom) Willendorf, Gargarino and Grimaldi. (After Leroi-Gourhan 1968 (1976), p. 92)

figures around the Arnhem Land plateau. In addition, Lewis has suggested that the striking similarities between Arnhem Land boomerang figures and the classic Bradshaw figures of the Kimberley region 600 kilometres to the southwest may reflect the former existence of an extended information network of the type documented historically in the harsh and unpredictable conditions of arid Australia. Later rock art styles tend to be more regional and differentiated, indicating a reduction in the extent of alliance networks and greater emphasis on territorial demarcation. These characteristics of the rock art sequence in northwest Australia strongly indicate that the earliest art styles predate 10 000 BP, but archaeological excavations are needed to confirm this.

In fact, Aboriginal rock art sequences in many regions of Australia show the same change from an early widespread art tradition to rock art styles that are far more regional in character. The Panaramitee rock engraving tradition, for instance, appears to have been pan-Australian in distribution. What is particularly significant, however, is that the emergence of regionally distinctive art systems in the mid-to-late Holocene coincides with evidence for an abrupt increase in number of sites (that is, number of people); the initial appearance of labour-intensive economic strategies, such as seed grinding and the use of cycads; and the spread of a suite of new stone artefact types and technologies. Regions where this correlation is evident include the central Queensland highlands, southeast Cape York Peninsula, the north Queensland highlands and the Kimberley.

A number of studies have also shown that recent Aboriginal symbolic systems, including art and language, are homogeneous (uniform) and widespread in resource-poor, risky areas with low population densities, where they functioned to link scattered groups. In contrast, in fertile areas with high population densities, symbolic systems are heterogeneous (diverse) and localized. Such inter-group differences help maintain territorial boundaries and serve as a means of restricting access to resources.

To test this observed correlation, Claire Smith undertook a comparative study of 438 bark paintings from Arnhem Land and 309 acrylic paintings from the Western Desert. She found that the art of the Arnhem Land region was considerably more heterogeneous and that many of its features had very abrupt boundaries (see Figures 4.19 and 4.20). For instance, 79 per cent of Arnhem Land paintings with a plain bark background were done by people of the

Maung language group. In contrast, Western Desert artistic traits had clinal or relatively uniform distributions. For instance, the use of alternating bands of dots and solid colour is found in the art of nine of the ten Western Desert language groups.

Because Arnhem Land rock art uses more motif types than that of the Western Desert, the former was also found to have 1010 times the latter's potential for diversity as expressed by possible motif combinations. Furthermore, in Arnhem Land paintings are generally done by individuals, while Western Desert paintings are more often a cooperative effort involving a number of artists from different linguistic groups. These differences have to be seen in the light of the symbolic emphasis on closed social networks and exclusive rights to country of Arnhem Land versus the open networks and integrative mythologies of the Western Desert. In the latter case, maintaining long-distance alliances with other groups is essential for survival during times of hardship.

The function of Australian Aboriginal art (and other symbolic activities) is related to demographic and social context, and this is physically expressed in the extent of art areas and the nature of boundaries. I suspect that this is a general governing principle for all art systems. If so, then the correlation could be used in the archaeological investigation of art elsewhere in the world.

SPATIAL DISTRIBUTION OF ROCK ART SITES

Other studies of rock art have looked at the way in which patterns in the distribution of sites in relation to their natural and cultural context reflect function. As American rock art buff Polly Schaafsma notes in her assessment of the method: 'It is a basic assumption that rock art will be located in a patterned way in relationship to both the landscape and other cultural remains, as it is integrated with a variety of specific activities that are in themselves presumed to be non-random.'

For instance, engraving sites in the western United States have been found to be associated with good hunting areas such as game trails. That is, there was a quantifiable bias in the distribution of art sites in the natural environment. In addition, the cultural context of the engraving sites supported their association with hunting, in that they tended to be found with blinds, drift fences, and so on. Presumably, then, the making of rock engravings was once an aspect of the hunting ritual of local peoples. Some more specialized examples of American art site locational studies have shown that in certain cases rock art is positioned to act as an astronomical sighting device or to function as a calendar. For instance, three engraved spirals on La Fajada Butte, Chaco Canyon, New Mexico, are bisected by a ray of light at the summer solstice and the equinoxes.

In some regions, it is also clear that the distribution of rock art sites is discontinuous, and that the pattern apparent in the positioning of sites in relation to other sites, or site clusters, has social or territorial implications. For instance, in southwest France and northern Spain, extensively decorated caves tend to be surrounded by areas with few or no painted caves. Michael Jochim interpreted discontinuous distributions in Upper Palaeolithic rock art sites in terms of the distribution of communication networks. Assuming that clusters of decorated caves were network focuses, he used the recorded distribution of Late Solutrean and Early Magdalenian decorated caves to reconstruct the extent of individual networks by overlaying a grid of polygons. On this basis, network areas varied between 15 000 and 25 000 square kilometres. Similar discontinuous rock art distributions occur in the Drakensberg region of South Africa. In these cases the clustered distributions of rock art sites may reflect the former arrangement of group territories. On a more general level, Iain Davidson concluded that European Upper Palaeolithic art was restricted in geographical distribution to areas 'with low population densities, little pressure on resources, and no autochthonous intensification and specialisation', and that it was mostly absent from the eastern Mediterranean, where economic innovation occurred. Artistic continuity and economic conservatism in Europe between 32 000 and 10 000 years ago may therefore reflect strong social and economic control reinforced through a variety of mechanisms, including rock art rituals.

Rock art sites in Australia also tend to occur in clusters that are highly correlated with other types of archaeological sites, such as stone artefact scatters. In fact, site complexes are a much more useful unit for research and management purposes than individual sites. In arid and semi-arid areas, site complexes are located near water sources, such as rock holes, but the same pattern of clustered sites also occurs in tropical and temperate areas. What is particularly interesting, but not surprising, is that the distribution of symbolic sites comprising natural features, which have not been modified by humans, corresponds closely with that of archaeological sites.

In Central Australia, Ben Gunn mapped the distribution of six Arrernte site complexes with the assistance of Aboriginal elders. The complexes included 93 rock art sites, shelters without art, stone mounds, open occupation sites, stone arrangements and a stone quarry, while named but unmodified symbolic sites comprised boulders, rock holes, hillsides, ridges, trees, alluvial flats, depressions, pathways and rock faces. Few archaeological or symbolic sites occurred in the areas between site complexes. Within each site complex the general pattern was that rock painting and engraving sites occurred around a waterhole, with the main open campsite on the adjacent flat. With a few exceptions, all symbolic sites were located within the perimeter of the archaeological site complex (Figure 7.3): water was crucial for survival in the region, and this is clearly reflected in the distribution of both domestic and symbolic sites. One implication is that in areas of Australia where there is little evidence, concentrations of rock art sites should indicate locales that were economically and ideologically important.

DISTRIBUTION BETWEEN SITES

The range and number of rock art motifs, techniques and colours may vary significantly between sites depending on the way the art system works to reinforce group identity, ideology and territoriality; the anticipated audience; the specific significance of sites; their natural environmental contexts; differences between sites in their rock surfaces and degree of exposure; differences in age; and so on.

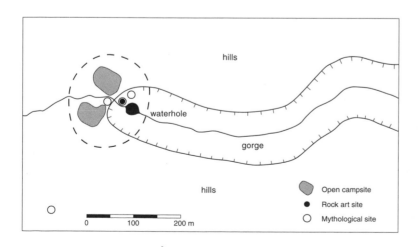

FIGURE 7.3

A Central Australian site complex. Note the high correlation between the location of water, open campsites, rock art and sites of mythological significance. (From Gunn 1997, Figure 2b)

In the case of European Palaeolithic rock art sites, for instance, Paul Bahn has argued that the amount and diversity of art evidence from Isturitz and Mas d'Azil suggested that these were 'super sites' central to occupation of the western and central Pyrenees respectively. Following this, Iain Davidson proposed that Spanish 'super sites', such as Altamira, Isuritz, Parpalló and Labastide, served as focuses for separate interaction networks, each controlled by a social hierarchy.

Although Meg Conkey's identification of past hunter–gatherer congregation sites was based on portable art objects, her regional scale of analysis and methodology are very relevant to the analysis of rock art. Conkey noted that most recent hunter–gatherers periodically came together in large groups not only to exploit resource abundances, but also for a variety of social and ritual purposes. She argues that this cycle of group fission and fusion is likely to have been a component of Upper Palaeolithic society in Europe, and the range of dietary and artefactual evidence from sites like Altamira and Castillo in Spain strongly suggests that these were Magdalenian aggregation sites. To test this idea, Conkey defined attribute categories, then analyzed the relative diversity in designs and structural principles on incised bone and antler pieces from five Magdalenian sites; Altamira, El Juyo, El Cierro, Cueto de la Mina and La Paloma. She predicted that if Altamira was an aggregation site, then art objects from it would show greater stylistic diversity than those from the other sites; most design elements of the core Magdalenian engraving repertoire would be present; and some design elements and structural principles would be unique to Altamira. In general these expectations were met.

Information on Australian Aboriginal art shows that factors determining the choice of motifs are often complex and dependant on circumstances. It is also worth remembering that the production of art was usually not a mechanical process with hard and fast rules, but often served political and social goals. The choice of motifs could depend on who was present, their social relationships and negotiation between those participating. However, one general principle is that Australian art produced in restricted contexts tends to be of geometric designs and tracks, whereas public art has a higher proportion of figurative motifs—meaning that two contemporaneous rock art sites in the same group territory, perhaps even done by the same artist, may differ greatly in the range of motifs portrayed. This is the case in Central Australia (see Chapter 4). On the other hand, if restricted art is mainly produced on media other than rock surfaces, then contemporaneous rock art sites in a region may be generally similar in the character of motifs used. This is the case with recent rock painting sites in the Kimberley, where the standardized format depicted Wandjina creative beings and their associated plants and animals. The quality, size and number of these paintings reflected the mythological significance of the site.

Specific rock art motifs in a region can be clustered, linear or dispersed in their pattern of distribution between sites, while the boundaries between areas where the motifs are present or absent may be gradual or abrupt. The various dispersal patterns can reflect factors, such as the function of the art, the membership of the groups producing and viewing it, or the distribution of suitable rock outcrops. For instance, June Ross' study of rock art in the Mt Isa region of northwest Queensland shows that the distribution of distinctive anthropomorph paintings corresponds to the territory of a particular tribal/language group, the Kalkadoons (see below), and the boundaries around this area are abrupt. Other elements of Kalkadoon rock art are much more widespread and the boundaries are clinal. Similarly, but on a larger scale, Wandjina rock paintings in the Kimberley correspond in distribution to the *wunan* exchange system (see Chapter 4), but some characteristics of Wandjina paintings, such as the use of a prepared white surface, and other types of painted figures found associated with Wandjinas, occur much further afield in the Baines and Victoria River districts to the east.

There are various means for examining differences between rock art sites. For instance, Bruno David assessed differences in motif, colour and technique preferences among rock art sites in southeast Cape York Peninsula, the Gulf country and the Mt Isa region of Queensland. He quantified the differences between sites for each of these attributes by calculating the root mean square of percentage differences: if one site had 20 per cent figurative, 50 per cent tracks and 30 per cent non-figurative motifs, and another site 40 per cent figurative and 55 per cent tracks and 5 per cent non-figurative motifs, then the measure of dissimilarity (distance) between the sites in motifs preference is $\sqrt{[(20 - 40)^2 + (50 - 55^2) + (30 - 5)^2]}$. The structure present in the calculated dissimilarity indices between 23 painting sites was then investigated using two multivariate techniques, multidimensional scaling and cluster analysis. In the case of motif preferences, David concludes that painting sites north of the Mitchell River are predominantly figurative, while those to the south are predominantly non-figurative motifs and tracks. This specific north–south difference is explicit in the raw data used in his analysis (that is, the percentage tables of motif types), but not in the dissimilarity indices or results of multivariate analysis, which confirm that northern and southern sites are different but do not indicate how they differ. Thirty years ago, Lesley Maynard undertook a very similar motif-preference comparison between three engraving sites of different age in western New South Wales. The findings were presented in an easily understood and informative way using bar graphs (Figure 2.26). There is a certain sophistication in such simplicity.

SPATIAL DISTRIBUTION WITHIN SITES

The first explicit structural analysis of rock art was undertaken by the doyen of French rock art research, André Leroi-Gourhan, in the 1960s. He and his colleague Annette Laming-Emperaire argued that the placement of animal depictions in French Upper Palaeolithic art sites such as Lascaux was not random. Leroi-Gourhan studied the layout of 60 sites and showed that the distribution of animal depictions and signs between entrance, periphery, main chamber, passageway and back areas was highly structured (Figure 7.4). Assuming a standard cave layout, he found that:

FIGURE 7.4

André Leroi-Gourhan's 'blue-print' for the distribution of animal species depicted in an idealized Upper Palaeolithic rock art site in Europe. Certain animal species tend to occur in particular sections of the cave. Horses and bovids, for instance, cluster in the central sections, whereas 'dangerous' animals, such as rhinos and lions, are usually at the rear. Leroi-Gourhan interpreted this spatial patterning in terms of religious beliefs. (After Leroi-Gourhan 1968 (1976))

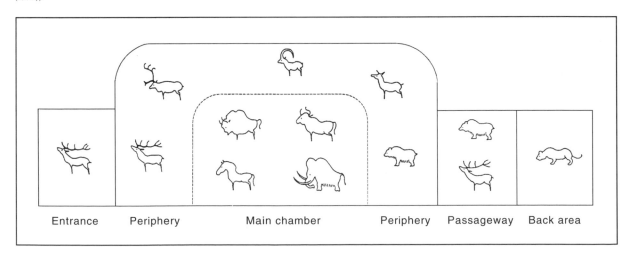

| Entrance | Periphery | Main chamber | Periphery | Passageway | Back area |

Topographical study discloses a clear division of the animals into three groups. The first comprises the large herbivores—bison, ox, mammoth, horse; the second, the small herbivores—stag and ibex; the third, the most dangerous animals—lion, bear, and rhinoceros, all of which occur by themselves in the rear portions of caves.

This pattern was interpreted in terms of religious beliefs, which included two fundamental groups of animals. This dualistic system was said to represent complementary components in a single symbolic scheme based on the division between the sexes, with Group A representing the male and Group B the female. The model was extended to include the signs found in the art, which were seen as derived either from the female figure (ovals, triangles, rectangles, lattice shapes, tectiforms, claviforms, brace shapes) or from the male sex organs (strokes, rows of dots, barbs).

Other researchers may disagree with these specific interpretations, and in later work Leroi-Gourhan became more cautious, although the Horse–Bovid pairing in the central portions of most rock art panels was still explained in terms of an oppositional–complementary principle. Even so, his work and that of Laming-Emperaire at Lascaux have clearly demonstrated that there was bias/selectivity/order in the way Palaeolithic artists placed motifs within sites. Despite the practical difficulties of distinguishing non-arbitrary, topographic sections and rock art associations in caves, as well as doubts about the quantitative analyses employed, these studies showed the research potential of considering rock art in context rather than in isolation.

González Garcia similarly demonstrated selectivity in the intra-site organization of European Palaeolithic rock art, but he avoided the problem of arbitrarily defining entrance, central and rear sections of caves by comparing art on rock surfaces of different shape. Garcia defined four types of rock art surface—concave, convex, flat and miscellaneous—then examined the distribution of art in four caves in the Monte del Castillo region of Spain. He found that most horses (89 per cent), hinds (93 per cent), ibex (88 per cent), deer (100 per cent) and hand stencils (100 per cent) occurred on concave surfaces, while most bison (79 per cent) and bovines (83 per cent) occurred on convex surfaces.

In Australia also there are many sites where distribution of motifs within sites is clearly not random. In some cases the selectivity

FIGURE 7.5

Specific colours and techniques tend to cluster within rock art sites because of a concern for colour contrast and the suitability of different rock art surfaces for different techniques. For instance, white paintings and stencils generally occur on darker rock surfaces, while red pigments are used for art on pale surfaces, as in the case of this stencil in the Carnarvon Range, Central Queensland highlands.

(Photo M. J. Morwood)

relates to the suitability of the rock surface for particular art techniques or colours. The distribution of different rock art techniques at major sites, like the Art Gallery in Carnarvon Gorge, illustrates this principle well: stencils and paintings mainly occur on smoother sections of the shelter wall, while engravings are concentrated on rougher areas (Figure 7.5). But there were clearly other factors at work in the same region, for example, ideology: stencilled hand signs tend to be located in parts of the site where they are visible from some distance, while discrete panels of rock art are often positioned around tunnels, shelves and crevices in which burial cylinders, animal bone or plant material have been placed (see Chapter 8). This aspect of rock art, however, has not yet been quantitatively investigated in Australia.

SPATIAL DISTRIBUTION WITHIN PANELS

Structural patterning of rock art motifs may also occur within single panels of art, as in the case of the famed 'Black Frieze' at the French Upper Palaeolithic site of Peche Merle. Here, using detailed analysis of style, technique and sequence of production (as revealed by superimpositions) Michel Lorblanchet demonstrated that all the paintings had been made by the same artist, and that there was a definite pattern to the sequence and placement of the various subjects: the artist began in the centre of the panel with a large painting of

FIGURE 7.6

The Black Frieze at the French Upper Palaeolithic site of Peche Merle. A detailed study by Michel Lorblanchet indicates that the panel was made by a single artist, who began in the centre of the panel then added other subjects in spiral fashion. Again this structural patterning is evidence for the associated belief system.

a horse, then progressively added, in spiral fashion, a few bison, a ring of mammoth, and finally four auroch (Figure 7.6).

Similarly, Alexander Marshack analysed the structure within panels of European Palaeolithic rock art and on art objects by using microscopic and ultraviolet-light techniques. He showed that steps in the production of art panels were often discontinuous, indicating use and re-use of the art in a way that reflects function. He argued that in cases where incised line series were made by different tools, at different angles and under different pressures, the composition accumulated sequentially, and was therefore 'time-factored' and probably notational—that is, the designs were added to a number of times and were a method of record keeping.

Marshack's argument that the engravings are structured in terms of placement and sequence of manufacture is convincing. However, he also tries to demonstrate that the markings are a lunar count which 'would be the simplest possibility for an early system of time reckoning'. His method is based on a comparison between phases of the moon (Figure 7.7) and subsets of engraved marks which are 'tested' in various combinations and orderings until a degree of correspondence is achieved. The problem with the method is that any series of numbers can be matched against a lunar model, if sufficient time and ingenuity are used in combining and ordering them.

The work of Sauvet and Sauvet on the distribution of motifs within panels of European Palaeolithic art is another good case study because they used simple quantitative techniques to

FIGURE 7.7

Using a high-powered microscope, Alexander Marshack showed that marks made on a bone plaque from the Upper Palaeolithic levels of Abri Blanchard in France had been made with a number of tools, in a serpentine shaped sequence, and probably over a period of time. He attempted to relate groups of marks with the same tool to phases of the lunar cycle. While most researchers would now question Marshack's astronomic interpretation, he has shown that the placement of marks on the plaque has meaningful structure.
(After Marshack 1972, Figure 10)

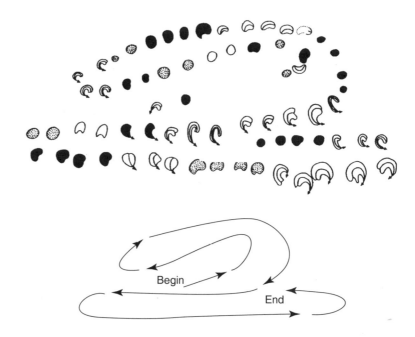

demonstrate non-random patterns of association. They then interpreted structural regularities in the art in terms of the 'grammar and syntax' by which information was encoded and communicated by the artists. The researchers calculated an index of association between animal species in the art by considering the number of species depicted on each panel. The mean number of species per panel was low (1.81), but different species exhibited statistically significant differences in the degree to which they shared panels with other species. What is significant is that exactly the same approach was used on twelve identified classes of non-figurative signs at the sites, and again it demonstrated artistic selectivity—in particular, most signs (60 per cent) were associated with animal motifs, while the absence of certain combinations of signs reflected the rules governing the production of the art.

In Australia, non-random placement of rock art motifs within panels is also evident, but has not been systematically investigated. It is most clearly seen in the frequent superimposition of hand stencils over other paintings. Other examples include the repeated association between specific motifs, such as Yam style rainbow serpents and flying foxes in Arnhem Land. The same pattern of association between rainbow serpents and flying foxes occurs in the Dreamtime stories of the region.

SPATIAL ANALYSIS OF PIGMENTS: SOURCING

Researchers can also study the distribution of materials associated with rock art production. For instance, the distribution of excavated pigments within a site can help identify activity areas and provide evidence for the age of specific panels of rock art (see Chapter 5), while the distribution of pigments away from the areas in which they were originally obtained can tell us about the operation of past art systems, ideology and trade.

Pigments for rock painting could be widely available, in creek beds and extensive geological layers, but sometimes occurred in very localized quarry sources. In the latter case, people often preferred to use pigments from more distant sources associated with Dreamtime mythology, rather than those from more mundane sources close at hand. Red ochre from the famed Wilga Mia quarry in the Murchison area of Western Australia was said to be the blood of an Ancestral kangaroo, and it was traded widely throughout Western Australia and possibly much further afield. Similarly, red ochre from the Bookartoo quarry in the Flinders Ranges of South Australia was traded throughout the Lake Eyre Basin as far north as Boulia in Queensland and the Darling River in New South Wales.

If geochemical 'fingerprinting' of pigment from known sources is undertaken, it is possible to determine whether lumps of ochre recovered from excavations, or samples from particular paintings, are from specific sources. The geographical distribution of pigments from known sources can then be used to infer past trade routes, the value of specific types of pigment, and so on.

Mike Smith and Barry Fankhauser fingerprinted the chemical composition of red ochres from a number of pigment sources, including Wilga Mia, Bookartoo, Karrku, Ulpunyali and Lawa, using inductively coupled plasma spectroscopy with mass spectrometry to identify trace elements as well as a scanning electron microscope to determine the major and minor oxides. Their work showed that these pigment sources are distinctive enough to make sourcing of red ochres possible.

Smith and Fankhauser then analysed small samples of pigment recovered from an archaeological excavation at Puritjarra in Central

Australia. Most of the recovered pigments from levels dated to between 30 000 and 7500 years ago came from the Karrku quarry about 150 kilometres away across a dune field. This indicates that by 30 000 years ago, the region had a well-established population that moved over a large territory or was in contact with groups using Karrku. Use of Karrku ochre decreased after 7500 years ago at the same time as far more intensive use of ochre began: presumably territorial bounding of country occurred as the population increased.

In the North Kimberley, Annie Thomas analyzed white pigments from two sources using X-ray diffraction and a scanning electron microscope. She found one source to be huntite and the other kaolinite, then analysed thirteen samples of white pigment from Wandjina rock art sites. Her results indicated that high-quality huntite from the north Kimberley, which was said to be the excreta or spittle of the Rainbow Serpent, was extensively traded throughout the region, but there was also localized use of low-quality materials.

Pigment sources are distinctive; fragments of pigment are commonly found in archaeological excavation, and analysis may be undertaken on extremely small samples obtained from rock paintings. Sourcing of pigments therefore has great potential for monitoring past exchange systems and the way in which these changed over time.

SPATIAL DISTRIBUTION: AN EXAMPLE FROM NORTHWEST QUEENSLAND

Although spatial patterns in rock art can provide useful information at many different levels of analysis, in only a few cases has this potential been systematically used. One exception is the work of June Ross on Aboriginal rock art around Mt Isa in northwest Queensland, where there is a regional rock art style in the Argylla, Leichhardt and Selwyn Ranges, characterized by distinctive anthropomorphic motifs (Figure 7.8).

The fact that these anthropomorphs are clustered within Kalkadoon tribal territory means that they probably had an emblematic function concerned with communicating group identity and maintaining Kalkadoon boundaries, a role emphasized by repetition of these motifs at some sites. The motifs are also found just outside the Kalkadoon tribal area to the north and south, but only in areas where local Aboriginal groups were Kalkadoon 'mess-

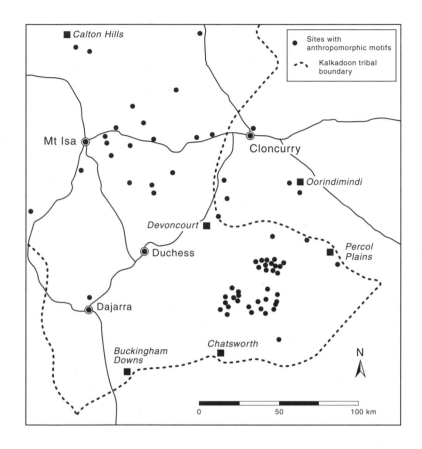

FIGURE 7.8

Distribution of distinctive anthropomorphic motifs in the rock art of northwest Queensland. These occur within the boundaries of the Kalkadoon tribe or their adjacent 'messmates'. The primary role of Kalkadoon figures appears to have been as territorial demarcations, restricting 'outsider' access to the highly valued stone axe quarries of the region. Other components of Kalkadoon rock art panels, such as concentric arcs, were much more widespread and may have functioned to emphasize social links between widespread groups.
(After Ross 1997, Figure 5.1)

mates', who had good social relations with the Kalkadoon, intermarried with them and met with them for ceremonies.

Furthermore, Ross was able to distinguish two types of Kalkadoon anthropomorphs: Basic and Detailed (Figure 7.18). Basic Anthropomorphs are small (<459 millimetres), monochrome and relatively standardized in form—they are depicted from a full frontal perspective, with arms out and down, body elongated and legs splayed. In addition, they rarely have feet, hands, facial features or head-dresses. In contrast, Detailed Anthropomorphs are larger and bichrome or polychrome, while the combination of decorative features, such as outline, head-dresses, underarm ovals, facial features, hands, feet and wing-like arms, make each figure unique.

The two types of Kalkadoon anthropomorph have very different distributions within the region: Basic motifs tend to occur within rockshelters and are not highly visible (Figure 7.9), whereas Detailed motifs tend to be located on waterholes with reliable water and are

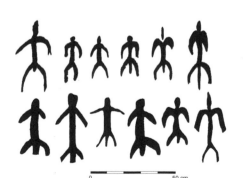

FIGURE 7.9

A range of Basic Kalkadoon anthropomorphs. These tend to be located discretely within rockshelters and were probably intended for local, Kalkadoon audiences as a way of reinforcing regional identity. (From Ross 1997, Figure 4.8)

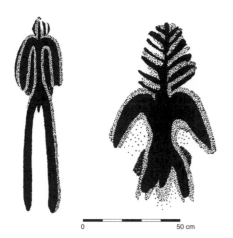

0   50 cm

FIGURE 7.10

Detailed Kalkadoon anthropomorphs were prominently positioned at water sources, where they could be seen by visitors to Kalkadoon territory. They appeared in the local rock art when extensive trading systems developed about 1000 years ago, and may have functioned to regulate access to the highly valued stone axe quarries of the area.

(From Ross 1997, Figures 4.9, 4.10)

highly visible (Figure 7.10). The implication is that the two variants of the Kalkadoon Anthropomorph served different social roles: Basic anthropomorphs were produced for local viewers as a way of reinforcing regional identity, while Detailed motifs were produced at locales likely to be used by large groups, including visitors and travellers. They thus seem to have functioned as prominent fixed emblems that marked Kalkadoon territory.

It is significant, though, that most motifs featuring in the rock art of the Mt Isa region were not localized in distribution, but also occur at sites hundreds of kilometres away. These motifs, such as lizards, concentric arcs, barred circles and tridents, may have served as a symbolic linking device between widespread groups—meaning that different parts of the same rock art system played different roles, some linking and some bounding.

Although there is not a lot of evidence for the time depth of the Kalkadoon regional art style, direct dating of one local anthropomorph and basal carbon-14 dates from an extensively decorated rock art site both indicate that the style is probably less than 1000 years old. Archaeological evidence also suggests that the extensive trading networks observed in historic times emerged at around this time. Stone axe heads from the Mt Isa region were highly valued in this trade. Increased social and economic interaction required stronger symbolic markers of local group identity, which also served to regulate access to the associated stone quarries. Looked at in this way, the distinctive Kalkadoon anthropomorphs served as a tool for making interactions between groups more predictable.

Ross' study of Mt Isa rock art thus shows not only how analysis can be undertaken at many but complementary levels, but also that information on the wider context is essential for assessing the 'meaning' of the art.

Compositional structure

SELECTIVITY IN SUBJECTS

In Vinnicombe's study of San rock paintings in the Drakensberg region of South Africa, quantitative bias in the depiction of animal species could be explained in terms of the ideological concerns evident in San ethnography. Analyses along similar lines have been undertaken elsewhere. For instance, Jésus Altuna compared the relative proportions of faunal species present in the rock art with those in the occupation deposits at three Magdalenian sites in Cantabria, Spain—Ekain, Tito Bustillo and Altxerri. He found notable discrepancies, such as the artistic emphasis on horses at Ekain and Tito Bustillo, where horses scarcely occur in the deposits, and the emphasis on bison and reindeer at Altxerri near the coast, where these species were not common in the natural environment (Figure 7.11). Altuna concluded that the factors responsible for species depiction in the art were very different from the economic behaviour responsible for bone deposition in middens, while the selectivity evident in human art and hunting means that neither will

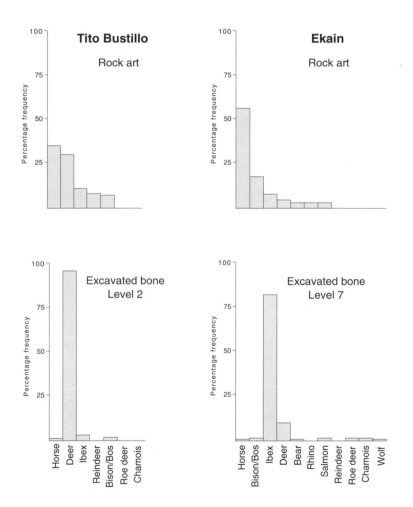

FIGURE 7.11

The relative proportions of animal species present in the rock art compared with the animal remains excavated from two Magdalenian sites—Tito Bustillo and Ekain—in Cantabria, Spain. In both cases, horses were the most commonly depicted subjects in the rock art, but they were not common in the artists' diet. The artists were mainly depicting animals which were symbolically, not just economically, important to them. (After Altuna 1983)

'mirror or reflect directly the spectrum of resources available in the environment'.

In these analyses the researchers demonstrated selectivity in the depiction of animals by comparing the relative numbers of species in the art with those in the diet or in the natural environment. Bob Layton also investigated 'selectivity' in the depiction of fauna in rock art by the structural method, but he chose to contrast species frequencies in three different rock art traditions—European Palaeolithic, southern San and Australian Aboriginal (Figure 7.12). In the first two traditions, rock art assemblages emphasized a limited number of species that were found in sites throughout the region (horses and bison in Europe, eland in South Africa), whereas Australian Aboriginal rock art of the Laura region depicts a wide range of species with approximately equal frequency.

Layton suggested that the Australian case reflects a segmentary cognitive system (that is, local totemism). He based his case on the well-documented rock art system of the Kimberley, where each land-owning clan had responsibility for maintaining certain food species by ceremonies, which included portrayal of the relevant species in painted rockshelters within the clan territory. The fact that all food species are so maintained results in a relatively equal depiction of all species overall, but each species only occurs at a limited number of locations.

Species representation in European Palaeolithic and South African rock art sites is quite different in character, and Layton suggests that this resulted from a different organizational and ideological structure (that is, non-totemic). He concludes by comparing other structural regularities found in rock art systems from different parts of the world—including the relative frequency of human depictions, emphasis upon narrative scenes, and whether rock art sites are clustered or not—to show that European Palaeolithic art represents a unique configuration of structural elements that are comparable in complexity to the art of modern hunter–gatherers.

SELECTIVITY IN MEDIA USE

In recent art traditions, different art media usually show different preferences in use of motifs. The same selectivity in motif use is apparent in the archaeological record. For instance, in European Upper Palaeolithic art, horses and bovids are the dominant figurative component on cave walls; the horse is the most common figure in

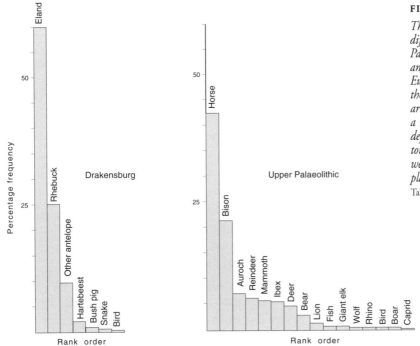

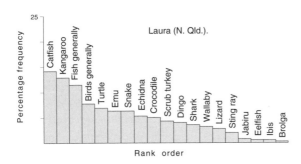

FIGURE 7.12

The frequency of animal species in three different rock art traditions—European Palaeolithic, southern San (South Africa) and Australian Aboriginal. In the case of Europe, horses and bovids are dominant in the rock art, while in South Africa the San artists targeted eland. In Australian rock art a wider range of animals was more evenly depicted. The Australian pattern reflects a totemic belief system, which involved the welfare and symbolic representation of all plant and animal species. (After Layton 1987, Table 11.1)

art on portable objects (except on harpoons and half-rounded rods); while bison predominate on plaques, are uncommon on pierced staffs and do not occur on spears.

As yet few analyses have been undertaken involving systematic documentation and interpretation of these significant differences, but Count Bégouën and Jean Clottes have examined differences in the range of motifs used on different media within a prehistoric art system. Their research involved excavation at the cave of Enlène, in the Ariège region of France, which contains hundreds of engraved plaques associated with a Magdalenian IV occupation but no rock art. However, Enlène is part of the same cave system as Trois-Frères, which does not have occupation deposits but contains Magdalenian IV rock paintings, engravings, stencils and clay figurines with stylistic similarities to the Enlène plaques. Furthermore, Trois-Frères has evidence for fairly intensive human use (such as amount of rock art, number of fires), in marked contrast to the nearby Magdalenian site of Tuc d'Audoubert, where the gallery containing clay models of bison has evidence (including footprints) for only fleeting visits. Bégouën and Clottes note that this situation presents considerable potential for the investigation of synchronous differences in motif use between different artistic media and contexts.

Studies of Australian Aboriginal art (see Chapter 2) have shown pronounced media-dependant differences in motif use. Some of these differences are due to physical constraints. For instance, linear designs predominate on baskets because they are more easily woven into the fabric. But they are also an important structural component of art function (such as the use of geometrically decorated boards by senior men in restricted contexts in the Kimberley, where rock paintings are predominantly public and figurative). Local Aboriginal populations could be subdivided on the basis of clan, resident group, moiety, section, matri-totemic group, initiation grade, sex, and so on. Symbolic markers denoting membership of these various groups involved a range of media, some for public display (such as shield motifs); others for use in restricted contexts (such as *churinga*). The nature and distributional structure of each symbolic subsystem were determined by the distribution, role and information requirements of their membership. Just as the membership of different groups often overlapped, so did their use of symbols. For instance, in Central Australia 'restricted' art, used and seen only by senior initiated men, emphasized the use of geometric and track motifs, whereas public art tended to be figurative. Despite this, there was considerable overlap (see Chapter 4).

In Aboriginal Australia, different but contemporaneous (rock) art techniques tend to emphasize different motifs. In the central Queensland highlands, for instance, motif preferences in stencilling, painting and engraving were very different. In fact, differences in motif use between contemporaneous rock art techniques were as great as those between rock art phases of different age (see Chapter 8). Similarly, in the Sydney Basin, the range of motifs found at open engraving sites is quite different from that used in rockshelters.

Choosing analytical techniques

The same basic principle was employed in all the structural analyses cited above, despite the fact that each analysis featured different variables and had very different implications. In all cases, the distribution of rock art variables was shown to differ from the pattern expected as a result of random processes. This artistic selectivity was then interpreted in terms of past human behaviour, social institutions or ideologies—the ultimate aim in any type of archaeological research.

The above examples also indicate that structural patterns in rock art can be identified using many different analytical techniques (such as pie charts, maps, histograms, cross-tabulations, chi-squared analyses, principal components analysis). Such analyses can also use one variable at a time (univariate analyses), or two (bivariate), or many (multivariate). It is fairly standard in regional rock art studies to begin with univariate analyses as a way to describe general characteristics of the art—for instance, the range of colours used, the techniques, the motifs, the contexts. These simple analyses will yield structural patterns that provide insights into factors determining the nature of the art—engravings rather than pigmented art usually predominates at open rock art sites, shelter sites tend to occur on hill slopes or at the base of escarpments rather than on ridge-tops, specific motifs may be clustered or linear or random in their distribution across the countryside, and so on. Some of the patterns identified are of trivial interest, while others provide information on the behaviour and beliefs of the artists.

Knowledge gained from univariate analyses can then be used to apply bivariate analyses. For instance, one can ask: Are there differences in colour use between different motifs? Are motif preferences in the different rock art techniques similar?, and so on. In turn, the results of these analyses can be used to design multivariate analyses to probe further the complexity of the rock art system and how it changed spatially or over time. These analytical steps are cumulative in impact, with each leading logically to a higher level of interpretation.

A major problem with many current rock art analyses is that they short-circuit this interactive process. Complex statistical calculations can now be done at the touch of a computer key, but it seems that multivariate techniques are often used more for effect than as a means for generating credible data, while some mathematical techniques that have been used in analyses of rock art seem totally inappropriate. For instance, if we accept that the identification and explanation of chronological and spatial patterns is the aim in any quantitative investigation of rock art, then we should avoid mathematical techniques that summarize, conflate and obscure structural patterning. Cluster analysis and correspondence analysis, for example, have often been applied to Australian rock art data in 'fishing expeditions' where the researchers have little understanding of how the techniques manipulate data or what mathematical assumptions they are based on.

This is not to say that multivariate analysis cannot be a useful tool for rock art research if it is thoughtfully and appropriately applied, but in most instances this has not been the case. In general, the simpler the analytical technique, the more effective it is. KISS (Keep It Simple Stupid) is a very useful, and frequently ignored, guiding principle.

CHAPTER 8

Central Queensland highlands

Known colloquially as the 'the mother of rivers' and 'roof of Queensland', the central Queensland highlands comprise an uplifted fault block of sandstones rising steeply from the surrounding blacksoil and sand plains about 500 kilometres northwest of Brisbane (Figures 8.1 and 8.2). They cover 82 000 square kilometres and feature 24 separate ranges radiating out from the Great Divide, including the Chesterton, Drummond, Expedition, Shotover, Bigge, Blackdown and Carnarvon Ranges. The highlands are also an important watershed: the Mitchell, Warrego, Ward, Langlo, Nive, Barcoo, Belyando, Nogoa and Comet Rivers all begin here.

This region has played a pivotal role in the history of Australian archaeology and rock art research, principally because it contains thousands of rock art sites, many of which have associated cultural deposits that can be excavated. Many decorated rockshelters also contained Aboriginal skeletal remains, often in elaborate bark coffins, which excited first amateur, then professional, interest.

Research in the central Queensland highlands shows the importance of a contextual approach to the study of rock art. In fact, previous ethnographic and archaeological research provided an essential platform for studying what Aboriginal rock art can tell us about the prehistory of the region.

FIGURE 8.1

General location of the central Queensland highlands, also known as 'The Mother of Rivers' and 'The Roof of Queensland'. It comprises an uplifted fault block of sandstones capped with basalt which arises abruptly from the plains of western Queensland.

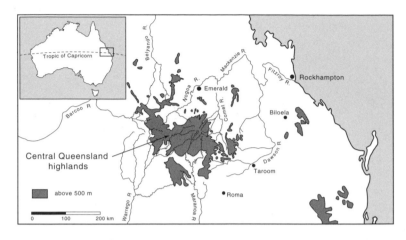

FIGURE 8.2

Carnarvon Gorge in the central Queensland highlands was a permanent water source and has many rockshelters at the base of the cliffs. The gorge contains a major concentration of rock art. (Photo M. J. Morwood)

Social context

Information on Aboriginal groups in the central Queensland highlands is not just a backdrop for the study of the local rock art, but in some instances provides means for relating archaeological evidence, including rock art, to the activities of people and their social institutions.

In 1844, when Ludwig Leichhardt became the first European to visit the region, it was occupied by Aboriginal tribes such as the Pitjara of the upper Warrego and Nogoa Rivers, the Wadgalang of the upper Barcoo, Bulloo and Langlo Rivers, and the Mandandji of the upper Maranoa (Figure 8.3). Each tribe of about 500 people was grouped into several patrilineal clans, which owned tracts of land,

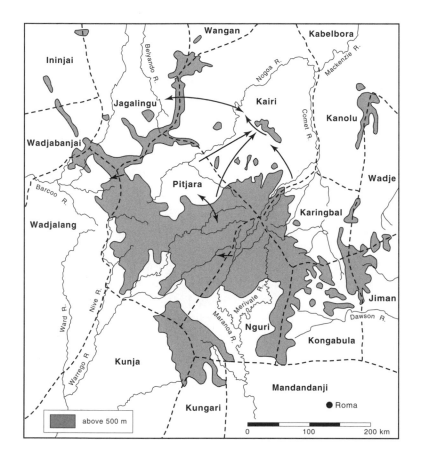

FIGURE 8.3

Distribution of Aboriginal tribes and local groups in the central Queensland highlands. People moved frequently between different river catchments to attend fights and ceremonies. Economic strategies for supporting large-scale gatherings, such as the leaching of cycads and grinding of grass seeds, only appeared in the region about 5000 years ago. (After Tindale 1974; Morwood 1984a, Figure 2)

lived in contiguous regions, spoke the same language, usually intermarried, and habitually met for economic and other reasons. For instance, the Kanaloo tribe of the Comet River headwaters included the Bemburraburra patri-clan of Lake Nuga Nuga and the Goon-garee of Carnarvon Gorge.

Localized groups over the entire region interacted regularly for fights, trade and ceremonies. Gatherings could be local or regional, as when people from the upper Comet, Warrego and Nogoa Rivers gathered once a year near Springsure.

Details are sparse, but it is known that people in the region had exogamous moieties called Yangaru and Wuturu and that affiliation to these was inherited from one's mother. All people and things, both animate and inanimate, were ascribed to one of the moieties. In turn, each matri-moiety was divided into two sections—meaning that everyone belonged to one of four sections that prescribed possible marriage partners. The Yangaru moiety contained the Kulgila and Bunbari sections, while the Wuturu had Wungo and Kupuru sections.

Subdividing the moieties were totemic groups. A person's totem was also inherited through the mother, and was commonly referred to as 'meat', symbolizing the sharing of a common life based on inheritance of one flesh and blood. Across the region, totems were consistent in their moiety affiliation. For instance, a Pitjara informant stated that 'nearly always cold skin went Wuturu and feather Yangaru'; the former totemic group included water, lizard, goanna and frog matri-totems and the latter included emu, duck, eaglehawk and native companion. People were prohibited from eating their totemic species, and matri-totemic clans also played a prominent role in initiation, marriage and mortuary ceremonies.

Matri-totemic clan affiliation was determined by one's mother, but the preferred residential pattern was patri-local—that is, on marriage, women customarily moved to live on the clan estates of their husbands. In combination, this meant that members of matri-totemic clans were not localized, but dispersed across the region.

Archaeological context

Professional archaeology in the region began with excavations by John Mulvaney at Kenniff Cave on the upper Comet River in 1960 and 1964 (Figure 8.4). These revealed a 19 000-year cultural sequence with two broad phases of stone artefact use. From 19 000 to 5000 years ago local people made use of unhafted flakes and core tools. A variety of new artefact types and technologies then appeared and many of these, such as backed blades, pirri points, adzes and axes, would have been hafted.

The same two-part technological sequence was identified at other sites in the region, such as the Tombs, Native Well 1 and Native Well 2. In fact, regional variants of the two-part sequence are found throughout mainland Australia. Australian stone artefact assemblages older than 5000 years are now generally assigned to the Australian Core Tool and Scraper tradition, whereas the later technologies, characterized by backed blades, points and adzes, are part of the Australian Small Tool tradition.

During 1974–76 John Beaton excavated Cathedral, Wanderers' and Rainbow Caves, in the Carnarvon Gorge area, to show that large-scale consumption of cycad nuts started around 5000 years ago. The

FIGURE 8.4

Above: *John Mulvaney at Kenniff Cave in 1964. His excavation showed that the region had been occupied before 19 000 BP and that major changes in stone artefact technology had occurred over that time.* (Photo D. J. Mulvaney)

Below: *Local people near Springsure, central Queensland highlands, in 1889. The palm-like cycad,* Macrozamia moorei, *has a bountiful supply of nuts, but they are extremely toxic and require complex processing if they are to be consumed. From 5000 BP cycad nuts were used intensively in the highlands to support large-scale ceremonial gatherings. This coincided with the first large-scale use of grass and acacia seeds, evidence for a major population increase, innovations in stone artefact technology and the development of a regionally distinctive rock art.* (Photo Billington and Company, courtesy P. Keegan)

nuts cannot be eaten without first removing their toxins by grinding and leaching. In historic times such labour-intensive economic activities were associated with large-scale ceremonial gatherings. Beaton suggested that the appearance of cycad use at this time marked the appearance of extensive social and ceremonial networks in the central Queensland highlands.

It is significant that the first Aboriginal use of cycads in the region coincided with the appearance of specialized seed grindstones in the archaeological record. Processing of acacia and grass seeds is another labour-intensive activity, which could support large numbers of people. These economic developments also occurred at the same time as a major increase in the number of occupied sites and in the intensity of their use (Figure 8.5). Both lines of evidence indicate rapid population growth. Similar patterns of technological, economic and demographic change occurred in many other parts of Australia over the past 5000 years.

The rock art

Central Queensland highland rock art is characterized by the predominance of stencilled hands, feet, implements and grid patterns; by simple, geometric painted designs such as grids and zigzags; and by a variety of simple engraved motifs, such as lines, tracks, grids and vulvas. This style of rock art extends throughout central Queensland, as far north as the river headwaters of the Gulf Country.

Local rock art sites were first discovered in the 1860s, when European pastoralists took up vast land holdings (Figure 8.6).

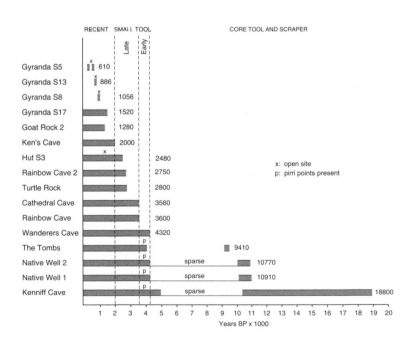

FIGURE 8.5

Dated sites in the central Queensland highlands. The figure shows initial occupation of the region by 19 000 years BP, with a rapid increase in population in the last 5000 years. This was also the time when people began to use resources more intensively, and changes in rock art indicate greater concern with exclusive ownership of territories.

FIGURE 8.6
The Buckland Tableland rock art site described by Thomas Worsnop in 1897. This was one of the earliest published reports on rock art in the central Queensland highlands and immediately established its regional character. (Photo M. J. Morwood)

Sporadic reports of the finds quickly established the character of rock art in the region, as in 1897 when Thomas Worsnop noted:

> In Central Queensland, on Buckland's Tableland is Nardoo Creek on the bank of which is a high cliff and, on its face is a magnificently executed picture, representing a sea of fire, out of which are stretched dusky-brown arms in hundreds in every conceivable position, the muscles knotted and the hands grasping convulsively, some pointing a weird finger upwards, others clenched as in agonies of death as though a host were engulfed in a seething lake of fire.

Depicted subjects clearly show that some of the rock art post-dates European contact in age, but early attempts to collect information on its significance were unsuccessful. Worsnop continued: 'The natives in the neighborhood have a horror of the place, and when questioned declare that they can give no information about it, saying that their white-headed blacks know nothing about it, nor even their fathers.'

The violence of the European contact period, which involved widespread massacres of local Aborigines, is the main reason for this lack of information. Whatever the reason, the fact remains that this art body is as 'dead' as the 20 000-year-old Upper Palaeolithic art of Europe.

Between 1909 and 1918, there was a surge of interest in rock art sites and visits to them increased, as indicated by dated graffiti.

W. G. Drane, a staff surveyor, was one visitor to the famed 'Blacks' Palace' on the upper Belyando River. He reports: 'The place is merely of historic value. It is admitted that no one even in the wildest flights of imagination could discern the slightest traces of art...I am forwarding per parcel post a painting of a hand, which may be of interest.'

Since that time, many popular accounts of central Queensland rock art have been published and several systematic site recording programs have been undertaken.

In 1976, I began an archaeological study in the region, involving extensive surveys, the recording of sites and four excavations. The aim was to see how rock art could add to our understanding of the region's cultural history. Fieldwork included the recording of 92 art sites, which comprised 84 rockshelters, six open engraving sites and two carved trees. A total of 17 025 motifs were counted—3975 stencils, 532 paintings, 10 634 abraded engravings, 1850 pecked engravings, 25 pebraded engravings, six drawings and three designs carved into trees.

As part of the recording process, site plans and cross-sections were drawn, the art was counted and photographed, and information on the natural and cultural contexts of the sites was collected. For each recorded motif, numeric or alphanumeric data on the site, section within the site, grid reference in relation to the surveyed plan, motif, technique, colour, side (for hands and feet), size and orientation, were put onto computer coding sheets and analyses undertaken using the Statistical Package for the Social Sciences on a Dec-10 computer: a total of 87 motif types, fifteen colours and eight techniques were distinguished.

Establishing a chronology

The first major step in the analyses was dating the regional rock art sequence with a number of relative and absolute dating techniques, including superimposition analysis, spatial analysis, differential weathering, depicted subjects and excavation of art evidence.

The superimposition analyses used data from Blacks' Palace 1, where 291 colour and 889 technique superimpositions were recorded (Figure 8.7). The idea was to first examine patterns of super-imposition on the basis of simple variables such as colour and

FIGURE 8.7

Superimpositions at Blacks' Palace, upper Belyando River, central Queensland highlands. The predominance of white stencils and paintings in the most recent rock art is seen at many sites in the region.
(Photo M. J. Morwood)

technique, then move on to look at composite variables, such as motif-technique combinations, after basic trends had been established.

The data was arranged in matrix form to show that superimposition frequencies vary greatly from what would be expected on the basis of random association. For instance, an avoidance of red/red associations and a preference for white/red ones are very clear. Similarly, there is only one case of a pecked motif occurring over another technique, but 92 cases in which other techniques covered or cut through peckings.

Some of the artists' selectivity in superimposing colour reflects their concern with contrast. They superimposed paintings and stencils so as to highlight rather than obscure their work. For instance, a number of composite paintings show that the rock art surface was first primed with red pigment before a white painting or stencil was applied (Figure 8.8). The durability of different colours and techniques may also have influenced the observed superimposition sequence. Red pigments adhere to rock surfaces better than white ones do, and engravings usually last longer than paintings. Even so, the superimpositions indicated that white pigment was used more often in recent paintings and stencils, and that pecked engravings were among the earliest surviving rock art in the region.

Because of the range of factors determining superimposition trends in central Queensland rock art, it was essential to obtain

213 :

FIGURE 8.8

A white grid over red primer at Blacks' Palace. In this case the rock artist has deliberately superimposed colours to increase contrast and impact. This has to be taken into account when interpreting trends in colour superimpositions: the fact that there are many more examples of white rock paintings over red does not necessarily mean that use of white increased late in the rock art sequence. (Photo M. J. Morwood)

comparative data from other relative age dating techniques. I therefore used principal components analysis (PCA) to see what colours and techniques tended to occur together at the 92 recorded sites. The basis of this relative dating method is that colours and techniques which tend to occur together in sites are probably contemporaneous: this is certainly the case when colours are superimposed for ideological reasons, or because of a concern for colour contrast.

PCA showed that red, orange, purple and brown tend to occur together, as do white and pink, but these two colour suites differ significantly in their distribution between sites. When they do occur, one of the two tends to dominate. Similarly, the way pecked engravings are distributed between sites is unrelated to the distribution of all other rock art techniques.

Both relative dating techniques therefore indicated that 'pecked engravings' and 'white paintings and stencils' were of different age than all the other techniques and colours respectively. Superimposition analyses also demonstrated the direction of the changes (that is, from early pecked engravings to a range of other techniques, and from emphasis on use of red to a later emphasis on white).

In addition, differential weathering confirmed that most pecked engravings were much more patinated and eroded than abraded and pebraded engravings, even when they occurred within the same site. It is significant that such 'old' pecked engravings differed significantly in their motif range, cultural context and natural context from relatively 'fresh' pecked, pebraded and abraded engravings: most notably they emphasized circles, lines, arcs and tracks, but lacked the distinctive human vulva motif typical of recent engravings in the region. The three-phase sequence defined on the basis of superimpositions, spatial analysis and differential weathering is shown in Figure 8.9.

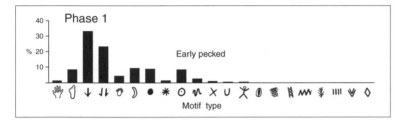

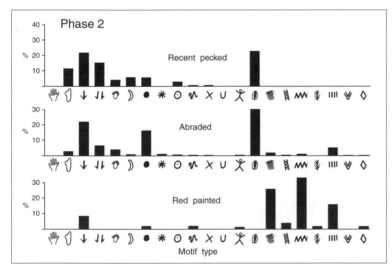

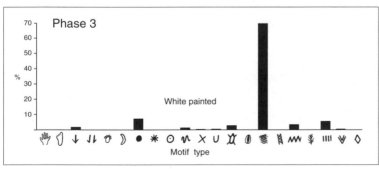

FIGURE 8.9

The three-phase rock art sequence in the central Queensland highlands, based on superimpositions, differential weathering and association. Absolute dating methods were required to 'anchor' major turning points in this relative sequence.

Phase 1 comprises pecked engravings of tracks, circles and other geometric motifs. Similar Panaramitee style engraving sites are found throughout most of Australia. By contrast, the rock art of Phases 2 and 3 is only found in the central Queensland highlands. The change in motif and technique emphasis between phases is accompanied by a change in the cultural and natural contexts of the sites, with the two later phases being associated with a distinctive type of burial cylinder found only in the central Queensland highlands.

FIGURE 8.10

Top: *A panel of pecked engravings at Buckland Creek showing hafted axes. These indicate that this panel, which is transitional in character between Central Queensland Rock Art Phase 1 and 2, is less than 5000 years old.* (After Morwood 1976, figure 2)

The three phases were then dated on the basis of subjects depicted and excavated evidence (Figure 8.10). For instance, Phases 2 and 3 both include representations of subjects that only existed after European contact, such as stencils of metal axes, and abraded depictions of cow tracks. In addition, a panel of pecked engravings, which are transitional between Phase 1 and 2, depict hafted stone axes, and therefore on the basis of excavated evidence cannot be more than 5000 years old. Another panel of Phase 2 engravings exposed

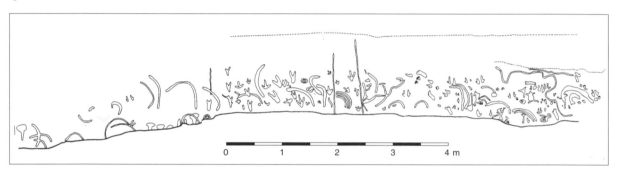

Middle: *A panel of deeply patinated, pecked engravings at the Plateau Site, upper Belyando River. The track-line composite is typical of Central Queensland Rock Art Phase 1, a regional variant of the panaramitee tradition, but use of the engraved vulva motif is more characteristic of the following, regionally distinctive Phase 2. The panel is therefore transitional in character and about 5000 years old.*

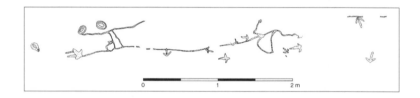

Bottom: *Excavated evidence for painting at sites (but not necessarily rock painting) included pigment fragments and ochre-stained grindstones. The examples shown were recovered in my excavations at Native Well 2 on the upper Warrego River. These and other finds showed that a major increase in artistic activity at many sites in the region began 5000 years ago.*

FIGURE 8.11

Pecked and abraded engravings at Cathedral Cave emphasize depiction of the human vulva and animal tracks. Excavations by John Beaton found that the engravings continued beneath the present floor level and that the earliest are about 4000 years old. (Photo M. J. Morwood)

FIGURE 8.12

A large engraved slab at Ken's Cave. The slab fell from the shelter ceiling onto occupation deposits dated to 530 years BP, which thereby provides a maximum age for the engravings. Such examples of stratified art enable the rock art sequence in the central Queensland highlands to be dated and therefore it can be related to changes in stone artefact technology and evidence for population increase. (Photo M. J. Morwood)

by excavations at Cathedral Cave appears to date from initial occupation of the site 4000 years ago (Figure 8.11), while similar engravings at Ken's Cave occur on a rock slab over occupation deposits dated to 530 BP (Figure 8.12).

In combination, the evidence indicates that the change from Phase 1 pecked engravings, which are very similar to 'old' Panaramitee engraving sites found throughout much of Australia, to the highly regional Phase 2 rock art, with its emphasis on stencils and engravings of tracks and human vulvas, occurred 5000 years ago. The change from Phase 2 to Phase 3, with its emphasis on the use of white stencils, grids and lizards, occurred in the European contact period after 1847 CE. Historical accounts also indicate that the most recent Aboriginal rock art in the region may date to around 1920 CE (that is, 36 BP). The chronology for central Queensland rock art is therefore as follows.

CENTRAL QUEENSLAND PHASE I (>5000 BP)

Deeply pecked engravings pecked into case-hardened surfaces of tracks, arcs, circles, lines and pits. These motifs were incorporated into complex patterns such as compositions of circles, arcs, lines and tracks (Figures 8.13 and 8.14). The sites are consistent in context. All are near permanent water and associated with stone artefact scatters. The range of motifs, motif compositions and context of Phase 1 sites indicate that they are a regional variant of an old art tradition that occurs all over Australia: the Panaramitee. Pigments recovered from excavations in the region indicate that rock paintings and/or stencils were also produced, but because of the friability of the central Queensland sandstones none of these appear to have been preserved.

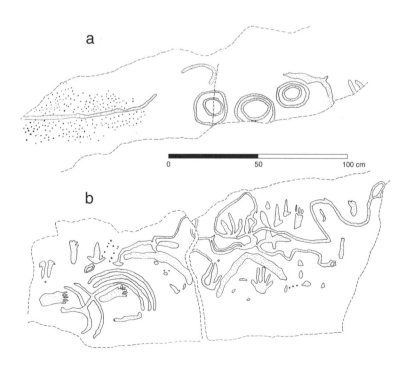

FIGURE 8.13

Panel of Central Queensland Rock Art Phase 1 pecked engravings at the Bull Hole and Twelve Mile Crossing. These appear to be a variant of the widespread Panaramitee tradition. They usually depict tracks, circles and other geometric motifs, whereas more recent (and regionally distinctive) engravings emphasize the human vulva motif.

FIGURE 8.14

Panel of Central Queensland Rock Art Phase 1 pecked engravings at the Bull Hole. These sites are invariably located near water and are quite different in their natural and cultural contexts than later rock art sites.
(Photo M.J. Morwood)

FIGURE 8.15

A panel of engravings at Blacks' Palace. These include the regionally distinctive human vulva motif, characteristic of Central Queensland Rock Art Phase 2 engravings. Some examples are flanked by tracks or knee-marks and contain red or yellow pigment. (Photo M. J. Morwood)

CENTRAL QUEENSLAND PHASE 2 (5000–36 BP)

Most surviving rock art in the region is from this phase. Techniques included stencilling, imprinting, painting, pecking, abrasion and pebrasion. The full range of colours was also used. The range of engraved motifs is significantly different from that of Phase 1, especially in the addition of the human vulva motif (Figure 8.15). There is also less composition in the engravings and they lack the narrative quality of Phase 1 assemblages. Instead, motifs are repetitively clustered.

FIGURE 8.16

White grids and hand stencils at Carnarvon Site 6. Similar white motifs, characteristic of Central Queensland Rock Art Phase 3, are the last rock art undertaken at many major sites in the central Queensland highlands. (Photo M. J. Morwood)

FIGURE 8.17

Charcoal drawings of lizards and grids from a small rockshelter on the upper Barcoo River, central Queensland highlands. These distinctive motifs were usually done in white pigment and represent the final phase, Phase 3, of rock art during the European contact period.

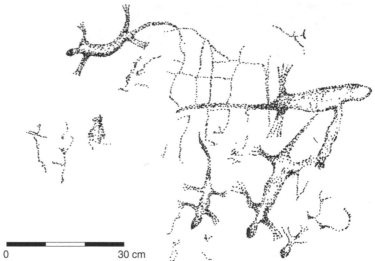

0   30 cm

CENTRAL QUEENSLAND PHASE 3 (<140–36 BP)

This is characterized by increased emphasis on the use of white and the depiction of grids. A number of distinctive motifs and compositions also appear, especially lizards, tortoises and lizard/grid compositions (Figure 8.16). In one case, a lizard/grid combination was drawn in charcoal (Figure 8.17).

It should be emphasized that this dated rock art sequence was not an end in itself but evidence requiring explanation. Why were the chronological distribution of motifs, colours, techniques and their combinations structured in this way? The sequence also allowed me to distinguish broadly contemporaneous groups of rock art types, which was essential for examining spatial and structural patterning in the rock art.

Subject analyses

STENCILS

The stencil component of central Queensland rock art provides useful insight into local Aboriginal practices and material culture. For instance, hand stencils of children are found at sites containing human skeletal remains and caches of animal bone in direct association with rock art: these special sites were obviously not restricted to adult males.

Thirty types of hand stencil variation occur in the rock art, invariably in prominent positions at sites that appear to have served as mortuaries (Figure 8.18). Many of the hand stencil variations tally closely with the hand signals reported by Walter Roth for the Mt Isa area of northwestern Queensland (Figure 6.17). They are not described in central Queensland ethnographic records but are attested to in the rock art.

Stencils also provide evidence for a wide range of Aboriginal material culture in the region, much of which was never noted during historic times. Stencils of boomerangs, axes, clubs, spears, dilly bags, containers and shields accurately show the range and dimensions of these items (Figure 8.19). They also include some real surprises. Stencils of spearthrowers, for instance, are uncommon, but

FIGURE 8.18

Hand stencil variations in the central Queensland highlands. These can be closely matched with hand signs used in northwest Queensland to communicate during hunting and other periods of enforced silence. They almost always occur in prominent positions at known burial sites and may have conveyed the totemic affiliations of deceased persons or visitors. (Photos M. J. Morwood)

FIGURE 8.19

Material culture stencils in the central Queensland highlands. As full-sized outlines, such stencils greatly extend our knowledge of the range of traditional tools, weapons and ceremonial objects used in the region. Because of the violent nature of the early European contact period, few such items were ever collected. (Photos M. J. Morwood)

do occur. Yet a number of historical sources tell us that local Aboriginal people did not use the spearthrower. These stencils must document long-distance exchange, as do stencils of Melo shell pendants, which must have originated from the north Queensland coast (Figure 6.16).

Structural analyses

CONTEXT

Contextual information collected for the 92 art sites used in the study included:

- evidence for human occupation (e.g. stone artefacts)
- evidence for mortuary use (e.g. human bones, burial cylinders, fragments of bark from cylinders)
- the presence of caches of animal bone and/or wood
- proximity to water.

Considered together with the dated rock art sequence, this information shows that there have been significant changes in the cultural and natural context of the art over time. In particular, Phase 1 assemblages of pecked engravings are all near permanent water sources and are associated with evidence of occupation (Figure 8.20). In contrast, later Phase 2 and 3 rock art sites are less consistent in context: twenty (23 per cent) were not associated with

FIGURE 8.20

The Bull Hole, showing the context of early pecked engravings, specifically their close association with water. Scatters of stone artefacts also occur in the vicinity. (Photo M. J. Morwood)

water sources; 50 per cent of the 80 rockshelter sites contained definite evidence for a mortuary function; and only six of these had associated evidence of occupation.

The relationship between central Queensland rock art and death was recognized by early European observers. It is also significant that the largest rock art site in the central Queensland highlands, Blacks' Palace, is associated with the largest recorded mortuary site, and contains no evidence of occupation. Other major art sites in the region known to have housed burials at the time of European contact are Cathedral Cave in Carnarvon Gorge and 'the Tombs' on the upper Maranoa River, where Archibald Meston, an early official protector of Aborigines, observed:

> These sandstone caves were the cemeteries of the aboriginals. On the roof or sides of all caves containing the dead were the imprints of hands done in red or white ochres. These hands were the unfailing signs of the rock sepulchre … all caves bearing those hand impressions were sacred and none dared to disturb or desecrate them under penalty of certain death.

This association between burial niches and clusters of rock art within sites is common, with the exact relative positioning being

FIGURE 8.21

A sandstone tunnel at Blacks' Palace that formerly contained a burial cylinder. The tunnel has a rock art panel located immediately above the entrance. This pattern of association between burial cylinders and rock art within sites is common. In addition, 50 per cent of decorated rockshelters in the region contain evidence for disposal of the dead. Recent rock art in the central Queensland highlands played a mortuary function.
(Photo M. J. Morwood)

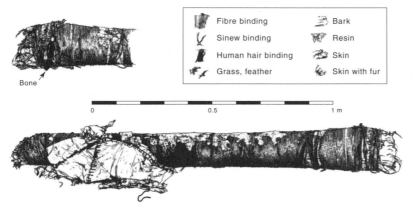

	Fibre binding		Bark
	Sinew binding		Resin
	Human hair binding		Skin
	Grass, feather		Skin with fur

Bone

0   0.5   1 m

FIGURE 8.22

Left: *A burial cylinder from near Carnaruun Gorge, made from hydgeroo bark wrapped in skins, with binding of fibre, sinew and human hair.*

determined by the configuration of the site. This pattern, plus the highly specific positioning of some motifs, tells us that panels of art within sites often relate directly to the placement of human remains and thus that rock art had a mortuary role (Figure 8.21). The same relationship is seen in the painted designs evident on many burial cylinders (Figure 8.22), and in the clear correlation between the distribution of distinctive central Queensland bark burial cylinders and rock art.

Rock art is also often associated with caches of animal bone and/or wood. Such caches were found at six Phase 2 and 3 sites (four also had mortuary evidence) and similar finds have occurred at other sites in the region. For instance, at Native Well a cache of macropod bone and twigs was found immediately behind an abraded vulva motif (Figure 8.23). The lack of any other art nearby makes it clear that the vulva, a fertility symbol of universal significance, was deliberately placed next to the cache.

Interaction between art, death and animal/plant species is also seen in the painting of motifs on some burial cylinders and the placement of branches, cycad nuts and even mummified animals in with the cylinder. The material evidence therefore indicates that central Queensland rock art, which emphasizes the vulva motif, is often associated with burials, and that both are sometimes associated with caches of animal and plant remains. This in turn suggests that there was probably a non-material system in which similar patterns of association operated—an ideology that embraced art, fertility, death, animal species and plants. Totemism is such an ideology, and the following observations are relevant:

FIGURE 8.23

A cache of animal bone and sticks found immediately behind an engraved vulva at Native Well, central Queensland highlands. The consistent association between rock art emphasizing engraved vulva motifs, disposal of the dead and caches of animal and plant remains suggests that there was a non-material system in which similar patterns of association operated—an ideology that embraced art, fertility, death, animal species and plants. Totemism, as historically recorded for the region, is such an ideology.
(Photo M. J. Morwood)

- Members of a totemic group had a specific relationship to certain animal species.
- Some totemic groups in the central Queensland area were also related to plant species.
- A forked branch from a totemically associated tree species could be placed in the grave with the deceased, or the burial platform could be made from wood of that species.
- Totemic designs of the deceased, or certain relatives, could feature at funeral rites.

These specific observations fit well with many of the contextual features of Phase 2 and 3 rock art, and suggest that some of the painted, abraded and pecked motifs may relate to the totemic affiliations of deceased persons or their relatives.

If we accept that the context of rock art reflects ideological principles, then a major change in physical context is also evidence for a major change in ideological context. Such a change can be seen when we compare Phase 1 pecked engravings with later assemblages. All early assemblages are associated with water and occupation debris, and in many cases the placement of motifs is specifically related to the water source, such as when a series of tracks appears to emerge from the water. Later art assemblages may or may not be associated with water, frequently lack occupational evidence, are often associated with mortuary evidence, and are sometimes associated with caches. The contextual shift suggests that the changes in technique, motif use and degree of composition probably reflect substantial changes in belief systems.

Similarities in content and context also indicate that the earliest engravings in the central Queensland highlands are of the widespread Panaramitee tradition found throughout central and eastern Australia, whereas later rock art phases are far more regional in character. The general archaeological sequence indicates that the development of a localised, regionally specific rock art tradition about 5000 BP coincided with a rapid increase in the number of sites, the appearance of a range of new technologies and artefact types, and the development of labour-intensive practices, such as the large-scale processing of toxic cycads and seed grinding.

The archaeological context of rock art in the central Queensland highlands suggests that significant regional variations in styles and functions occurred in eastern Australia at a time of rapid population growth, new systems for exchange of information, and greater demands upon food production systems.

DISTRIBUTION OF MOTIFS BETWEEN SITES

The distribution of motif types in Phase 2 and 3 art assemblages shows that most are dispersed throughout the study area rather than clustered (Figure 8.24). This strongly suggests that most are related to dispersed cultural institutions—in marked contrast to designs on shields, which were reported to have been highly localized, with each 'main encampment' using distinctive designs.

The analysis of site context above, indicates that aspects of central Queensland rock art can be explained in terms of the function and responsibilities of local totemic groups. During historic times, as we have seen, totemic affiliation in this region was inherited through the mother. Since the prescribed pattern of residence was patrilocal, with women moving to the territory of their husbands, matri-totemic groups—and designs—were widely dispersed. Rock art distribution and chronology thus suggest that the matrilineal, social organization recorded in the region during historic times dates back to at least 5000 BP.

Over much of Australia, where patrilineal or conceptional totemic systems operated, totemic groups coincided with patrilineal, landowning clans—meaning that individual totemic art motifs could be very localized in distribution. In this light the distribution of paired tortoise motifs in the central Queensland highlands is significant. Although each pair of tortoises has a different decorative infill, they are a highly distinctive motif set found at only four sites associated with water sources on the upper Warrego and upper Nogoa Rivers. These 'tortoise' sites are on a line some 75 kilometres long across the Great Dividing Range, which served as a territorial boundary between Aboriginal groups on the upper Warrego River and in the Lake Salvator–Wharton Creek area of the upper Nogoa. However, people made frequent crossings of the Range for meetings, and the two areas are also known to have been linked by a mythological track, as noted by Hazel Donovan:

> The big springs in the hills to the south, known as Major Mitchell Springs, were never swum in for fear of illness. It was also believed that a big snake called Moonda murra left its home in the reed filled Barngo Lagoon in the upper reaches of the Warrego River

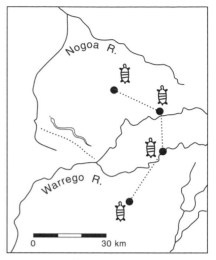

FIGURE 8.24

Most rock art motifs in central Queensland occur in sites throughout the region, but a few are very restricted in distribution. For instance, there are four known sites with paired tortoise motifs. These sites form a line, which crosses the Great Dividing Range from the upper Warrego to the upper Nogoa river catchment. A Rainbow serpent storyline is known to run parallel to the line of rock art sites, suggesting that they mark points of significance along another mythological track. (After Morwood 1979)

and found its way into the springs at the foot of Mount Farraday... and then to Major Mitchell Springs. It is reported that a trail, as if a big log had been dragged through the grass from Barngo Lagoon to the springs near Mt. Farraday can still be seen in the area, as if the grass growth pattern had been disturbed.

In 1976, I collected another myth that said Barngo Lagoon (or Dugganbuganan) was made by men digging in pursuit of a goanna. This hunt was unsuccessful and the goanna escaped to the northwest, creating the distinctive grass plain still to be seen there. The paths taken by these mythological beings runs parallel to that delineated by the 'tortoise' art sites, while both paths also link sites at which water was available.

These similarities between known mythological tracks and the linear distribution of a distinctive rock art design strongly suggest that the rock art sites mark points of significance along the path taken by another creative being, while differences in the infill used for the tortoise pairs seem to correlate with recorded local group distribution in the area. In the first creation myth the snake is referred to as a *murra* being and is said to have remained in Major Mitchell Springs. *Murra* myths have been termed 'western' myths, and are generally associated with cult totems and with a philosophy of localized totemic centres and clans.

The *murra* myth and the distribution of tortoise motifs both suggest that a similar philosophy was found in central Queensland. Although other evidence for this is sketchy, central Queensland may have been an overlap area between matrilineal totemism (with non-localized clans) and patrilineal cult-totemism (with localized clans). The fact that most rock art motifs are non-localized but a few are clustered or linear in distribution supports this interpretation.

DISTRIBUTION OF MOTIFS BETWEEN TECHNIQUES

There were considerable variations in the distribution of motifs produced using different techniques. Some of these seem to be due to technical factors (for instance, abrasion may be a more suitable way than pecking to make linear motifs), but many of the differences cannot be explained in this way.

The point is best illustrated by the particular kinds of techniques used in making a well-defined subset of motifs, such as hands, feet

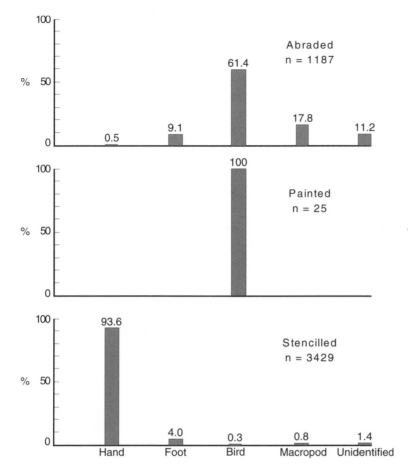

FIGURE 8.25

Although the same artists probably made stencils, paintings and engravings at rock art sites in the central Queensland highlands, each technique emphasizes different motifs. For instance, in the case of track/hand motifs, the absence of painted macropod and human tracks is in marked contrast to their frequency in panels of engravings, and shows selectivity on the part of the artists. Some of the selectivity is due to the nature of the different techniques, such as the emphasis on hands in stencilling, but some must relate to strict rules governing production of the rock art.

(After Morwood 1979)

and tracks (Figure 8.25). Hands were mainly depicted by stencilling. In other parts of Australia, such stencils were generally used to express individuality or as a mark of ownership. The individuality of many hand stencils is stressed by their positioning in prominent places, which are often hard to reach, while 'ownership' or 'affiliation' is reflected in the way some stencils are superimposed over non-stencilled motifs.

Tracks are mainly pecked, abraded and pebraded, and all of these engraving techniques are used with similar frequency for the different track types; they are also seldom used in depiction of the human hand. In contrast, painting is seldom used for tracks, and then only for bird tracks; the tracks of humans, macropods and other species are never painted. Given the emphasis on tracks of all varieties in engraved art, which occurs near paintings at many sites, this bias must result from cultural rules about what technique is appropriate for what subject. It is not evident in the other artistic techniques of the region, nor is it shared by the rock painting traditions of adjacent regions.

This comparison of techniques suggests that there were three artistic subsystems operating in the depiction of hands and tracks, each with a different set of rules: stencils are primarily of hands, paintings are exclusively of bird tracks, and engravings focus on the tracks of animals, especially birds. Similar patterns of variance in other subsets of motifs can be explained in the same way. For instance, in the case of geometric motifs, 'stars' were pecked and abraded but never painted or stencilled; most circles were pecked; most lines were abraded; the vulva motif was only engraved; and so on.

Motif use in different rock art techniques may have served different but overlapping roles within the artistic system. This evidence suggests that central Queensland rock art assemblages are highly structured and are likely to reflect a complex interplay of functional and ideological factors.

Conclusions

This case study from the central Queensland highlands shows how structural analyses of rock art can illustrate differences in the natural and cultural context of sites, the distribution of motifs between sites, the distribution of motifs between techniques, and so on. All the analyses point to structural biases in the art, and some of these relate to the nature of the social institutions and ideology observed in the region during the European contact period.

Rock art assemblages also provide evidence for the age of non-material aspects of local Aboriginal culture, strongly suggesting that before the development of a distinctive central highland rock art tradition about 5000 BP, social organization and ideology in the region were very different and part of a far more widespread system. Although such extrapolations must be treated with caution, two points should be stressed: rock art appears to document aspects of cultural change not otherwise reflected in the archaeological record; and the nature of the rock art sequence fits well with other archaeological evidence for demographic, economic and technological change.

CHAPTER **9**

North Queensland highlands

In the central Queensland highlands case study (Chapter 8), we saw that rock artists were very selective in the way they created art, as well as in the cultural and natural contexts of the sites. We also saw how major changes in the character, extent and cultural context of the art could be related to evidence for population increase, the appearance of more labour-intensive economic strategies, larger ceremonial gatherings, and so on. But this study took little account of the role of individual sites in local Aborigines' land use, and barely considered the material resources at the sites and how they might have altered in the past.

To make full use of the potential of rock art as evidence for past cultures, one needs to look at it in a much wider context. This was attempted in my archaeological study of the north Queensland highlands (1980–85), which utilized archaeological surveys, excavations, the recording of many rock art assemblages, the mapping of different terrain units, and a stock-take of plant and animal species.

For me this was a pivotal project, because it permanently transformed my approach to research. The project initially focused on individual sites, but then changed to a greater concern with Aboriginal use of areas, how patterns of resource use may have changed over time, and the strategies required to collect evidence for answering these questions. It was in this context that the age and distribution of seed grindstones provided crucial evidence for developments in local Aboriginal land use, economic activity, and symbolic and ceremonial systems. I now believe it is impossible to carry out serious archaeological research, including rock art research, without information on the environmental contexts of the sites. This requires input from many sources and scientific disciplines.

The region

The north Queensland highlands is an elevated region of complex geology and rugged topography (Figure 9.1). It is the largest upland region in Queensland and forms a major watershed with rivers radiating out east to the coast (the Burdekin), south to the Cooper Creek system (the Thomson) and northwest into the Gulf of Carpentaria (the Flinders, Norman and Gilbert).

The study focused on the upper Flinders River about 350 kilometres west of Townsville and immediately north of Hughenden. The geology here comprises an uplifted block of Mesozoic sandstones, which has been heavily dissected, then capped in some areas with Tertiary basalt flows.

FIGURE 9.1

General location of the north Queensland highlands, the largest upland area in Queensland and the least known.

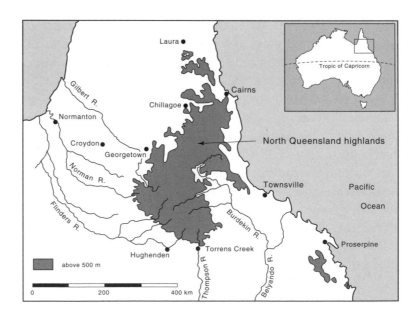

The history of European Aboriginal contact in the region began with the expeditions of Frederick Walker in 1861 and William Landsborough in 1862—both parties looking for the missing explorers Burke and Wills. European settlement began soon after with the taking up of extensive pastoral leases, such as Hughenden and Lammermoor Stations. With a few exceptions, local Aborigines were excluded from these leases.

In 1868 the first of a number of gold rushes began on the Gilbert River. This led to a further influx of Europeans and increased pressure on local Aborigines, who responded by spearing intruders and their stock. 'Dispersals' by the Native Mounted Police and local settlers resulted. It is estimated that during the 1860s, 10 to 15 per cent of the white population were killed by Aborigines, and local residents are able to identify many sites where Aborigines were massacred in retaliation. For instance, in late 1873 or early 1874, after a mailman was killed on the present-day Hann highway and horses from Mt Emu Station were speared, the Native Police and local settlers trapped a group of Aborigines on a spur overlooking the precipitous eastern side of Prairie Gorge. The whole group was shot.

By 1874, traditional life in the area appears to have collapsed and local Aborigines began to occupy fringe-camps around stations. Displacement, violence, introduced diseases, opium and alcohol all led to a rapid decline in the Aboriginal population. Finally the survivors were forced onto reserves, such as Woorabinda, under the 1897 *Aborigines Protection and Restriction of the Sale of Opium Act*.

As a result of the violent European contact period and the rapid disintegration of traditional Aboriginal life, we have only sketchy details on local group clans, their distribution, economy and material culture. We know, for instance, that the *Quippenburra* occupied the basalt country north of Hughenden, the *Dalleburra* Tower Hill Creek on the upper Thomson, the *Mungooburra* desert uplands further to the east, and the *Mootaburra* the Mitchell grass downs to the south. As to the significance of rock art in the region, we have no information at all.

The rock art

Until 1980, the north Queensland highlands was a large archaeological 'unknown' lying between the previously researched areas in southeast Cape York Peninsula, the central Queensland highlands, the Gulf Country of northwest Queensland and Townsville. There had been no prior excavations in the region, but brief reports in the early 20th century by John 'Along the line' Chisholm described stencil and 'carving' sites on the upper Thomson and Flinders rivers at Mt Sturgeon, Torrens Creek and Tattoo Hole. In 1913, Robert Gray had written of his discovery 46 years earlier of a site along the main channel of the Flinders River:

> We crossed some remarkable flat sandstone rocks, where the blacks at some time or other had employed themselves in cutting out the smooth surface representations of iguanas, men's hands and feet, and boomerangs, the footprints of emus and suchlike objects, and had evidently taken a good deal of trouble over it.

Later reports indicated that there were many rock art sites in the region, and that the art was similar to that of the central Queensland highlands.

My team's work in the region began with a wide-ranging reconnaissance and recording project between Torrens Creek and Richmond in the south, and Georgetown and Croydon in the north. This showed that the rock art of the north Queensland highlands is characterized by the predominance of stencilled hands, feet and implements; by the painting of simple, geometric designs, such as grids and zigzags; and by the engraving of a variety of simple motifs, such as lines, tracks, grids and pits (Figure 9.2). To judge by differential weathering, the earliest surviving rock art comprises

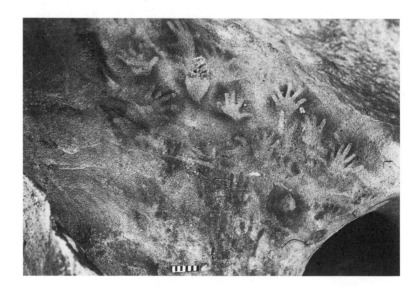

FIGURE 9.2

A panel of hand stencils in the north Queensland highlands. Stencilling and engraving are the main rock art techniques in the region. (Photo M. J. Morwood)

deeply pecked engravings of circles, spoked circles, radiating lines, arcs pits and tracks (Figures 9.3). Pigment fragments recovered from excavations indicate that paintings and/or stencils were also being produced at this time, but the subjects are unknown. More recent engraved panels comprise shallowly pecked circles, arcs and tracks, but they have a greater figurative component. Superimpositions show that these engravings were done in the same period as surviving paintings, stencils and drawings.

Excavations at Mickey Springs

To establish a cultural sequence of the region, we carried out a series of excavations focusing on two areas on the upper Flinders River where sites with good excavation prospects were identified: Mickey Springs and the Prairie–Porcupine Creek system.

Mickey Springs lies about 400 metres downstream from the head of Mickey Gorge, itself a tributary of the main Flinders River channel northeast of Hughenden. The sandstone gorge is shallower at the northern end, where rugged sandstone scarps are fronted by rock fall slopes down to the creek bed. Most of the sandstones in the area are coarse-grained and friable, although scarps of fine-grained sandstone occur below the springs on the eastern side. These local sandstones contain conglomerate layers from which quartz pebbles are readily available for stone artefact manufacture. The scrubby vegetation consists mostly of ironbark and acacias, but there are stands of melaleuca at the springs.

The springs are the only permanent water source for a considerable distance, although a rockhole at the head of the gorge and nearby Mickey and Carbine Swamps contain water at certain times of the year. Our survey of the gorge turned up fourteen rockshelters in the sandstone scarp with evidence for Aboriginal use, an axe-grinding site in the creek bed and a basalt grindstone stored on a sandstone ledge. Burials are also reported to have been once present in the area, but all surface evidence for such has been removed. Rockshelters close to the springs contain abraded and pecked engravings and stencils. Most also contain evidence of occupation—flaked stone artefacts, grindstones and charcoal-rich deposits. Significantly, all of the archaeological sites we recorded are within 400 metres of the springs; although there are many rockshelters further down the gorge, we

FIGURE 9.3

Two panels of pecked engravings of geometric motifs and a 'kangaroo'(?) in the north Queensland highlands. Both panels are in very protected positions in rockshelters but are still very patinated and weathered. Pecked engravings of this type, with an emphasis on tracks and circles but with some figurative motifs, are the oldest surviving rock art in the region.

(From Morwood 1992a: figure 2)

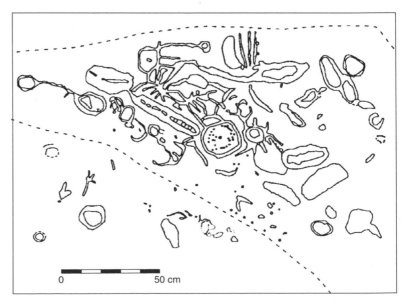

found no evidence of human occupation. This suggests that Aborigines only made use of sites close to the permanent water source.

MICKEY SPRINGS SITE 34

Our excavation program at Mickey Springs concentrated on Site 34, which contained a large and varied rock art assemblage, cached material, and occupation deposits that appeared to be both rich and deep. To confirm that the trends we saw were not specific to that site alone, we also did some smaller-scale excavations at Sites 31, 33 and 38.

Site 34 has an extensive rock art assemblage, dominated by series of vertical abraded lines that in some sections disappear beneath the present floor level. Other motifs include abraded bird and macropod tracks, and pits. Pecked engravings of tracks, arcs, circles and line series occur only on case-hardened sections of the shelter wall and appear to be the oldest surviving rock art at the site. We also recorded twelve hand stencils, including those of a very young child, although the faintness of some examples suggests that others had faded from view. On the sand floor of the cave there was abundant charcoal and flaked stone artefacts, while two sandstone grinding stones had been placed against the wall, presumably for later re-use. Hidden in a crevice towards the rear of the shelter, we also found a small boomerang, two quartz pebbles, a bone from a red flying fox, a possum mandible, and fragments of wallaby longbone, rib and vertebrae.

Excavations were done at various places within the site to sample different activity areas, to investigate deeper sections of the deposits, and to obtain minimum ages for some of the rock engravings, which appeared to continue beneath ground level. Deposits reached a maximum depth of 160 centimetres. Six radiocarbon dates showed the site had been occupied from about 11 000 years ago until the European contact period.

Throughout this time, the main meat staple of the shelter's occupants seems to have been large and medium-sized macropods (such as wallaroo and rock wallaby), although small-bodied species were also present, including bandicoots and possums. Some of these animals, especially rodents, may have been naturally deposited on site, but the presence of cut-marks and extensive charring of macropod bones suggests that these were a large part of the Aboriginal occupants' diet. Four bone points found in the shelter suggest that they also ate fish—in historic times, local Aborigines fastened prongs of bone to the shaft of their fishing spears just below the tip. Remains of the red kangaroo, an animal of the open plains, show that people brought some foodstuffs to the site from a considerable distance. We found no direct evidence as to what plant foods the occupants might have eaten, but a seed grindstone fragment in the excavation and two mullers on the shelter floor indicate that the labour-intensive processing of seeds had taken place there during the past 3700 years.

We also noticed signs of major changes in the way the site was used over time. For instance, from the discard rates of stone tools (calculated on the basis of their radiocarbon dates), the site shows low density and sporadic occupation up until about 9000 years ago, after which deposition of artefacts became more consistent. Also, until around 3700 years ago, hearths were simple, shallow holes averaging 20 to 30 centimetres in diameter. After that the number, range and complexity of hearth structures increased.

Stone artefact technology also varied over time. Tools were mostly made by flaking quartz, and the size of the discarded quartz cores does not change much over time. However around 9000 years ago there was a substantial change in raw material use, with an abrupt increase in the range of materials used. About 3700 years ago, a range of new implements appeared, including backed blades, adzes, seed grindstones and edge-ground axes (Figure 9.4).

Fragments of ochre with sections ground down were probably used to make pigments. The fact that these occur throughout the full depth of the deposit suggests that the occupants of the shelter were painting, although not necessarily rock painting, since the site was first occupied. During the excavation we also uncovered a group of pecked engravings on the shelter wall. The lowermost engravings, comprising a series of seven vertical lines, were located between charcoal samples radiocarbon dated to 11 000 BP and 9000 BP (Figure 9.5 and 9.6). These were covered over by a rockfall and must be associated with initial Aboriginal use of the site. Also buried were engravings of another vertical line series and a bird track. Similar deeply weathered pecked engravings occur on the case-hardened wall at floor level; these include paired macropod tracks, bird tracks, pits and circles.

Our excavations at Mickey Springs Sites 34, 33 and 31, also indicate that the area was first occupied around 11 000 years ago.

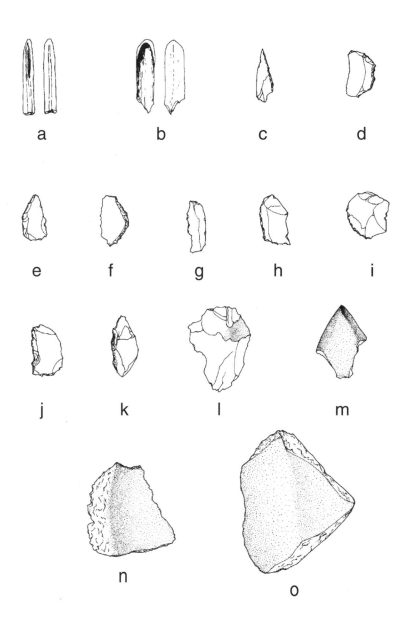

FIGURE 9.4

A range of stone and bone artefacts from Mickey Springs 34 and Quippenburra Cave: (a),(b) bone points; (c)–(f) backed microliths; (g),(h) blades with use wear; (i) thumbnail scraper; (j) burren adze slug; (k) tula adze slug; (l) ground adze axe fragment; (m) piece of ground ochre; (n),(o) piece of seed grindstone.
(After Morwood 1990: Figures 9,19)
The appearance of seed grindstones in the local sequence is particularly significant: it indicates that people were prepared to work harder to make a living over the last 3700 years ago. This is also the time when there was population expansion and a more regionally distinctive style of rock art emerged. (Drawing Kathy Morwood)

Given the closeness of the occupied rockshelters to the springs, it seems likely that systematic use of the area began when the springs were activated by climate changes.

The first occupants of the area were involved in a range of artistic activities. The pecked engravings buried by rockfall by 9000 years ago at Site 34 were probably made at about the same period as

FIGURE 9.5

The stratigraphic location of buried pecked engravings, which were exposed during archaeological excavations at Mickey Springs 34. The earliest engravings at this site and adjacent rockshelters were produced soon after initial human use of Mickey Gorge around 11 000 years ago. Pieces of used red ochre of similar age were also recovered, but any associated paintings have not survived. Human use of the site remained very ephemeral until around 3700 years ago, when a major increase in the intensity of occupation began. The extensive panels of abraded lines and pits at the site date from this time. (After Morwood 1990: figure 4)

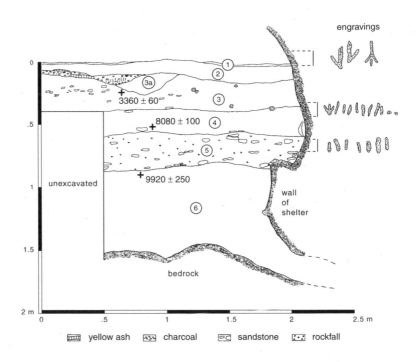

another set of deeply pecked and weathered engravings of an arc and line-track maze at Site 31. At this site, sections of the rock art surface have exfoliated, and three pieces of sandstone bearing peckings were recovered. The uppermost fragment about halfway down the sequence was associated with the radiocarbon date of 5900 BP, suggesting that the lowermost one just above bedrock is around 11 000 years old. Although the engraved fragments were too small for the original motifs to be recognizable, the nature of the peckings and matrix suggest that all probably came off a deeply pecked and weathered panel on the wall immediately above our excavation. The position of these fragments in the deposits indicates that people were doing this sort of engraving as long as the site was in use.

With their emphasis on tracks and geometric motifs, the pecked engravings at Mickey Springs 31 and 34, as well as the undated ones in other shelters, appear to be regional variants on the widespread and relatively homogeneous Panaramitee rock engraving tradition.

A range of evidence indicates that the first people to use the Mickey Springs sites at the end of the Pleistocene, 11 000 years ago, came in small transient groups. For instance, the rate of stone artefact

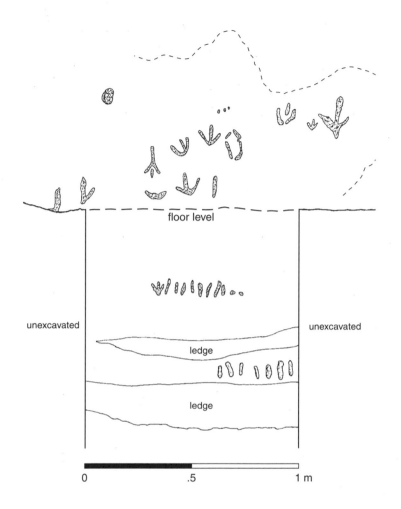

FIGURE 9.6

The panel of pecked engravings exposed in the excavations at Mickey Springs 34. These include circles, line series and tracks and are a regional variant of the widespread Panaramitee tradition. Patination and weathering of pecked engravings at the site indicated that they are older than the extensive panels of abraded lines and grooves. The excavation showed that the earliest pecked engravings date to around 11 000 BP, whereas abraded engravings are less than 3700 years old.
(After Morwood 1990)

floor level

unexcavated

unexcavated

ledge

ledge

0   .5   1 m

discard was generally low and episodic, while the only hearths at this time were small. The faunal evidence is also suggestive: most bone in the earliest deposits is of rodents, lizards and small birds, reflecting use of the site by natural predators. Human economic refuse is sparse but shows an emphasis upon hunting of large and medium-sized macropods, although some small-bodied species were also taken.

The pattern of site use began to change around 9000 years ago with increases in the rate of stone artefact discard and hearth construction, as well as a greater emphasis upon use of higher-quality flaking material; all possible indications of heavier site use. However, on the basis of evidence from Mickey Springs 34, significant technological, economic and artistic change did not occur until 3700 BP. The range of new artefact types and technologies included backed blades, and adzes of burren and tula type, edge-ground axes, and seed grindstones. From this time there were further increases in stone artefact and ochre discard rates, use of conservation strategies in knapping high-quality stone, and rate of hearth manufacture. Evidence from Mickey Springs 31 shows that the nature and timing of this change is not site-specific: here a total of 934 stone artefacts was recovered including three burren adze slugs, two tula adze slugs and two fragments of edge-ground axe, all of which occurred in deposits above the date of 5900 BP.

At both Mickey Springs 34 and 38, the uppermost cultural deposits of the 'late' stone artefact industry cover the bases of abraded panels of engravings. Together with a massive increase in the amount of recovered ochre, this evidence strongly suggests that the extensive panels of abraded engravings that predominate in the shelters post-date the change in site use that occurred around 3700 years ago. Evidence collected during the 1920s on the significance of the Mickey Springs engravings shows that these continued to be of cultural significance until the European contact period. The range of domestic activities present in the uppermost deposits, and the presence of hand stencils of very young children at Mickey Springs 34, show that the most recent rock art was public and that family groups occupied the shelters. In addition, a fragment of human molar from the uppermost spit of Mickey Springs 38 supports the claims of local informants that some of the shelters formerly contained burials. Overall, the evidence suggests larger groups used the shelters, for longer periods, and for a wider range of activities over the past 3700 years.

Survey and excavation at Prairie Gorge

Excavations at Mickey Springs indicate that significant changes in site use, technology, economy and art had occurred in this area over the past 11 000 years. The implications of this sequence for changes in the pattern of land use were investigated along the Prairie-Porcupine Creek system located 15 kilometres to the west. This area was selected because it was known to have a wide range of site types, such as the Tattoo Hole art sites, which appear to span a considerable time period, and Quippenburra Cave, where datable deposits are associated with evidence for large ceremonial gatherings.

In addition, the area has a number of distinct landforms: plateau, scarps and gorge; sandstone and basalt country; narrow, deeply incised gorges and other less rugged sections. Finally, traditional Aboriginal life seems to have come to an abrupt end in the early European contact period, after the massacre on the eastern side of Prairie Gorge in late 1873 or early 1874. Since that time, many of the sites have been left almost intact and have a wide range of material evidence.

The study area comprises the gorges, scarps and adjacent plateaux from Tattoo Hole on Porcupine Creek, north to the Porcupine—Prairie Creek junction and up Prairie Gorge, a total distance of 21 kilometres. A total of twelve land units was distinguished, comprising the main plateau; blacksoil plains, breakaways and scree slopes on basalt country; upper slopes, lateritic edges and footslopes on the Cretaceous sandstones; and upper scarps, talus, lower scarps and creek bed on the Jurassic sandstones (see Figure 9.7).

Then we set out to examine the relationship between the distribution of archaeological sites, different types of terrain and resources, and, via dating evidence, to monitor changes in the pattern of land use. Fieldwork involved mapping the distribution of each land unit using aerial photographs, recording plant and animal species present in each land unit, systematically surveying for archaeological sites, and excavation at Quippenburra Cave. We took special care during the surveys to look for rock holes that might have

FIGURE 9.7

This figure shows the distribution of twelve land units across Prairie Creek Gorge on the upper Flinders River. The units are defined on the basis of geology, slope and vegetation. Such information on the distribution of plant and animal foods is crucial for interpreting the archaeological evidence. For instance, the remains of freshwater mussels, bandicoots and other animals found in our excavations at Quippenburra Cave show that the site occupants exploited all major resource areas, including the bottom of the gorge which would have involved climbing down precipitous cliffs. (After Morgan and Terry 1990)

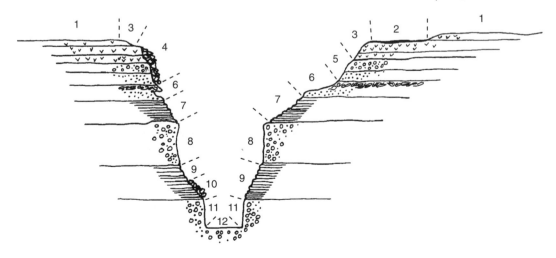

FIGURE 9.8

Distribution of archaeological sites recorded along the Porcupine–Prairie Creek system, upper Flinders River. Native millet on the black soil plains (shaded) and kurrajong trees on the basalt scarps seem to have provided the economic staples for Aboriginal use of the deeply incised gorge country along Prairie Creek from 3700 years ago. Sites occur in association with these plant staples near rockholes that hold water for some time after rain. Smaller sites comprizing one or two grindstones probably reflect the activities of family groups, but Quippenburra Cave, with 89 seed grindstones, was a site where large numbers of people came together for ceremonies. (After Morwood 1990: figure 12)

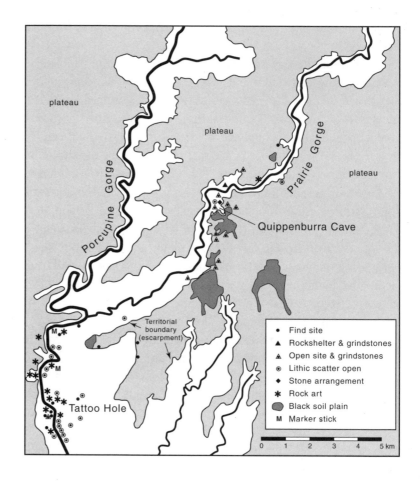

served as transient water sources on the edges of the plateau. Traverses were also made up to 5 kilometres out from the gorge country to sample the full range of resources in the plateau zones.

The archaeological survey showed significant patterns in the distribution of sites (Figure 9.8). Large sections of the plateau, plateau margins and sandstone scarps in the study area have no or very few sites, even where ground visibility is excellent. The majority of sites are clustered in the shallow incised areas of Porcupine Creek, in the general area of Tattoo Hole. Here open engraving sites, rockshelters with stencils and abraded engravings, caches, marker sticks in sandstone pipes, and open artefact scatters are all located near permanent waterholes.

Near Tattoo Hole, most open sites contained only flaked stone tools and the remnants of their manufacture. The only site where we found grindstones was near to a small, swampy, blacksoil area in the basalt country to the west. We concluded that Aboriginal occupation of the area around this section of the Prairie–Porcupine Creek system did *not* depend upon seed processing. Differential weathering of the engravings here indicates that the area has probably been a focus for local Aboriginal groups from a time predating the appearance of new technologies and intensive economic strategies 3700 years ago. The oldest engravings comprise deeply pecked geometrics (circles, lines, radiating lines, line-track compositions) and track motifs (Figure 9.9). These are similar in technique and motif range to the deeply pecked engravings dated at Mickey Springs 34, suggesting that they are of similar age.

Although the more recent, lightly pecked and unpatinated engravings at Tattoo Hole include many of the motifs used in older engravings, there are also distinct differences, such as the appearance of stylized 'humanoid' and club motifs (Figure 9.10). At an engraving site in the White Mountains to the east of Mickey Springs, similar lightly patinated engravings include depictions of humans, clubs, boomerangs, shields and edge-ground axes (Figure 9.11). On the basis of the Mickey Springs excavations, the axe motifs provide a chronological marker—these lightly patinated engravings are less than 3700 years old. One implication of this is that the early engraving tradition predates the mid-Holocene appearance of seed grindstones, at Mickey Springs. In contrast, recent, unpatinated engravings with an increased figurative component seem to postdate these developments. It is significant

FIGURE 9.9

A panel of deeply pecked and weathered engravings at Tattoo Hole, Flinders River. These engravings of circles and tracks are more than 3700 years old and are similar in content and context to early engravings found over most of Australia. (From Morwood 1992: figure 7)

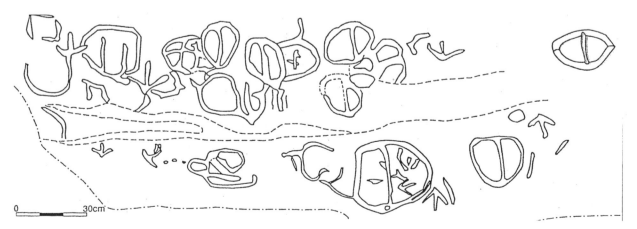

FIGURE 9.10

Recent abraded and lightly pecked engravings at Tattoo Hole, Flinders River. These are less than 3700 years old and some of the motifs are very localized in distribution: they are only found in this section of the upper Flinders River catchment. (Photo M. J. Morwood)

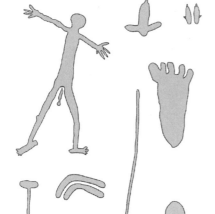

FIGURE 9.11

A range of unpatinated pecked engravings from a site in the White Mountains which include depictions of women, weapons and tracks. The engraving of a hafted axe indicates that the group is less than 3700 years old. (Morwood 1992: figure 8)

that the two rock engraving sites located in the deeply incised gorge north of Quippenburra Cave were of the latter type.

The distribution of sites along the edges of the deep gorge country to the north along Prairie Creek is very different from that around Tattoo Hole. With the exception of widely spaced, small surface scatters of flaked stone (or findsites of individual artefacts), all contain grindstones and occur in areas with ready access to water and two specific plant resources: stands of native millet on areas of blacksoil alluvium, and groves of kurrajong on the basalt scarps. Small, open sites with two or three grindstones which probably served the normal domestic requirements of small family groups are all located next to groves of kurrajong, or on red-soil flats (good campsites) near areas with large stands of native millet—but only where there are also water sources nearby.

Quippenburra Cave, which has evidence for large gatherings of people, has a similar pattern of resource use to other sites along Prairie Creek: the cave contains a large number of basalt grindstones and is next to a large, permanent rock hole and extensive blacksoil plains. Large-scale seed processing at this site seems to have underwritten ceremonial activities at a nearby stone arrangement, and the only seeds in the area available in sufficient density to be considered as a staple are those of native millet.

The distribution and content of both domestic and large-scale ceremonial sites along the margins of the deep gorge and the basalt plateau reflect a dependence on seed grinding. The evidence from Mickey Springs, confirmed by the results of excavations at Quippenburra Cave, shows that this pattern of land use and site distribution is less than 3700 years old.

QUIPPENBURRA CAVE

This site is located on the east side of Prairie Gorge on a sandstone ledge about 100 metres wide. Apart from clumps of spinifex where sandy soil has accumulated, and western bloodwood scrub along the outer edge, the ledge is mainly flat bare rock. Behind it rises a steep scarp of deeply weathered coarse sandstone, partially obscured by a scree slope of basalt boulders that have tumbled from the plateau some 60 metres above.

Near the cave, the ledge is crossed by a creek line, which emerges from a small gorge at right angles to Prairie Creek. The normally dry creek bed has a large rock hole just before it drops into the main gorge. If properly maintained, this would have been the only permanent water source along the margins of the gorge. This is confirmed by the number of Aboriginal sites nearby: on the east a stone arrangement constructed from basalt boulders rests on the sandstone platform flanking the eastern side of the creek line (Figure 9.12), while scatters of grindstones and flaking debris occur on the western side, as does Quippenburra Cave.

Quippenburra Cave has formed by weathering of the softer, lower parts of the lateritic strata. The roof is formed of ironstone lattice,

FIGURE 9.12

A stone arrangement located 100 metres north of Quippenburra Cave. Hand stencils of children, youths and men in the cave mean that it was a public area, whereas the stone arrangement was probably used for ceremonies by senior men and initiates. It is located just out of sight of the cave. (Photo M. J. Morwood)

FIGURE 9.13

Quippenburra Cave showing some of the grindstones, as left by the last site occupants. The number of grindstones present shows that the site was used for large gatherings of people, presumably for ceremonies involving use of the nearby stone arrangement. (Photo M. J. Morwood)

but the cave matrix is mostly white sandstone stained with patches of orange and red from oxidized ironstone. The site measures 40 metres by 30 metres with a maximum roof height of 5 metres (Figure 9.13). The southern end of the cave has collapsed to form a crater-like opening with a scrub-covered scree slope, which provides the back entrance. The two other entrances, to the north and northwest, are fronted by a sandstone shelf, then a precipitous drop into the main gorge. A small watercourse begins at the back entrance of the cave and exits at the northern entrance. Its channel is filled with bedrock and rubble, which contains many grindstone fragments. On each side of the watercourse there are areas of dry deposit rich in organic material and artefacts.

The cave contains stencilled rock art—202 hands (including ten of young children), one hand-plus-forearm, one foot, two axes, three boomerangs and four unidentified objects (Figure 9.14). The majority are red, but yellow (two), brown (one), purple (thirteen) and black (three) also occur. The only sign of European vandalism is two

FIGURE 9.14

A panel of rock stencils at Quippenburra Cave. The presence of children's hand stencils show that the use of the cave by local people was not restricted to adults. (Photo M. J. Morwood)

scratched names dated to 1924. A range of art materials is available in the cave: the sandstone matrix contains patches of ironstone suitable for making red pigment, and an abraded area on the western wall documents removal of the white matrix which is also suitable for use as pigment.

The most obvious evidence of Aboriginal occupation is the large number of grindstones lying on the top of the deposits. These total 89 complete or fragmented lower grindstones and 52 mullers, many of which are grouped (for instance, a line of eight, a parallel line of seven, a pile of four). Outside, around the crater entrance, we found a further 31 slab and 31 muller grindstones, together with scattered flaking debris. With the exception of four specimens of sandstone and one of granite, all grindstones are of local basalt, obtainable from the plateau scarps 100 metres to the south. The cave also contains evidence for quarrying: an outcrop of chert near the northern entrance has been flaked and battered, and is surrounded by flaking waste and large hammer stones.

Other artefacts found on the surface include an edge-ground axe head, a riding spur and a mouth organ reed-frame (Figure 9.15 a,b,c). These last are very common on post-contact Aboriginal sites in western Queensland and, given the very small number of European visitors, the Quippenburra Cave reed-frame probably dates from the last phase of Aboriginal occupation. The spur is also interesting: it is a 'hunting spur' of a type quite common in the latter half of the

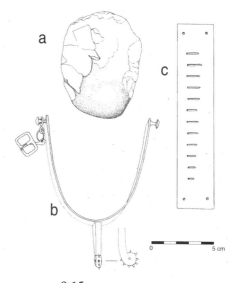

FIGURE 9.15

Objects found on the surface inside Quippenburra Cave: (a) edge-ground axehead; (b) military riding spur; (c) mouth-organ reed. (Morwood 1990, figure 16) *The spur suggests that the massacre of local people by European settlers and the Native Mounted Police on the east side of Prairie Gorge in 1874 took place in the immediate vicinity of the site.* (Drawing Kathy Morwood)

19th century, and bears a 'broad arrow' stamp indicating that it is of British military issue. Information received from elderly informants about the early contact history of the area, the location of the cave and the range of material evidence recovered, strongly suggests that the reported massacre of local Quippenburra people by the Native Mounted Police occurred close to this site.

I first learned of Quippenburra Cave when discussing Aboriginal sites of the Hughenden region with George Pearce, who had driven a Model-T Ford there with a group of people in 1924. Although he could not remember whether the cave contained rock art or other evidence of Aboriginal use, his photographs of the site looked tantalizing. During the excavations at Mickey Springs 34 in 1984, we drove across country to the general area of Prairie Gorge that he had indicated, and relocated the site. Its research potential was clear.

In June 1986, we excavated, two 1-metre squares. These were located in dry areas where there are many grindstones, and where probing had indicated that the deposits were deepest—up to a depth of 63 centimetres (Figure 9.16). The upper unit of the excavation (Layers 1 to 3) contained a compact sand with lenses of charcoal and ash, and was rich in charcoal, bone, plant materials and stone artefacts. It also contained a large number of well-defined hearths, and the divisions between layers largely corresponded to ash from hearths.

In contrast, the lower unit (Layer 4), comprised a coarse-grained sand between sandstone talus and the occasional water-rolled basalt pebble, and was similar in composition to the talus/scree slope in the 'crater'. Much of this material appears to have been deposited by running water and, although the density of stone artefacts was

FIGURE 9.16

Stratigraphic cross-section for the main excavation at Quippenburra Cave. A fragment of seed grindstone was found on bedrock, meaning that seed grinding was done here right from initial occupation of the site 3600 years ago Cave. (After Morwood 1990: figure 17)

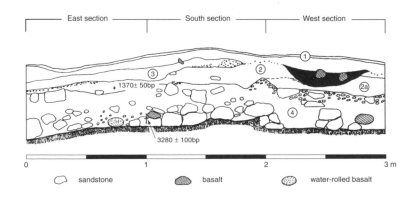

similar to that found in the upper unit, there was minimal charcoal, bone or other organic material. The basal units of both excavation areas may document a period when the cave deposits were periodically much wetter, before a well-defined drainage channel had formed through the site.

The two main stratigraphic units are also reflected in the distributions of charcoal, bone and stone artefacts within the deposits, all of which indicate a major change in the depositional regime.

Two radiocarbon dates show that Quippenburra Cave was first used by Aboriginal people about 3600 years ago. The earliest evidence of human use of the site included a fragment of grindstone with traces of red ochre, indicating that it had been used for both seed grinding and preparation of paint.

Among the plant remains recovered from the excavation were the Burdekin plum and the green plum. Both species occur on the lower scarp areas, which suggest that the occupants of the site foraged for food along the bottom of adjacent Prairie Gorge. The large number of grindstones in the cave also suggests that they relied heavily on the processing of plant resources. Both starch grains and green plant matter were identified on grindstone specimens, while the distribution of sites along this section of gorge indicates that the seeds of native millet and kurrajong were staples. The evidence shows that the occupants used plants from every area of the local landscape, from the lower scarp areas of the gorge to the basalt scree slopes, the breakaways and the blacksoil plains on the plateau. The exploitation of these plant resources most probably occurred between February and April, following good summer rains.

The range of animal remains is also drawn from the full range of habitats in the surrounding area: the red-earth woodlands of the main plateau (red kangaroo), the escarpments (wallaroo, rock wallaby) and the gorge (freshwater mussel, water rat, bandicoot). Our faunal resource survey indicates that all these species are still extant in the area.

Most of the 557 stone artefacts recovered were the waste products of hammer and anvil working of quartz pebbles from nearby conglomerates, but chert, petrified wood, silcrete and basalt also occur. Formal artefact types included four grindstone fragments, comprising two undiagnostic specimens, the edge of a muller with adhering red ochre, and a large fragment of faceted grindstone. The presence of specialized seed grindstones from the lowermost deposits, as well as on the cave floor, shows that seed processing was an economic staple at the site from the time it was first occupied 3600 years ago. Other stone tools we recovered included a backed point, three Bondi points, two chert tula adze slugs and a chert burren slug. With the exception of a tula adze slug, these 'formal' flaked tools occur in the uppermost layer of the cave deposits. Their vertical spread in the deposits indicates that backed blades and tula adzes were in use up to the time of European contact.

In the excavated deposits we also found two flattened lead bullets from a Winchester Model 1892 2/20 calibre rifle (a weapon not found in Australia in great numbers until after World War I), fourteen Remington-Peters cartridge primers of a design not in existence until the 1920s, and a piece of lead foil. We concluded that a member of George Pearce's group had probably reloaded his gun in the cave during their 1924 visit.

Assessment of Prairie Creek evidence

The distribution and content of both domestic and ceremonial sites in the deeply incised country along Prairie Creek reflects the extensive, systematic practice of seed grinding. Work at Mickey Springs showed that this type of food production and the related patterns of land use are less than 3700 years old. The results of our excavations at Quippenburra Cave, which was first occupied about 3600 BP, support this interpretation. Aboriginal occupation of the north Queensland highlands generally goes back at least 40 000 years, but at Mickey Springs and Prairie Creek humans did not appear until around 11 000 and 3700 BP respectively. These dates correspond to extensive environmental and cultural changes, which have consequences for local resource use.

In summation, a range of evidence indicates that the distribution of archaeological sites in the region is highly correlated with the distribution of resources, and that resource levels and structure have effectively changed at least twice over the past 11 000 years. The proposed scenario is:

1 Environmental changes at the end of the Pleistocene, such as increased rainfall, activated Mickey Springs about 11 000 years ago, and allowed people to move into the area.

2 Large-scale processing of grass and kurrajong seeds with grindstones appeared about 3700 BP. It was used to meet both increased domestic and social demands upon the production system, and allowed occupation of previously marginal country along Prairie Creek. This expansion of occupation and use of labour-intensive foods indicates an overall increase in population.

It is significant that these two different patterns of land use are associated with different types of rock art.

Conclusions

The earliest rock engravings of the region—currently dated to a minimum of 9000 BP, but almost certainly older—appear to have been a regional variant of the Panaramitee style, which, as we have seen, is found throughout much of mainland Australia. Later changes in motif range and emphasis, as well as engraving technique, appear to have been of more regional character and to have been associated with increases in population and more labour-intensive patterns of resource use, including the large-scale processing of seeds.

Studies of recent hunter–gatherer groups have shown that populations in environments that are harsh, unpredictable and/or of low population density require open social networks for ensuring flexibility of population distribution over large areas. The result is a widespread cultural and stylistic homogeneity not found among hunter–gatherers living in richer, more predictable environments that can support larger populations. On this basis, we can expect the geographical spread of a rock engraving style to contract when population density increases significantly and people become more concerned with ownership of resources on designated tracts of land. In such circumstances, the role of art changes from a primary concern with 'linking' people in a high-risk, low-population-density system, to one emphasizing territorial bounding.

The local rock art sequence indicates that, prior to 3700 years ago, the upper Flinders region was occupied by relatively few people who ranged widely and had extensive social and ceremonial links to other groups. In contrast, after this time, the population increased and people became more concerned with use and ownership of localized resources. Some marginal areas were regularly used for the first time; labour-intensive economic activities such as seed processing appeared; and the character of rock art and ceremonial gatherings changed accordingly. Clearly, the rock art adds to, but is also informed by, other aspects of the archaeological record.

Much of the information potential of archaeological sites in the region, including rock art sites, only became evident when we shifted the focus of our research from what was found at specific sites and began to consider the broader changes in Aboriginal land use. In turn this necessitated—in fact, developed from—the mapping of local resource structures by specialists from other disciplines, as a basis for interpreting site distribution and contents. Little rock art research has been undertaken in Australia with this in mind.

CHAPTER 10

Southeast Cape York Peninsula

Studies of Aboriginal art show that the best way to understand its meaning and social role is to examine its context of production. That is, when was the art produced, where and by whom? Such an approach is essential if we are to utilize the potential of rock art as archaeological evidence. Clues to the social and economic role of rock art lie in its natural and cultural context—yet few archaeological studies of art have attempted to systematically apply this principle.

One of the exceptions—my archaeological study of Aboriginal art in southeast Cape York Peninsula—was explicitly contextual and multi-disciplinary in approach. The investigation was concerned with the way people occupied and modified the landscape from earliest times until European contact. It used a range of environmental and archaeological evidence, including rock art.

Following on from lessons learnt during a previous project in the north Queensland highlands (Chapter 9), our intention right from the beginning of the project was to target the ways in which people used resources, the part that individual sites played in this land use system and how the system might have developed over time in response to changes in climate, resource levels and distribution, population, technological innovations, and so on. Much of the information required for the investigation came from researchers in other scientific disciplines, including palynology (the study of pollen), geology, geomorphology, zoology and botany. This work was carried out in conjunction with archaeological surveys and excavations, and the recording and dating of rock art. It proved crucial to understanding the context and significance of the archaeological record.

The study demonstrated that major developments in Aboriginal population levels and resource use occurred in southeast Cape York Peninsula during occupation spanning at least 34 000 years. The evidence of rock art definitely added a social dimension to the archaeological scenario.

Land and history

On the southern and eastern edges of the Laura Basin in southeast Cape York Peninsula, a great arc of coarse sandstones curves south then west from Princess Charlotte Bay to form a dissected plateau some 12 500 square kilometres in area (Figure 10.1). These sandstones contain one of the largest and most spectacular bodies of Aboriginal rock art in Australia—the very distinctive Quinkan rock painting tradition, which is comparable in richness and diversity to the better-known rock art traditions of western Arnhem Land and the Kimberley.

FIGURE 10.1

General map of southeast Cape York Peninsula showing resource zones. A major concentration of rock art sites occurs throughout Resource Zone 5, the Battle Camp Sandstones. (1) Karumba Plains, (2) Coastal Lowlands, (3) Mitchell-Gilbert Fans, (4) Holroyd Plains, (5) Battle Camp Sandstones, (6) Cohen-Yamba Inliers, (7) Hodgkinson Hills, (8) Wet Tropics, (9) Merluna Plain. (From Morgan et al. 1995, Figure 1.1)

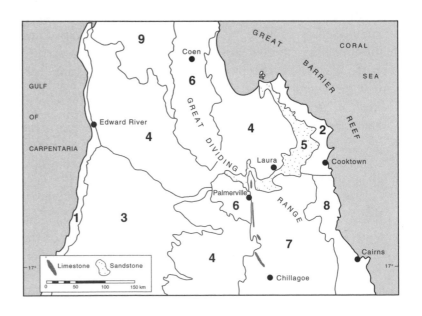

The history of European–Aboriginal contact in the region is largely one of violence. An expedition led by Edmund Kennedy passed through the Laura area in 1848, but the first large-scale contact occurred with the finding of gold on the Palmer River in 1873. The resulting gold rush led to clashes between miners and Aborigines, and the rapid destruction of traditional Aboriginal society. As a result, ethnographic information on the local groups, such as the Kokojawa, Koko Minni, Koko Yimidir and Koko Yellanji, is very sparse (Figure 10.2). Similarly, there is little specific information on Quinkan rock art, although there are reports of rock paintings being made as late as the 1920s, in association with sorcery.

The rock art

Quinkan rock paintings are almost entirely figurative and comprise outline or solid silhouettes of a great variety of subjects, such as spirit beings, men and women, dingos, macropods, echidnas, birds, reptiles, fish, tracks and yams. Aboriginal informants have identified the painted spirit beings as Quinkans, who also feature prominently in local myths and traditional lore, and it is these figures that have given the name to this regional art style.

Despite this variety in subject matter, most of the paintings are depicted in a highly standardized 'Simple Figurative' format. For instance, humans are almost invariably shown from the front, macropods and birds from the side, and reptiles from above. Although they often have interior patterning, the paintings also lack fine anatomical details. Painting is the predominant technique, but stencils of hands and weapons are also found, along with pecked engravings, which emphasize lines, pits, circles and tracks (Figure 10.3).

The time depth of the Quinkan painting style is unknown, but some of the earliest examples, as assessed on the basis of superimpositioning and relative weathering, include depictions of the Australian native dog, which is a relatively recent addition to the range of Australian animals (Figure 10.4). Evidence from archaeological and fossil sites indicates that the dingo first came to Australia about 4000 years ago, and this is a probable maximum age for the Quinkan rock painting tradition. It is significant, however, that at sites with particularly stable rock surfaces, earlier 'non-Quinkan' styles of painting are occasionally preserved.

FIGURE 10.2

Aboriginal tribes and their movements around Laura in southeast Cape York, as recorded by Walter Roth, Protector of Aborigines for North Queensland, in 1989. Our study of historical documents yielded a range of information on local peoples and how they responded to seasonal changes in the availability of fresh water, food and other resources. In turn this was used to model how people may have responded to long-term fluctuations in climate—especially during the arid period between 25 000 and 15 000 years ago. (After Roth 1898, 1899)

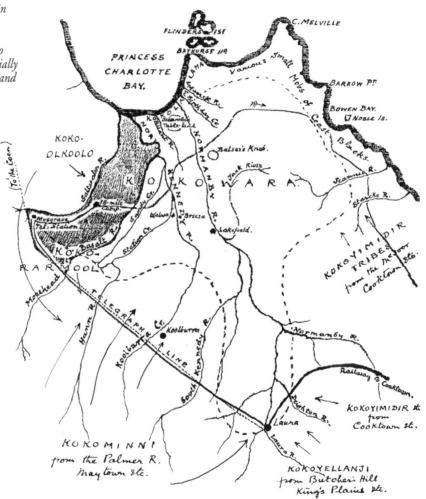

FIGURE 10.3

Part of the main panel of rock paintings at Magnificent Gallery, southeast Cape York Peninsula. Archaeological excavations at the site have shown that the majority of the 500 paintings are less than 1000 years old. (Photo M. J. Morwood)

The depiction of post-European contact subjects in some painted panels shows that the most recent Quinkan paintings postdate 1848, when the Kennedy expedition passed through the region. Post-contact subjects include horses, pigs, cattle, Europeans and Native Mounted Police with firearms.

The lack of relevant ethnographic information means that it is no longer possible to 'read' individual Quinkan rock paintings. The literal meanings are therefore beyond recall. However, clues to their role in local Aboriginal society, and how this may have changed over time, can still be found by careful examination of evidence for other activities that occurred in decorated rockshelters. The principal way of obtaining this evidence is by investigating the associated sandy deposits which have slowly accumulated on rockshelter floors, and which often contain the remains of Aboriginal fires, meals and stone artefacts.

FIGURE 10.4

A panel of engravings at the Amphitheatre site, southeast Cape York Peninsula. The depiction of a dingo must be less than 4000 years old, when the species was introduced to Australia from Southeast Asia. (From Cole et al. 1995, Figure 13 4b)

The project

The main reason for selecting southeast Cape York Peninsula for a regional archaeological project was that it has a large number of rock art sites and there appeared to have been major changes in the rock

FIGURE 10.5

Excavations at Giant Horse Shelter showed that the site was first used 4000 years ago. Rock paintings of horses and pigs, as well as the occurrence of artefacts made from flaked bottle glass at the site, indicate that it continued to be used during the European contact period. (Photo M. J. Morwood)

art over time. Art has unique potential for shedding light on social processes, as well as types of behaviour and material culture sparsely represented in other categories of archaeological evidence.

A second reason was the fact that at many sites, occupation deposits of considerable depth were closely associated with the rock art (Figure 10.5). This circumstance was particularly suited to the archaeological investigation of the art's cultural context—what activities took place in decorated rockshelters and how did these activities change? In addition, much of the region has not been heavily impacted since European settlement, and it is still possible to map the natural contexts of the sites. Such information is required for assessing the likely role of individual sites in a regional pattern of land use.

Finally, the work of previous researchers in the general area provided a minimum timespan for occupation of the region and demonstrated that changes in Aboriginal stone-working technology, art and general patterns of site use had occurred during this time. Previous work served as an established platform for more detailed assessment.

The first reports on Quinkan rock paintings by Robert Logan Jack, a government geologist, appeared in the 1890s, but local rock art sites are best known through the recording work of Percy Trezise, as outlined in his books *Rock Art of Southeast Cape York, Quinkan Country* and *Last Days of a Wilderness.* Over the past forty years Trezise has amply demonstrated the abundance and character of this cultural heritage. Trezise's work led directly to the creation of the Quinkan Reserve, an area of 1000 square kilometres near the township of Laura that has been set aside specifically for the protection of rock art sites. It is now owned by the Ang-gnarra Aboriginal Corporation and has been renamed Ang-gnarra Lands.

From the 1960s, Trezise's recording work also prompted a number of archaeological investigations of decorated rockshelters in the region, beginning with the work of Richard Wright at Mushroom Rock near Laura in 1963 and 1964. Wright excavated areas on the east and west side of Mushroom Rock, and found that stone artefacts on the west side occurred to a depth of 4.5 metres (Figure 10.6). Two radiocarbon dates were obtained—the older, of about 7000 BP, came from a depth of 2 metres. Only preliminary analyses were undertaken on the large stone artefact assemblage recovered from Mushroom Rock, but Wright was able to demonstrate that two main stone artefact industries were represented. The more recent industry consisted of smaller artefacts made to repeated patterns, and was dated to approximately the last 3000 years. In contrast, the older industry mainly comprised larger artefacts with flaked edges irregular in form and disposition. Older stone tools were also less frequently produced on flakes.

Later Andrée Rosenfeld excavated at Early Man rockshelter, and Josephine Flood excavated at Green Ant and Echidna Dreaming rockshelters on the Koolburra Plateau (Figure 10.7). By the mid-1970s scientific excavations had pushed back the time depth of Aboriginal occupation in the region to about 14 000 years BP and demonstrated that major changes in stone artefact technology, such as the introduction of burren adzes, had occurred late in the sequence, in association with an increase in the intensity of rockshelter use.

Rosenfeld's work at Early Man also showed that a panel of deeply weathered, pecked engravings, with some similarities to the widespread Panaramitee engraving tradition, was at least 14 400 years old. Noting a significant increase in the amount of pigment being deposited in the site and the position of paintings truncated by occupation deposits (Figure 10.8), she suggested that the change from an early rock art tradition of pecked engravings of mostly geometric designs and tracks, to the figurative Quinkan rock painting tradition, occurred between 4000 and 5000 years ago. However, the implications of these changes in stone artefact technology, intensity

FIGURE 10.6

Part of Richard Wright's 1964 excavation on the west side of Mushroom Rock, southeast Cape York Peninsula. He found stone artefacts and used fragments of pigment in the sand deposits to a depth of 4.5 metres. Thermoluminescence dating of the deposits indicate that the shelter was first used by Aboriginal people about 40 000 years ago. (Photo Richard Wright)

FIGURE 10.7

Andrée Rosenfeld's 1974 excavation at Early Man Shelter. She found that the site was first occupied around 14 400 BP, with a major change in stone artefact technology at 4000 BP. (Photo A. Rosenfeld)

FIGURE **10.8**

Buried engravings exposed during Andrée Rosenfeld's excavation at Early Man Shelter, southeast Cape York Peninsula. These are a minimum of 14 400 years old and may be a regional variant of the widespread Panaramitee tradition. Note also the truncated paintings of flying foxes, which must be at least 1000 years old. (After Rosenfeld et al. 1981, Figure 22a)

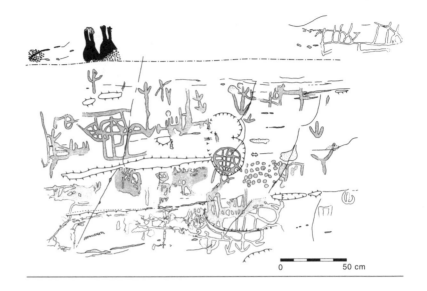

of shelter use and rock art for Aboriginal population levels, social organization and economy remained unclear.

Useful comparative data was provided by another researcher, John Beaton, who worked around Princess Charlotte Bay at the northern end of the Laura Basin sandstone plateau. His excavations at three rockshelters (Endaen, Walaemini and Alkaline Hill) and thirteen shell mounds demonstrated that Aboriginal occupation of this area commenced only 4700 years ago, well after the rise and stabilization of sea level at the end of the last Ice Age. Furthermore, the first systematic use of marine resources, as practised by local Aboriginal people in historic times, began just 2500 years ago. Beaton claimed that these developments resulted from a major increase in the Aboriginal population late in the occupational sequence.

More recently, Bruno David completed archaeological research on changes in Aboriginal social relations and resource use in the region just south of Quinkan country. His study focused on the limestones of the Mitchell–Palmer and Chillagoe areas and the volcanics and coarse sandstones on the northern edge of the Featherbed Ranges, about 100 kilometres west of Cairns. The work includes a series of excavations and the dating of the local rock art sequence. At Nurrabullgin Cave, the earliest cultural deposits found are dated to 'older than 37 000 years', which provides a minimum age for occupation of the region. However, the highest deposition rates for all cultural materials at this site, including ochre, occurred over the last 5000 years. David concluded that the increase in the intensity of Aboriginal site and regional land use that occurred in the mid-to-late Holocene was not prompted by an increase in resources, but resulted from 'social processes'.

The work of Wright, Rosenfeld, Flood, Beaton and David established a minimum time depth for human occupation of southeast Cape York Peninsula, and identified major changes in stone artefact technology, art and economy. In the context of general trends in Australian prehistory, the distinctive Quinkan rock painting tradition might have appeared around 4000 to 5000 BP, at the same time as an abrupt increase in population and the development of more intensive local economies in both coastal and inland areas. One of the main aims of my project was to refine and test this hypothesis.

PREPARATION AND COLLABORATION

The basic approach taken to analysis of all categories of evidence collected in the project was structural—that is, the identification and explanation of distributional patterning in the archaeological record— whether in stone artefact assemblages, economic remains, settlement patterns or rock art.

The importance of an integrated, multi-disciplinary approach was also emphasized. Different lines of evidence provide different but complementary perspectives on the past. Furthermore, considering evidence for human technology, material culture, economy and art in unison, rather than in isolation, must provide a stronger basis for reconstructing past land use systems, especially in the context of changes in the abundance and distribution of resources. Although archaeological excavations take place at individual sites, the aim of the work is to investigate occupation of areas.

The size and complexity of the database required to investigate the human past in any meaningful manner also negates a naive empirical approach, in which evidence is collected then interpreted. Instead, it requires an appreciation of possible connections between environment, human population levels, technology and art—and how these might be manifest in the archaeological record. In this study, ethnographic information on how Aboriginal groups in Cape York Peninsula reacted to short-term changes in social circumstances and resource availability was used to model the recent pattern of land use.

In turn, this was used as a basis for predicting how Aboriginal land use might have changed over time, and the archaeological implications.

This project on the archaeology of the Quinkan region, southeast Cape York Peninsula, began in 1989. Its primary aim was to investigate a range of evidence for the changing nature of Aboriginal culture throughout the occupation sequence. The evidence included food remains and stone artefacts recovered from archaeological excavations, as well as rock art.

RESOURCE MAPPING

This involved the mapping of major resource zones in southern Cape York Peninsula and local environments around excavated sites. The mapping of environmental units was combined with a stock-take of local plants and animals. Information was obtained on the traditional uses of plants and their seasonal availability from the Laura Aboriginal community, as well as from published ethnographic sources and archives.

Data on local resource structure were deemed essential for understanding the scheduling of Aboriginal economic activities, and the part that individual sites played in the overall pattern of land use. The study identified key resource zones for Aboriginal occupation. For instance, the upper sections of sandstones and conglomerates on the plateau scarps and sandy outwash plains were particularly rich in plant foods such as yams and plums, which formed the staple of the local Aboriginal diet. Springs and swamps, many of them geologically permanent, also occur around the plateau scarps. These resource-rich spring areas would have been a focus of Aboriginal occupation in the region, and would have enabled low-density use of some sections of the country throughout the most arid periods of the late Ice Age.

Past environments

Prior to our fieldwork, the environmental history of southeast Cape York Peninsula was reconstructed on the basis of the general Australian climatic sequence. There was no specific evidence from southeast Cape York Peninsula itself. We felt that this had to be rectified, and that more local data was required as a basis for reconstructing likely patterns of past land use in the region.

Information on local environmental changes was collected by Lesley Head and Karen Stephens, who studied pollen and charcoal particle sequences recovered from archaeological sites and from swamps. These show a basic stability in the local vegetation throughout the whole period of Aboriginal occupation. The evidence suggests that the eucalypt woodland back to 34 000 BP was similar to, but more open than, that found today, and that only minor changes have occurred since this time. It also suggests that regular Aboriginal burning of local vegetation, as observed by Europeans during historic times, had commenced by 5000 years ago.

Although dry-land vegetation remained relatively stable, the number of freshwater swamps in both coastal and inland sections of the Laura Basin increased during the past 10 000 years. The trend appears to have accelerated after 2700 BP. These swamps provided reliable water sources and were rich in plant foods. In association with the development of food-rich estuaries along the coast following the stabilization of sea level from 6000 BP, this would have led to a major increase in the range of resources, with high potential for population growth.

In addition, sand samples taken by David Price were dated by thermoluminescence to provide data on the rates of build-up for the extensive sand sheets that form such a prominent feature of the landscape (Figure 10.9). He showed that the sand plains had been accumulating well before initial Aboriginal occupation of the region, and that the rate of build-up was greatest when the climate was particularly cold and dry about 18 000 years ago.

FIGURE 10.9

Left: *Lesley Head and Doug Hobbs taking care of sediments from a swamp in southeast Cape York Peninsula. Changes in the types of pollen and numbers of charcoal particles at different depths were used to reconstruct changes in vegetation and firing regimes over time,* (Photo M. J. Morwood)

Right: *David Price, of Wollongong University, using an auger to take samples from the sand plain outside Mushroom Rock Shelter. Sand from different depths was then dated using thermoluminescence, which enabled the rate of sand accumulation to be calculated. The work showed that sand plains in the area accumulated fastest at times when the climate was much drier, and that Mushroom Rock was first occupied around 40 000 years ago. Information on past changes in the local environment is crucial for interpreting the archaeological record, including the rock art sequence.* (Photo M. J. Morwood)

Ethnographic research

Ethnographic information describes how local Aboriginal groups responded to short-term changes in resources such as droughts. This information was used to model how people might have responded to long-term environmental changes, such as the onset of the last glacial maximum. This assisted greatly with the interpretation of the cultural changes apparent in the archaeological record. Although data on Aboriginal groups in the Quinkan region is sparse, people from the Laura Aboriginal community advised us on the traditional use and availability of plant foods, medicines and raw materials. In addition, some of the most detailed accounts of Aboriginal land use, the seasonality of economic activities, and material culture come from nearby regions, especially on the west coast of Cape York Peninsula.

Despite regional differences in the way resources were exploited, there were common features in Aboriginal land use throughout Cape York Peninsula. Coastal groups occupied smaller territories, had higher population densities and were more sedentary. In contrast, 'inland' groups had large estates, relatively low population densities, low linguistic diversity, and less seasonal variation in economic strategies. There was, however, extensive population movement to meet social and economic obligations—for warfare, trade and to arrange marriages.

People were most mobile, and most widely dispersed, during the early dry season when surface water was freely available, falling back to more permanent waters as the country dried out. Rockshelters were most intensively used during the heavy rains of the wet, when travel was difficult and more or less permanent camps were established. At the end of the wet these camps were abandoned and groups became progressively smaller and more mobile as the dry progressed. In the late dry, groups congregated at more permanent water sources close to strategic resources.

On the basis of these ethnographic observations, the following scenario for Aboriginal occupation of the region is likely. The earliest human presence in the region would have involved transient visits by wide-ranging exploratory groups. Between 40 000 and 25 000 years ago, when conditions were relatively cool and wet, the population increased.

When conditions became much colder and drier from 25 000 to 15 000 years ago, human habitation would have contracted to refuge areas where permanent water sources occurred within convenient walking distance of each other—that is, along the plateau margin. At the same time the regional population would have declined and some areas, such as the alluvial and outwash plains, which lack geologically permanent water sources, were probably abandoned.

From 15 000 years ago, as the climate improved, there was potential for regional population growth and expansion. As this happened, groups would have become less mobile and more tied to particular tracts of country. The environmental evidence indicates a continuing increase in the region's biological carrying capacity throughout the Holocene. The trend is likely to have accelerated 6000 years ago, when sea levels stabilized—especially from 2700 years ago, when there was a further increase in number of freshwater swamps. This would have culminated in the high population levels; intensive resource use and partitioning of the country into tightly packed clan territories of the type observed by Europeans in historic times. These changes would have been accompanied by a trend towards increased linguistic and artistic diversity.

Rock art recording and dating

The detailed recording of rock art sites provided data on geographical and chronological variation in the art, which were compared with changes evident in other categories of archaeological evidence. At the start of the project, Percy Trezise had already recorded over 1000 rock art sites, and Noelene Cole continued the slow, painstaking work of recording rock art panels in detail using photography and scaled drawings (Figure 10.10). As part of her research, Cole compared the representation of animal subjects in the rock art with their frequency in the natural environment, their importance in local Aboriginal mythology and their numbers in dietary remains excavated from rockshelter deposits. Alan Watchman assisted with the technological study of rock art production by taking very small samples of pigment for geological identification, and for comparison with pigment fragments recovered from the excavations.

The ability to integrate the record provided by rock art with other types of archaeological evidence and past environmental changes

FIGURE 10.10

Noelene Cole, of James Cook University, using an artist's grid to record rock paintings at Red Horse Shelter near Cooktown. The paintings were copied at 1:10 scale with annotated notes on colours used. (Photo M. J. Morwood)

depends upon having a good, dated rock art sequence. Since the precise dating of rock art is difficult, a number of approaches were employed. Many of the excavations yielded evidence for the antiquity of rock art—for example, fragments of pigment and sections of decorated rockshelter wall, which had subsequently become covered by occupation deposits. Some subjects, such as dingos and Europeans depicted in the paintings, also provided dating evidence. Watchman collected samples of rock art paint and mineral crusts in which minute traces of organic materials occurred—some of these organics, including fibres from the paintbrushes used by the Aboriginal artists, were radiocarbon dated. In total, the evidence suggested the following rock art sequence for the region.

LATE PLEISTOCENE (34 000 TO 18 000 BP)

Used ochres, indicative of painting, occur in the Sandy Creek 1 deposits back to 34 000 BP. However, the earliest definite evidence of rock painting or stencilling is the layer of haematite at the base of an oxalate crust sampled from Sandy Creek 2. This dates to 27 000 BP.

TERMINAL PLEISTOCENE (18 000 TO 10 000 BP)

Evidence from Early Man rockshelter shows that an engraving tradition of deeply pecked pits, tridents or bird tracks, rectilinear mazes, rings and rounded enclosures existed by 14 000 years ago. Deeply pecked engravings of similar age occur at Sandy Creek 1. Used ochres excavated at Sandy Creek 1 and 2, Early Man, Mushroom Rock and Magnificent Gallery also suggest that painting occurred widely throughout the region at this time. More specifically, a layer of pigment in a gypseous crust at Sandy Creek 2 is evidence of rock painting or stencilling around 16 000 BP. However, what was actually portrayed in the paintings is unknown.

EARLY HOLOCENE (10 000 TO 4000 BP).

Aboriginal artists practised both rock painting and engraving in this period. Used ochres recovered from deposits of this age in excavated art sites suggest that painting was widespread. At Sandy Creek 2, a layer of red pigment on the rear wall has been dated to 7500 BP, but the motif and technique of application are unknown. More speculatively, a panel of rock paintings at Magnificent Gallery is stylistically different from the majority of Quinkan rock paintings at the site. The panel is covered by a silica skin, and comprises small anthropomorphs, hand stencils and a cross. Archaeological excavation at this site found that there were two phases of pigment use at the site; production of the distinctive panel is likely to have been associated with the earliest phase, which occurred around 10 000 years ago (Figure 10.11).

Josephine Flood and Nicky Horsfall showed that the patinated engravings (circles, pits, 'mazes', lines, and bird and macropod tracks) in the panel at Green Ant shelter are about 10 000 years old. A sandstone slab with engraved bird tracks excavated from Early Man shelter shows that the techniques of shallow pecking and pounding were also part of the rock artist's repertoire by 4000 BP.

LATE HOLOCENE (4000 BP) TO EUROPEAN CONTACT (80 BP)

The Quinkan painting style dominated during this period. Stencilling, mainly of hands, coexisted with painting as a widely used technique. Stencilling of boomerangs may have lapsed with the loss of this artefact from the cultural repertoire, whereas the appearance of stencilled spearthrowers shows that these were introduced to the region relatively recently.

Depictions of the dingo in the lower (sometimes lowest) superimposition levels of Quinkan paintings imply that this painting style is less than 4000 years old. Similarly, at the Early Man site paintings of red flying foxes were partly covered by cultural deposits 1000 years old, thereby providing a minimum age for the Quinkan rock painting style (see Figure 10.8). However, AMS dates for layers of pigment obscured by oxalate crusts indicate that rock paintings more than 3000 years old have mostly been covered over by dust and salts. In other words, with a few exceptions, all the rock paintings still visible on the surface are less than 3000 years old. This makes it difficult to construct a detailed rock painting sequence for earlier times.

In a few cases unpatinated engravings, both figurative and non-figurative, overlie Quinkan style paintings, showing that they are at least partially contemporaneous. Other engravings likely to be contemporaneous with Quinkan paintings include open-air site assemblages, such as the Laura Crossing sites, the Amphitheatre (which contains a dingo), and the figurative engravings infilled with paint at the Kennedy, Little Kennedy, Death Adder and Hann River

FIGURE 10.11

A panel of paintings that is overlain by silcrete skins and recent Quinkan-style paintings at Magnificent Gallery. Evidence recovered during excavations at the site suggests that the earliest painted panel may be 10 000 years old. (Photo M. J. Morwood)

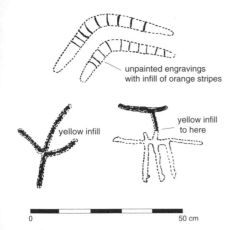

FIGURE 10.12

Figurative engravings infilled with paint at the Little Kennedy River shelters. Many engravings may have been originally highlighted with pigment. (After unpublished records by Eddy Oribin 1982)

FIGURE 10.13

Excavations at Sandy Creek 1 showed that the site was first used prior to 34 000 BP, and that painting had been a feature of site use throughout the entire cultural sequence. However, a range of archaeological evidence indicates that use of the site became far more intensive over the past 4000 years, with more people staying for longer. (Photo M. J. Morwood)

shelters (Figure 10.12). These all show great stylistic similarity with motifs in rock painting assemblages. In addition, non-figurative motifs continued to be of significance to Aboriginal people. For instance, AMS dating of an oxalate crust immediately overlying non-figurative pecked engravings at the Deighton Lady site indicates that they are about 3000 years old.

THE EUROPEAN CONTACT PERIOD (1873 CE TO THE 1920s)

Depictions of European subjects show that Aboriginal rock painting and stencilling in the Laura region continued well into the contact period, and isolated reports indicate that rock painting in the general region continued into the 1920s. Contact-period paintings are in the same Quinkan style typical of earlier paintings, even though Aboriginal culture and lifestyle were being devastated at the time.

Archaeological excavations

Excavations were undertaken in a range of natural and cultural contexts at nine rockshelters around Laura and one near Cooktown: Yam Camp, Red Bluff, Magnificent Gallery, Sandy Creek 1, Sandy Creek 2, Giant Horse, Mushroom Rock East, Mushroom Rock West, Red Horse and Hann River. In addition, stone artefacts were collected from the surface at one open site, Yam Camp Artefact Scatter, for comparative analysis.

Sites were selected for investigation so as to maximize the range of economic and technological information; to provide comparative samples from different contexts; and to extend the known time-depth of Aboriginal occupation. For instance, Magnificent Shelter was excavated because the site has a major rock painting assemblage associated with occupation deposits containing a range of artefacts and economic remains; Yam Camp because of the excellent preservation of organic remains in the uppermost levels; and Sandy Creek 1 because its deep deposits were likely to span a considerable time period (Figure 10.13).

Material excavated from local rockshelters by previous researchers was also analyzed. Overall, the excavation program enabled previously identified changes in stone artefact technology, economy, art and general site use to be defined and dated with greater resolution. It also pushed back the time depth of Aboriginal occupation of the region to a minimum of 34 000 years.

Conclusions

Although early evidence is sparse, it suggests that Aboriginal people made brief and infrequent visits into the region between 34 000 and 25 000 years ago, in small groups equipped with edge-ground axes and high quality stone for making flaked stone artefacts. Used pigment fragments, which provide indisputable evidence of painting, occur throughout deposits of this age, and evidence from Sandy Creek 2 shows that rock painting was definitely part of the artistic repertoire. Clearly, the first Aboriginal colonists of the region included artists, and their use of some sections of the plateau margin continued right through the coldest and driest conditions of the last glacial period 18 000 years ago.

As the climate began to improve about 15 000 years ago, the number of sites being occupied for the first time progressively increased (Figure 10.14), and there were changes in stone artefact

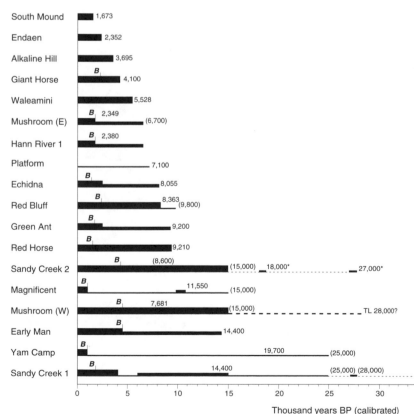

FIGURE 10.14

Basal radiocarbon dates for excavated sites in southeast Cape York Peninsula. The figure shows a rapid increase in number of sites (and therefore people) over the past 15 000 years as the climate became wetter and more productive. The regionally distinctive Quinkan rock painting tradition seems to have developed late in the cultural sequence, when there was increasing pressure on resources and people became more concerned with formal ownership of territory. Key: B = introduction of burren adze technology, * = dated rock paintings at Sandy Creek 2. Dates in brackets are inferred from the age-depth graphs.
(From Morwood and Hobbs 1995)

technology, plant exploitation and art. For instance, before this period there is little evidence for economy of raw material use in making stone artefacts. With the exception of edge-ground axes, most tools also appear to have been of expedient type. The most common woodworking implements were heavy flake and core tools made from stone of variable quality, and they were thrown away immediately after use (Figure 10.15).

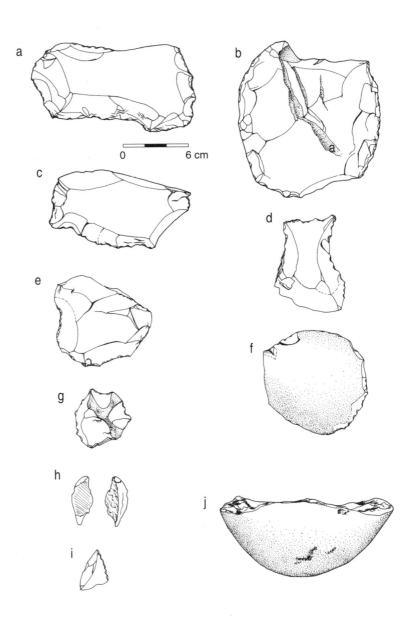

FIGURE 10.15

A range of tools of the Early Industry of southeast Cape York Peninsula: (a–g), flake tools; (h, i) edge-ground axe fragment; (j) split pebble. Prior to 15 000 BP, such stone tools were often made with little concern for conserving raw materials, and they were discarded soon after use. There were few people in the area at the time and there was little pressure to conserve resources.

(Drawing Kathy Morwood, from Morwood and L'Oste-Brown 1995, Figure 14.7)

Later, however, the sequence was marked by people becoming more selective in their choice of stone used for the manufacture of tools, and more economical in their use of cores. In addition, they resharpened tools more and developed curated tools, which took time and trouble to make but had a long working life. Many of these technological innovations appear to have been a response to regional population growth and increases in the intensity of individual site use. These placed increased demands on stone suitable for tool making. As a result, people developed ways of flaking to economise on the use of good-quality stone and to extend the use-life of some tools use (Figure 10.16). For instance, the first heavily retouched woodworking tools that were made from chert flakes fixed with resin onto wooden handles (known as burren adzes), appeared around 6000 years ago. By 4200 years ago adzes had become standardized

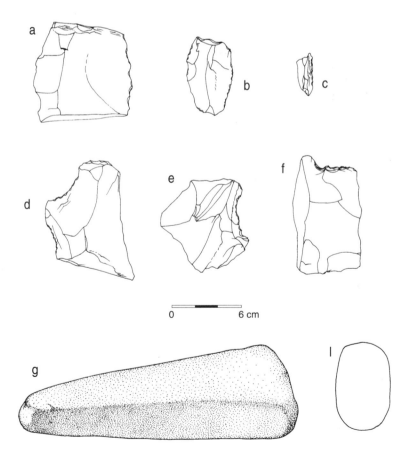

0   6 cm

FIGURE 10.16

A range of tools of the Middle Industry of southeast Cape York Peninsula: (a–b), (d–f) flake scrapers; (c) adze slug; (g) 'file'. From 15 000 years BP, stone tools in the region were mostly made using highly efficient flaking techniques on good quality material. Many tools were also retained for reuse. These innovations provide evidence for the beginnings of a major population increase. (Drawing Kathy Morwood, from Morwood and L'Oste-Brown 1995, Figure 14.9)

in size and shape, and by 2500 BP they were the predominant woodworking implements (Figure 10.17).

Further evidence for a progressive increase in the local Aboriginal population is provided by the expansion of settlement to the coast

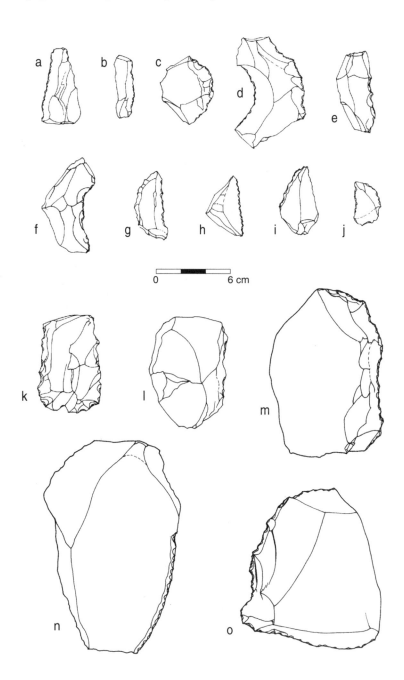

FIGURE 10.17

A range of tools of the Recent Industry of southeast Cape York Peninsula: (a) unifacial point; (b) microblade; (c) thumbnail scraper; (d–f), (k) burren adze slugs; (g–h) elouerae; (i) backed point; (j) geometric microlith; (l–m) core tools; (n–o) large flake tools. From 4200 BP, burren adzes had become standardized and rapidly became the most common woodworking implements. The stone adze slugs would have been hafted onto wooden handles with gum. They represent an extremely efficient use of good quality stone for artefact manufacture. Population build-up resulted in more intensive use of resources and at the same time the rock art became far more regionally distinctive.
(Drawing Kathy Morwood, from Morwood and L'Oste-Brown 1995, Figure 14.12)

around Princess Charlotte Bay 4700 years ago. Also, labour-intensive economic strategies to meet increased demands upon production did not appear until very late in the sequence. Excavations at the site of Red Horse near Cooktown showed that the use of grindstones for plant food preparation did not begin until after 1100 years ago, nor did the use of cycads, which were a food staple in historic times, but which are extremely toxic and require elaborate processing before consumption.

The rock art sequence for southeast Cape York Peninsula has to be seen in the context of this evidence for progressive increases in population over the past 15 000 years. It is significant that the earliest rock engravings, comprising the pecked panels of bird tracks, lines and other geometric motifs at Early Man and Sandy Creek 1, date from this time. These panels and other recorded examples can be seen as regional variants of the widespread Panaramitee engraving tradition. The extent and relative degree of homogeneity of this tradition suggests that it may have served an important function in linking small, widely dispersed territorial groups.

Dated examples of rock paintings, the subjects they depicted, and a major increase in pigment discard rates at excavated sites all suggest that the regionally distinctive Quinkan rock painting tradition appeared around 4000 years ago. If so, then ethnographic information on the way Aboriginal art systems work strongly suggests that the role of rock art changed over time, from an early role of linking groups, to one more concerned with limiting territorial boundaries. This shift is associated with a range of archaeological evidence for larger populations and more intensive use of resources. Bruno David similarly concluded that this late 'regionalisation' of rock art styles in southeast Cape York Peninsula marks increased differentiation and delineation of territories.

Quinkan rock art provides one line of evidence about the processes by which Aboriginal society was transformed into that observed during the European contact period. It can be seen that archaeological research is just as complicated as the human affairs it seeks to document. Clearly, the archaeological investigation of rock art in southeast Cape York Peninsula can provide insights into the Aboriginal past, especially when looked at within the context of information from a range of disciplines on the local resources, climate change, and evidence for changes in population, economy and technology.

CHAPTER 11

A future for the past: conservation of rock art

Literature on the conservation of rock art is extensive, but it is often technical and tends to be dry. One way of getting a general overview, before examining problems and solutions in detail, is to begin with the basic questions: 'Why preserve rock art sites?' and 'Is it possible to preserve rock art sites in the long term?'. Such questions are important because there are many sites and many ways in which they can be damaged, yet only limited funds and resources available for their management and conservation.

The amount of money allocated to rock art conservation, and the way in which it is divided up, is ultimately a political decision, and thus subject to dispute. But various organizations have worked out some general guidelines for the assessment of priorities in preserving natural and cultural resources. Since rock art is a division of this very large field, it is worth looking at general conservation principles before we move on to specific issues in rock art conservation.

The case for protecting rock art sites is ultimately based on respect for the historic fabric of an area and, in the words of G. Young, 'the need to conserve representative evidence of the total historical development pattern'. This in turn cannot be separated from a broader concern for the natural and cultural environment and a sense of obligation to future generations.

The 1972 World Heritage Convention of the United Nations Educational, Scientific and Cultural Organisation (UNESCO) formulated an international code of ethics for the conservation of monuments and sites (both cultural and natural) that are considered worth preserving for humankind. This convention was built on principles set out in the 1954 Hague Convention for the protection of cultural property in the event of armed conflict.

The World Heritage Convention is based on the idea that, 'deterioration or disappearance of any item of the cultural or natural heritage constitutes a harmful impoverishment of the heritage of all the nations of the world'. Under this convention a World Heritage list is gradually being prepared to be administered and supported by the World Heritage Committee and World Heritage Fund. Rock art areas and sites listed to date include the Palaeolithic decorated caves of the Vézère (France), Altamira Cave (Spain), rock engravings of the Val Camonica region (Italy), rock drawings of Alta (Norway), Tassili n' Ajjer (Algeria), and rock art sites of Tadart Acacus (Libya) and Kakadu National Park (Australia).

UNESCO also sponsors the International Council on Monuments and Sites (ICOMOS), whose 1964 Venice Charter provides guidelines for conservation and management of places of cultural significance in member countries. The Australian ICOMOS charter, known as the Burra Charter, defines conservation as the process of looking after a place so as to retain its cultural significance—that is, its aesthetic, historic, scientific or social value—for present and future generations.

Signatories to the ICOMOS charter agree to take into account all aspects of a given site's cultural significance; maintain an appropriate visual setting; ban the removal of culturally significant contents, unless this is the sole means of ensuring their preservation and survival; and allow the site to be altered only where there is no other way to achieve conservation, and where the change does not detract significantly from cultural value. ICOMOS also has an International Committee on Rock Art (CAR), whose aims include promoting the general cause of rock art studies, disseminating information and publishing a 'who's who' in rock art.

Most countries also formulate heritage legislation and guidelines. In Australia the 1975 Heritage Commission Act set up a commission to promote the conservation of places of natural and/or cultural value that have aesthetic, historic, scientific or social significance, or other special value for future generations as well as for the present community. One of the commission's roles is to compile a Register of the National Estate—a comprehensive list of nationally significant places—to provide objective information for decision makers and a focus for national heritage research programs. Each Australian state also has legislation protecting archaeological sites, including rock art sites, regardless of land tenure, and these are backed up by the federal *Aboriginal and Torres Strait Islander Heritage Protection Act 1984*.

In many countries, state ownership of all archaeological sites provides the fundamental basis for their conservation. But in the United States, federal legislation only protects archaeological sites on federal and Indian lands, or areas affected by federally funded projects (the *Antiquities Act 1906* and the *Archaeological and Historical Conservation Act 1974*). Similarly, state legislation only protects sites on state land. Sites on private land are the property of the landholders, who in most cases can deal with them as they wish. This has led to the 'legal' destruction or wholesale looting of very significant sites. In the few places where the law treats archaeological sites on private land as public property—as in Alabama or in Inyo County, California (which has an ordinance restricting excavation of ancient Indian cemeteries to professional archaeologists with a permit)—the general feeling is that such legislation is probably unconstitutional, although this remains to be tested in court.

In France, most archaeological sites are on private property and are also privately owned. Very few Palaeolithic sites are owned by the state: among these are Lascaux, Font de Gaume and Les Combarelles in the Dordogne. The world-famous site of Pech Merle is owned and managed by the commune of Cabrerets, a small village, even though it has been declared a historic monument under the control of the Ministry of Culture. A number of researchers have criticized the inadequacy of archaeological conservation laws in France—a country where, paradoxically, research on Palaeolithic sites has played a key role in the general history of archaeology, especially rock art studies.

Henry Cleere has discussed some of the factors responsible for differences in the nature and effectiveness of archaeological legislation in different countries. For instance, centralized governments are likely to produce a more even system of protection than federal, decentralized systems. In places such as France, a long archaeological tradition can be an obstacle to the rationalization of conservation infrastructure; in others, like Scandinavia, such traditions have resulted in very effective protection of sites and their surrounds. The issue of cultural identity also plays a key role in determining a nation's level of commitment to its archaeological heritage. For instance, post-colonial Mexico, India and China have all allocated considerable resources to the protection and interpretation of archaeological sites.

Despite such differences, all international, national and regional charters, legislation and organizations concerned with conservation of cultural resources operate on the same premise: that it is socially desirable to preserve places of aesthetic, historic, scientific or social significance. Other reasons commonly given for preserving archaeological sites are: they are a limited, non-renewable resource essential for documenting human prehistory; they have a significant role in establishing ethnic or national identity; they are repositories of palaeo-environmental information useful in a range of disciplines; and they have recreational and monetary value. Although the various charters and laws stipulate general conservation procedures and requirements, the onus for assessing cultural significance and working out specific conservation priorities clearly lies with expert organizations and individuals.

Significance is relative and has many dimensions. Deciding how significant a site is and how it should be conserved may involve weighing up conflicting assessments by different interest groups. Judgements about whether a site should be open to the public, fenced, left unmodified or destroyed by development will have to take into account the relative scientific, historical, ethnic, public and/or monetary significance of the site, its conservation needs, and possible conflicting patterns of site use.

In addition, the significance of a site can change. For instance, Sandra Bowdler has observed that scientific significance is a measure of the site's relevance to 'timely and specific research questions' and of its representativeness, both of which may change as the discipline develops. Given this situation, it is little wonder that conservation issues, priorities and measures vary from country to country, from region to region, and from organization to organization.

Rock art conservation problems

Many of the key problems in conserving rock art reflect the fact that it is positioned on an unstable interface between a body of rock and air. This is especially apparent in rockshelters, which are formed by weathering in rock outcrops. The surfaces of rock outcrops are where chemical and physical weathering is most pronounced, where salts in water moving through the rock tend to be precipitated, where airborne particles are deposited, and where a variety of animals build nests, rub themselves or leave their marks. Some rock art conservation problems can be rectified easily; others are beyond the help of the technologies currently available. But most of them can be divided into two broad categories: those caused by people, and those caused by natural agencies and processes.

THE EFFECTS OF PEOPLE

People can damage rock art sites indirectly, such as during development in an adjacent area, or directly, such as where the site itself attracts visitors.

Development

Many rock art sites have been affected by developments such as mining and the construction of dams and roads. Even distant development can affect a site: Whale Cave, near Wollongong in New South Wales, is collapsing because of subsidence resulting from mining of a coal seam beneath it. Development may also affect rock art sites by changing the general pattern of land use within an area: the Ranger uranium mine in Kakadu National Park, Northern Territory, does not impinge directly on art sites but has led to the establishment of a small town in a once sparsely populated region.

To counter the effects of developments like these, some groups have salvaged the art. For example, on the Burrup Peninsula in Western Australia, rock engravings on tumbled boulders were threatened by the Woodside offshore petroleum-drilling project. Boulders were accurately plotted, then removed by crane and trailer and taken to a salvage yard. Where removal was not possible, tracings and/or moulds were made of selected panels. A similar procedure was adopted at the Bundaberg rock engraving site in Queensland before a dam was built nearby: after a thorough recording program some engraved sections were removed by drilling out large slabs and transporting them with heavy equipment (Figure 11.1). In cases where salvage was not possible or not tried, the sites were merely recorded prior to destruction.

Visitors

Visitors can damage rock art by drawing graffiti, chalking or wetting motifs to 'improve' photographs, trying to remove motifs for private

FIGURE 11.1

Removal of an engraved block from the Dampier region, Western Australia. Industrial development in the area would have resulted in the destruction of the engravings, so many were taken to a place of safety, where they are currently stored.
(After Vinnicombe 1987, Figure 13)

FIGURE 11.2

Left and below: *Vandalism at the Bull Hole, central Queensland. The offender, a local girl, was 'reprimanded' although court action could have been taken under the Queensland Heritage Legislation. Subsequent attempts by local residents to remedy the damage with plastic filler merely added to the damage. The engravings are more than 5000 years old.* (Photo M. J. Morwood)

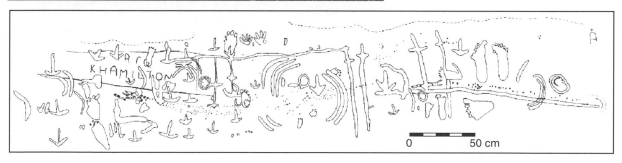

collections or commercial gain, and deliberately vandalizing sites (Figure 11.2). Visitors may also stir up dust which settles on the art, destabilize associated cultural deposits, inadvertently touch and brush against the art, introduce micro-organisms to previously sealed caves and alter pigments by using photographic flashes in poorly lit areas.

Removal of existing graffiti from rock art sites is now a standard site management practice, as it discourages copy-cat behaviour.

However, some graffiti at rock art sites—such as that left by the explorers Burke and Wills at Burke's Cave in western New South Wales, and by Aboriginal stockmen in Central Australia—is itself of historical importance. Such graffiti can only be removed after a difficult consideration of conflicting priorities. Dated graffiti can also provide useful data for monitoring changes in public awareness and appreciation of rock art sites, so it should be recorded by conservationists before removal (Figure 11.3).

Researchers

Researchers have not always used the most appropriate methods when recording and 'conserving' rock art. Applying chalk, ink and crayon to make faint rock art motifs more photogenic, for example, not only detracts from the integrity and aesthetics of a site, but also distorts the original form of the motifs. Where subsequent bonding with the rock matrix has occurred, such 'touching up' cannot be removed without damaging the art.

Tracing rock art onto plastic sheets using ink pens is still a common practice, as is the use of artist's grids for scale drawings (Figure 11.4). Recording the art thus has a physical—and sometimes damaging—impact. Although much excellent recording work has been done in Australia using these techniques, caution is clearly

FIGURE 11.3

Changes over time in the rate of vandalism at rock art sites in the central Queensland highlands based upon dated graffiti. The earliest examples were done at a time when large pastoral stations were divided up and more Europeans moved into the area. Some of this early vandalism is itself of historical significance. There was a major increase in vandalism in the 1950s as people became more affluent and mobile. This peaked just after 1967, when cultural heritage legislation protecting Aboriginal sites was introduced in Queensland. It is significant that this legislation preceded rather than resulted from a general change in community attitudes to Aboriginal sites.
(After Morwood and Kaiser-Glass 1991, Figure 4)

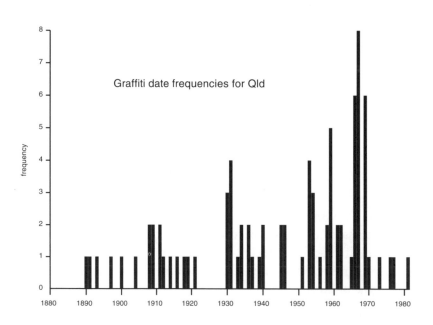

FIGURE 11.4

Below: *Chalked engravings at the Bundaberg engraving site, central Queensland coast. This recording technique is now discouraged as the chalk can permanently affect the rock surface. Most journals will no longer accept photographs of chalked engravings for publication.* (Photo K. A. Sutcliffe)

Left: *Engravings can be traced onto plastic sheets, then photographically reduced for publication. However, this method is now generally discouraged because there is direct contact between the plastic and the rock art surface. Alternatively, the engraved area can be gridded and scale drawings made directly, or photographs can be taken and annotated on-site. In all cases the results need to be checked under oblique lighting conditions.* (Photo M. J. Morwood)

FIGURE 11.5

Using latex to take a mould of rock engravings in the central Queensland highlands. This technique should only be undertaken by technical specialists as a means of replicating a threatened site. It can cause serious damage to the rock art surface. (Photo M. J. Morwood)

required. Some European researchers prefer to minimize contact with the art by annotating large-scale photographs of the surface under a range of lighting conditions.

Some researchers take moulds of rock engravings with latex, aluminum foil or other media so that casts can be made for display purposes. But this has often had unacceptable effects, even when undertaken by technically skilled people (Figure 11.5). Taking moulds can only really be justified when the engravings are under threat and a replica is needed for future research and education.

Removing the art is an even more drastic measure and is usually undertaken only in cases of a real or perceived threat to the art. For instance, the well-known engraved 'crocodile head' panel at the Panaramitee site in Northeast South Australia was drilled and blasted from the outcrop by the South Australian Museum because of concern about vandalism. The Queen Victoria Museum took similar steps at the Mt Cameron West engraving site in Tasmania. In the past, some rock art removals were not well thought out and so they became a conservation problem rather than a solution. These days, rock art is removed only if there is no other way to save it.

Archaeologists digging in rockshelters have also played a part in damaging rock art. Team members may inadvertently knock against rock surfaces, while the dust from excavation, sieving and backfilling can cover the art. Yet few excavators make an effort to minimize their

FIGURE 11.6

Use of a calico curtain around the sieve during excavations at Magnificent Gallery reduced production of dust by 90 per cent. The sieving area was also curtained off and located downwind and some distance from the rockshelter. These measures were essential to prevent dust from the work settling on the rock paintings or being breathed in by people. (Photo M. J. Morwood)

impact on rock art—largely because 'dirt' archaeologists tend to focus on the deposits and are more or less oblivious to the art.

All archaeologists need do, however, is take a few simple remedial measures, such as screening the art, covering the surface of the deposit around the excavation area with plastic, using plank boardwalks, placing sieves outside and downwind from the site, screening the sieving area, attaching a 'skirt' around the sieves, and backfilling with previously bagged deposits (Figure 11.6). These measures reduce physical contact with the art, dust production and general site disturbance. They also serve to remind the participants about the site's heritage value and conservation requirements.

MANAGING PEOPLE

Legislation

A wide range of management techniques has been tried to minimize the amount of damage inflicted on rock art sites. But a sure deterrent is to punish those who cause such damage with fines and/or imprisonment, and all legislation concerned with preserving cultural resources stipulates penalties for the destruction or disturbance of sites. Fay Gale and Jane Jacobs have stressed that an important part of making archaeological legislation effective is ensuring that the fine is large enough to discourage would-be offenders.

In practice, however, prosecution is seldom used as a way to limit deliberate damage to rock art sites. Apart from the practical difficulties in catching offenders red-handed, many management bodies are reluctant to take legal action, arguing that it would be bad for public relations and might lead to a backlash. They advocate public education as the best long-term solution to the problem. Charles McGimsey, for instance, has made the point that conservation laws must be designed 'to facilitate, develop, and encourage public support and to avoid, insofar as possible, situations whereby the law is likely to be honoured principally in the breach'.

But sometimes authorities seem so attached to this useful general guideline that they overlook the importance of demonstrating official commitment by enforcing the law. In Australia, there have only been six successful prosecutions in this area, mostly involving graffitists who have signed and dated their work. Grahame Walsh has suggested that, given the frequency of deliberate vandalism, the policy of going easy on offenders has not paid dividends and it therefore needs to be reassessed.

Restricting access to information

The most common official ways of protecting rock art from visitors involve restricting access to sites and/or controlling the movement of visitors at sites. An easy and widely used method of restricting access is not to tell the general public where rock art sites are. In an extreme example, Western Australian authorities do not promote any art sites as tourist attractions and withhold all location information from the public.

More often, a few 'sacrificial' rock art sites are developed, promoted and closely monitored, while others are kept safe by ensuring that they do not appear on maps or official brochures. Allowing access tracks to deteriorate, declaring 'restricted access' buffer zones, and so on can also actively discourage visitors. Experience at Carnarvon Gorge National Park has demonstrated how the public visibility of even heavily visited sites can be changed. Here a decision was made to salvage one of the three main galleries in the gorge from heavy visitation. All reference to the site was deleted from brochures and maps, the access track was camouflaged and the main track up the gorge was rerouted to permit natural vegetation to grow back. This went hand in hand with active promotion of the other two 'sacrificial' galleries, where structural changes had been made to cope with visitor pressure. Visits to the salvaged site dwindled surprisingly quickly.

Land tenure

Access and visitor behaviour can also be controlled by the creation of national parks, wilderness areas and restricted areas. The most notable area where entry is restricted solely because of the number of rock art sites is the Ang-gnarra Lands (formerly Quinkan Reserves) in southeast Cape York, an area of about 97 000 hectares (400 square miles), which is administered by the Ang-gnarra Aboriginal Corporation. The access gate on the main road into the reserves is kept locked. This, the size of the reserves, and the fact that the locations of the art sites are not published, ensure that the area gets very few unauthorised visitors. The limited demand to see Quinkan rock art has been satisfied by allowing access to the Split Rock art complex on adjacent Crocodile Station, which is closely monitored and has been developed with trails, signposting and a car park to minimize visitor impact.

Transferring areas with rock art sites from private to public lands can result in increased visitor numbers, but this need not lead to damage if there are enough resources and staff to properly manage the areas. Depending upon the goodwill of landholders to look after significant sites is risky in the long term, as not all landholders are equally sympathetic to conservation aims.

Restricting access

Another way to control the number of people visiting art sites is to impose a quota system. Among the many well-known rock art sites where daily visitor numbers are restricted in this way is Lascaux, in the Perigord region of France. Since the cave was 'closed' in 1963 a full-sized replica of one section, termed Lascaux II, has curbed much of the public demand to see the original. In Australia, Carnarvon Gorge National Park in Queensland admits a maximum of 800 visitors a day on a first-come basis. All visitors must book in advance and pay a camping fee.

Visitor access can also be controlled by placing barriers around the sites to prevent entry while still letting people see and photograph the art. In some areas, such as the Grampians in Victoria, all publicly accessible rock art sites are caged in mesh with slots for cameras (Figure 11.7). A similar approach was taken at the Red Hands site in the Blue Mountains, New South Wales, where perspex and grilles

FIGURE 11.7

The security cage at Glen Isla Gallery in the Grampians, Victoria, was constructed to prevent visitors accidentally or deliberately damaging the rock paintings. Some visitors regard such cages as a challenge and will go to extraordinary steps to gain entry to the gallery. (Photo G. L. Walsh)

protect the art. Such barriers are unattractive and alter the appearance of a site, and determined individuals may simply see them as a challenge. However, they offer reliable protection and dismantling them would now be seen as irresponsible. Fugoppe Cave, on Hokkaido Island in Japan, has an unusual variation on the barrier theme. An air-conditioned building has been erected across the cave mouth and visitors view the rock engravings through the windows of a pod which projects into the cave (Figure 11.8).

Reducing visitor impact

Barriers are the most visible but not the only way to control the numbers of visitors to a site and the way they move through it. Boardwalks, signposting and information centres can influence visitor interest and access, as can the location of car parks and toilet facilities. Designers need to give careful thought to the length and width of paths, types of stairs and barriers, handrail heights, placement and wording of informative or warning signs, and the location of photographic vantage points, rest and gathering areas, visitors' centres and toilets. At the Rainbow Serpent Gallery at Ubirr, Kakadu National Park, the boardwalk railing obstructed views of a rock art motif, encouraging would-be photographers to stand on or cross the railing. As Gale and Jacobs note, preliminary studies and monitoring

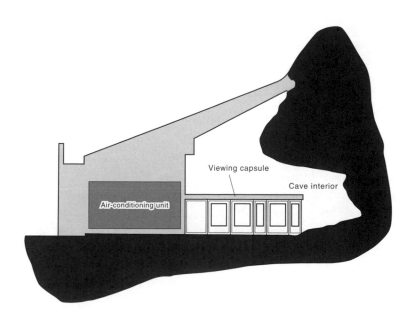

FIGURE 11.8

Conservation facilities at Fuggope Cave, Hokkaido Island, Japan. Visitors see the engravings through windows in a capsule, which intrudes into the cave. It is a surreal experience! (After Ogawa 1992, Figure 9)

FIGURE 11.9

General view of the boardwalks at Cathedral Cave, Carnarvon Gorge, Queensland. The facilities put in place at this site to reduce visitor impact have served as role models for developments at other rock art sites, such as Kakadu National Park. For instance, the boardwalk sits on top of the site causing minimum disturbance. Also, the boardwalk is constructed in sections chained together which can be moved to allow for future archeological excavations at this site.
(Photo G. L. Walsh)

of the effectiveness of crowd control mechanisms may be costly, but having to alter poorly planned facilities is even more so.

The boardwalks and interpretive signs at the Art Gallery and Cathedral Cave in Carnarvon Gorge National Park have been particularly successful and have strongly influenced the planning of infrastructure at other Australian rock art sites (Figure 11.9). These accessories were primarily designed to prevent people touching the art, stirring up dust and eroding archaeological deposits, but the boardwalks were also designed to blend with the setting and provide a gently sloping, safe access route, an attractive walk and a spectacular introduction to the art. Special photography positions were worked out after experimentation with camera shots using a range of lenses, and rest seats were placed so as not to interfere with pedestrian traffic. The handrails help constrain visitor movement within the site and are reinforced by psychological barriers: the floors of the shelters away from the boardwalks are kept free of litter and footprints, and 'no-go areas' are maintained at times when no visitors are present. A visitors' book allows people to record their visit and impressions for posterity, and thereby reduces the frequency of graffiti at the site. The book is closely monitored by park staff for comments requiring action and for information on visitor origins. Negative comments are routinely removed, since they have a flow-on effect to later entries.

The integrity of the archaeological deposits at both sites has also been ensured by using cross-mounting bearer supports laid on the surface of the deposits, and by constructing the boardwalks in short sections coupled by chains so they can be removed for future archaeological excavations. Elsewhere, however, the integrity of cultural deposits has not always been given due consideration. When National Parks and Wildlife staff built steps and a wooden viewing platform at the Yarrowich art site in northeast New South Wales in 1987, they dug out the majority of associated deposits and thereby destroyed much of the evidence for the art's cultural context (Figure 11.10).

Gale and Jacobs have demonstrated that effective site management depends upon careful monitoring of the nature and scale of visitor pressure; assessment of visitor profiles, attitudes and behaviour; and measurement of visitors' physical impact upon the site and its surrounds. Their study focused on Uluru in Central Australia and Kakadu National Park in the north of Australia, and employed a variety of survey techniques (for example, counters, observers, interviews) developed by organisations such as the Tourist and Recreation Research Unit in Britain. They found that differences in the intensity of visitor use between sites (even those very close to each other) over the long term, seasonally, daily and even hourly,

FIGURE 11.10

Most of the cultural deposits were dug out when the steps and wooden viewing platform were constructed at the Yarrowich art site in northeast New South Wales. The viewing platform and associated barriers have been very successful in reducing the impact of animals and visitors on the rock art, but evidence for the history of site use has been destroyed. (Photo M. J. Morwood)

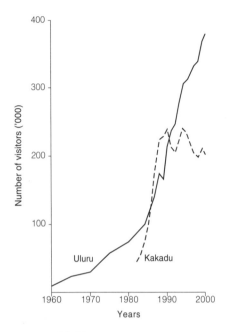

FIGURE 11.11

Number of visitors at Uluru and Kakadu National Parks between 1960 and 2000. In both parks strategies to reduce the impact of rapidly increasing visitor numbers include putting in 'hard' infrastructure, such as boardwalks, barriers, visitors' books and informative signs. Restricting public access to sites in Kakadu since 1988 has also stabilized the number of visitors to around 220 000 per year; visitor numbers at Uluru, however, have continued to grow rapidly. (Data from Gale and Jacobs 1987b, Figure 12; Uluru-kata Tjuta National Office; Sarah Pizzey of the Kakadu National Park Office)

depend upon a whole range of factors. Visitor numbers at the well-known, much promoted sites at Uluru and Kakadu—as at other such sites worldwide—have increased rapidly over the past 25 years, along with ease of access, leisure time and general awareness of the cultural heritage (Figure 11.11). Numbers also vary seasonally—falling during the monsoonal wet season at Kakadu, for example—and from day to day, depending on the ratio of local to long-distance visitors: Uluru is not near a major population centre and lacks the pronounced 'weekend' peak in visitors seen at Kakadu, which is near Jabiru and Darwin.

Gale and Jacobs also found that visitor age, mode of travel (private or organized) and place of origin (local or distant) are associated with very different attitudes and behaviour, and that different sectors of the visitor population have different and varied impacts upon sites. The most destructive categories of visitors are poorly supervised children; large, poorly-led organized tour groups who tend to overcrowd confined sites; and local residents with feelings of 'ownership' and over-familiarity. Walsh has also noted that different stages in the public awareness of a site tend to attract different types of visitors and give rise to very different management problems.

1 *'Pioneer' visitors* seek out remote areas and often overcome considerable obstacles to locate virgin sites. They are 'high risk' visitors and as a group have been responsible for the worst desecration, vandalism, graffiti and souveniring at art sites. Controlling them is difficult, but reasonably effective measures include restricted-access areas, mobile patrols, strict law enforcement and official tagging of known sites to make it clear that the 'pioneers' are not the first discoverers.

2 *'Individual' visitors* prefer to avoid more developed areas in the quest for a less 'commercial' experience. They cause considerable damage, especially with graffiti, but their relatively small numbers make costly management strategies, such as boardwalks, uneconomical. Appropriate management strategies include restricted-access areas, withholding information on site locations and provision of adequate information on the significance and vulnerability of sites.

3 *'General' visitors* are content with fully managed sites and are generally law-abiding and self-policing. They comprise the bulk of visitors to rock art sites, and any associated damage they do is largely unintentional (for example, erosion of deposits, touching

of art). General visitors are easiest to control and their large numbers justify costly management strategies. Walsh suggests that the sooner a site attains 'high visitation' status, the easier it is to manage and protect from human damage.

THE EFFECTS OF NATURAL AGENCIES AND PROCESSES

Even if people never visit them, rock art sites are still subject to the depredations of geological and biogenic weathering. On a geological time scale, all rock art sites are deteriorating, but some are deteriorating more rapidly than others. The factors responsible, and the rate of weathering, depend upon the composition of the rock art support, the macro- and micro-configuration of the site (for example, cave, shelter, open), the climatic and biological environment, and the artistic techniques used. In the central Queensland highlands, for instance, Hutton sandstone weathers rapidly and the Murphy Range, in which Hutton sandstone predominates, has lost almost all of its known rock art during the past 50 years. In contrast, the hardness and stability of rock art surfaces in the Kimberley has ensured excellent preservation of some paintings and engravings for more than 25 000 years.

Rock art weathering involves many factors but generally proceeds in three ways.

Disintegration of the rock support

This can occur through block collapse, exfoliation, grain-by-grain disintegration, or a combination of these. The form of the weathering process depends on the characteristics of the rock and the principal factors responsible. Block collapse and exfoliation tend to be episodic in nature and are caused by stresses set up within the rock as a result of faults, rapid changes in temperature (for example, frosts, bushfires), the pressure of deposited salts building up beneath the rock surface, seismic activity or subsidence (Figure 11.12).

Grain-by-grain disintegration, which may be continuous, results from chemical weakening of the minerals cementing the rock matrix (Figure 11.13). Such weakening is caused by processes including hydrolysis and mobilisation of salts and can be promoted by the corrosive products of bacteria, algae, fungi, lichens and industrial pollution. These work in conjunction with physical processes such as gravity, wind, water flow, wave action and rubbing by animals, which remove the grains. For instance, Phil Hughes has demonstrated that the rate of weathering in rockshelters is directly

FIGURE 11.12

This block fracture has split an early rock painting in the Kimberley, Western Australia. Rock in the region is so hard that very little grain-by-grain disintegration occurs and sediment does not accumulate in most rockshelters. Hence, the geological circumstances responsible for long-term survival of Kimberley rock art militate against the formation of sites with deeply stratified deposits. (Photo G. L. Walsh)

proportional to the intensity of human use of the shelters, not only because of physical contact between people and rock surfaces, but also because of changes in temperature and humidity due to fires, sweaty bodies and so on. In mineral-deficient areas, animals sometimes use rock art surfaces as salt licks. This has occurred in the central Queensland highlands, where horses and cattle are literally eating rock art sites.

Disintegration of the art

Rock paintings are more susceptible to weathering than rock engravings, and Andrée Rosenfeld has observed that paintings on rock surfaces exposed to the atmosphere are seldom more than 8000 to 10 000 years old. The resilience of a pigment depends upon its ability to penetrate the rock. This in turn depends upon factors such as rock porosity, humidity, viscosity and the size and shape of pigment particles. Since rock artists used a variety of materials for pigment manufacture—including haematite, goethite, limonite, malachite, sericate, huntite, china clay, gypsum, pounded white quartz and charcoal—considerable variation in pigment resilience is to be expected.

In general, red pigments have higher penetration power because of their small particle size and plate-like form. In contrast, clay-rich pigments do not penetrate the rock surface to any extent but form an impervious layer, bond only weakly to the rock and soak up

FIGURE 11.13

Top: *The effects of cattle rubbing on the painted surface can be seen at Maidenwell Rockshelter, southeast Queensland. Some of the red pigment has been rubbed off, and there is a layer of 'grease' at rump level along the back wall of the shelter. Fencing of the site has stopped further damage of this type occurring.* (Photo M. J. Morwood)

Bottom: *Grain by grain disintegration of the painted surface at Blacks' Palace, central Queensland highlands. The movement of water and deposition of salts near the surface are major factors in the disintegration of the rock support.* (Photo M. J. Morwood)

moisture. The continual absorption of water followed by drying out of the pigment layer leads to exfoliation. Paint that adheres poorly to the rock surface is vulnerable to removal by animals rubbing against it and by waterwash, flooding, and so on. As a result, some colours in rock art assemblages tend to survive much longer than others: the oldest rock paintings in many parts of the world are red monochromes. The weathering of rock art and the implications for the interpretation of sequence are a topic requiring detailed research.

Engravings, which are cut into the rock matrix, deteriorate in the same way as the natural rock does (that is, by granular disintegration and exfoliation). In more exposed sites, they will therefore generally last longer than paintings, drawings or stencils. Even so, engravings can trap moisture, which promotes geological and biogenic weathering (Figure 11.14). Certain engraving techniques tend to weather faster than others: pecking, for example, can lead to the formation of microfractures and increase the effective surface area available for weathering.

The effects of rock type and climate can be illustrated by comparing engravings at the Early Man site on the southeast Cape York Peninsula and at the Mt Cameron West site in Tasmania. At Early Man, where the rock is mostly sandstone, engravings below ground level are badly weathered, probably because moisture trapped in the covering deposits created mild acids that corroded the rock surface. The engravings above ground level, on the other hand, remained dry throughout much of the year and are consequently far less weathered. At Mt Cameron West the engravings are on soft aenaceious calcarenite, which is physically damaged by wind, vegetation and animals when exposed. Only the covering of calcareous beach sand provided stable enough conditions to protect the art, which was accordingly reburied after excavation.

FIGURE 11.14

Because they are cut into the rock, engravings can lead to accelerated erosion through retention of water and accumulation of soil—as shown at the Weir on the upper Barcoo River, central Queensland highlands. (Photo M. J. Morwood)

FIGURE 11.15

Examples of micro-organisms over rock art in the central Queensland highlands: (a) mudwasp nests over a hand stencil at Blacks' Palace; (b) lichen over pecked engravings at the Weir. Although these biological deposits cause deterioration of the art, they can also provide minimum dates for underlying rock art. In the Kimberley, for instance, a mudwasp nest over a late Bradshaw rock painting was found to be about 17 000 years old by using the OSL dating technique. The painting could be much older. (Photo M. J. Morwood)

Rock engravings are also buried to preserve them from frost damage and vandalism during winter in the Northern Hemisphere.

Masking of the art

Rock art may be covered by salts flushed out of the rock, dust, micro-organisms such as lichens and bacteria, plant roots and the mud constructions/nests of mudwasps, termites and birds (Figure 11.15). In some cases these agents corrode the rock as well as covering it. However, on the positive side, mineral and biological deposits over rock art may also allow it to be dated. For instance, a flake from an apparently unpainted rock surface at Sandy Creek 2, Cape York Peninsula, contained layers of rock painting pigment 'buried' in layers of oxalate crust, which could be dated using accelerater mass spectrometry (AMS): these showed that the surface had been painted 7500, 16 000 and 27 000 years ago. Similarly, mudwasp nests over and under rock paintings can be dated using optically stimulated luminescence (see Chapter 5).

The single most important cause of deterioration of rock art is moisture, which underpins many chemical, physical and biogenic weathering processes. Paradoxically, moisture also plays a crucial role in the formation of the weather-resistant mineral skins beneath which many of the oldest rock paintings and engravings have been preserved. In some cases water within the rock dissolves the cementing minerals, which it carries to the surface and precipitates to form a crust/patina/skin. The nature and extent of such skins depend on the composition and structure of the rock, the moisture regime, acidity and biological processes, but the most interesting variety for rock art conservationists are silica skins, which are hard, clear, relatively impervious and chemically stable. These can stabilize paintings, which then essentially become part of the rock matrix. Silica skins and other mineral deposits can also derive from external sources, such as water flow across the rock surface, but these deposits are opaque and thus tend to obscure underlying rock paintings.

Conserving rock art

Only a handful of conservation measures have been commonly applied to the broad generality of rock art sites, and all of them have been remedies for external damage to the rock surface. They include the installation of silicone driplines and diversion lines to redirect waterwash away from painted panels; fencing to keep out large animals that might rub against the surface, destabilize it, lick it for the salt content and churn up dust in rockshelters; and the removal of vegetation, wasp and termite nests, lichen and graffiti. But it is not always obvious when to apply even these commonly used measures. For instance, mudwasp nests on rock art surfaces may be disfiguring and encourage the construction of new nests, but they can also be dated and thus give us maximum or minimum ages for the art they overlie or underlie (see Chapter 5). In addition, mudwasp nests contain a range of evidence about past climatic changes.

Other conservation techniques have been designed to meet the needs of particular (significant) sites and/or have only been used experimentally. Examples include the attempt to stabilize engraved slabs at the Mootwingee site in western New South Wales using steel pins driven into the underlying bedrock, and the use of epoxy resins to reattach pieces of engraved rock at Mootwingee and Trotman's Cave in Western Australia.

Dealing with weathering processes operating within the rock matrix has proved far more difficult, and the few successful strategies have all involved limiting internal moisture levels by controlling external sources of groundwater. For instance, at the Mt Grenfell site in western New South Wales, the installation of guttering, and the removal of vegetation, which retained water in depressions immediately above the shelter, significantly reduced the amount of water seeping through the roof. Some have suggested that rain shelters be built and entire outcrops be roofed over at sites of particular importance. Where groundwater sources are not so immediate and accessible, drilling drainage channels in the bedrock is a possibility, but this is expensive, and there are a great many sites whose conservation problems can be solved much more simply. By way of interest, the Peterborough Petroglyph site in Ontario, Canada was fully enclosed at great expense, but to little positive effect.

Alan Watchman has commented on the lack of research into the reasons for the breakdown of the rock substratum at many sites:

> During the next fifty years a large proportion of Australian Aboriginal rock art will disintegrate behind crude and visually appalling barriers because rock art conservators have addressed only those agents causing superficial damage to the art.

In the past, attempts to stabilize rock surfaces by impregnating them with consolidating agents failed because the resulting layer was impermeable and inclined to exfoliate, or became brittle and discoloured. More recently developed silicone-based products offer some potential, particularly for fixing poorly bonded clay-rich pigments. The silica skins found naturally over some rock paintings may be one way of protecting rock faces from deterioration, provided a method is found to duplicate them artificially. But the complexity of the problem can be gauged from detailed mineralogical analyses of 'silica-like' coatings over rock art in Kakadu National Park. The analyses showed that most coatings were a complex mixture of minerals, usually comprising a succession of thin layers rich in sulphates, phosphates and carbonates but comparatively silica-deficient. The fact that silica skins were found only on orthoquartzite rock surfaces suggests that artificial skins capable of protecting rock faces in the long term may, even when they become available, be useful only on specific rock types.

RESTORATION

Repainting, retouching and restoration have been suggested as ways of conserving old or worn-out rock art. This approach appears to contravene the ICOMOS Charter for the conservation of places of cultural significance, and therefore should not be considered as a conservation measure. This issue can become contentious where a continuing rock art tradition includes repainting, as in the Kimberley region of Western Australia (see case study at the end of this chapter).

TAKING STOCK

One of the main problems in conserving rock art generally is that much information is not known. Without basic details on the number of sites in an area, their distribution, and the range of styles and ages represented, their natural and cultural contexts, ethnic value and conservation status, informed management and funding decisions are impossible. Rock art recording projects, which canvass the number and variety of art sites in a region to identify sites of particular significance, priority areas and problems—are crucial to rock art conservation. This is recognized in many laws on archaeological conservation, which require that the authorities responsible for managing sites also maintain a site inventory.

The rapid deterioration of many rock art sites makes obtaining a representative sample of such recordings an urgent priority. In their assessment of conservation needs in Kakadu National Park, Hughes and Watchman note that because of the large number of sites in this area, the time needed to implement conservation measures and the often limited effectiveness of these measures, the amount and quality of surviving art are bound to decline rapidly. They call for the urgent listing of all known sites in order of conservation priority on the basis of significance to Aborigines, scientific and aesthetic value, tourist potential, state of preservation and amenability to conservation measures.

In most parts of the world archaeological sites are legally protected, meaning that archaeological surveys are now a standard part of environmental impact studies. As a result, most 'management' orientated site-recording projects have been undertaken in direct response to proposed developments. This has resulted in a significant increase in the number of known art sites. For instance, the Dampier Archaeological Project, which documented archaeological resources on the Burrup Peninsula (Pilbara region, Western Australia) before the commercial development of the area, recorded 544 engraving sites, as well as middens, manufacturing sites, stone arrangements and stone artefact scatters; the survey of the Alligator River region in response to the proposal to mine uranium yielded over 300 rock art sites.

In a few instances, rock art resources in an area have been documented with long-term management in mind, rather than in response to the immediate threat of development. Examples include the assessment by Grahame Walsh of art sites in the central Queensland highlands for the Queensland National Parks and Wildlife Service, and Josephine McDonald's synthesis of Sydney Basin rock art data for the Australian Heritage Commission. The former project involved an extensive site recording program, while the latter collated information collected previously by a number of site recorders. However, both studies produced reports useful for management and further research.

Long-term prospects

Most experts agree that prospects for the long-term survival of much of the world's rock art are poor. In fact, a large amount of this art is likely to vanish within decades or centuries, rather than millennia. Where rock art is known to be extremely ancient, such as in Franco-Cantabrian caves, attempts have been made to re-establish the original conditions that led to the works' long-term preservation. If the procedures adopted are successful, then long-term survival of some Palaeolithic art is assured.

At many rock art sites, simple measures to curb natural and man-made damage have greatly slowed the rate of deterioration. Rather than just postponing the inevitable, such rearguard action may provide the time needed to develop technologies for the long-term consolidation of rock art surfaces generally or, more realistically, of specific types of rock art surfaces in specific contexts. Remedial measures taken now may also increase the proportion of rock art panels that become relatively geologically stable.

Systematic recording programs are crucially important for rock art conservation. Without them, we cannot make informed judgements about the extent of the problems, or decisions about the allocation of scarce resources for solving them. The rapidity of rock art deterioration in many areas also means that site recordings undertaken now may end up being all that remains for future research.

Conservation of rock art does not occur in a political or ethical vacuum. Rock art means different things to different people and interest groups, who may have conflicting priorities, as in the question of copyright. Here an important distinction needs to be made between the preservation of Aboriginal cultural heritage and the protection of intellectual property rights, which have commercial implications. In Australia this issue first emerged in 1966 with the introduction of decimal currency. A design from a painting by David Malangi was used on the one-dollar note without permission of the artist, on the basis that the work was probably the work of 'some anonymous and probably long-dead artist'. As compensation Malangi received $1000, a fishing rod and a silver medallion. A later case of similar nature shows how complex the issues really are. In 1991 the Aboriginal artist Terry Yumbulul made a Morning Star Pole, as authorised by his Galpu clan. The pole was sold to the Australian Museum and reproduction rights were licensed to the Aboriginal Artists Agency, which in turn licensed the Reserve Bank of Australia to depict the item on the Bicentennial ten-dollar note. Galpu clan members argued that this use exceeded the authority granted to Mr Yumbulul and that featuring a sacred item on money was culturally inappropriate. A Federal Court action taken by Mr Yumbulul against the Aboriginal Artists Agency and the Reserve Bank failed.

Australian Aboriginal rock art motifs now feature prominently on T-shirts, tea-towels, coasters and a host of other knick-knacks. They are also widely used as institutional logos for Aboriginal land councils, corporations and medical services, as well as for organizations concerned with Australian archaeology and rock art (Figure 11.16). In most cases, designs are based on the work of long-dead artists— but not always. Aboriginal artists have already launched successful court actions under the federal *Copyright Act 1968* (though not specifically concerning rock art). In one case, the Federal Court found that designs on a batch of carpets breached copyright in that they substantially reproduced traditional Central Australian clan designs without the artists' permission. Damages of $188 000 were awarded and the court ordered unsold carpets to be handed over to the plaintiffs.

Some art motifs are owned by clans rather than individuals and play an important role in defining clan corporate identity. The question of copyright in such circumstances is complex. In fact, the artist Wandjuk Marika, as chairman of the Aboriginal Artists Agency,

FIGURE 11.16

Worldwide, rock art is a powerful symbol for expressing group identity. Examples of logos based on Aboriginal rock art: (top) Australian Rock Art Research Association, Sites Department of the Western Australian Museum, Takarakka Rock Art Research Centre; (bottom) Quinkan Reserves Trust, Ang-gnarra Aboriginal Corporation, Ang-gnarra Aboriginal Corporation.

had to advise the federal government about legal ways of protecting Aboriginal ceremonies and arts not easily covered by copyright laws.

It is also relevant to the questions of copyright and intellectual property rights that many 'Aboriginal' designs produced for mass consumption by Aboriginal and non-Aboriginal artists are based on the two best-known art styles, those of the Western Desert and Arnhem Land, regardless of the artists' place of origin.

Some of the political and ethical problems involved are illustrated in the controversy surrounding the repainting of Wandjina rock art sites in the Kimberley region of northwest Australia. Aspects of this repainting program have been over-simplified in the published literature. I will therefore include previously unpublished information showing that the Kimberley repaint issue was much more complicated than is generally recognized.

Case study: the Kimberley repaint controversy

In 1987, the Wanang Ngari Aboriginal Corporation from Mowanjum, near Derby in the southern Kimberley, obtained a federal government grant of \$109 019 under the Commonwealth Employment Project to train young unemployed people to repaint Wandjina rock paintings.

FIGURE 11.17

A traditionally repainted Wandjina panel in the Caroline Ranges, West Kimberley. Paint layers exposed by animal scratching are almost 7 millimetres thick in places showing that the panel was repainted many times.
(Photo G. L. Walsh)

Wandjinas are anthropomorphic (human-like) figures without mouths, painted on a prepared white background (Figure 11.17). The paintings themselves are traditionally believed to be the 'shadows' of ancestral beings rather than human handiwork, and to have power to create rain, lightning and thunder. Their repainting was rigorously controlled, and done in a strictly prescribed way at specific times of the year.

The project involved senior custodians and young Aborigines from Derby in the repainting of several major rock art galleries in the Gibb River area, about 300 kilometres to the northeast of the town. The original proposal provided for consultation with traditional site custodians and on-site supervision of the rock art renewal by elders. In the event, twelve young men and women of the Ngarinyin community (Figure 11.18) repainted ten Wandjina sites. Some of these sites contained art said to be of World Heritage significance.

However, the project was first suspended and later discontinued when Lorin Bishop, the non-Aboriginal lessee of nearby Mt Barnett Station, and others complained about the low level of consultation with local Aboriginal people and the standard of the repainted art.

The Kimberley repaint project and its fate generated much debate both locally and further afield. The issue is still controversial and no consensus on the merits of the project has emerged either in academia or in local Aboriginal communities.

FIGURE 11.18

Contemporary-style Wandjina and other motifs added to the Low (Crocodile) Gallery during the 1987 repaint, West Kimberley. Critics of the federally-funded project argued that the repainting of major sites by novices should not have taken place, but some local Aboriginal people were very supportive. It also emerged that the Australian Heritage Commission, to which all such heritage projects proposed for federal funding should have been referred for prior approval, had never been consulted. When complaints about the poor quality of the work were made to the Federal Government, the project was first suspended and later discontinued after the review by the State Sites Authority, which had originally approved the work. (Photo G. L. Walsh)

The intensity of the debate, which involved Aboriginal groups, graziers, anthropologists, archaeologists and state and federal authorities, reflected the complexity of the issue and the enormous divergence in the views of special interest groups. It cost some participants dearly in terms of reputation as well as money. For instance, Nic Green, an anthropologist with the Western Australian Museum, successfully sued Lorin Bishop for defamation over the latter's comments about the project.

Points of contention included whether only persons of Aboriginal descent have the right to make decisions about Aboriginal rock art sites, whether the work was a continuation or a parody of the traditional system, whether the poor condition of the original paintings diminished the loss caused by the repainting, and whether unskilled novices should have been allowed to do the work.

For the local Aboriginal communities the main concern was the relative custodial rights and responsibilities of different individuals to cultural heritage sites. For instance, David Mowaljarlai, a Ngarinyin elder and chairman of the Wanang Ngari Aboriginal Corporation which organized the repaint, said:

We need to teach the young men and women; to teach them about bush learning, the old stories and about the messages of the images, so that they can continue to look after the country. That's why we, the old men, started to train the young people. A very important part of this training was for them to learn about repainting—body painting for ceremonies and to renew the painted images on rock.

In general, the academic community assumed that this view reflected the consensus among Kimberley Aborigines. But they were wrong. Billy King, a Ngarinyin elder and chairman of the Kupungarri Community at Mt Barnett, owners of the land on which the repainting occurred, presented a very different perspective:

When these kids were brought from Derby we didn't know they were a painting crew and they just ruined all our paintings; we've got no decent paintings to take our kids for learning our law. We doing now our own law during the wet.

The 'positive' Wanang Ngari view was promoted through a number of publications and seminars, most notably by David Mowaljarlai, an articulate man with good contacts in academia and elsewhere. In contrast, Billy King had difficulty making the 'negative' Kupungarri view more widely known. He tried unsuccessfully to have a paper on the matter read before the 1992 Australian Rock Art Research Association (AURA) Congress in Cairns. An attempt to have the paper published also failed. To prevent similar repainting of rock art sites in their area, people from Kalumburu in the far northern Kimberley wrote a letter to a local grazier stating that they did not want their rock art sites repainted by Wanang Ngari (Figure 11.19).

The controversy surrounding the Kimberley repaint project reminds us that rock art research and management do not take place in an ethical or political vacuum. In this case, there were many agendas at work, hidden and otherwise, within local Aboriginal communities and among wider interest groups such as graziers and researchers. But questions of rock art protection, management and control will almost invariably involve debate. Within bounds, this is healthy. What is particularly interesting in this case is the way in which most published discussions of the Kimberley repaint debate presented it as a simple black-versus-white issue. Indeed, alternative Aboriginal views were in effect censored.

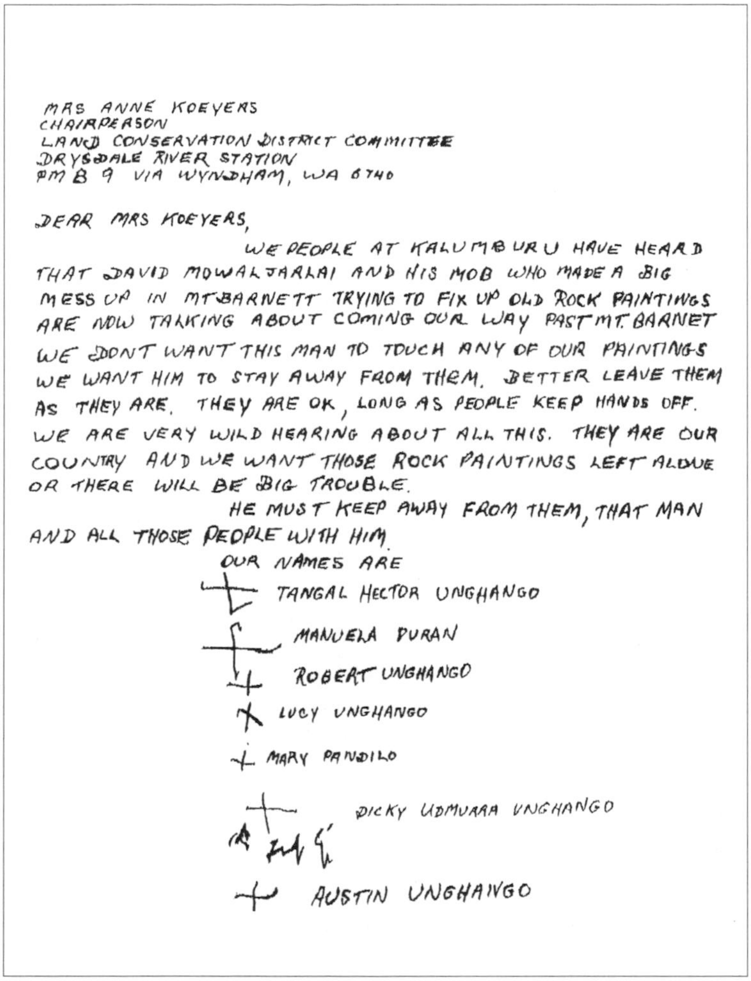

MRS ANNE KOEYERS
CHAIRPERSON
LAND CONSERVATION DISTRICT COMMITTEE
DRYSDALE RIVER STATION
PMB 9 VIA WYNDHAM, WA 6740

DEAR MRS KOEYERS,

WE PEOPLE AT KALUMBURU HAVE HEARD THAT DAVID MOWALJARLAI AND HIS MOB WHO MADE A BIG MESS UP IN MT BARNETT TRYING TO FIX UP OLD ROCK PAINTINGS ARE NOW TALKING ABOUT COMING OUR WAY PAST MT. BARNET. WE DONT WANT THIS MAN TO TOUCH ANY OF OUR PAINTINGS WE WANT HIM TO STAY AWAY FROM THEM. BETTER LEAVE THEM AS THEY ARE, THEY ARE OK, LONG AS PEOPLE KEEP HANDS OFF. WE ARE VERY WILD HEARING ABOUT ALL THIS. THEY ARE OUR COUNTRY AND WE WANT THOSE ROCK PAINTINGS LEFT ALONE OR THERE WILL BE BIG TROUBLE.

HE MUST KEEP AWAY FROM THEM, THAT MAN AND ALL THOSE PEOPLE WITH HIM.

OUR NAMES ARE

✝ TANGAL HECTOR UNGHANGO

✝ MANUELA DURAN

✝ ROBERT UNGHANGO

✗ LUCY UNGHANGO

✝ MARY PANDILO

✝ DICKY UDMURRA UNGHANGO

✝ AUSTIN UNGHANGO

FIGURE 11.19

Letter from Aboriginal custodians at Kalumburu, in the north Kimberley, voicing concern over the 1987 repainting of Wandjina sites under Commonwealth Employment Project funding. This makes it clear that there was widespread concern among Kimberley communities over the repainting. (Courtesy Land Conservation District Committee)

Aboriginal ownership and control of rock art sites, if accepted without qualification, have implications for the conservation of rock art throughout Australia. But the issue also needs to be seen in terms of the wider international debate about control of archaeological sites in other places where an economically and politically dominant group has dispossessed an indigenous population.

Concluding remarks

Rock art has played, and continues to play, many roles. It can show cultural similarities or differences, can connect or divide, and can facilitate or restrict information flow. But it is also worth remembering that rock art is a miniscule part of the total range of human activity and achievement. It is the connections and context of these paintings and engravings that give them an importance way beyond simple marks on rock. This applies at all levels. For instance, the meaning of Aboriginal (rock) art produced today can only be understood in terms of its functional relationship with other symbolic systems, ideology, social organisation, territoriality, and so on. Similarly in archaeological studies, art evidence and its meaning can only be interpreted in the context of other archaeological and environmental evidence, as well as information gleaned from the study of recent art systems.

Turning to issues of rock art conservation and management, the same need for a wider perspective applies. Spending time and money on preservation of rock art can only be justified by appealing to a more basic principle—the need to preserve natural and cultural sites as part of our responsibility to future generations, as well as respect from other cultures and other life forms. Arguments for preservation of rock art are founded on the same fundamental premises as arguments for ensuring the long-term survival of the Egyptian pyramids, whales and rainforests.

Rock art has always provided a cultural focus which fostered, maintained and reinforced connections between people. And it still serves this purpose—as anyone who has participated in meetings of the Australian Rock Art Research Association will testify. However, because it involves people, art and the study of art is undertaken within a political and social context which is subject to change. The indigenous landrights movement, recognition of Native Title, indigenous control of their cultural heritage sites, and questions of copyright and intellectual property, are just some of the issues that have emerged in Australia over the past 30 years.

As a consequence, Australian rock art researchers have had to revise the way that they work and communicate their results. The trend is well-illustrated by recent rock art recording projects, such as the work of Noelene Cole with the Ang-gnarra Aboriginal Corporation in southeast Cape York Peninsula and Andrée Rosenfeld with the Wallace Rockhole community in Central Australia. Both these projects were initiated by local people, who want their sites scientifically documented for the purposes of conservation and management. The new information complements, rather than detracts from, traditional knowledge about the sites.

Clearly, some aspects of the tradition of scholarly inquiry need to be retained in rock art research, including the need for technical expertise, objectivity, peer review and intellectual tolerance. These aspects provide the credibility that researchers and rock art organizations need in order to speak out on controversial issues, and to advise or criticize governments on matters concerning rock art, cultural heritage and indigenous rights. Also, if undertaken with due respect and sensitivity, research is inherently good. It can provide answers to the basic human curiosity about the past, can foster cross-cultural understanding and may have immediate social benefits. In this light, ethical guidelines for rock art research should be seen as formalizing respect for other peoples' rights and views—not just as a series of 'Thou shall nots'.

In rock art research there is therefore a need for continuity as well as the ability to respond to changing political circumstances. 'Elders' of the rock art community, who have spent their professional lives working with Aboriginal people to document their remarkable artistic and intellectual achievements and who have great knowledge and experience, have an important role to play here—in passing on knowledge, commenting on issues, defining standards of practice and raising public appreciation of rock art.

A balance between continuity and change, between established and up-coming, and between retaining and releasing knowledge, has probably always been a feature of Australian Aboriginal art. The same dynamic tensions are evident in the archaeological study of Australian Aboriginal art. These should not be discouraged; they are signs of a healthy discipline.

Glossary

Abraded—made by repeated rubbing.

Adze—a tool for shaving or adzing wood. In Australia this would usually comprise a distinctly shaped chert flake mounted on a wooden handle with resin.

Alphanumeric—a coding system which uses letters of the alphabet as well as numbers.

Ambilineal—an inheritance system in which rights (or property) can be passed down from the mother or father.

AMS (accelerator mass spectrometry)—a technique for dating carbon atoms requiring very small samples (i.e. 1/50 000 gm).

Anthropomorphic—human shaped.

Artefact—any object made or modified by people.

Aurignacian–Perigordain—two Upper Palaeolithic cultures in Europe, defined on the basis of their stone artefact assemblages. They date to around 30 000 years ago.

Auroch—the ancestor of modern cattle. Now extinct.

Australian Aboriginal—people of Australoid racial type who were the first to colonize Australia.

Australopithecines—literally 'southern ape man'. The earliest recognized members of the hominid family tree, dating from about 5 million to 1 million years ago in East and South Africa. About 2.5 million years ago, the genus *Homo* evolved directly from a species of Australopithecine in East Africa.

Austronesian—one of the world's major language families. It includes at least 700 languages spoken in island Southeast Asia, Melanesia, Polynesia, Micronesia and Madagascar.

Autochthonous—original, earliest known inhabitants; Aboriginals.

Bichrome—produced in two colours.

Bilateral asymmetry—two halves not having exact mirror images.

Biogenic (coating)—living organisms are responsible for its formation.

Biogeographical boundary—marks a major change in the distribution of plant and/or animal species.

Biologically viable—a population large enough to ensure its own long-term survival.

Blitzkrieg model—refers to the rapid and destructive advances of the Nazis in Poland and France at the beginning of World War II.

Bolas—a hunting weapon in which three stone balls are tied to each other by lengths of rope or leather thongs. When hurled at an animal, it can entangle the animal's legs.

Bondaian—a previous Aboriginal culture defined on the basis of the occurrence of a distinctive type of stone point—the Bondi Point. The term was first used by Fred McCarthy when describing the cultural sequence in the Blue Mountains west of Sydney.

BP—before present in calendar years (BP means before present in radiocarbon years where present is taken as 1950).

Bradshaw (paintings)—a style of Kimberley rock painting, which includes exquisitely depicted human figures, usually in red. It was named after the explorer Joseph Bradshaw, who in 1891 was the first European to observe such paintings.

Burren adze—a small chert flake, usually of triangular cross-section, often with heavy damage along the lateral margins indicating use in woodworking. Some burren adzes retain traces of resin, showing that they were originally mounted on a wooden handle.

Calcite—natural carbonate of lime.

Capture technologies—the various hunting and trapping methods used by humans.

Cation dating—a now discredited technique for dating of a type of mineral coating, called desert varnish. It was based on different leaching rates of the cations K+, Ca+ and Ti+.

Caudal fin—a fish tail fin.

Caudal penducle—the fleshy part of a fish fin.

Chert—a smooth, homogeneous type of rock with a conchoidal fracture pattern, widely used for making flaked stone tools.

Churinga—a Central Australian sacred object made of stone or wood and bearing incised and/or painted geometric motifs.

Claviform—club-shaped.

Clinal—a gradual, as opposed to abrupt, change in distribution.

Cluster analysis—a mathematical technique for quantifying similarities and differences between things. The results are usually depicted in a family tree format.

Comparative method—involving comparisons (especially of sciences).

Compositional patterning—structure inherent in the components (e.g. of a site, a panel of rock paintings or engraved design) rather than its context.

Contextual analysis—analysis of the structure inherent in the surrounds of a site or a panel of art, rather than in the item itself (cf. compositional patterning).

Contiguous—touching, adjoining, neighbouring.

Continental shelf—the submerged coastal section of a continent, such as Australia.

Core tools—tools made on a piece of stone from which flakes have been detached.

Crania—a skull.

Crosstabulation—a table of figures which examines the interaction between two variables at the same time (e.g. site by motif— the distribution of rock art motifs between sites).

Cultural meta-landscape—the way that a people view the landscape, in terms of creation stories, ancestral figures, etc.

Cupules—cup-shaped engravings, usually made first by pecking, then abrasion.

Curated tools—tools which are quite time-consuming to make, but which are then retained for use over a relatively long period of time (as compared to expedient tools, which are used then almost immediately discarded).

Deductive logic—a formal logic system in which if the premises are true, then the conclusion must be true.

Demographic flexibility—the ability of local populations to cluster or disperse depending on social and economic circumstances.

Desert varnish—a black mineral coating which can form on rock surfaces in arid regions. Micro-organisms probably play a part in its formation.

Didgeridoo—a musical instrument about 1.5 metres in length, made from a hollow branch or section of bamboo with a wax or resin mouthpiece. The sound is produced by blowing.

Differential weathering—uneven rates of erosion or patination.

Dispersed cultural institutions—social groups in which the membership is not localised.

Dissimilarity indices—a quantitative measure expressing relative differences between things (e.g. sites, panels of rock art).

Efflorescence—literally, a flowering.

Emblematic function (emblemic)—the use of symbols to distinguish one human group from another (e.g. football jerseys, national flags, shield designs).

Empirical—based on the senses.

Ethnography—anthropological description of 'traditional' or non-industrial culture and society.

Exfoliation—a type of rock weathering characterised by detachment of large sections of the surface layer.

Exogamous—members must select their marriage partners from outside the group.

Factor analysis—a mathematical technique which attempts to show the determinates causing variation in a sample. First used in psychology.

FLECS-AMS (focused laser extraction of carbon-bearing substances)—a technique in which an organic material is oxidised to carbon dioxide with a laser which can target samples very precisely. The carbon dioxide is then collected for radiocarbon dating by AMS.

Formal attributes—definable characteristics.

Frequency calculations—quantitative methods for estimating numbers.

Geo-chemical fingerprinting—analytical techniques that enable a sample to be uniquely identified by its chemical and geological composition.

Gesture language—use of body movement, usually hands, as a form of communication.

Glacial maximum—the coldest period in any Ice Age. For instance, the last glacial maximum occurred around 18 000 BP.

Goethite—an iron oxide from which yellow pigment can be made.

Greater Australia—the combined areas of Australia, Tasmania, New Guinea and associated continental shelves. At times of very low sea level these areas would have formed a single land mass.

Gypseous crust—a mineral layer containing calcium sulfate.

Haematite—an iron oxide from which red or purple pigment can be made.

Heterogeneity (heterogeneous)—relatively varied.

Hierarchically consistent—a predictable way of ordering different levels.

Holocene—a geological time period from 10 000 years ago to the present.

Homogeneity (homogeneous)—relatively uniform.

Hydrolysis—movement of water.

Iconography—representation of a subject by means of drawings or figures.

Inductively coupled plasma spectroscopy—an analytical technique where samples are made into a plasma (gaseous) state to enable their composition to be identified.

Infrared spectroscopy—a technique for analysing the composition of materials, using the infra-red portion of the light system.

Intaglio—a fully pecked (incised) design technique.

Integrative methodologies—research methods which emphasise combining different lines of evidence.

Intensification—increase in produce or productivity in a given area.

Intra-site—within a site, as opposed to between sites.

Lateritic strata—a layer of red, iron-rich clay.

Lichenometry—a method for estimating the age of rock surfaces by measuring the size of covering lichens. It requires a calibrated growth curve for specific lichen species.

Lingua franca—a common language used to allow communication between different language groups.

Littoral—region along a shoreline.

Mass-spectrometry—an analytical technique to identify the composition of materials based on different element weights.

Matrilineal—inheritance through the female line.

Matri-totemic—a system in which membership of totemic groups (i.e. with a special relationship to a plant or animal) is inherited through the mother.

Matrix—mass in which something is developed or contained.

Maul—a kind of hammer, commonly made of wood.

Megafauna—large extinct animals, birds and reptiles.

Mental construct—a complete picture in the mind before a plan is carried out.

Mesolithic—literally, Middle Stone Age. These were hunter–gatherer cultures with increased emphasis on smaller game and the processing of plant foods. Associated equipment includes grindstones, edge-ground axes and bows and arrows. In Europe, the Mesolithic occurred between the end of the Ice Age (around 10 000 years ago), and the appearance of farming communities with pottery.

Micro-environmental—environmental conditions within a small area.

Micro-erosion analysis—describing the wear on individual mineral crystals.

Micro-fractures—minute cracks.

Microliths—small stone artefacts less than 3 centimetres in maximum dimension.

Micro-stratified—minute layering as found in mineral coating.

Middle range theory—theory which connects the (archaeological) evidence to its interpretation in terms of human activities.

Mineral accretions—layers of inorganic material, such as silica skins and oxalate crusts.

Mitochondrial DNA—genetic material found in mitochondria within individual cells.

Moiety—one of two social divisions into which a whole population is divided. Generally, in a culture with such a system, individuals from one moiety division must choose a spouse from the other.

Monochrome—of one colour.

Montane—of mountains.

Morphology—study of the form of animals and plants.

Mullers—upper grindstones, generally round or oval, used in the wet milling of seeds on millstones.

Multi-dimensional scaling—a type of mathematical manipulation in which the relative size of measurements for different variables is adjusted.

Multi-disciplined—looking at evidence from a range of scientific studies.

Multi-media—different types of communication vehicles.

Multivalent—a single item representing more than one meaning.

Multivariate analysis—statistical study of relationships between three or more variables.

Multivariate statistical techniques—tests of significance simultaneously applied to several variables.

Narrative quality—story-telling quality.

Non-contiguous—not in proximity/not adjoining.

Non-Pama-Nyungan—about 60 Aboriginal languages from nine language families found in the northwest of Australia. They are characterised by adding prefixes to verbs to indicate tense, nature of subject and object, etc.

Non random (placement)—of patterned distribution.

Obsidian—vitreous lava/volcanic glass.

Orthoquartzite—sedimentary quartzite.

OSL (optically stimulated luminescence)—a dating technique which measures how long quartz grains have been buried away from sunlight. Laser light of specified wavelengths is used to force the release of electrons trapped in micro-fissures in the quartz grains. The number of trapped electrons is determined by the length of time since last exposed to sunlight and the background radioactivity.

Oxalate—a salt of oxalic acid.

Oxalate crusts—a geological deposit containing oxalic acid.

Palaeolithic (or Old Stone Age)—The period dating from the first appearance of stone tools until the end of the last Ice Age and beginnings of the Mesolithic.

Palaeontology—the study of fossils.

Palynology—the study of pollens.

Pama-Nyungan—about 190 Aboriginal languages which form a coherent grouping across 85 per cent of Australia. They are characterized by the addition of suffixes to verbs to show grammatical relationships, nature of subject and object, etc. There is evidence that Pama-Nyungan languages began to disperse around 6000 years ago from an area near the Gulf of Carpentaria.

Panaramitee—an ancient style of pecked engravings characterized by an emphasis on circles and tracks. It is the earliest rock art phase in Lesley Maynard's three-part pan-Australian sequence and is named after the type site on Panaramitee Station, South Australia.

Patinated—having surface 'finish' caused by chemical or physical weathering.

Patrilineal (clan)—with inheritance through the father.

Pebraded—an engraving made by pecking (i.e. direct percussion) then completed by abrasion.

Petrology—study of origin, structure, etc. of rocks.

Phyla (language phyla)—linguistic grouping which includes languages having between 5 and 12 per cent shared cognates.

Piedmont—lower mountain slopes.

Pleistocene—glacial period preceding the Holocene, from 10 000 to approximately 2 million years ago.

Primogeniture—first born.

Principal components analysis (PCA)—a mathematical technique that assumes variability in a complex characteristic, such as intelligence, is due to a number of distinct causes or factors.

Proto-modern—the earliest modern.

Quantifiable—a state or characteristic that can be measured.

Quantification—the assignment of a numerical value to a state or characteristic.

Quinkans—distinctive ancestral beings in southeast Cape York Peninsula and often depicted in the rock paintings of the region.

Radiocarbon dating—using the relative proportion of an unstable (radioactive) isotope of carbon, (carbon-14), to estimate the age of organic materials. It utilises the fact that carbon-14 in the organic component of life diminishes at a fixed rate after the animal or plant dies.

'Restricted art'—art which is produced in a context to which some members of the community are denied access.

Scarps—steep slopes.

Schematisation—a simplified depiction which captures the key elements of a subject.

Scree slopes—mountain slopes covered with small, unstabilised stones.

Secondary carbonate deposits—calcium carbonate (limestone) which has been dissolved by carbolic acid in water, then redeposited elsewhere.

Segmentary cognitive system—a partitioned system of knowledge.

Sexual dimorphism—pronounced physical differences between the sexes in size or secondary characteristics, such as beards in humans, manes in lions, etc.

Shaman—a religious leader who communicates with the other world by going into a trance.

Silica—silicon dioxide, most commonly occurring as quartz.

Silica skins—thin layers of silicates in which organic matter may be trapped.

Social processes—the way institutions in a society work.

Sociolinguistic territories—areas owned by a language group.

Solutrean–Magdalenian—two cultures of the European Palaeolithic period identified on the basis of distinctive styles of tools, especially those of stone, bone and antler.

Spatial patterning—non-random dispersal.

Spatial variation—differences between areas.

Spearthrower (woomera)—a length of wood, bone or other material with a hook at one end, designed to fit into the end of spearshaft to give increased leverage in throwing.

Stone knapping—flaking off pieces of stone with a hammer.

Structural analysis—the identification and explanation of patterning in evidence.

Structural patterning—the non-random distribution of evidence.

Style zones—areas in which particular characteristic features are found.

Stylistic analysis—analysis which focuses on the different ways that individuals, communities or ethnic groups depict or decorate.

Subgroup affiliation—membership of a recognized group within a community or population.

Subject analysis—identifying what is depicted in art.

Superimposition(s)—overlaying of one motif by another in rock art.

Superimposition analysis—analysis of patterns of superimposition(s) in rock art.

Symbol—an item, activity or behaviour that is conventionally understood as standing for, or representing, something else. Generally, the symbol and its referent have analogous qualities.

Symbolic subsystems—distinct areas of symbol use within the same community or population. Their audiences correspond to different gender or social groupings within the larger population.

Synchronous—at the same time or contemporary. Synchronous differences can be contrasted with differences that occur over time.

Talus slope—slope at the foot of a cliff or below a rock shelter, often covered with rock debris.

Tectiforms—motifs made up of straight lines, such as rectangular shapes.

Temporally ordered—arranged in the sequence in which things occurred.

Territorial demarcation—boundaries between tribal areas.

Territoriality—the claiming and defense of boundaries between tribal areas.

Tertiary—a specific geological period.

Theoretical—concerned with theories or ideas as opposed to empirical evidence.

Thermoluminescence—a dating technique where a sample of quartz grains is heated to give off electrons.

'*Threshold discovery*'—new evidence which leads to a breakthrough in research or knowledge.

Thylacine (Tasmanian tiger)—carnivorous, dog-like marsupial which became extinct on the Australian mainland about 3000 BP, but survived in Tasmania until the 1930s.

'*Time-factored*'—relating to the passing of time.

Time-specific subjects—subjects that can be closely dated.

Totemic ancestors—mythological beings—who were both anthropomorphic and animal—responsible for the creation of the present-day landscape and social order.

Totemism—'The use of animal or plant (or other) emblems to stand for individuals or groups. The commonest forms of totemism in Australia are Clan and Personal totems. Clan totems were conferred during the creation period and are inherited. Personal totems are conferred at conception or birth, when the spirit of the unborn child announces its identity.' (Layton 1992)

Ultra-violet light—a non-visible portion of the light spectrum.

Undiagnostic specimens—specimens lacking defining character.

Uniformitarianism—the principle that the past can only be explained on the basis of our knowledge of the present.

Upper Palaeolithic—an archaeological period defined on the basis of stone-knapping techniques and type implements. It is based in Europe, the Middle East and India and is characterized by use of blades as blanks for a range of implements.

Uranium series dating—a dating technique based on the constant rate of fission for uranium isotopes.

Volcanic tuff—volcanic ash.

Waisted blade—a stone tool bearing notches or a groove on its lateral margins, indicating that a handle was hafted to it.

Wandjina—a type of anthropomorphic ancestral figure found in the West Kimberley. Wandjinas and associated beings created the landscape, and were appealed to for rain and the maintenance of animal and plant species. They could punish transgressions with flood and storm. Rock paintings of Wandjinas, which always lack mouths, were thought to be their 'shadows'—not merely human constructs. There is a regionally distinctive Wandjina rock painting style.

'Wunan'—the formalised exchange system found in the Kimberley involving the movement of women, sacred items, weapons and materials between clans.

X-ray diffraction—an analytical technique that beams X-rays at the sample. The bending of the rays is used to infer the sample's structural composition.

Zoomorphic—of animal form.

Notes

1 Aboriginal archaeology in context

General overview of Australian archaeology Flood 1995; Lourandos 1977; Mulvaney and Kamminga 1999

The first humans Bellwood 1997; Lahr and Foley 1998; Morwood et al. 1999; Rightmire 1994; Stoneking and Camm 1989; Thorne and Wolpoff 1981

Southeast Asia and colonization of Australia Bednarik and Kuckenberg 1999; Bellwood 1997; Birdsell 1977; Bowdler 1993; Chappell 1993; Davidson and Noble 1992; Kuhn et al. 2001; Thorne 1976

Dating initial Australian colonization Allen and Holdaway 1995; Brown 2000; Roberts et al. 1990, 1994; Smith and Sharp 1993

Modes of dispersal Birdsell 1977; Bowdler 1977; Davidson 1990; Flood 1995; Horton 1981; Irwin 1992; Veth 1989

Early Australians Allen and O'Connell 1995; Brown 1989; Chaloupka 1993; Flannery 1994; Lewis 1988, 1997; Luebbers 1975; McConnell and O'Connor 1997; Morse 1988; Morwood and Hobbs 1995a,b; Morwood and Trezise 1989; Mountford and Edwards 1963; O'Connor 1990, 1996; Smith et al. 1998; Smith and Sharp 1993; Walsh 1994; Watchman and Campbell 1996

A world in transition: the past 10 000 years Beaton 1983, 1985, 1994, 1995; Bellwood 1997; Brown 1989; Dixon 1980; Gollan 1984; Golson 1993; Lourandos 1985; McConvell 1996; McConvell and Evans 1997; Morwood 1986, 1987; Morwood and Hobbs 1995a; Pardoe 1995; Porch and Allen 1995; Ross 1985; Smith 1989b; Taçon and Brockwell 1995

Close-up: southeast Queensland Morwood 1986, 1987
Contact across Torres Strait Harris 1977, 1995; McCarthy 1953; Moore 1978; Tanks 1987
Recent Indonesian contact Campbell and Wilson 1993; Clarke 1994; Crawford 1969; Healey 1980; Macknight 1976, 1986; McCarthy 1953; Mitchell 1994; Morwood and Hobbs 1997; Swadling 1996
European archaeology in Australia Connah 1988; Mulvaney 1989

2 Australian Aboriginal rock art

Antiquity of Australian rock art Layton 1992a; Maynard and Edwards 1971; O'Connor 1995; Roberts et al. 1997; Watchman and Campbell 1996; Wright 1971a
Central Australia Davidson 1937; Edwards 1971; Mountford 1937, 1965a, 1976; Smith 1989a; Strehlow 1964
Tasmania Brown 1991; Porch and Allen 1995; Sims 1977
Sydney Campbell 1899; Clegg 1979; McCarthy 1959; McDonald 1985, 1994; McMah 1965
Southeast Cape York Peninsula Cole 1998; Cole and David 1992; David and Chant 1995; Flood 1987; Flood and Horsfall 1986; Morwood and Hobbs 1995a,b; Rosenfeld et al. 1981; Trezise 1971; Wright 1971b
Victoria River District David et al. 1994; Flood 1997; McNickle 1991
Arnhem Land Brandl 1973; Chaloupka 1993; Chippindale et al. 2000; Edwards 1979; Lewis 1988; Mountford 1956; Taçon and Brockwell 1995
Kimberley Crawford 1968, 1977; Elkin 1930; Layton 1992a; Morwood et al. 1994; Walsh 1994, 2000; Welch 1990, 1993
Pilbara Dix 1977; McNickle 1984; Mountford 1965b; Walsh 1988; Wright 1968
The big picture David and Chant 1995; Davidson 1937; Dixon 1980; Franklin 1992; Lommel 1961; Maynard 1979; McCarthy 1962, 1967; Mountford 1959; Mountford and Edwards 1963; Rosenfeld 1991; Walsh and Morwood 1999; Wright 1968

3 Australian rock art research

International beginnings
Europe: Anati 1976; Bahn and Vertut 1988; Beltrán 1982; Breuil 1952; Clottes et al. 1998, 2001; Coles 2000; Layton 2000; Leroi-Gourhan 1968 (1976); Ucko and Rosenfeld 1967
North America: Grant 1983; Mallery 1972 (1893); Schaafsma 1985; Wellmann, 1979; Whitley 1987; Whitley and Loendorf 1994

South America: Dubelaar 1986; Prous 1986
South Africa: Lewis-Williams 1981, 1983a, b; Lewis-Williams and Loubser 1986; Vinnicombe 1976
India: Neumayer 1983
General syntheses for Australian Aboriginal rock art Davidson 1937; Dix 1989; Edwards 1971; Layton 1992a; Lewis and Rose 1988; Lommel 1961; Maynard 1979; McCarthy 1967; Mountford 1959; Walsh 1988
Trends and developments Chippindale et al. 2000; Dix 1989; Lewis and Rose 1988; Maynard 1979; Morwood and Smith 1994; Pearson and Swartz 1991; Sales 1992; Thorn and Brunet 1995; Taçon 2001

4 How we study Australian Aboriginal rock art

Explaining the evidence Binford 1967, 1978; Davidson 1988; Frazer 1890; Hempel 1945; Layton 1992b; Leroi-Gourhan 1965; Morwood 1975, 1988; Morwood and Hobbs 1992; Spencer and Gillen 1899; Tylor 1871
Australian Aboriginal art: general use Conkey 1980; Elkin 1961; Gamble 1982; Gould 1969; Horton 1994; Jochim 1983; Layton 1992a,b; Macintosh 1977; Maynard 1977; Munn 1966, 1973; Spencer and Gillen 1899
Meaning and function
Central Australia: Davidson 1937; Edwards 1966, 1971; Gould 1969; Layton 1985; Mountford 1955, 1965a, 1976; Munn 1973; Pfeiffer 1982; Spencer and Gillen 1899; Strehlow 1964, 1965, 1970; Taylor 1979
West Kimberley: Blundell 1974, 1980, 1982; Capell 1972; Crawford 1968, 1977; Layton 1985, 1992a; McCarthy 1939–40; Mowaljarlai and Malnic 1993; Mowaljarlai and Vinnicombe 1995; Thomas 1998; Walsh 1988
Arnhem Land: Chaloupka 1993; Galindo 1997; Morphy 1977, 1991; Mountford 1956; Taçon 1989; Taylor 1987
Producing rock art Chaloupka 1993; Mountford 1956; Sagona and Webb 1994; Smith and Fankhauser 1996; Thomas 1998
General points Berndt 1958, 1964; Biernoff 1978; Brandt and Carder 1987; Chase 1984; Elkin 1961; Fisher 1961; Gamble 1982; Godwin 1990; Gould 1969, 1986; Johnson and Aplin 1978; Layton 1985, 1992a; Lewis 1988; Macintosh 1977; Mathew 1910; Maynard 1979; Morphy 1977, 1991; Morwood 1979, 1984a, 1987, 1992, 1994, 1998; Mountford 1976; Munn 1973; Petrie 1904; Rose 1992; Smith 1989a, 1992, 1994; Spencer and Gillen 1899; Strehlow 1970; Sutton and Rigsby 1982; Taçon 1989; Taylor 1979, 1987; von Sturmer 1978; Wiessner 1984, 1990; Wobst 1974; Wolfe 1969; Yengoyan 1976

5   A question of time: dating Australian rock art

Relative dating methods
Differential weathering: Lewis 1986; Lorblanchet 1992;
 Maynard 1976, 1979; Quinnell 1975; Trezise 1971;
 Wright 1968
Superimposition analysis: Crosby 1968; Leroi-Gourhan
 1968(1976); Lewis-Williams 1974; McCarthy 1960a,b,
 1961, 1962, 1974, 1976; Morwood 1979; Quinnell
 1975; Trezise 1971; Wright 1968
Spatial analysis: Morwood 1979, 1980
Stylistic dating: Rosenfeld and Smith 1997; Walsh 1994, 2000
Absolute dating methods Bednarik 2001
Historical information: Chaloupka 1993; Mulvaney 1989
Subjects: Chaloupka 1993; Gollan 1984; Lewis 1988; Wright
 1968
Weathering: Bednarik 2000; Edwards 1965a, 1965b, 1966,
 1971; Maynard 1976; Maynard and Edwards 1971;
 McCarthy 1962; Mountford and Edwards 1963; Trezise
 1971
Stratified art: Beaton and Walsh 1977; Beck et al. 1998;
 Bednarik 1985; Clegg 1987; David and Chant 1995;
 Dragovich 1984a, b, 1986; Florian 1978; Gould 1977;
 Hale and Tindale 1930; Jones and Johnson 1985; Joubert
 et al. 1983; Kamminga and Allen 1973; Lorblanchet
 1992; Macintosh 1965; Malakoff 1998; Morwood 1979,
 1988, 1995; McBryde 1974; Morwood et al. 1994;
 Mulvaney 1975; Mulvaney and Joyce 1965; Nobbs and
 Dorn 1988, 1993; Roberts et al. 1997; Rosenfeld et al.
 1981; Watchman 1985, 1987, 1990, 1993; Watchman
 and Campbell 1996; Whitley and Dorn 1987
Association: Cosgrove and Jones 1989; Jones 1987; Kiernan et
 al. 1983; Lorblanchet 1992; Maynard and Edwards 1971;
 Prous 1986
Direct dating: Chaloupka 1993; Cole and Watchman 1992;
 Cole et al. 1995; Denninger 1971; Loy et al. 1990;
 McDonald et al. 1990; Nelson 1993, 2000; Nelson et al.
 1995; Rosenfeld and Smith 1997; Russ et al. 1993; Taçon
 and Garde 2000; Walsh et al. in prep; Watchman 1993
The antiquity of Aboriginal art Allen and Holdaway 1995;
 Bahn and Vertut 1988; Bednarik 1986; Bowler and
 Thorne 1976; Cole et al. 1995; Davidson and Noble
 1992; Fankhauser et al. 1997; Lewis 1997; Maynard
 1979; Maynard and Edwards 1971; Morwood and Jung
 1995; O'Connor 1995; Roberts et al. 1990, 1994, 1997;
 Rosenfeld et al. 1981; Smith and Fankhouser 1996;
 Walsh 1994; Watchman and Campbell 1996
Dating Kimberley art Crawford 1968, 1977; Gelatley and
 Sofoulis 1969; Morwood et al. 1994; Morwood and
 Hobbs 2000; O'Connor 1995; Roberts et al. 1997; Walsh

1994; Walsh and Morwood 1999; Watchman et al. 1997;
 Welch 1993;
Conclusions Chippindale and Taçon 1998: Cole et al. 1995;
 d'Errico 1994; David and Chant 1995; Loy et al. 1990;
 McDonald et al. 1990; Morwood et al. 1994; Nelson
 1993; Roberts et al. 1997; Tuniz and Watchman 1994;
 Watchman 1989/90, 1993; Watchman and Cole 1993

6   Subject analyses

The method Anati 1976; Beltrán 1982; Camps 1982; Huyge
 1998; Lewis-Williams 1981; Lhote 1982; Lorblanchet
 1977; Muzzolini 1990; Neumayer 1983; Rosenfeld 1977;
 Vinnicombe 1976
Limitations Bahn 1986; Biesele 1983; Clegg 1981, 1985;
 Clottes 1989; Gould 1969; Layton 1985; Leroi-Gourhan
 1965; Lewis-Williams 1981, 1983a,b, 1987; Macintosh
 1952, 1977; Marshack 1972; Martineau 1973; Saussure
 et al. 1959; Vinnicombe 1976
The cultural context Beaton and Walsh 1977; Birdsell 1977;
 Brandl 1973; Crawford 1968, 1977; David and David
 1988; Donovan 1976; Flood 1987; Huchet 1990; Lewis
 1988; Maynard 1979; Morwood 1979; Taçon and
 Chippindale 1994; Taçon et al. 1996; Trezise 1971;
 Walsh 1979; Walsh and Morwood 1999; Welch 1990;
 Wright 1985
The natural context Basedow 1914; Brandl 1972, 1980;
 Calaby and Lewis 1977; Chaloupka 1993; Chaloupka
 and Murray 1986; Clegg 1978; Guthrie 1984; Lewis
 1977; Macintosh 1977; McDonald 1982; Mithen 1987;
 Murray and Chaloupka 1984; Rosenfeld 1982, 1984;
 Taçon 1988; Tindale 1951; Trezise 1977; Wright 1968
General points Roberts et al. 1997; Vinnicombe 1972, 1976

7   Structural analyses

The method Conkey 2001; Vinnicombe 1972, 1976
Patterns in time Conkey 1978, 1984; Davidson and Noble
 1989; Davis 1986; Gamble 1980, 1982, 1983; Gowlett
 1984; Mithen 1996; Morwood 1979; Noble and
 Davidson 1996; Walsh 1994; Wynn 1979
An example from the Sydney region McDonald 1994
Patterns in space
Spatial distribution of rock art styles: Davidson 1937; Gamble
 1982; Lewis 1988; Smith 1992
Spatial distribution of rock art sites: Davidson 1988; Gunn
 1997; Heizer and Baumhoff 1962; Jochim 1983;
 Rosenfeld 1982; Schaafsma 1985; Straus 1987;
 Vinnicombe 1976

Distribution between sites: Bahn 1982; Conkey 1980, 1985; David and Chant 1995; Maynard 1979; Rosenfeld 1997; Ross 1997

Spatial distribution within sites: González Garcia 1987; Laming 1959; Leroi-Gourhan 1965, 1968 (1976), 1982; Ucko and Rosenfeld 1967

Spatial distribution within panels: Lewis-Williams 1974; Marshack 1972, 1975; 1977; Sauvet and Sauvet 1979; Sauvet et al. 1977

Spatial distribution of pigments: sourcing David et al. 1993; Smith and Fankhouser 1996, Smith et al. 1998: Thomas 1998

An example from northwest: Queensland Ross 1997

Compositional structure

Selectivity in subjects: Altuna 1983; Layton 1987; Vinnicombe 1972, 1976

Selectivity in media use: Bégouën and Clottes 1987; Bégouën et al. 1984/5; Conkey 1981; David et al. 1999; González Garcia 1987; Leroi-Gourhan 1965; Morwood 1979

Choosing analytical techniques Franklin 1991; McDonald 1994; Ross 1997

8   Central Queensland highlands

Beaton 1977; Beaton and Walsh 1977; Crosby 1968; Donovan 1976; Drane 1918; Meston 1901; Morwood 1979, 1981; 1984a,b; Morwood and Kaiser-Glass 1991; Mulvaney and Joyce 1965; Quinnell 1975; Walsh 1984, 2000; Worsnop 1897

9   North Queensland highlands

Gray 1913; Morgan and Terrey 1990; Morwood 1990, 1992, 1992a; Morwood and Godwin 1982; Walsh 1985

10   Southeast Cape York Peninsula

Beaton 1985; Cole 1998; David 1994; David and Chant 1995; Flood 1987; Flood and Horsfall 1986; Morgan et al. 1995; Morwood and Hobbs 1995a,b; Morwood and L'Oste-Brown 1995; Rosenfeld et al. 1981; Roth 1898, 1899; Trezise 1971, 1993; Wright 1971b

11   A future for the past: conservation of rock art

General rationale for conservation Bates 1993; Bowdler 1984; Brunet *et al.* 1995; Byrne 1991; Cleere 1989; Elliot and Gare 1983; Lipe 1984; Lorblanchet 1986; Mangi 1989; Marika 1975; McGimsey III 1972; Mulvaney 1985; Pearson and Sullivan 1995; Schiffer and Gumerman 1977; Ward 1983; Yencken 1979, 1985; Young 1984

Rock art conservation problems

The effects of people: Gale and Jacobs 1986, 1987a,b; Morwood 1994; Morwood and Kaiser-Glass 1991; Mulvaney 1970; Rosenfeld 1985; Sullivan 1984; Vinnicombe 1987; Walsh 1984, 1988

Managing people: Dragovich 1995; Gale and Jacobs 1987a,b; Lorblanchet 1986; McGimsey 1972; Ogawa 1992; Walsh 1984, 1988

Effects of natural agencies: Beltrán 1982; Crawford 1977; Florian 1978; Hughes and Watchman 1983; Lewis 1988; Morwood 1984a; Roberts et al. 1997; Vinnicombe 1976; Walsh 1988

Conserving rock art: Brunet et al. 1987; Clarke 1984; Edwards 1979; Gillespie 1983; Hughes and Watchman 1983; Lambert 1989; McDonald 1985; Pearson and Swartz Jr. 1991; Rosenfeld 1985; Sullivan 1995; Vinnicombe 1987; Wainright 1985; Walsh 1984; Walston 1976; Watchman 1985, 1987; Watson and Flood 1987

Intellectual property Janke 1998

The Kimberley repaint controversy Bowdler 1988; King 1992; Mowaljarlai 1992; Mowaljarlai and Peck 1987; Mowaljarlai et al. 1988; Mowaljarlai and Vinnicombe 1995; Walsh 1992; *West Australian* 9 June 1990

Long-term prospects Wallace and Wallace 1977

Bibliography

Allen, J. and S. Holdaway 1995. The contamination of Pleistocene radiocarbon determinations in Australia. *Antiquity*, 69:101–112.

Allen, J. and J. F. O'Connell (eds) 1995. *Transitions: Pleistocene to Holocene in Australia and Papua New Guinea. Antiquity*, 69: Special Number 265.

Altuna, J. 1983. On the relationship between archaeofaunas and parietal art in the caves of the Cantabrian region. In J. Clutton-Brock and C. Grigson (eds), *Hunters and their prey*, pp. 227–238. BAR International Series 163. British Archaeological Reports, Oxford.

Anati, E. 1976. *Evolution and style in Camunian rock art*. Archivi 6. Edizioni del Centro Camuno di Studi Preistorici, Capo di Ponte.

Bahn, P. G. 1982. Inter-site and inter-regional links during the Upper Palaeolithic: the Pyrenean evidence. *The Oxford Journal of Archaeology*, 1:247–268.

Bahn, P. G. 1986. Comment on Dragovich's 'A plague of locusts or manna from Heaven?'. *Rock Art Research*, 3(2):144–146.

Bahn, P. G. and J. Vertut 1988. *Images of the ice age*. Windward, Leicester.

Basedow, H. 1914. Aboriginal rock carvings of great antiquity in South Australia. *Journal of the Royal Anthropological Institute of Great Britain and Ireland*, 44:195–211.

Bates, G. M. 1993. *Environmental law in Australia*. Butterworths, Sydney.

Beaton, J. M. 1977. Dangerous harvest. PhD thesis, ANU, Canberra.

——1983. Does intensification account for changes in the Australian Holocene archaeological record? *Archaeology in Oceania*, 18(2):94–97.

——1985. Evidence for a coastal occupation time-lag at Princess Charlotte Bay (North Queensland) and implications for coastal colonisation and population growth theories for Aboriginal Australia. *Archaeology in Oceania*, 20(1):1–20.

——1994. Seven ways of seeing rock art. *Antiquity*, 68: 158–162.

——1995. The transition on the coastal fringe of Greater Australia. In J. Allen and J. F. O'Connell (eds), *Transitions: Pleistocene to Holocene in Australia and Papua New Guinea*, pp. 798–806. *Antiquity*, 69: Special Number 265.

Beaton, J. M. and G. L. Walsh. 1977. Che-ka-ra. *Mankind*, 11(1):46–48.

Beck, W., D. J. Donahue, A. J. T. Jull, G. Burr, W. S. Broecker, G. Bonani, J. Hajdas and E. Malotki 1998. Ambiguities in direct dating of rock surfaces using radiocarbon measurements. *Science*, 280:2132–2135.

Bednarik, R. G. 1985. Parietal finger markings in Australia. *Bollettino del Centro Camuno di Studi Preistorici*, XXII:83–88.

——1986. Cave use by Australian Pleistocene man. *Proceedings of the University of Bristol Spelaeological Society*, 17(3): 227–245.

——1998. The technology of petroglyphs. *Rock Art Research*, 15(1):23–35.

——1999. The speleothem medium of finger flutings and its isotropic geochemistry. *The Artefact*, 22:49–64.

——2000. Microerosion analysis—a recap. In G. K. Ward and C. Tuniz (eds), *Advances in dating Australian rock-markings: papers from the first Australian rock-picture dating workshop*, pp. 52–54. Occasional AURA Publication 10. AURA, Melbourne.

——2001. The dating of rock art: a critique. *Journal of Archaeological Science* (in press).

Bednarik, R. G. and M. Kukenburg 1999. *Nale Tasih: eine floßfahrt in die steinzeit*. Jan Thorbecke Verlag, Stuttgart.

Bégouën, R. and J. Clottes 1987. Les Trois-Fréres after Breuil. *Antiquity*, 61:180–187.

Bégouën, R., J. Clottes and H. Delporte 1984/5. Art mobilier sur support lithique d'Enléne. *Bulletin Societe Préhistoire Francais*, 74:112–120.

Bellwood, P. 1997. From bird's head to bird's eye view: long term structures and trends in Indo-Pacific prehistory. In J. Miedema, C. Odé and R. A. C. Dam (eds), *Perspectives on the Bird's Head of Irian Jaya, Indonesia: proceedings of the conference Leiden, 13–17 October*, pp. 951–975.

Beltrán, A. 1982. *Rock art of the Spanish Levant*. Cambridge University Press, Cambridge.

Berndt, R. M. 1958. Some methodological considerations in the study of Australian Aboriginal art. *Oceania*, 29(1): 26–43.

——1964. *Australian Aboriginal art*. Ure Smith, Sydney.

Biernoff, D. 1978. Safe and dangerous places. In L. R. Hiatt (ed.), *Australian Aboriginal concepts*, pp. 93–105. AIAS, Canberra.

Biesele, M. 1983. Interpretation in rock art and folklore: communication systems in evolutionary perspective. In J. D. Lewis-Williams (ed.), *New approaches to southern African rock art*, pp. 54–60. Goodwin Series Vol. 4. The South African Archaeological Society, Cape Town.

Binford, L. R. 1967. Smudge-pits and hide-smoking: the use of analogy in archaeological reasoning. *American Antiquity*, 32:1–12.

——1978. *Numamiut ethnoarchaeology*. Academic Press, New York.

Birdsell, J. H. 1977. The recalibration of a paradigm for the first peopling of Greater Australia. In J. Allen, J. Golson and R. Jones (eds), *Sunda and Sahul: prehistoric studies in Southeast Asia Melanesia and Australia*, pp. 113–168. Academic Press, London.

Blundell, V. 1974. The Wandjina cave paintings of northwest Australia. *Arctic Anthropology*, 11(supp.):213–223.

——1980. Hunter–gatherer territoriality: ideology and behaviour in northwest Australia. *Ethnohistory*, 27: 103–117.

——1982. Symbolic systems and cultural continuity in northwest Australia: a consideration of Aboriginal cave art. *Culture*, 2:3–20.

Bowdler, S. 1977. The coastal colonisation of Australia. In J. Allen, J. Golson and R. Jones (eds), *Sunda and Sahul: prehistoric studies in Southeast Asia, Melanesia and Australia*, pp. 205–246. Academic Press, London.

——1984. Archaeological significance as a mutable quality. In S. Sullivan and S. Bowdler (eds), *Site surveys and significance assessment in Australian archaeology*, pp. 1–9. Department of Prehistory, Research School of Pacific Studies, ANU, Canberra.

——1988. Repainting Australian rock art. *Antiquity*, 62:517–523.

——1993. Sunda and Sahul: a 30 kyr BP culture area? In M. A. Smith, M. Spriggs and B. Fankhouser (eds), *Sahul in review: Pleistocene archaeology in Australia, New Guinea and island Melanesia*, pp. 60–70. Department of Prehistory, Research School of Pacific Studies, ANU, Canberra.

Bowler, J. M. and A. G. Thorne 1976. Human remains from Lake Mungo: discovery and excavation of Lake Mungo III. In R. L. Kirk and A. G. Thorne (eds), *The origin of the Australians*, pp. 127–140. AIAS, Canberra.

Brandl, E. J. 1972. Thylacine designs in Arnhem Land rock paintings. *Archaeology in Oceania*, 7(1):24–30.

——1973. *Australian Aboriginal paintings in western and central Arnhem Land: temporal sequences and elements of style in Cadell River and Deaf Adder Creek art*. Prehistory and Material Culture Series 9. AIAS, Canberra.

——1980. Some notes on faunal identification and Arnhem Land rock paintings. *Australian Institute of Aboriginal Studies Newsletter*, New Series 14: 6–13.

Brandt, S. A. and N. Carder. 1987. Pastoral rock art in the Horn of Africa: making sense of udder chaos. *World Archaeology*, 19(2):194–213.

Breuil, H. 1952. *Four hundred centuries of cave art*. Centre d'etudes et de documentation prehistoriques, Montignac, France.

Brown, P. 1989. *Coobal Creek: a morphological and metrical analysis of the crania, mandibles and dentitions of a prehistoric Aboriginal population*. Terra Australis 13. Department of Prehistory, Research School of Pacific Studies, ANU, Canberra.

——2000. The first Australians: the debate continues. *Australian Science*, 21(4):28–31.

Brown, S. 1991. Art and Tasmanian prehistory: evidence for changing cultural traditions in a changing environment. In P. Bahn and A. Rosenfeld (eds), *Rock art and prehistory: papers presented to symposium G of the AURA Congress, Darwin 1988*, pp. 96–108. Oxbow Monograph 10. Oxbow Books, Oxford.

Brunet, J., P. Vidal and J. Vouvé 1987. *The conservation of rock art*. Studies and Documents on the Cultural Heritage 7, UNESCO.

Brunet, J., J. Vouvé, P. Vidal, P. Malaurent and G. Lacazedieu 1995. Theories and practice of the conservation of our heritage of rock art: concrete examples of interventions in natural climatic environment. In A. Thorn and J. Brunet (eds), *Preservation of rock art*, pp. 1–11. Occasional AURA Publication 9. AURA, Melbourne.

Byrne, D. 1991. *Western hegemony in archaeological heritage management*. History and Anthropology 5. Harwood Academic Publishers, Great Britain.

Calaby, J. and D. Lewis 1977. The Tasmanian Devil in Arnhem Land rock art. *Mankind*, 11(2):150–151.

Campbell, B. C. and V. E. Wilson 1993. *The politics of exclusion: Indonesian fishing in the Australian fishing zone*. Monograph No. 5. Indian Ocean Centre for Peace Studies, Perth.

Campbell, W. D. 1899. *Aboriginal carvings of Port Jackson and Broken Bay*. Memoirs of the Geological Survey of NSW, Ethnological Series No. 1. Department of Mines and Agriculture, Sydney.

Camps, G. 1982. Le cheval et le char dans la prehistoire nord-Africaine et Saharienne. In G. Camps and M. Gast (eds), *Les chars prehistoriques du Sahara*, pp. 9–20. University of Provence, Aix-en-Provence.

Capell, A. 1972. *Cave painting myths: northern Kimberley*. Oceania and Linguistic Monographs No. 18. University of Sydney, Sydney.

Chaloupka, G. 1993. *Journey in time*. Reed Books, Sydney.

Chaloupka, G. and P. Murray. 1986. Dreamtime or reality? Reply to Lewis. *Archaeology in Oceania*, 21:145–147.

Chappell, J. 1993. Late Pleistocene coasts and human migrations in the Austral region. In M. Spriggs, D. E. Yen, W. Ambrose, R. Jones, A. Thorne and A. Andrews (eds), *A community of culture: the people and prehistory of the Pacific*, pp. 43–49. Department of Prehistory, Research School of Pacific Studies, ANU, Canberra.

Chase, A. K. 1984. Belonging to country: territory, identity and environment in Cape York Peninsula, northern Australia. In L. R. Hiatt (ed.), *Aboriginal landowners: contemporary issues in the determination of traditional Aboriginal land ownership*, pp. 104–122. University of Sydney, Sydney.

Chippindale, C., B. Smith and P. S. C Taçon. 2000. Visions of dynamic power: archaic rock-paintings, altered states of consciousness and 'clever men' in western Arnhem Land (NT), Australia. *Cambridge Archaeological Journal*, 10(1):63–101.

Chippindale, C. and P. S. C. Taçon 1998. The many ways of dating Arnhem land rock-art, north Australia. In C. Chippindale and P. S. C. Taçon (eds), *The archaeology of rock-art*, pp. 90–111. Cambridge University Press, Cambridge.

Clarke, A. 1994. Winds of change: an archaeology of contact in the Groote Eylandt Archipelago, northern Australia. PhD thesis, ANU, Canberra.

Clarke, J. 1984. 'Rock art conservation': a research project in Western Australia. *Rock Art Research*, 1(2):135–136.

Cleere, H. 1989. Introduction: the rationale of archaeological heritage management. In H. Cleere (ed.), *Archaeological heritage management in the modern world*, pp. 1–17. Unwin Hyman, London.

Clegg, J. 1978. Pictures of striped animals: Which ones are thylacines? *Archaeology and Physical Anthropology in Oceania*, 13(1):19–29.

——1979. Prehistoric pictures. In P. Stanbury (ed.), *10,000 years of Sydney life*, pp. 156–163. Southwood Press, Sydney.

——1981. *Notes towards Mathesis art*. Clegg Calendars, Sydney.

——1985. Comment on 'The interpretation of prehistoric art' by D. Groenfeldt. *Rock Art Research*, 2(1):35–45.

——1987. Style and tradition at Sturt's Meadow. *World Archaeology*, 19(2):236–255.

Clottes, J. 1989 The identification of human and animal figures in European Palaeolithic art. In H. Morphy (ed.). *Animals into art*. pp. 21–56. Unwin Hyman, London.

Clottes et al. 2001. *La Grotte Chauvet l'art des origines*. Seuil, Paris.

Clottes, J., D. Lewis-Williams and S. Hawkes 1998. *The shamans of prehistory: trance and magic in the painted caves*. Abrams, London.

Cole, N. A. 1998. Eel and boomerang: an archaeological study of stylistic order and variability in Aboriginal rock art of the Laura Sandstone Province, Cape York Peninsula, Australia. PhD thesis, James Cook University, Townsville.

Cole, N. A. and B. David 1992. 'Curious drawings' at Cape York Peninsula. *Rock Art Research*, 9(1):3–26.

Cole, N. A. and A. Watchman 1992. Painting with plants: investigating fibres in Aboriginal rock paintings at Laura, north Queensland. *Rock Art Research*, 9(1):27–36.

Cole, N. A., A. Watchman and M. J. Morwood 1995. Chronology of Laura rock art. In M. J. Morwood and D. Hobbs (eds), *Quinkan Prehistory: the archaeology of Aboriginal art in S.E. Cape York Peninsula, Australia*, pp. 147–160. Tempus Volume 3. Anthropology Museum, University of Queensland, St Lucia.

Coles, J. 2000. *Patterns in a rocky land: rock carvings in south-west Uppland, Sweden*. Department of Archaeology and Ancient History, Uppsala.

Conkey, M. W. 1978. Style and information in cultural evolution: toward a predictive model for the Paleolithic. In C. L. Redman, M. J. Berman, E. V. Curtin, W. T. Langhorne Jr., N. M. Versaggi and J. C. Wanser (eds), *Social archaeology: beyond subsistence and dating*, pp. 61–85. Academic Press, New York.

——1980. The identification of prehistoric hunter–gatherer aggregation sites: the case of Altamira. *Current Anthropology*, 21(5):609–629.

——1981. A century of Palaeolithic cave art. *Archaeology*, July/August:20–28.

——1984. To find ourselves: art and social geography of prehistoric hunter-gatherers. In C. Shrire (ed.), *Past and present in hunter–gatherer studies*, pp. 253–276. Academic press, New York.

——1985. Ritual communication, social elaboration and the variable trajectories of Paleolithic material culture. In T. D. Price and J. A. Brown (eds), *Prehistoric hunter–gatherers: the emergence of cultural complexity*, pp. 299–323. Academic Press, New York.

——2001. Structural and semiotic approaches. In D. S. Whitley (ed.), *Handbook of rock art research*. Altamira Press, New York.

Connah, G. E. 1988. *'Of the hut I builded': the archaeology of Australia's history*. Cambridge University Press, Cambridge.

Cosgrove, R. and R. Jones 1989. Judds Cavern: a subterranean Aboriginal painting site, southern Tasmania. *Rock Art Research*, 6(2):96–104.

Crawford, I. M. 1968. *The art of the Wandjina: Aboriginal cave paintings in Kimberley, Western Australia*. Oxford University Press, Melbourne.

——1969. Late prehistoric changes in Aboriginal culture on Kimberley, Western Australia. PhD thesis, University of London.

——1977. The relationship of Bradshaw and Wandjina art in north-west Kimberley. In P. J. Ucko (ed.), *Form in indigenous art: schematisation in the art of Aboriginal Australia and prehistoric Europe*, pp. 357–369. AIAS, Canberra.

Crosby, E. 1968. An archaeological site survey near Taroom, south-eastern Queensland. *Memoirs of the Queensland Museum*, xv(pt.2):73–78.

d'Errico, F. 1994. Birds of Cosquer Cave: the Great Auk (*Pinguinus impennis*) and its significance during the Upper Palaeolithic. *Rock Art Research*, 11(1):45–57.

David, B. 1994. A space-time odyssey: rock art and regionalisation in North Queensland prehistory. PhD thesis, Department of Anthropology and Sociology, University of Queensland, St. Lucia.

David, B. and D. Chant 1995. Rock art and regionalisation in North Queensland prehistory. *Memoirs of the Queensland Museum*, 37(2):357–528.

David, B. and M. David 1988. Rock pictures of the Chillagoe-Mungana limestone belt, north Queensland. *Rock Art Research*, 5(2):147–156.

David, B., M. Lecole, H. Lourandos, A.J. Baglioi and J. Flood 1999. Investigating relationships between motif forms, techniques and rock surfaces in north Australian rock art. *Australian Archaeology*, 48: 16–22.

David, B., I. McNiven, V. Attenbrow, J. Flood and J. Collins 1994. Of Lightning Brothers and white cockatoos: dating the antiquity of signifying systems in the Northern Territory, Australia. *Antiquity*, 68:241–251.

David, B., A. Watchman, R. Goodall and E. Clayton 1993. The Maytown ochre source. *Memoirs of the Queensland Museum*, 38(2):441–445.

Davidson, D. S. 1937. *A preliminary consideration of Aboriginal Australian decorative art*. Memoirs of the American Philosophical Society, Volume 9. American Philosophical Society, Philadelphia.

Davidson, I. 1988. The naming of parts: ethnography and the interpretation of Australian prehistory. In B. Meehan and R. Jones (eds), *Archaeology with ethnography: an Australian experience*, pp. 17–32. Department of Prehistory, Research School of Pacific Studies, ANU, Canberra.

——1990. Prehistoric Australian demography. In B. Meehan and N. White (eds), *Hunter–gatherer demography: past and present*, pp. 41–58. University of Sydney, Sydney.

Davidson, I. and W. Noble 1989. The archaeology of perception: traces of depiction and language. *Current Anthropology*, 30(2):125–155.

——1992. Why the first colonisation of the Australian region is the earliest evidence of modern human behaviour. *Archaeology in Oceania*, 27(3):135–142.

Davis, W. 1986. The origins of image making. *Current Anthropology*, 27(3):193–216.

Denninger, E. 1971. The use of paper chromatography to determine the age of albuminous binders and its application to rock painting. *South African Journal of Science*, Special Publication 2:80–84.

Dix, W. C. 1977. Facial representations in Pilbara rock engravings. In P. J. Ucko (ed.), *Form in indigenous art: schematisation in the art of Aboriginal Australia and prehistoric Europe*, pp. 277–285. AIAS, Canberra.

——1989. Foreword. In D. Lambert, *Conserving Australian rock art: a manual for site managers*, pp. vi. Aboriginal Studies Press, Canberra.

Dixon, R. M. W. 1980. *The languages of Australia*. Cambridge University Press, Cambridge.

Donovan, H. L. 1976. The Aborigines of the Nogoa Basin: an ethno-historical/archaeological approach. BA (Hons) thesis, Department of Anthropology, Queensland University.

Dragovich, D. 1984a. Desert varnish as an age indicator for Aboriginal rock engravings: a review of problems and prospects. *Archaeology in Oceania*, 19(2):48–56.

——1984b. Varnished engravings and rock weathering near Broken Hill, western New South Wales. *Australian Archaeology*, 18:55–62.

——1986. Minimum age of some desert varnish near Broken Hill, New South Wales. *Search*, 17(5–6):149–150.

——1995. Site management and the visitor book, Mootwingee. In G. K. Ward and L. A. Ward (eds), *Management of rock imagery*, pp. 103–106. Occasional AURA Publication 9. AURA, Melbourne.

Drane, W. G. 1918. Letter to Surveyor-General, Brisbane, 27 April 1918. Ref. 18/5244 L.S.D.

Dubelaar, C. N. 1986. *South American and Caribbean petroglyphs*. Foris Publications, Holland.

Edwards, R. 1965a. Prehistoric rock engravings at Thomas Reservoir, Cleland Hills, western central Australia. *Records of the South Australian Museum*, 15:647–670.

——1965b. Rock engravings and incised stones: Tiverton Station, north-east South Australia. *Mankind*, 6(5):223–231.

——1966. Comparative study of rock engravings in South and Central Australia. *Proceedings of the Royal Society of South Australia*, 90:33–38.

——1971. Art and Aboriginal prehistory. In D. J. Mulvaney and J. Golson (eds), *Aboriginal man and environment in Australia*, pp. 356–367. ANU Press, Canberra.

——1979. *Australian Aboriginal art: the art of the Alligator Rivers region, Northern Territory*. AIAS, Canberra.

Elkin, A. P. 1930. Rock-paintings of north-west Australia. *Oceania*, 1(3):257–279.

——1961. Art and meaning: a review article. *Oceania*, 32:54–59.

Elliot, R. and A. Gare 1983. *Environmental philosophy: a collection of readings*. University of Queensland Press, St Lucia.

Fankhauser, B., S. O'Connor and Y. Pittelkow 1997. The analysis of pigments on rock surfaces, *Conference Handbook: sixth Australasian Archaeometry Conference*. Australian Museum, Sydney.

Fischer, J. L. 1961. Art styles as cultural cognitive maps. *American Anthropologist*, 63:79–93.

Flannery, T. F. 1994. *The future eaters*. Reed Books, Sydney.

Flood, J. M. 1987. Rock art of the Koolburra Plateau, North Queensland. *Rock Art Research*, 4(2):91–126.

——1995. *Archaeology of the Dreamtime: the story of prehistoric Australia and its people*. Angus and Robertson, Sydney.

——1997. *Rock art of the Dreamtime: images of ancient Australia*. Angus and Robertson, Sydney.

Flood, J. M. and N. Horsfall 1986. Excavations at Green Ant and Echidna Shelters. *Queensland Archaeological Research*, 3:4–64.

Florian, M. L. E. 1978. A review: the lichen role in rock art—dating, deterioration and control. In C. Pearson (ed.), *Conservation of rock art*, pp. 95–98. Institute for the Conservation of Cultural Material, Sydney.

Franklin, N. 1991. Explorations of the Panaramitee style. In P. Bahn and A. Rosenfeld (eds), *Rock art and prehistory: papers presented to symposium G of the AURA Congress, Darwin 1988*, pp. 120–135. Oxbow Monograph 10. Oxbow Books, Oxford.

——1992. Explorations of variability in Australian prehistoric rock engravings. PhD thesis, La Trobe University, Bundoora.

Frazer, J. G. 1890. *The golden bough: a study in comparative religion.* Macmillan, London.

Gale, F. and J. M. Jacobs 1986. Identifying high-risk visitors at Aboriginal art sites in Australia. *Rock Art Research,* 3(1):3–19.

——1987a. Aboriginal art—Australia's neglected heritage. *World Archaeology,* 19(2):226–235.

——1987b. *Tourists and the National Estate.* Australian Heritage Commission, Canberra.

Galindo, J. L. 1997. Scales of human organization and rock art distributions: an ethnoarchaeological study among the Kunwinjku people of Arnhem Land, Australia. MA thesis, University of Lincoln, Nebraska.

Gamble, C. 1980. Information exchange in the Palaeolithic. *Nature,* 283:522–523.

——1982. Interaction and alliance in Palaeolithic society. *Man,* 17:92–107.

——1983. Culture and society in the Upper Palaeolithic Europe. In G. Bailey (ed.), *Hunter–gatherer economy in prehistory: a European perspective,* pp. 201–211. Cambridge University Press, Cambridge.

Gellatley, D. C. and J. Soulis 1969. *Drysdale and Londonderry W.A. 1:250,000 Geological Series—explanatory notes.* Bureau of Mineral Resources and Geophysics, Government Printer, Hobart.

Gillespie, D. A. 1983. The practice of rock art conservation and site management in Kakadu National Park. In D. A. Gillespie (ed.), *The rock art sites of Kakadu National Park—some preliminary research findings for their conservation and management,* pp. 191–214. Special Publication 10. Australian National Parks and Wildlife Service, Canberra.

Godwin, L. 1990. Inside information: settlement and alliance in the late Holocene of northeastern New South Wales. PhD thesis, Department of Archaeology and Palaeoanthropology, UNE, Armidale.

Gollan, K. 1984. The Australian dingo: in the shadow of man. In M. Archer and G. Clayton (eds), *Vertebrate zoogeography and evolution in Australasia,* pp. 921–926. Hesperian Press, Carlisle, WA.

Golson, J. 1993. Kuk and the development of agriculture in New Guinea: retrospection and introspection. In D. E. Yen and J. M. J. Mummery (eds), *Pacific production systems: approaches to economic prehistory,* pp. 139–147. Department of Prehistory, Research School of Pacific Studies, ANU, Canberra.

González Garcia, R. 1987. Organisation, distribution and typology of the cave art of Monte del Castillo, Spain. *Rock Art Research,* 4(2):127–136.

Gould, R. A. 1969. *Yiwara: foragers of the Australian desert.* Charles Scribner's Sons, New York.

——1977. *Puntutjarpa rockshelter and the Australian desert culture.* American Museum of Natural History, New York.

——1986. Cave art of the Australian Desert Aborigines: a code to survival. In H. J. Shafer (ed.), *Ancient Texans: rock art and lifeways along the Lower Pecos,* pp. 204–209. Texas Monthly Press, San Antonio.

Gowlett, J. A. J. 1984. Mental abilities of early man. In R. Foley (ed.), *Hominid evolution and community ecology: prehistoric adaptation in biological perspective,* pp. 167–192. Academic Press, London.

Grant, C. 1983. *The Rock art of the North American Indians.* Cambridge University Press, Cambridge.

Gray, R. 1913. *Reminiscences of India and north Queensland.* Constable and Company, London.

Gunn, R. G. 1997. Rock art, occupation and myth. The correspondence of symbolic and archaeological site within Arrernte rock art complexes in central Australia. *Rock Art Research,* 14(2):124–136.

Guthrie, R. D. 1984. Ethological observations from Palaeolithic art. In H. G. Bandi, W. Huber, M. R. Sauter and B. Sitter (eds), *La contribution de la zoologie et de l'éthologie à l'interprétation de l'art des peuples chasseurs préhistoriques,* pp. 35–74. 3rd Colloque de la Société Suisse des Sciences Humaines, Editions Universitaires Fribourg Suisse, Fribourg.

Hale, H. H. and N. B. Tindale 1930. Notes on some human remains in the Lower Murray Valley, South Australia. *Records of the South Australian Museum,* 4(2):145–218.

Harris, D. R. 1977. Subsistence strategies across Torres Strait. In J. Allen, J. Golson and R. Jones (eds), *Sunda and Sahul: prehistoric Studies in Southeast Asia, Melanesia and Australia,* pp. 421–463. Academic Press, London.

——1995. Early agriculture in New Guinea and the Torres Strait divide. In J. Allen and J. F. O'Connell (eds), *Transitions: Pleistocene to Holocene in Australia and Papua New Guinea,* pp. 848–854. *Antiquity,* 69: Special Number 265.

Healey, C. J. 1980. The trade in bird plumes in the New Guinea region. *Occasional Papers of the Queensland University Anthropological Museum,* 10:249–276.

Heizer, R. F. and M. A. Baumhoff. 1962. *Prehistoric rock art of Nevada and eastern California.* University of California Press, Berkeley.

Hemple, C. 1945. Studies in the logic of confirmation. *Mind,* 54:1–26.

Horton, D. R. 1981. Water and woodland: the peopling of Australia. *AIAS Newsletter,* (16):21–27.

— (ed.) 1994. *The Encyclopaedia of Aboriginal Australia: Aboriginal and Torres Strait Islander history, society and culture*. Aboriginal Studies Press, Canberra.

Huchet, B. M. J. 1990. The identification of cicatrices depicted on anthropomorphs in the Laura region, north Queensland. *Rock Art Research*, 7(1):27–43.

Hughes, P. J. and A. Watchman 1983. The deterioration, conservation and management of rock art sites in Kakadu National Park. In D. A. Gillespie (ed.), *The rock art sites of Kakadu National Park—some preliminary research findings for their conservation and management*, pp. 37–86. Special Publication 10. Australian National Parks and Wildlife Service, Canberra.

Huyge, D. 1998. Possible representations of Palaeolithic fish-traps in upper Egyptian rock art. *Rock Art Research*, 15(1):3–11.

Irwin, G. 1992. *The prehistoric exploration and colonisation of the Pacific*. Cambridge University Press, Cambridge.

Janke, T. 1998. *Our culture, our future: report on Australian indigenous cultural and intellectual property rights*. Michael Frankel and Co., Sydney.

Jochim, M. A. 1983. Palaeolithic cave art in ecological perspective. In G. Bailey (ed.), *Hunter–gatherer economy in prehistory*, pp. 212–219. Cambridge University Press, New York.

Johnson, I. and K. Aplin 1978. Excavations at Capertee and Noola, January/February 1978: preliminary report prepared for National Parks and Wildlife Service. ANU, Canberra.

Jones, R. 1987. Ice-age hunters of the Tasmanian wilderness. *Australian Geographic*, 8:26–45.

Jones, R. and I. Johnson 1985. Deaf Adder Gorge: Linder Site, Nauwalabila 1. In R. Jones (ed.), *Archaeological research in Kakadu National Park*, pp 165–227. Australian National Parks and Wildlife Service, Canberra.

Joubert, J. J., W. C. Kriel and D. C. J. Wessels 1983. Lichenometry: its potential application to archaeology in southern Africa. *The South African Archaeological Society Newsletter*, 6(1):1–2.

Kamminga, J. and H. Allen 1973. *Report on the archaeological survey. The Alligator River fact-finding study*. Government Printer, Darwin.

Kiernan, K., R. Jones and D. Ranson. 1983. New evidence from Fraser Cave for glacial age man in southwest Tasmania. *Nature*, 301:28–32.

King, B. 1992. Retouching rock paintings. Unpublished letter to the 2nd AURA Congress, Cairns 1992.

Kuhn, S. L., M. C. Satiner, D. S. Reese and E. Gulec 2001. Ornaments of the earliest Upper Paleolithic: new insights from the Levant. *Proc. National Academy of Science*, 98(130): 7641–6.

Lahr, M. M. and R. A. Foley 1998. Towards a theory of modern human origins: geography, demography and diversity in recent human evolution. *Yearbook of Physical Anthropology*, 41:137–176.

Lambert, D. J. 1989. *Conserving Australian rock art: a manual for site managers*. Aboriginal Studies Press, Canberra.

Laming, A. 1959. *Lascaux: paintings and engravings*. Penguin, Harmondsworth.

Layton, R. 1985. The cultural context of hunter–gatherer rock art. *Man*, 20(3):434–453.

——1987. The use of ethnographic parallels in interpreting Upper Palaeolithic rock art. In L. Holy (ed.), *Comparative anthropology*, pp. 210–239. Blackwell, Oxford.

——1992a. *Australian rock art: a new synthesis*. Cambridge University Press, Cambridge.

——1992b. Ethnographic analogy and the two archaeological paradigms. In S. Goldsmith, S. Gavrie, D. Selin and J. Smith (eds), *Ancient images, ancient thought: the archaeology of identity. Proceedings of the 23rd Chacmool Conference*, pp. 211–221. Proceedings of the 23rd Chacmool Conference. Archaeological Association, University of Calgary, Calgary.

——2000. Shamanism, totemism and rock art: les chamanes de la préhistoire in the context of rock art research. *Cambridge Archaeological Journal*, 10:169–186.

Leroi-Gourhan, A. 1965. *Treasures of prehistoric art*. H.N. Abrams, New York.

——1968 (1976). The evolution of Paleolithic art. From Avenues to Antiquity. *Readings from Scientific American*: 55–65.

——1982. *The dawn of European art: an introduction to Palaeolithic cave painting*. Cambridge University Press, Cambridge.

Lewis, D. 1977. More striped designs in Arnhem Land rock paintings. *Archaeology and Physical Anthropology in Oceania*, 12(2):98–111.

——1986. 'The Dreamtime animals': a reply. *Archaeology in Oceania*, 21(2):140–145.

——1988. *The rock paintings of Arnhem Land, Australia: social ecological and material culture change in the post-glacial period*. BAR International Series 415. British Archaeological Reports, Oxford.

——1997. Bradshaws: the view from Arnhem Land. *Australian Archaeology*, 44:1–16.

Lewis, D. and D. Rose 1988. *The shape of the Dreaming*. Aboriginal Studies Press, Canberra.

Lewis-Williams, J. D. 1974. Superimpositioning in a sample of rock paintings from the Barkly East District. *South African Archaeological Bulletin*, 29:93–103.

——1981. *Believing and seeing: symbolic meanings in southern San rock paintings*. Academic Press, London.

——1983a. Introductory essay: science and rock art. *New approaches to southern African rock art*, pp. 3–13. Goodwin Series Volume 4. South African Archaeological Society, Cape Town.

——1983b. *The rock art of southern Africa*. Cambridge University Press, Cambridge.

——1987. A dream of eland: an unexplained component of San shamanism and rock art. *World Archaeology*, 19(2):165–177.

Lewis-Williams, J. D. and J. H. N. Loubser 1986. Deceptive appearances: a critique of southern African rock art studies. In F. Wendorf and A. Close (eds), *Advances in world archaeology* Volume 5, pp. 253–289. Academic Press, New York.

Lhote, H. 1982. Les chars rupestres du Sahara et leurs rapports avec le peuplement dans les temps protohistoriques. In G. Camps and M. Gast (eds), *Les chars prehistoriques du Sahara*, pp. 10–23. University of Provence, Aix-en-Provence.

Lipe, W. D. 1984. Value and meaning in cultural resources. In H. Cleere (ed.), *Approaches to archaeological heritage*, pp. 1–11. Cambridge University Press, Cambridge.

Lommel, A. 1961. Rock art of Australia. In H. G. Bandi and others (eds), *The art of the stone age: forty thousand years of rock art*, pp. 205–231. Methuen, London.

Lorblanchet, M. 1977. From naturalism to abstraction in European prehistoric rock art. In P. J. Ucko (ed.), *Form in indigenous art*, pp. 44–58. Australian Institute of Aboriginal Studies, Canberra.

——1986. Comment on Dragovich's 'A plague of locusts, or manna from heaven?'. *Rock Art Research*, 3(2):152–155.

——(ed.) 1992. *Rock art in the Old World*. Indira Gandhi National Centre for the Arts, New Delhi.

Lourandos, H. 1977. Aboriginal spatial organization and population: south-western Victoria reconsidered. *Archaeology and Physical Anthropology in Oceania*, 12(3):202–225.

——1985. Intensification and Australian prehistory. In T. D. Price and J. A. Brown (eds), *Prehistoric hunter–gatherers: the emergence of cultural complexity*, pp. 385–423. Academic Press, Orlando.

Loy, T. H., R. Jones, D. E. Nelson, B. Meehan, J. Vogel, J. Southon and R. Cosgrove 1990. Accelerator radiocarbon dating of human blood proteins in pigments from Late Pleistocene art sites in Australia. *Antiquity*, 64:110–116.

Luebbers, R. A. 1975. Ancient boomerangs discovered in South Australia. *Nature*, 253:39.

Macintosh, N. W. G. 1952. Paintings in Beswick Creek Cave, Northern Territory. *Oceania*, 22(4):256–274.

——1965. Dingo and horned anthropomorph in an Aboriginal rock shelter. *Oceania*, 36(2):85–101.

——1977. Beswick Creek Cave two decades later: a reappraisal. In P. J. Ucko (ed.), *Form in indigenous art: schematisation in the art of Aboriginal Australia and prehistoric Europe*, pp. 191–197. AIAS, Canberra.

Macknight, C. C. 1976. *The voyage to Marege: Macassan trepangers in Northern Australia*. Melbourne University Press, Melbourne.

——1986. Macassans and the Aboriginal past. *Archaeology in Oceania*, 21(1):69–75.

Malakoff, D. 1998. Rock art dates thrown into doubt, researcher under fire. *Science*, 280:2041–2042.

Mallery, G. 1972 (1893). *Picture-writing of the American Indians Vols. 1 and 2*. Dover Publications, New York.

Mangi, J. 1989. The role of archaeology in nation building. In R. Layton (ed.), *Conflict in the archaeology of living traditions*, pp. 217–227. Unwin Hyman, London.

Marika, W. 1975. Statement on sacred sites. In R. Edwards (ed.), *The preservation of Australia's Aboriginal Heritage: report on national seminar on Aboriginal antiquities in Australia, May 1972*, pp. 77–82. AIAS, Canberra.

Marshack, A. 1972. *The roots of civilization: the cognitive beginnings of man's first art, symbol and notation*. Weidenfeld and Nicolson, London.

——1975. Exploring the mind of ice age man. *National Geographic*, pp. 62–89.

——1977. The meander as a system: the analysis and recognition of iconographic units in upper Palaeolithic compositions. In P. J. Ucko (ed.), *Form in indigenous art: schematisation in the art of Aboriginal Australia and prehistoric Europe*, pp. 286–317. AIAS, Canberra.

Martineau, L. V. 1973. *The rocks begin to speak*. KC Publications, Las Vegas, Nevada.

Mathew, J. 1910. *Two representative tribes of Queensland*. Unwin, London.

Maynard, L. 1976. An archaeological approach to the study of Australian rock art. MA thesis, University of Sydney.

——1977. Classification and terminology in Australian rock art. In P. J. Ucko (ed.), *Form in indigenous art: schematisation in the art of Aboriginal Australia and prehistoric Europe*, pp. 387–403. AIAS, Canberra.

——1979. The archaeology of Australian Aboriginal art. In S. M. Mead (ed.), *Exploring the Visual Art of Oceania*, pp. 83–110. University of Hawaii Press, Honolulu.

Maynard, L. and R. Edwards 1971. Wall markings. In R. V. S. Wright (ed.), *Archaeology of the Gallus Site, Koonalda Cave*, pp. 61–80. AIAS, Canberra.

McBryde, I. 1974. *Aboriginal prehistory in New England: an archaeological survey of northeastern New South Wales.* Sydney University Press, Sydney.

McCarthy, F. D. 1939–40. 'Trade' in Aboriginal Australia. *Oceania*, 9: 405–38, 10: 80–104, 171–95.

——1953. The Oceanic and Indonesia affiliations of Australian Aboriginal culture. *Journal of the Polynesian Society*, 62:243–261.

——1959. Rock engravings of the Sydney–Hawkesbury district. *Records of the Australian Museum*, 24(5):37–58.

——1960a. Rock art of Central Queensland. *Mankind*, 5:400–404.

——1960b. The cave paintings of Groote Eylandt and Chasm Island. In C.P. Mountford (ed.), *Records of the American and Australian scientific expedition to Arnhem Land, Volume 2*, pp. 297–414. Melbourne University Press, Melbourne.

——1961. The rock engravings of Depuch Island, north-west Australia. *Records of the Australian Museum*, 25:121–148.

——1962. *The rock engravings at Port Hedland, north-western Australia.* Kroeber Anthropological Society, Papers No. 26.

——1967. *Australian Aboriginal rock art.* 3rd ed. Australian Museum, Sydney.

——1974. Space and superimposition in Australian Aboriginal art. In A. K. Ghosh (ed.), *Perspectives in palaeoanthropology*, pp. 113–128. Firma K.L. Mukhopadhyay, Calcutta.

——1976. *Rock art of the Cobar pediplain in central western New South Wales.* AIAS, Canberra.

McConnell, K and S. O'Connor 1997. 40,000 year record of food plants in the southern Kimberley Ranges, Western Australia. *Australian Archaeology*, 45 20–32.

McConvell, P. 1996. Backtracking to Babel: the chronology of Pama-Nyungan expansion in Australia. *Archaeology in Oceania*, 31(3):125–144.

McConvell, P. and N. Evans 1997. *Archaeology and linguistics: Aboriginal Australia in global perspective.* Oxford University Press, Melbourne.

McDonald, J. 1982. On the write track. BA (Hons) thesis, University of Sydney, Sydney.

——1985. Sydney Basin Aboriginal Heritage Study: rock engravings and shelter art sites. Report to Australian Heritage Commission, Australian National Parks and Wildlife Service.

——1994. Dreamtime superhighway: an analysis of Sydney Basin rock art and prehistoric information exchange. PhD thesis, ANU, Canberra.

McDonald, J., K. Officer, T. Jull, D. Donahue, J. Head and B. Ford. 1990. Investigating C14 AMS: dating prehistoric rock art in the Sydney Sandstone Basin, Australia. *Rock Art Research*, 7(2):83–92.

McGimsey III, C. R. 1972. *Public archaeology.* Seminar Press, New York and London.

McMah (Maynard), L. 1965. A quantitative analysis of the Aboriginal rock carvings of Sydney and the Hawkesbury River. BA (Hons) thesis, Sydney University, Sydney.

McNickle, H. P. 1984. Variation in style and distribution of rock engravings in the Pilbara region (Western Australia). *Rock Art Research*, 1(1):5–24.

——1991. A survey of rock art in the Victoria River District, Northern Territory. *Rock Art Research*, 8(1):36–46.

Meston, A. 1901. Among the Myalls. Maranoa Aborigines. *The Queenslander*, 12 January.

Mitchell, S. 1994. Culture contact and indigenous economies on the Cobourg Peninsula, northwestern Arnhem Land. PhD thesis, Department of Anthropology, Northern Territory University, Darwin.

Mithen, S. J. 1987. Looking and learning: upper Palaeolithic art and information gathering. *World Archaeology*, 19(3):297–327.

——1996. *The prehistory of the mind: a search for the origins of art, religion and science.* Thames and Hudson, London.

Moore, D. R. 1978. Cape York Aborigines: fringe participants in the Torres Strait trading system. *Mankind*, 11(3):319–325.

Morgan, G. and J. Terrey 1990. Lands of the Prairie/Porcupine Gorge system, upper Flinders River, North Queensland Highlands. *Queensland Archaeological Research*, 7:41–52.

Morgan, G., J. Terrey and M. Abel 1995. The biophysical environment. In Morwood and Hobbs (eds), Quinkan prehistory: the archaeology of Aboriginal art in south-east Cape York Peninsula, Australia. *Tempus*, 3, pp. 5–17. Anthropology Museum, University of Queensland, Brisbane.

Morphy, H. 1977. Too many meanings: an analysis of the artistic system of the Yolngu of north-east Arnhem Land. PhD thesis, ANU, Canberra.

——1991. *Ancestral connections: art and an Aboriginal system of knowledge.* Chicago University Press, Chicago.

Morse, K. 1988. Mandu Mandu Creek rock-shelter: Pleistocene coastal occupation of North West Cape, Western Australia. *Archaeology in Oceania*, 23:81–88.

Morwood, M. J. 1975. Analogy and the acceptance of theory in archaeology. *American Antiquity*, 40(1):111–116.

——1979. Art and stone: towards a prehistory of central western Queensland. PhD thesis, ANU, Canberra.

——1980. Time, space and prehistoric art: a principal components analysis. *Archaeology and Physical Anthropology in Oceania*, 15(2):98–109.

——1981. Archaeology of the Central Queensland Highlands: the stone component. *Archaeology in Oceania*, 16(1):1–52.

——1984a. The prehistory of the Central Queensland Highlands. In F. Wendorf and A. Close (eds), *Advances in world archaeology*, Volume 13, pp. 325–379. Academic Press, New York.

——1984b. The Mt. Inglis cache: a new perspective on Aboriginal material culture in the Central Queensland Highlands. *Memoirs of the Queensland Museum*, 21(2):541–559.

——1986. Australian Aboriginal archaeology. In A. Cameron (ed.), *The Second Australian almanac*, pp. 532–543. Angus and Robertson, Sydney.

——1987. The archaeology of social complexity in south-east Queensland. *Proceedings of the Prehistoric Society*, 53: 337–350.

——1988. Rock Art and ethnography. *Rock Art Research*, 5(1):67–68.

——1990. The prehistory of Aboriginal landuse on the upper Flinders River, North Queensland Highlands. *Queensland Archaeological Research*, 7:3–56.

——1992. Aboriginal rock art in S.E. Cape York Peninsula: an archaeological approach. In S. Goldsmith, S. Gavrie, D. Selin and J. Smith (eds), *Ancient images, ancient thought: the archaeology of ideology*, pp. 417–426. Proceedings of the 23rd Chacmool Conference. Archaeological Association, University of Calgary, Calgary.

——1992a. Changing art in a changing landscape: a case study from the North Queensland Highlands. In J. McDonald (ed.), *State of the Art*, AURA Occasional Publication No. 6: 25–40.

——1994. Handy household hints for archaeological excavations at rock art sites. *Rock Art Research*, 11(1): 10–12.

——1995. Introduction: the archaeology of Quinkan rock art. In M. J. Morwood and D. R. Hobbs (eds), *Quinkan prehistory: the archaeology of Aboriginal art in S.E. Cape York Peninsula, Australia*, pp. 1- 4. Tempus, Volume 3. Anthropology Department, University of Queensland.

——1998. Sex, lies and symbolic behaviour. *Rock Art Research*, 15(1):17–22.

Morwood, M. J., F. Aziz, Nasruddin, D. R. Hobbs, P. B. O'Sullivan and A. Raza 1999. Archaeological and palaeontological research in central Flores, east Indonesia: results of fieldwork, 1997–98. *Antiquity*, 73:273–286.

Morwood, M. J. and L. M. Godwin 1982. Aboriginal sites in the Hughenden region, North Queensland Highlands: research prospects. *Australian Archaeology*, 15:49–53.

Morwood, M. J. and D. R. Hobbs (eds) 1992. *Rock art and ethnography*. Occasional AURA Publication 5. AURA, Melbourne.

——(eds) 1995a. *Quinkan prehistory: the archaeology of Aboriginal art in S.E. Cape York Peninsula, Australia*. Anthropology Museum, University of Queensland, St Lucia.

——1995b. Themes in the prehistory of tropical Australia. In J. Allen and J. F. O'Connell (eds), *Transitions: Pleistocene to Holocene in Australia and Papua New Guinea*, pp. 747–768. *Antiquity*, 69: Special Number 265.

——1997. The Asian connection: preliminary report on Indonesian trepang sites on the Kimberley coast, N.W. Australia. *Archaeology in Oceania*, 32:197–206.

——2000. The archaeology of Kimberley art. In G. L. Walsh (ed.), *Bradshaw art of the Kimberley*, pp. 34–37. Takarakka Nowan Kas Publications, Toowong, Queensland.

Morwood, M. J. and S. Jung 1995. Excavations at Magnificent Gallery. In M. J. Morwood and D. R. Hobbs (eds), *Quinkan prehistory: the archaeology of Aboriginal art in S.E Cape York Peninsula, Australia*, pp. 93–100. Tempus Volume 3. Anthropology Museum, University of Queensland, St Lucia.

Morwood, M. J. and Y. Kaiser-Glass 1991. The use of graffiti in the monitoring of community attitudes towards Aboriginal rock art. *Rock Art Research*, 8(2):94–98.

Morwood, M. J. and S. L'Oste-Brown 1995. Excavations at Mushroom Rock. In Morwood and Hobbs (eds), Quinkan prehistory: the archaeology of Aboriginal art in south-east Cape York Peninsula, Australia. *Tempus*, 3, pp. 161–77. Anthropology Museum, University of Queensland, Brisbane.

Morwood, M. J. and C. E. Smith 1994. Rock art research in Australia 1974–94. *Australian Archaeology*, 39:19–38.

Morwood, M. J. and P. J. Trezise 1989. Edge-ground axes in Pleistocene greater Australia: new evidence from S.E. Cape York Peninsula. *Queensland Archaeological Research*, 6:77–90.

Morwood, M. J., G. L. Walsh and A. Watchman. 1994. The dating potential of rock art in the Kimberley, N.W Australia. *Rock Art Research*, 11(2):79–87.

Mountford, C. P. 1937. Aboriginal crayon drawings from the Warburton Ranges in Western Australia relating to the wanderings of two ancestral beings, the Wati Kutjara. *Records of the South Australian Museum*, 6(1):5–28.

——1955. An unrecorded method of Aboriginal rock marking. *Records of the South Australian Museum*, 11:345–352.

——1956. *Records of the American-Australian scientific expedition to Arnhem Land Vol. 1: art, myth and symbolism*. Melbourne University Press, Melbourne.

——1959. The rock art of Australia. MA thesis, Department of Anthropology, Cambridge University.

——1965a. *Ayers Rock: its people, their beliefs and their art*. Angus and Robertson, Sydney.

——1965b. Aboriginal rock poundings on Gallery Hill, north-western Australia. *Records of the South Australian Museum*, 1:89–108.

——1976. *Nomads of the Australian desert*. Rigby, Sydney.

Mountford, C. P. and R. Edwards. 1963. Rock engravings of Panaramitee Station, north-eastern South Australia. *Transcripts of the Royal Society of South Australia*, 86:131–148.

Mowaljarlai, D. 1992. Wayrrull—Aboriginal traditional responsibility in cultural resource management in the northwest Kimberleys of Western Australia. In J. Birckhead, T. de Lacy and L. J. Smith (eds), *Aboriginal involvement in parks and protected areas*, pp. 176–189. Aboriginal Studies Press, Canberra.

Mowaljarlai, D. and J. Malnic 1993. *Yorro Yorro, everything standing up alive: spirit of the Kimberley*. Magabala Books, Broome, Western Australia.

Mowaljarlai, D. and C. Peck 1987. Ngarinyin cultural continuity: a project to teach the young people the culture, including the re-painting of Wandjina rock art sites. *Australian Aboriginal Studies*, 2:71–78.

Mowaljarlai, D. and P. Vinnicombe 1995. Perspectives of the origin of rock images in the Western Kimberley. In G. K. Ward and L. A. Ward (eds), *Management of rock imagery*, pp. 42–52. Occasional AURA Publication 9. AURA, Melbourne.

Mowaljarlai, D., P. Vinnicombe, G. K. Ward and C. Chippindale. 1988. Repainting of images on rock in Australia and the maintenance of Aboriginal culture. *Antiquity*, 62:690–696.

Mulvaney, D. J. 1970. Human factors in the deterioration and destruction of antiquity and their remedy. In F. D. McCarthy (ed.), *Aboriginal antiquities in Australia: their nature and preservation*, pp. 115–125. AIAS, Canberra.

——1975. *The prehistory of Australia*. Penguin Books, Ringwood.

——1985. A question of values: museums and cultural property. In I. McBryde (ed.), *Who owns the past?*, pp. 86–98. Oxford University Press, Melbourne.

——1989. *Encounters in place: outsiders and Aboriginal Australians 1606–1985*. University of Queensland Press, St Lucia, Brisbane.

Mulvaney, D. J. and E. B. Joyce 1965. Archaeological and geomorphological investigations on Mt. Moffat Station, Queensland, Australia. *Proceedings of the Prehistoric Society*, 31:147–212.

Mulvaney, D. J. and J. Kamminga 1999. *The prehistory of Australia*. Allen & Unwin, Sydney.

Munn, N. 1966. Visual categories: an approach to the study of representational systems. *American Anthropologist*, 68:936–950.

——1973. *Walbiri iconography: graphic representation and cultural symbolism in a central Australian society*. Cornell University Press, New York.

Murray, P. and G. Chaloupka. 1984. The Dreamtime animals: extinct megafauna in Arnhem Land rock art. *Archaeology in Oceania*, 19(3):105–116.

Muzzolini, A. 1990. The sheep in Saharan rock art. *Rock Art Research*, 7(2):93–109.

Nelson, D. E. 1993. Second thoughts on a rock art date. *Antiquity*, 67:893–895.

——(ed.) 2000. *The beeswax art of northern Australia*. Simon Fraser University, Burnaby.

Nelson, D. E., G. Chaloupka, C, Chippindale, M.S. Alderson and J. Southron 1995. Radiocarbon dates for beeswax figures in the prehistoric rock art of northern Australia. *Archaeometry* 37(1): 151–156.

Nelson, E. (ed.) 2000. *The beeswax art of northern Australia*. Simon Fraser University, Burnaby.

Neumayer, E. 1983. *Prehistoric Indian rock paintings*. Oxford University Press, Delhi.

Nobbs, M. F. and R. I. Dorn. 1988. Age determinations for rock varnish formation within petroglyphs: cation-ratio dating of 24 motifs from the Olary region, South Australia. *Rock Art Research*, 5(2):108–146.

——1993. New surface exposure ages for petroglyphs from the Olary Province, South Australia. *Archaeology in Oceania*, 28(1):18–39.

Noble, W. and I. Davidson 1996. *Human evolution, language and mind*. Cambridge University Press, Cambridge.

O'Connor, S. 1990. 30,000 years in the Kimberley: a prehistory of the islands of the Buccaneer Archipelago and adjacent mainland, west Kimberley, Western Australia. PhD thesis, Department of Archaeology, University of Western Australia.

——1995. Carpenter's Gap rockshelter 1: 40,000 years of Aboriginal occupation in the Napier Ranges, Kimberley, W.A. *Australian Archaeology*, 40(June):58–59.

——1996. Thirty thousand years in the Kimberley: results of excavation of three rockshelters in the coastal west Kimberley, W.A. In P. Veth and P. Hiscock (eds), *Archaeology of northern Australia: regional perspectives*, pp. 26–49. Tempus Volume 4. Anthropology Museum, University of Queensland, Brisbane.

Ogawa, M. 1992. Rock engravings in Fugoppe Cave, Japan. In M. J. Morwood and D. R. Hobbs (eds), *Rock art and ethnography*, pp. 71–74. Occasional AURA Publication 5. AURA, Melbourne.

Pardoe, C. 1995. Riverine, biological and cultural evolution in southeastern Australia. In J. Allen and J. F. O'Connell (eds), *Transitions: Pleistocene to Holocene in Australia and Papua New Guinea*, pp. 696–713. *Antiquity*, 69: Special Number 265.

Pearson, C. and B. K. Swartz Jr. (eds) 1991. *Rock art and posterity: conserving, managing and recording rock art.* Occasional AURA Publication 4. AURA, Melbourne.

Pearson, M. and S. Sullivan 1995. *Looking after heritage places. The basics of heritage planning for managers, landowners and administrators.* Melbourne University Press, Melbourne.

Petrie, C. C. 1904. *Tom Petrie's reminiscences of early Queensland.* Watson, Fergusson and Co., Brisbane.

Pfeiffer, J. E. 1982. *The creative explosion: an inquiry into the origins of art and religion.* Cornell University Press, New York.

Porch, N. and J. Allen 1995. Tasmania: archaeological and palaeoecological perspectives. In J. Allen and J. F. O'Connell (eds), *Transitions: Pleistocene to Holocene in Australia and Papua New Guinea*, pp. 714–732. *Antiquity*, 69: Special Number 265.

Prous, A. 1986. L'archéologies au Brésil: 300 siecles d'occupation humaine. *L'Anthropologie*, 90(2):257–306.

Quinnell, M. C. 1975. Aboriginal rock art in Carnarvon Gorge, south-central Queensland. *Anthropological Society of Queensland Newsletter*, 69:2–10.

Rightmire, G. P. 1994. The relationship of Homo erectus to later Middle Pleistocene hominids. In J. L. Franzen (ed.), *100 years of Pithecanthropus: the Homo erectus problem*, pp. 319–326. Courier Forschungs, Frankfurt.

Roberts, R. G., R. Jones and M. A. Smith. 1990. Thermoluminescence dating of a 50,000-year-old human occupation site in northern Australia. *Nature*, 345(10 May):153–156.

——1994. Beyond the radiocarbon barrier in Australian prehistory. *Antiquity*, 68:611–616.

Roberts, R. G., G. Walsh, A. Murray, J. Olley, R. Jones, M. Morwood, C. Tuniz, E. Lawson, M. Macphail, D. Bowdery and I. Naumann 1997. Luminescence dating of rock art and past environments using mud-wasp nests in northern Australia. *Nature*, 387(12):696–699.

Rose, D. B. 1992. *Dingo makes us human: life and land in an Aboriginal Australian culture.* Cambridge University Press, Melbourne.

Rosenfeld, A. 1977. Profile figures: schematisation of the human figure in the Magdalenian culture of Europe. In P. J. Ucko (ed.), *Form in indigenous art: schematisation in the art of Aboriginal Australia and prehistoric Europe*, pp. 90–109. AIAS, Canberra.

——1982. Style and meaning in Laura art: a case study in the formal analysis of style in prehistoric art. *Mankind*, 13(3):199–217.

——1984. The identification of animal representations in the art of the Laura region, North Queensland (Australia). In H. G. Bandi, W. Huber, M. R. Sauter and B. Sitter (eds), *La contribution de la zoologie et de l'éthologie à l'Interprétation de l'art des peuples chasseurs préhistoriques*, pp. 399–422. 3rd Colloque de la Société Suisse des Sciences Humaines, Editions Universitaires Fribourg Suisse, Fribourg.

——1985. *Rock art conservation in Australia.* Special Australian Heritage Publication No. 2. Australian Government Publishing Service, Canberra.

——1991. Panaramitee: dead or alive? In P. Bahn and A. Rosenfeld (eds), *Rock art and prehistory: papers presented to symposium G of the AURA Congress, Darwin 1988*, pp. 136–144. Oxbow Monograph 10. Oxbow Books, Oxford.

——1997. Archaeological signatures of the social context of rock art production. In M. Conkey, O. Soffer, D. Stratmann and N.G. Jablonski (eds), *Beyond art: Pleistocene image and symbol*. Memoirs of the California Academy of Sciences.

Rosenfeld, A., D. Horton and J. Winter 1981. *Early Man in North Queensland: art and archaeology in the Laura area.* Terra Australis 6. Department of Prehistory, Research School of Pacific Studies, ANU, Canberra.

Rosenfeld, A. and C. E. Smith 1997. Recent developments in radiocarbon and stylistic methods of dating rock-art. *Antiquity*, 71:405–411.

Ross, A. 1985. Archaeological evidence for population change in the middle to late Holocene in southeastern Australia. *Archaeology in Oceania*, 20:81–89.

Ross, J. 1997. Painted relationships: an archaeological analysis of a distinctive anthropomorphic rock art motif in northwest central Queensland. BA (Hons) thesis, Department of Archaeology and Palaeoanthropology, UNE, Armidale.

Roth, W. E. 1897. *Ethnological studies among the north-west central Queensland Aborigines.* Government printer, Brisbane.

——1898. On the Aboriginals occupying the 'Hinter-land' of Princess Charlotte Bay, together with a preface containing suggestions for their better protection and improvement. Unpublished report to the Commissioner of Police, Mitchell Library, Sydney.

——1899. An account of the Koko Minni Aboriginals occupying the country drained by the (middle) Palmer

River. Unpublished report to the Commissioner of Police, Mitchell Library, Sydney.

Russ, J., M. Hyman and M. W. Rowe 1993. Direct radiocarbon and chemical analysis of ancient rock paintings. *Archaeology and Natural Science*, 1:127–142.

Sagona, A. G. and J. A. Webb. 1994. Toolumbunner in perspective. In A. G. Sagono (ed.), *Bruising the red earth: ochre mining and ritual in Aboriginal Tasmania*, pp. 133–151. Melbourne University Press, Melbourne.

Sales, K. 1992. Ascent to the sky: a shamanic initiatory engraving from the Burrup Peninsula, northwest Western Australia. *Archaeology in Oceania*, 27(1):22–35.

Saussure, F., C. Bally, A. Sechehaye and A. Riedlinger 1959. *Course in general linguistics*. Philosophical Library, New York.

Sauvet, G. and S. Sauvet 1979. Fonction sémiologique de l'art pariétal animalier franco-cantabrique. *Bulletin de la Société Préhistorique Francaise*, 76:340–354.

Sauvet, G., S. Sauvet and A. Wlodarczyk. 1977. Essai de sémiologie préhistorique (Pour une thÈorie des premiers signes graphiques de l'homme). *Bulletin de la Société Préhistorique Francaise*, 74:545–558.

Schaafsma, P. 1985. Form, content and function: theory and method in North American rock art studies. In M. B. Schiffer (ed.), *Advances in archaeological method and theory Vol. 8*, pp. 127–177. Academic Press, New York.

Schiffer, M. B. and G. J. Gumerman 1977. *Conservation archaeology: a guide for cultural resource management studies*. Academic Press, New York.

Sims, P. C. 1977. Variations in Tasmanian petroglyphs. In P. J. Ucko (ed.), *Form in indigenous art: schematisation in the art of Aboriginal Australia and prehistoric Europe*, pp. 429–438. AIAS, Canberra.

Smith, C. 1989a. Designed dreaming: assessing the relationship between style, social structure and environment in Aboriginal Australia. BA (Hons) thesis, Department of Archaeology and Palaeoanthropology, UNE, Armidale.

——1992. The use of ethnography in interpreting rock art: a comparative study of Arnhem Land and the Western Desert of Australia. In M. J. Morwood and D. R. Hobbs (eds), *Rock art and ethnography*, pp. 39–45. Occasional AURA Publication 5. AURA, Melbourne.

——1994. Situating style: an ethnoarchaeological analysis of social and material context in an Australian Aboriginal artistic system. PhD thesis, Department of Archaeology and Palaeoanthropology, UNE, Armidale.

Smith, M. A. 1989b. Seed grinding in inland Australia. Current evidence from seed-grinders on the antiquity of the ethnohistorical pattern of exploitation. In D. R. Harris and G. C. Hillman (eds), *Foraging and farming: the evolution of plant exploitation*, pp. 305–317. Unwin Hyman, London.

Smith, M. A. and B. Fankhauser 1996. An archaeological perspective on the geochemistry of Australian red ochre deposits: prospects for fingerprinting major sources. Unpublished report. Australian Institute of Aboriginal and Torres Strait Islander Studies, Canberra.

Smith, M. A., B. Fankhauser and M. Jercher 1998. The changing provenance of red ochre at Puritjarra rock shelter, Central Australia: Late Pleistocene to present. *Proceedings of the Prehistoric Society*, 64:275–292.

Smith, M. A. and N. D. Sharp 1993. Pleistocene sites in Australia, New Guinea and island Melanesia: geographic and temporal structure of the archaeological record. In M. A. Smith, M. Spriggs and B. Fankhouser (eds), *Sahul in review: Pleistocene archaeology in Australia, New Guinea and island Melanesia*, pp. 37–59. Department of Prehistory, Research School of Pacific Studies, ANU, Canberra.

Spencer, B. and F. J. Gillen. 1899. *The native tribes of Central Australia*. Macmillan and Co., London.

Stoneking, M. and R. L. Cann 1989. African origin of mitochondrial DNA. In P. Mellars and C. Stringer (eds), *The human revolution: behavioural and biological perspectives on the origins of modern humans Vol.1*, pp. 17–29. Edinburgh University Press, Edinburgh.

Straus, L. G. 1987. The Paleolithic cave art of Vasco-Cantabrian Spain. *Oxford Journal of Archaeology*, 6(2):149–163.

Strehlow, T. G. H. 1964. The art of circle, line and square. In R. M. Berndt (ed.), *Australian Aboriginal art*, pp. 44–59. Ure Smith, Sydney.

——1965. Culture, social structure and environment in Aboriginal Central Australia. In R. M. Berndt and C. W. Berndt (eds), *Aboriginal man in Australia: essays in honour of Emeritus Professor A.P. Elkin*, pp. 121–145. Angus and Robertson, Sydney.

——1970. Geography and the totemic landscape in Central Australia: a functional study. In R. M. Berndt (ed.), *Australian Aboriginal anthropology: modern studies in the social anthropology of the Australian Aborigines*, pp. 92–140. University of Western Australia Press, Perth.

Sullivan, H. 1984. *Visitors to Aboriginal sites: access, control and management: proceedings of the 1983 Kakadu Workshop*. Australian National Parks and Wildlife Service, Canberra.

Sullivan, S. (ed.) 1995. *Cultural conservation: towards a national approach*. Special Australian Heritage Publication No. 9. Australian Government Publishing Service, Canberra.

Sutton, P. J. and B. Rigsby 1982. People with 'politicks': management of land and personnel on Australia's Cape York Peninsula. In N. M. Williams and E. S. Hunn (eds), *Resource managers: North American and Australian hunter-gatherers*, pp. 155–171. Westview Press, Boulder, Colorado.

Swadling, P. 1996. *Plumes from Paradise*. Papua New Guinea National Museum, Boroko.

Taçon, P. S. C. 1988. Identifying fish species in the recent rock paintings of western Arnhem Land. *Rock Art Research*, 5(1):3–15.

——1989. From rainbow snakes to 'X-ray' fish: the nature of the recent rock painting tradition of western Arnhem Land, Australia. PhD thesis, ANU, Canberra.

——2001. Australia. In D. S. Whitley (ed.), *Handbook of rock art research*, pp. 530–75. Altamira Press, New York.

Taçon, P. S. C. and S. Brockwell 1995. Arnhem Land prehistory in landscape, stone and paint. In J. Allen and J. F. O'Connell (eds), *Transitions: Pleistocene to Holocene in Australia and Papua New Guinea*, pp. 676–695. Antiquity 69, Special Number 265.

Taçon, P. S. C. and C. Chippindale. 1994. Australia's ancient warriors: changing depictions of fighting in the rock art of Arnhem land, N.T. *Cambridge Archaeological Journal*, 4:211–248.

Taçon, P. S. C. and M. Garde 2000. Dating beeswax figures on rock: the view from central Arnhem Land. In G. K. Ward and C. Tuniz (eds), *Advances in dating Australian rock-markings: papers from the first Australian rock-picture dating workshop*, pp. 71–75. Occasional AURA Publication 10. AURA, Melbourne.

Taçon, P. S. C., M. Wilson and C. Chippendale 1996. Birth of the Rainbow Serpent in Arnhem land rock art and oral history. *Archaeology in Oceania*, 31:103–124.

Tanks, G. 1987. Illusions of diffusion: the distribution of maritime technology along the northeast Queensland coast. BA (Hons) thesis, Department of Archaeology and Palaeoanthropology, UNE, Armidale.

Taylor, L. 1979. Ancestors into art: an analysis of Pitjanjatjara Kulpidji designs and crayon drawings. BA (Hons) thesis, Department of Prehistory and Anthropology, ANU, Canberra.

——1987. 'The same but different': social reproduction and innovation in the art of the Kunwinjku of western Arnhem Land. PhD thesis, Department of Prehistory and Anthropology, ANU, Canberra.

Thomas, A. M. 1998. Spit of the serpent: an ethnographic and scientific analysis of white pigments used in Wandjina rock art, Kimberley, Western Australia. BA (Hons) thesis, Department of Archaeology and Palaeoanthropology, UNE, Armidale.

Thorn, A. and J. Brunet (eds) 1995. *Preservation of rock art*. Occasional AURA Publication 9. AURA, Melbourne.

Thorne, A. G. 1976. Morphological contrasts in Pleistocene Australians. In R. L. Kirk and A. G. Thorne (eds), *The origin of the Australians*, pp. 95–112. AIAS, Canberra.

Thorne, A. G. and M. H. Wolpoff 1981. Regional continuity in Australasian Pleistocene hominid evolution. *American Journal of Physical Anthropology*, 53:337–349.

Tindale, N. B. 1951. Comments on supposed representations of giant bird tracks at Pimba. *Records of the South Australian Museum*, 9(4):381–382.

Trezise, P. J. 1971. *Rock art of south-east Cape York*. AIAS, Canberra.

——1977. Representations of crocodiles in Laura art. In P. J. Ucko (ed.), *Form in indigenous art: schematisation in the art of Aboriginal Australia and prehistoric Europe*, pp. 325–336. AIAS, Canberra.

——1993. *Dream road: a journey of discovery*. Allen and Unwin, Sydney.

Tuniz, C. and A. Watchman 1994. The ANTARES AMS spectrometer. Accelerators and lasers for dating rock art in Australia. *Rock Art Research*, 11: 71–73.

Tylor, E. B. 1871. *Primitive culture*. Henry Holt, New York.

Ucko, P. J. and A. Rosenfeld 1967. *Palaeolithic cave art*. Weindenfeld and Nicolson, London.

Veth, P. 1989. Islands in the interior: a model for the colonisation of Australia's arid zone. *Archaeology in Oceania*, 24:81–92.

Vinnicombe, P. 1972. Motivation in African rock art. *Antiquity*, 46:124–133.

——1976. *People of the Eland*. University of Natal Press, Pietermaritzburg.

——1987. *Dampier archaeological project. Resource document, survey and salvage of Aboriginal sites, Burrup Peninsula, Western Australia*. Western Australian Museum, Perth.

von Sturmer, J. R. 1978. The Wik region: economy, territoriality and totemism in western Cape York Peninsula, North Queensland. PhD thesis, University of Queensland.

Wainwright, I. N. M. 1985. Rock art conservation in Canada. *Bollettino del Centro Camuno di Studi Preistorici*, XXll:15–46.

Wallace, P. and N. Wallace 1977. *Killing me softly. The destruction of a heritage*. Thomas Nelson, Melbourne.

Walsh, G. L. 1979. Mutilated hands or signal stencils? *Australian Archaeology*, 9:33–41.

——1984. Archaeological site management in Carnarvon National Park. A case history in the dilemma of presentation or preservation. In H. Sullivan (ed.), *Visitors to Aboriginal Sites: access, control and management*, pp. 1–14. Australian National Parks and Wildlife Service, Canberra.

——1985. The archaeological significance of the White Mountains. Unpublished report to Queensland National Parks and Wildlife Service, Brisbane.

——1988. *Australia's greatest rock art*. E.J. Brill/Robert Brown and Associates, Bathurst, NSW.

——1992. Rock art retouch: can a claim of Aboriginal descent establish curation rights over humanity's cultural heritage? In M. J. Morwood and D. R. Hobbs (eds), *Rock art and ethnography*, pp. 46–59. Occasional AURA Publication 5. AURA, Melbourne.

——1994. *Bradshaws: ancient rock paintings of north-west Australia*. The Bradshaw Foundation, Carouge-Geneva, Switzerland.

——2000. *Bradshaw art of the Kimberley*. Takarakka Nowan Kas Publications, Toowong, Queensland.

Walsh, G. L. and M. J. Morwood 1999. Spear and spear-thrower evolution in the Kimberley region, N.W. Australia: evidence from rock art. *Archaeology in Oceania*, 34(2):45–58.

Walsh, G. L., M. J. Morwood and A. Watchman In prep. *AMS radiocarbon dates for beeswax rock art in the Kimberley, WA.*

Walston, S. 1976. Plans for the protection of the Mt Grenfell painted rockshelters. In C. Pearson and G. Pretty (eds), *Proceedings of National Seminar on the conservation of cultural material, Perth, 1973*, pp. 44–50. International Committee on Conservation of Monuments, Perth.

Ward, G. K. 1983. Archaeology and legislation in Australia. In G. Connah (ed.), *Australian field archaeology: a guide to techniques*, pp. 18–42. AIAS, Canberra.

Watchman, A. 1985. Mineralogical analysis of silica skins covering rock art. In R. Jones (ed.), *Archaeological research in Kakadu National Park*, pp. 281–290. Special Publication 13. Australian National Parks and Wildlife Service, Canberra.

——1987. Preliminary determinations of the age and composition of mineral salts on rock art surfaces in the Kakadu National Park. In W. R. Ambrose and J. M. J. Mummery (eds), *Archaeometry: further Australasian studies*, pp. 36–42. Department of Prehistory, Research School of Pacific Studies, ANU, Canberra.

——1989–90. New clocks on old rocks: dating Dreamtime art. *Australian Natural History*, 23(3):243–247.

——1990. A summary of occurrences of oxalate-rich crusts in Australia. *Rock Art Research*, 7(1):44–50.

——1993. Perspectives and potentials for absolute dating rock paintings. *Antiquity*, 67:58–65.

Watchman, A. and J. B. Campbell 1996. Micro-stratigraphic analyses of laminated oxalate crusts in northern Australia.

In M. Realini and L. Toniolo (eds), *The oxalate films in the conservation of works of art: proceedings of the 2nd International Symposium, Milan, 1996*, pp. 407–422. Bologne, Gruppo Editoriale, Milan.

Watchman, A. and N. A. Cole 1993. Accelerator radiocarbon dating of plant-fibre binders in rock paintings from northeastern Australia. *Antiquity*, 67:355–358.

Watchman, A., G. L. Walsh, M. J. Morwood and C. Tuniz 1997. AMS radiocarbon age estimates for early rock paintings in the Kimberley, N.W. Australia: preliminary results. *Rock Art Research*, 14(1):18–25.

Watson, J. A. L. and J. M. Flood. 1987. Termite and wasp damage to Australian rock art. *Rock Art Research*, 4(1):17–28.

Welch, D. 1990. The bichrome art period in the Kimberley, Australia. *Rock Art Research*, 7(2):110–124.

——1993. Early 'naturalistic figures' in the Kimberley, Australia. *Rock Art Research*, 10(1):24–37.

Wellmann, K. F. 1979. *A survey of North American Indian rock art*. Akademische Druck-u. Verlagsanstalt, Graz Austria.

Whitley, D. S. 1987. Socio-religious context and rock art in east-central California. *Journal of Anthropological Archaeology*, 6:159–188.

Whitley, D. S. and R. I. Dorn 1987. Rock art chronology in eastern California. *World Archaeology*, 19(2):150–163.

Whitley, D. S. and L. L. Loendorf (eds) 1994. *New light on old art: recent advances in hunter–gatherer rock art research*. Monograph 36. Institute of Archaeology, University of California, Los Angeles.

Wiessner, P. 1984. Reconstructing the behavioural basis for style: a case study among the Kalahari San. *Journal of Anthropological Archaeology*, 3:190–234.

——1990. Is there a unity to style? In M. W. Conkey and C. Hastorf (eds), *The uses of style in archaeology*, pp. 105–112. Cambridge University Press, Cambridge.

Wobst, H. M. 1974. Boundary conditions for Palaeolithic social systems: a simulation approach. *American Antiquity*, 39(2):147–178.

Wolfe, A. 1969. Social structural bases of art. *Current Anthropology*, 10:3–44.

Worsnop, T. 1897. *The prehistoric arts, manufactures, works, weapons etc. of the Aborigines of Australia*. Government printer, Adelaide.

Wright, B. J. 1968. *Rock art of the Pilbara region, north-west Australia*. AIAS, Canberra.

Wright, R. V. S. (ed.) 1971a. *The archaeology of the Gallus site, Koonalda Cave*. AIAS, Canberra.

——1971b. Prehistory in the Cape York Peninsula. In D. J. Mulvaney and J. Golson (eds), *Aboriginal man and environment in Australia*, pp. 133–140. ANU Press, Canberra.

——1985. Detecting patterns in tabled archaeological data by principal components and correspondence analysis: programs in BASIC for portable computers. *Science and Archaeology*, 27:35–38.

Wynn, T. 1979. The intelligence of later Acheulian hominids. *Man*, 14:371–391.

Yencken, D. 1979. Our universal heritage. *UNESCO Review*, 1:9–12.

——1985. *Australia's National Estate: the role of the Commonwealth*. Special Australian Heritage Publication No. 1. Australian Government Publishing Service, Canberra.

Yengoyan, A. A. 1976. Structure, event and ecology in Aboriginal Australia. In N. Peterson (ed.), *Tribes and boundaries in Australia*, pp. 121–133. AIAS, Canberra.

Young, G. 1984. *Environmental conservation: towards a philosophy*. Heritage Council of New South Wales, Sydney.

Index